The Torah
Portion by Portion

Seymour Rossel

The Torah: Portion by Portion
Copyright © 2007 by Seymour Rossel

ISBN: 978-1-891662-94-2
First Edition

Published by
Torah Aura Productions
4423 Fruitland Avenue
Los Angeles CA, 90058
(800)BE-TORAH (800-238-6724)
Fax: (323) 585-0327
Web: *http://www.torahaura.com*
Email: *misrad@torahaura.com*

Printed in Malaysia

Dedicated to

Rabbi Manuel Gold
Sharon L. Wechter
Exodus 17:12
S.R.

Note to Readers

"Turn it and turn it again, for everything is in it"—so the Rabbis spoke of the inheritance we call Torah. By their time, it already meant more than just the *Chumash* (the Five Books of Moses). It included all the teachings of prophets and sages that came to be known as Bible, Talmud, and Midrash. And more was added to Torah through the centuries. The earliest fruits of Jewish thought included *Pesher*, the running commentaries and emendations that have become most familiar to us through the Dead Sea Scrolls. Before long, Torah also included the works of the great commentators—from the Middle Ages right down to the present moment. It was further expanded by the Codes and the Responsa, which sought to clarify the laws and commandments and to turn them into the storehouse of legal thought we call *Halachah*, the "Path" to living a Jewish life.

In the last few hundred years, Torah has been widened through the work of historians, archaeologists, social historians, scientists, and philologists. Their explanations and comparative analysis help frame a new picture of the world of the Bible, explaining and annotating how the Torah sounded and what its words meant to its earliest readers. Modern Jewish scholarship has not been left behind. It has long participated in the many schools of critical Bible inquiry that flourish among non-Jews.

All liberal and progressive Jews now embrace (to one degree or another) modern scholarship—including what is sometimes called "the Documentary Hypothesis"—as a form of inquiry as valid as Responsa and as enlightening as commentary. We no longer wince when it is suggested that Moses might never have carried a scroll of Torah through the camp of a people that may never have numbered 600,000 warriors and their families wandering through the Sinai wilderness. The holiness of the Torah to us is as unimpaired by such knowledge as it is by the legends spun by the Rabbis to explain parts of Torah that could not be comprehended in a literal way.

We would not dream of denying the commentaries and the Codes to modern Jews young or old, just as there is no logical or philosophical reason for denying them the findings of the last three hundred years of Jewish scholarship. So this commentary sets the Rabbis beside the archaeologists, the commentators beside the critical scholars, to demonstrate anew that when we "Turn it, and turn it again," we find in Torah no emptiness or hypocrisy, but a continually self-renewing treasure. No matter how or when we encounter Torah, it helps us discover the secrets to Judaism's basic mysteries: what we should believe and how we should behave.

This, then, is a book dedicated to the new generation of Jews, those who were never "slaves" in any Egypt of the mind, but who are ready to conquer their modern world with respect for tradition and respect for modernity. It is presented in the faith that the Torah can be precious for them—and meaningful to them—as it was for all the generations of Jews before them.

Rabbi Seymour Rossel
Houston, Texas

Contents

בראשית, The Book of Genesis

Two Creations—*page 1*—בראשית, *Bereishit*, Genesis 1:1–6:8

Noah—*page 10*—נח, *Noach*, Genesis 6:9-11:32

Abram, Abraham; Sarai, Sarah—*page 19*—לך־לך, *Lech-Lecha*, Genesis 12:1-17:27

Testing God; Testing Abraham—*page 26*—וירא, *Vayeira*, Genesis 18:1–22:24

A Cave and a Wife—*page 33*—חיי שרה, *Chayei Sarah*, Genesis 23:1–25:18

The Twins—*page 39*—תולדות, *Toldot*, Genesis 25:19-28:10

The Great Dream—*page 46*—ויצא, *Vayeitzei*, Genesis 28:10-32:3

Wrestling—*page 53*—וישלח, *Vayishlach*, Genesis 32:4-36:43

The Interpreter of Dreams—*page 59*—וישב, *Vayeishev*, Genesis 37:1-40:23

Joseph and Pharaoh—*page 65*—מקץ, *Mikeitz*, Genesis 41:1-44:17

Joseph and Jacob—*page 72*—ויגש, *Vayigash*, Genesis 44:18-47:27

Israel in Egypt—*page 77*—ויחי, *Vayechi*, Genesis 47:28-50:26

שמות, The Book of Exodus

The Baby and the Bush—*page 83*—שמות, *Shemot*, Exodus 1:1-6:1

Let My People Go—*page 91*—וארא, *Va'eirah*, Exodus 6:2-9:35

Adonai and Pharaoh—*page 98*—בא, *Bo*, Exodus 10:1-13:16

Miracles, Song, Dance, and War—*page 105*—בשלח, *B'Shalach*, Exodus 13:17-17:16

Law and Order—*page 113*—יתרו, *Yitro*, Exodus 18:1-20:23

Rules—*page 119*—משפטים, *Mishpatim*, Exodus 21:1-24:18

Gifts—*page 126*—תרומה, *Terumah*, Exodus 25:1-27:19

Instructions—*page 132*—תצוה, *Titzaveh*, Exodus 27:20-30:10

A Golden Bull Calf—*page 137*—כי תשה, *Ki Tisah*, Exodus 30:11-34:35

Too Much—*page 145*—ויקהל, *Vayakheil*, Exodus 35:1-38:20

Creating God's Place—*page 149*—פקודי, *Pikudei*, Exodus 38:21-40:38

ויקרא, The Book of Leviticus

Offerings—*page 154*—ויקרא, *Vayikra*, Leviticus 1:1-5:26

Memory—*page 159*—צו, *Tzav*, Leviticus 6:1-8:36

Differences—*page 164*—שמיני, *Shemini*, Leviticus 9:1-11:47

Blood—*page 170*—תזריע, *Tazria*, Leviticus 12:1-13:59

From Unclean to Clean—*page 174*—מצרע, *Metzora*, Leviticus 14:1-15:33

Dangers—*page 181*—אחרי מות, *Acharei Mot*, Leviticus 16:1-18:30

The Heart of the Torah—*page 187*—קדשים, *Kedoshim*, Leviticus 19:1-20:27

Priests and Times—*page 193*—אמר, *Emor*, Leviticus 21:1-24:23

A Perfect World—*page 199*—בהר, *Bihar*, Leviticus 25:1-26:2

Terms of the Covenant—*page 205*—בחקתי, *Bichukotai*, Leviticus 26:3-27:34

במדבר, The Book of Numbers

In the Wilderness—*page 212*—במדבר, *Bemidbar*, Numbers 1:1-4:20

Mishkan and Tent—*page 220*—נשא, *Naso*, Numbers 4:21-7:89

Trumpets and Complaints—*page 228*—בהעלתך, *Beha'alotcha*, Numbers 8:1-12:16

Scouts—*page 236*—שלח-לך, *Shelach-Lecha*, Numbers 13:1-15:41

Rebellions—*page 243*—קרח, *Korach*, Numbers 16:1-18:32

Miriam and Aaron Die—*page 252*—חקת, *Chukkat*, Numbers 19:1-22:1

Balaam the Prophet—*page 261*—בלק, *Balak*, Numbers 22:2-25:9

Dividing the Land—*page 268*—פינחס, *Pinchas*, Numbers 25:10-30:1

As Good as Your Word—*page 274*—מטות, *Mattot*, Numbers 30:2-32:42

Marches and Boundaries—*page 279*—מסעי, *Masei*, Numbers 33:1-36:13

דברים, The Book of Deuteronomy

The Words—*page 286*—דברים, *Devarim*, Deuteronomy 1:1-3:22

Hear, O Israel!—*page 293*—ואתחנן, *Va-Etchanan*, Deuteronomy 3:23-7:11

All Depends on You—*page 300*—עקב, *Eikev*, Deuteronomy 7:12-11:25

One People, One Place—*page 306*—ראה, *Re'eih*, Deuteronomy 11:26-16:17

Judges, Prophets, Kings—*page 313*—שופטים, *Shoftim*, Deuteronomy 16:18-21:9

Laws upon Laws—*page 320*—כי תצא, *Ki Teitzei*, Deuteronomy 21:10-25:19

Covenants and Curses—*page 327*—כי תבוא, *Ki Tavo*, Deuteronomy 26:1-29:8

Choose Life—*page 332*—נצבים, *Nitzavim*, Deuteronomy 29:9-30:20

Josiah and Deuteronomy—*page 338*—וילך, *VaYeilech*, Deuteronomy 31:1-30

The Song of *Ha'azinu*—*page 347*—האזינו, *Ha'azinu*, Deuteronomy 32:1-52

The Death of Moses—*page 352*—וזאת הברכה, *VeZot HaBerachah*, Deuteronomy 33:1-34:12

The Torah—*page 359*—*A Few Notes in Closing*

Two Creations

ברֵאשִׁית
Bereishit
Genesis 1:1–6:8

A Story of Creation

Even today, most people recognize the first sentences of the Torah as they were translated into English in the year 1611 for the King James Version of the Bible:

> In the beginning, God created the heaven and the earth. And the earth was without form, and void; and darkness was upon the face of the deep. And the Spirit of God moved upon the face of the waters. And God said, Let there be light: and there was light.

The three English words "In the beginning" stand for one Hebrew word, *Bereishit*, which is made up of two parts: *Be-*, which means "in" or "when" or "as", and *reishit*. which means "head of" or "beginning of" or "start of". So the King James Version's "In the beginning" was a fair translation.

But things have changed since 1611. Archaeologists and linguists have decoded several ancient languages that were "close cousins" to Hebrew—in fact, a few existed before Hebrew and could be called "ancestors". Knowing these Semitic languages helps us better understand the Hebrew of the Torah. So today scholars believe that a closer English translation of the Torah's first sentence would be:

> *When God began* creating heaven and earth—the earth being shapeless and empty, with darkness above the deep, with God's spirit soaring over the water—God said, "Let there be light"; and there was light.

We might think that a book needs to be translated into English only once, but that has never been true for the Torah. Instead, every new translation of the Torah reveals a new understanding of ancient Hebrew. Each translation helps us hear the words in a fresh way. And that is just the beginning, because it is not only the *language* of the Torah that needs to be constantly refreshed.

Quote to Remember

בְּרֵאשִׁית בָּרָא אֱלֹהִים אֵת הַשָּׁמַיִם וְאֵת הָאָרֶץ.

In the beginning God created the heaven and the earth.

2 – The Torah: Portion by Portion

Plural Names for God

In the ancient world, many languages used plural-sounding names like *Elohim* to speak of a single god. In Mesopotamia both the word *il* (singular) and the word *ilm* (plural) could mean "god". In letters written by an ancient Egyptian, we hear the Pharaoh called "my *gods*, the sun *god*"—plural and singular in one sentence! And in the early days of Hebrew settlement in the Holy Land, Canaanites already spoke of their god as *elohim*. So the Hebrew habit of calling the One God by the plural word *Elohim* was not unusual in its time.

From days of old it was said that the Torah was "written by Moses" or that it was "given by God to Moses at Mount Sinai." People did not necessarily believe that every word was *true*, only that the Torah was *sacred* and every word in it was *important*. For instance, the Torah includes stories about a talking serpent and a talking donkey. Of course, we know that animals do not argue with us or offer us fruit. People have always known that. And people have always told tales about talking animals for the same reason the Torah does: to teach important lessons.

In every age and time there were serious Jewish scholars and rabbis who believed that the Torah was *not* "the word of God given to Moses." They found parts that did not quite make sense and other parts where scribes made obvious errors in copying the words. Often they hesitated to speak of this openly, thinking that it might cause other Jews to think less of the Torah or to stop treating it as sacred. And they did not want to be known as "doubters". So they shared their knowledge with other scholars in careful words, suggesting that they should study this verse or that story closely in order to find "a great secret" about the Torah.

In the past three hundred years or so Jewish and non-Jewish scholars have studied the Torah with new tools. They have discovered much about *how* the Torah was written, *who* wrote it, and *why*. Today we are free to bring together older ways of studying Torah with the newer tools of the last few centuries. This fresh look at the Torah helps us understand its deeper truths.

The best place to start is in the beginning. Almost everyone knows the first two stories of the Torah. The first one explains how God created all things in heaven and earth in six days. It ends with:

> The heaven and the earth were finished, and all they contain. On the seventh day, God [*Elohim*] finished the work God had been doing, and God rested on the seventh day from all the work that God had done. And God blessed the seventh day and declared it holy, because on it God rested from all that work of creation that God had done. Such is the story of heaven and earth when they were created.

The Mystery of God's Names

Throughout the first story of creation God is called *Elohim*, a name that comes from *El*, a word that meant "god" in many languages of the ancient Near East. In Hebrew the name **אלהים**, *Elohim*, looks and sounds like a plural word. The singular for *Elohim* is *Eloha*, and the Bible sometimes (but not often) uses *Eloha* as a name for the One God.

Yet we can tell from the first sentence that *Elohim* is a name and not a word meaning "many gods". The verb used with *Elohim* is singular—the Bible says "*Elohim* creates" (singular) and not "*Elohim* create" (which would be plural), and it says "*Elohim* speaks" and not "*Elohim* speak." So it is clear that *Elohim* is a name that ancient Hebrew speakers used for "the One God". It was also a name for God in other languages. For example, the Canaanites used it.

But in the Torah's second story of creation God is called *YHVH-Elohim*. The four-letter name **יהוה**, *YHVH*, was used only by Hebrews (and Jews call God by this name even now). As far as we know, no other nation ever shared this four-letter name for the One God.

Names are important. In fact, people have always believed that names hold magic power. It was said that knowing a god's "true" name could make it possible to control that god. The Torah does not agree. Our ancestors taught that the One God can not be controlled by humans, even through magic.

Nevertheless, ancient Hebrews considered God's name sacred and guarded the four-letter name of God by not speaking it out loud. Whenever they saw or read *YHVH* they substituted the word *Adonai*, a word meaning "my sovereign(s)" or "my ruler(s)"—as if to say "my every God."

As we study the Torah in English, we need to know which name of God is being used. So when the Hebrew text uses the word *Elohim*, we will translate it with the capitalized word "God". And when the Hebrew text uses *YHVH*, we will translate it as Jews have always spoken it throughout history, using the word "Adonai". Thus, in the Torah's second story of creation, the name *YHVH-Elohim* is translated into English as *"Adonai God"*.

Vowels and Vowel Letters

Look inside a Torah scroll and you will see that the writing contains no vowel points (the little dots and dashes that help us read Hebrew). In ancient times the Hebrew language used *vowel letters* instead of vowel points (just as English uses "a-e-i-o-u and sometimes y" as vowel letters). Mysteriously, God's four-letter name is made up entirely of Hebrew vowel letters! Even the "v" in *YHVH* is actually a Hebrew vowel letter (a close cousin to "u" and "o"—as every Hebrew student knows—and also to "y"—as scholars tell us). When Jewish scribes later added vowels to the Bible, they placed the vowels for *Adonai* around the four-letter name *YHVH* to remind us to pronounce this name of God as *Adonai*.

To Consider

Why did our ancestors decide to keep two Creation stories instead of choosing one or the other? If you were putting things together, would you choose to keep both? Would you combine them into one story? Or would you choose one over the other?

The Second Story of Creation

The second story in the Torah starts with the words: "These are the generations of heaven and earth as they were created, in the day that Adonai God made heaven and earth." According to this account, Adonai God creates the world in one day! And Adonai God creates the human first, not last. As the story says,

> No shrub of the field was yet on earth and no grasses of the field had yet sprouted, because Adonai God had not sent rain to the earth, and there was no human to farm the soil …. Adonai God shaped the human from the dust of the earth, and blew into [the human's] nostrils the breath of life. And the human became a living being.

Adonai God then plants "a garden in Eden" with "the tree of life in the middle of the garden and the tree of knowing good and evil." The Torah says that a river goes out of Eden and divides into four rivers—the Pishon, the Gihon, the Tigris, and the Euphrates. Adonai God put the human in the garden "to farm it and guard it." And Adonai God told the human to eat the fruit of every tree, but not of "the tree of knowing good and evil … you must not eat of it; for as soon as you eat of it, you shall certainly die."

> Adonai God said, "It is not good for the human to be alone; I will make a matching helper for it." Then Adonai God formed … all the wild beasts and all the birds …; and brought them to the human to see what it would call them …. Thus, the human gave names to all the cattle and to the birds of the sky and to all the wild beasts; but for the human no matching helper was found. So Adonai God put a deep sleep on the human; and while it slept, [Adonai God] took one of its ribs and closed up the flesh at that spot. And Adonai God built the rib that [Adonai God] had taken from the human (*adam*) into a woman, and brought her to Adam.

> Then Adam said, "This time, this is bone of my bone, and flesh of my flesh. This one shall be

named 'woman,' for from 'man' was she taken." It is because of this that a man leaves his father and mother and unites with his wife, so they become like one flesh.

The Mystery of Creations

For a long time people thought that the first story—the creation of the world in seven days—was a general picture of how God created the world and that the second story—about the garden of Eden and how the first human was separated into man and woman—just added more details. In other words, people thought that the two were the same story told in different ways. By the Middle Ages, though, Jewish and non-Jewish scholars looked more closely at the stories and saw the many differences in them.

In the first story God (*Elohim*) uses words to create things. God is distant—separate from the earth and the heavens. God fashions the human as both male and female in one body, "in our image," as God says. The second story, though, calls God by a different name: Adonai God (*YHVH-Elohim*). Surely these two stories of creation were not told by the same teller. They may not come from the same time or the same place. And we can also see that they were being told for different reasons.

Two Different Stories

The first story begins in the heavens and explains the beginnings of everything in the universe. God is behind it all, the creator of it all. The One God created human beings "in our image," to act on earth as God does in heaven, to "take charge of it" and rule it. Most important, this story explains the creation of the seventh day: a day of rest, Shabbat. God created Shabbat; and in fact, according to this story, God also created the seven-day week. So this story delivers a message: The One God is the creator of heaven and earth and all things and controls heaven and earth and all things.

The second story doesn't bother with the creation of heaven, sun, moon, or stars. It is interested only in what happened on earth. In this story Adonai God steps into the

Why Two Stories?

The Torah (the first five books of the Bible) was already hundreds of years old before the first rabbis appeared in the time of the Second Temple. (The term "Rabbis" with a capital "R" stands for these early sages down to the sixth century, C.E.) Looking back, the Rabbis tried to explain why there were two stories of Creation. One rabbi taught that a day for God was much longer than a human day, so when the Torah states the world was created in seven days, it does not mean seven of our days, but seven of God's much longer days.

Another rabbi said that there were two creation stories because there were two creations! God created many worlds before this one, he said. So the two stories are separated by the sentence "The heaven and the earth were finished, and all they contain." The word for "finished" could also mean "destroyed". God destroyed the first creation and started over. It is the second story, this rabbi said, that tells how *our* world came to be.

What Should We Eat?

In the creation stories God gives plants and trees as food for humans and beasts. But even in ancient times, when people first told these stories, they knew that many beasts were not plant-eaters, and neither were human beings. The stories take place in a kind of dream time, a time when things were better and kinder. As people listened they could dream of returning to that wonderful time—after all, the prophets spoke of a future time when the wolf would lie down beside the lamb and the lamb would not be afraid. Perhaps this is what the Torah had in mind in telling about a Garden of Eden.

world. Adonai God shapes a human being (*adam*) from dust and breathes life into the human's nose. Adonai God plants a garden, allows *adam* to name the animals, worries about loneliness, casts a deep sleep on *adam*, operates on and heals *adam*, shapes a rib bone into a woman, and brings the woman (Eve) to the new "Adam" that awakes.

The second story tells how a "wily" serpent tricked the woman into eating fruit from "the tree of knowing good and evil." A little further on—after Eve and Adam both eat from the forbidden tree—Adonai God is said to be "strolling in the garden at the breezy time of the day" and calling to Adam (the way we might call to a friend), "Where are you?" (Even the idea of Adonai God "strolling" seems quite natural in this story.)

So the second story explains why ordinary things are the way they are. It tells how the serpent (snake) lost its legs as a punishment. It tells how Adonai God punished the woman (Eve) by making her suffer pain in giving birth to children and punished Adam by making him sweat and toil to get his food. And the story tells us that Adonai God was worried that human beings might eat of "the tree of life" and live forever. Then Adonai God sent Adam and Eve out of the garden of Eden "and stationed *cherubim* [special angels] and the fiery ever-turning sword east of the garden of Eden, to guard the way to the tree of life." What else is missing here? This story of creation does not mention the Sabbath or the seven-day week.

Names and Stories

A so-called "archaeologist" once announced that he had uncovered the skeletons of Adam and Eve. Near Denver he found bones of male and female skeletons hugging each other in the grave. He claimed that the bones were prehistoric, and—wonder of wonders!—one rib bone of the male skeleton was found attached to the female skeleton. This "discovery" was front page news in the supermarket newspapers—the ones that report alien landings and scandals about movie and television personalities. But serious archaeologists just chuckled at the whole idea.

Discovering the truth about early human beings is the work of science. To students of Torah it is clear that the characters of Adam and Eve were invented to fit the second story of creation. The word *adam* in Hebrew means "human"—it is closely related to the Hebrew word *adamah*, which means "earth", which makes sense since the Torah's *adam* was shaped from the "dust of the earth." Once the woman was separated from *adam*, the Torah's male was still called Adam—the word became a name. The new female, though, was called Eve (*chavah* in Hebrew, meaning "life-giver"), because women give birth.

In the Torah, names are little stories in themselves. They are often tools for teaching. Take, for example, the names of the two sons of Adam and Eve. The name Cain means "acquired" (the Torah explains that Cain was "acquired with help from Adonai"), and the name Abel means "breath" or "nothingness". Their tale continues the Torah's teaching about "beginnings".

The Fertile Crescent

Below: The Torah locates the Garden of Eden somewhere in the Fertile Crescent. In this area of the ancient Near East, steady rivers like the Jordan, Tigris, and Euphrates (and the Nile, with its yearly floods) provided large amounts of water for farms and cities—the basis for early civilization.

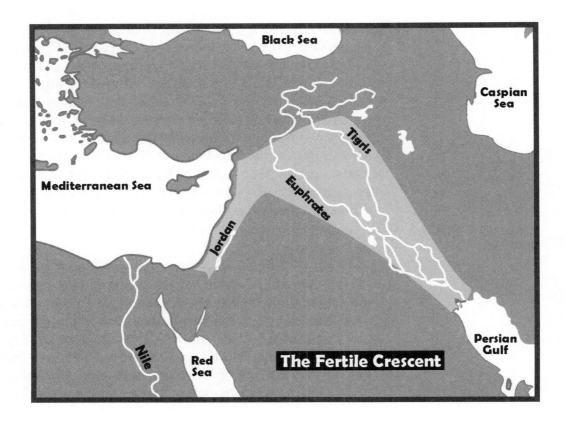

The Fertile Crescent

To Consider
How should we think of God? When should we think of God as being distant and commanding (as in the story of the seven days of creation)? And when should we think of God as being up close and personal like a good companion (as in the Garden of Eden creation story and in the story of Cain and Abel)?

Cain and Abel

Cain became a farmer while his younger brother, Abel, became a shepherd.

In time, Cain brought an offering from the first fruits of the soil to Adonai; and Abel, for his part, brought the best of the first young of his flock. Adonai noticed Abel and his offering, but paid no heed to Cain and his offering. Cain was very upset and his face fell.

Adonai told Cain not to fret. "If you do right," Adonai said, "things will go well. But if you do not do right, sin crouches at the door, urging you on. Yet you can be its master."

Cain hears Adonai's words but does not seem to understand. In the fields one day he invents revenge and murder by killing Abel. Adonai then calls out to Cain, "Where is your brother Abel?" And Cain speaks the famous words: "I do not know. Am I my brother's keeper?"

It is an angry Adonai who answers: "Hear now, your brother's blood cry out to me from the ground!" Adonai forces Cain to become a wanderer. But Cain is worried. What if someone tries to kill *him*? So Adonai puts a mark on Cain to warn other people not to kill him. And Cain goes away from Adonai to settle in the land of Nod, east of Eden.

Adam and Eve have a third son, Seth. Meanwhile, Cain's children and grandchildren discover and invent many of the world's "firsts": they become the first nomads, the first musicians, and the first blacksmiths. In all of this, just as in the second story of Creation, the Torah answers questions about how things began and how Adonai works in the world.

The Big Questions

Most people know these stories and know they come from the first book of the Torah, the Book of Genesis. What most people do not realize is that Genesis is not a book, but a "library of stories." When modern scholars look closely, they see the differences in the two stories of creation. They are the work of two different storytellers—the storytellers did not even call God by the same name. But these stories—and all the stories, the laws, and the teachings in the Torah—were woven together to answer two big questions that all of us must ask: What should a person think? and How should a person behave?

The Bible is divided into three units: the books of the Torah, the books of the Prophets, and the books we call Writings. Studying Bible is the work of a lifetime. In this book we will concentrate on the Torah, sometimes called "the Five Books of Moses." The Torah has been divided into fifty-four portions so that we can read it weekly in the synagogue.

As we discuss each portion we will have the help of those who studied before us—rabbis and Bible scholars through the ages. We will look closely at what is in the Torah, trying to explain things like "Why are there two stories of creation?" and "Why are there different names for God?" Above all, we will examine the greater questions that the Torah and the whole Bible try to answer: "What should we think?" and "How should we live?"

Portions

For reading in the synagogue, the Torah is divided into *parshiot*, ("portions"). Each weekly portion is called a *parashah*. These divisions appear only in printed copies of the Torah. They are not marked off in any way in the handwritten scroll of the Torah that we read from each week. To make it easier to find them in the Torah scroll, the *parshiot* are usually named by the first important word in the portion. That is why the first portion is called *Bereishit*. For each portion the Rabbis selected a *haftarah* or "parting [message]" from the books of the prophets (see *page 360*).

Haftarah: Isaiah 42:5-43:11

These words from the Book of Isaiah begin with the birth of the world, as the Torah portion does, and they connect the world's birth with the birth of the people of Israel. God, who created heavens and earth, tells Israel, "I am the One who created you and made you a covenant people, a light to the nations." God says, "I am Adonai—that is My name." And later God says:

> I have called you [Israel] by name, you are Mine. When you pass through waters I am with you; even rivers shall not overcome you.

God punished the Israelites by allowing the Babylonians to take them into slavery. But God, the mightiest of all warriors, now suffers for the Israelites "like a woman in labor." God will now "turn their darkness into light." "Have no fear," God says, "for I will redeem you."

God chose (and needs) Israel to be witnesses to all the other nations:

> So, know Me and trust Me. Understand that I am One. Before Me, no god was formed; after Me, there shall be none. Truly, I am Adonai; and I alone can bring you out.

Isaiah's words brought hope to the Israelites who had just seen the Babylonians defeated by the Persians and the Medes. And miraculously, within a few years the Israelites would be allowed to return to the Promised Land.

Adonai had said that Israel would know a prophet was true if the prophet's words came true. By coming true, the words of this late prophet added to the Book of Isaiah gained an honored place in the Bible.

Noah

Long before Torah times, stories about deadly floods were popular in Mesopotamia because great floods actually do happen there. One ancient story was about a man named Utnapishtim who was loved by one of the gods. When this god learned that a flood was about to wash away the whole earth, he warned Utnapishtim to build a huge boat to save himself and his family. Utnapishtim's boat landed on a mountain. Utnapishtim sent out a dove and then a raven. And finally Utnapishtim saw that the flood was over, so he came out of his ark. In time, the story says, Utnapishtim became so wise that the gods made him a god, too. Except for that last piece—how he became a god—the story of Utnapishtim sounds very much like the story of Noah.

Don't Bother Looking

The second weekly portion of the Torah is called *Noah*, and it contains the story of Noah's ark. Real people still get caught up in the frenzy of looking for the boat that Noah built. If you think about it, though, you will soon realize that the tale of Noah is a Torah story that has little to do with either science or boat-building. Modern scientists have a rough idea of how many species of animals and birds there are on earth—and we can guess how many have become extinct through the centuries. Surely no boat could hold them all, even in pairs, and even if we could do the impossible by collecting them all in one place and time. The fact is that the story of Noah is "a whale of a tale." But it is also a fact that it is a *sacred* tale, a story like those in our first weekly portion: meant to teach us lessons about how we should behave and what we should think.

You Already Know the Story

The story of Noah's ark is popular the world over. It has been told and retold, pictured by artists in thousands of ways, and it is often among the first stories that parents tell their children. But children's books about Noah's ark do not tell the tale the way it is told in the Torah. They can't. In the Torah there are actually *two* stories of Noah, just as there are two stories of creation. So you may think you know the story, but let us see what happens when we break the tale of Noah into its two pieces (both of which tell the whole tale).

One Telling of the Noah Story

Adonai (*YHVH*) saw how great was the evil of the human being on earth, and that the human heart leaned toward doing only evil all the time. So Adonai was upset that [Adonai] had made the human being in the earth, and [Adonai's] heart was filled with pain. And Adonai said, "I shall wipe away the human being which I have created from the face of the earth—from humans to beasts, to crawling things, to birds of the skies—for I am saddened that I have made them." But in Adonai's eyes, Noah seemed good.

Adonai said to Noah, "Come—you and all your household—to the ark, for I see that, in this generation, you are righteous before Me. Of all the clean beasts, take with you seven pair (seven males and their mates). And of all the beasts that are unclean, take two pair (two males and their mates). Also seven pairs of the birds of the skies … to keep their kind on the face of the earth. For in seven days, I am sending rain on the earth for forty days and forty nights, and I shall wipe away all that I have made from the face of the earth."

Noah did everything just as Adonai commanded.

Noah and his sons and his wife and the wives of his sons came to the ark before the waters of the flood. A week passed, then the waters of the flood came on the earth. And the rain fell on the earth, forty days and forty nights. And Adonai closed [the ark] for [Noah].

Now the flood was on the earth forty days, and the waters increased and raised the ark—it was lifted from the earth. And the waters grew strong and increased greatly on the earth, and the ark traveled on top of the waters. And the waters grew stronger and stronger on the earth, and they covered all the high mountains that are under all the heavens. Fifteen cubits above, the waters grew stronger, and they covered the mountains. From all that had the spirit of life in its nostrils to everything that was on the dry ground—it died. And [Adonai] wiped away all that was on the face of the earth—from humans to beasts, to crawling things, to birds of the skies—they were wiped away. Only

The Noah Project

The story of Noah is so popular that people often own more than one picture book about Noah and the ark. Gather up all the picture books of the story of Noah that you can find. Or do a quick search on the web for pictures of Noah and the ark. Set them all side by side. Though we seldom think about it, the differences in the way we imagine the story can be very surprising.

As You Read

Watch carefully for the big differences between one story of Noah and the next. Pay attention to what the stories say, but also pay attention to how the two stories are being told. What reason does God give for destroying the world in each story? What reason does God give for saving Noah and his family in each story?

Noah and those who were with him in the ark were left.

Then [Adonai] stopped the rain from the heavens. And the waters kept going back from the earth. Then, at the end of forty days, Noah opened the window of the ark which he had made. And he sent out a dove to see if the waters had eased from the face of the earth. But the dove found no resting place for its foot, for the waters were on the face of the earth. So Noah put out his hand and took it and brought it to him to the ark.

And [Noah] waited seven more days, then he again sent out a dove from the ark. And the dove came to him at evening time, and there was a freshly-plucked leaf from an olive tree in its beak, and Noah knew that the waters had eased from the earth. And he waited seven more days. Then he sent out a dove and it did not return to him ever again. And Noah removed the cover from the ark and looked: behold, the face of the earth had dried.

Then Noah built an altar to Adonai, and he took some of each clean beast and of each clean bird, and he offered sacrifices on the altar. Adonai smelled the pleasant aroma, and Adonai said to [Adonai's] heart, "I shall never again curse the ground because of the human being, for the human heart leans toward evil from its childhood— but I shall not strike all the living again, as I have done. In all the remaining days of the earth, seed and harvest, cold and heat, summer and winter, day and night shall never rest."

Another Telling of the Noah Story

These are the generations of Noah: Noah was a righteous person, perfect among those of his time. Noah walked with God [*Elohim*]. And Noah had three sons: Shem, Ham, and Japhet. Now the earth was spoiled before God [*Elohim*] and the earth was filled with violence. And God saw the earth, behold, it was spoiled, for all flesh had spoiled its way on the earth.

God said to Noah: "The end of all flesh has come before Me, for the earth is filled with violence because of them, and, behold, I will destroy them with the earth. Make yourself an ark of gopher wood, make rooms within the ark, and coat it with pitch inside and outside. Here is how you shall make it: The length of the ark [shall be] three hundred cubits; its width, fifty cubits; and its height, thirty cubits. Make a window for the ark, and finish it up to a cubit from the top. Make an entrance to the ark in its side. Make lower, second, and third stories for [the ark].

Behold, I am bringing the flood, water over the earth, to destroy all flesh that contains the breath of life from under the heavens. Everything which is on the land will die. But I shall establish My covenant with you. You shall come to the ark, you and your sons, your wife and your sons' wives. And of all the living, of all flesh, you shall bring two to the ark to keep alive with you, they shall be one male and one female. Of all the kinds of birds, and of the kinds of beasts, and of the kinds of crawling things of the earth, two of each will come to you to keep alive. And you must take for yourself of every food that is eaten and gather it for yourself, and it will be for you and for them for food." And Noah did all that God commanded him, thus he did.

Noah was six hundred years old, and the flood was on the earth. Of the clean beasts and of the beasts which were not clean, and of the birds and of all those which crawl upon the earth, two of each came to Noah to the ark, male and female, as God had commanded Noah. In the six hundredth year of Noah's life, in the second month, in the seventeenth day of the month—on this day all the fountains of the great deep burst out, and the windows of the heavens were opened. In this very

Quote to Remember

נֹחַ אִישׁ צַדִּיק תָּמִים הָיָה בְּדֹרֹתָיו.

Noah was a righteous person—he was without blame in his generation.

To Discuss

After the flood, in the second Noah story, God repeats the command given in the first story of creation, "Be plentiful and multiply," but adds that from now on humans can eat any fish or bird or animal for food, as long as it is dead and, as God says, as long as there is no "lifeblood in it." At the very end of this telling of the Noah story God commanded human beings to put to death any person who commits murder, "for in the image of God has God made the human." Why do we think of murder as the greatest evil that a person can do? In what way does murder harm the image of God?

day, Noah and Shem, Ham, and Japhet, the sons of Noah, and Noah's wife and his sons' three wives came to the ark. They and all the kinds of living things, and all the kinds of beasts, and all kinds of crawling things that crawl on the earth, all kinds of fowl, and all the winged birds. And they came to Noah to the ark, two of each, of all flesh in which is the breath of life. And those which came were male and female, some of all flesh came, as God had commanded.

All flesh—those that crawl on the earth, the birds, the beasts, and the wild animals, and all the swarming things that swarm on the earth, and all the human beings—died. And the waters grew strong on the earth for a hundred and fifty days.

Then God remembered Noah and the living things and all the beasts that were with him in the ark, and God passed a wind over the earth, and the waters ebbed. And the fountains of the deep and the windows of the heavens were shut. And the waters were cut off at the end of a hundred and fifty days. And the ark rested, in the seventh month, in the seventeenth day of the month, on the mountains of Ararat. And the waters continued to go back and forth until the tenth month. In the tenth month, on the first day of the month, the tops of the mountains appeared. And [Noah] sent out a raven, and it went back and forth until the waters dried up from the earth.

It was in the six hundred and first year, in the first month, on the first day of the month, the waters dried up from the earth. And in the second month, on the twenty-seventh day of the month, the earth dried up. And God spoke to Noah, saying, "Go out from the ark, you and your wife and your sons' wives with you. All the living things that are with you—of all flesh, of the birds, of the beasts, of all the crawling things that crawl on the earth—that go out with you, they shall swarm in the earth and be plentiful and multiply in the earth."

And Noah and his sons and his wife and his sons' wives went out. All the living things, all the crawling things, all the birds, and all that crawl on the earth, by their families, they went out of the ark.

Two Stories of Noah

In the Torah, the story of Noah does not look like either of the two stories above. Yet every word and every sentence above comes directly from the Torah story of Noah's ark. Taken apart like this, you can see both stories, each on its own. In the Torah the two are woven together so that they read like a zebra's skin—a few lines from one storyteller and a few lines from another—back and forth. Actually, though, each story has its own ideas about what is important, and each storyteller has something special to say.

The first storyteller calls for *seven pairs* of clean animals and *one pair* of unclean animals. The second teller calls for only two (*one pair*) of each animal. The first teller says the flood lasted forty days and forty nights. The second teller says the flood lasted one hundred fifty days. The first teller says that Adonai wanted to destroy the world because it was a mistake to create people with hearts that could lean toward doing evil. The second teller says that God wanted to destroy the world because people were spoiling it with violence.

Taking the stories apart, you can also see that each uses a different name for God. One calls God by the name *Elohim,* while the other uses the name Adonai (*YHVH*). Modern Bible scholars believe that the stories told about *Elohim* were told by priests. They speak about these storytellers as coming from the "P" (Priestly) source. Stories told about Adonai (*YHVH*), they say, came from a "J" source, since Hebrew words like *YHVH* that begin with "Y" or *yod* come into English starting with "J" (*Yehudah* becomes Judah, *Yonah* becomes Jonah, *Yehoshua* becomes Joshua, and so on). In J-stories, Adonai operates in our world. So Adonai closes the ark for Noah. Adonai smells a pleasant aroma, the way you smell a nice perfume. Adonai speaks to Adonai's heart, talking about the heart of the humans—just the way you sometimes talk to yourself.

To Consider

Someone worked very hard to weave these two different tales of Noah into one story. It had to be someone who knew both stories. Can you guess what reasons this person had for combining the two stories into one?

Not Quite So Simple

It is not always easy for scholars to know what storyteller is at work in the Torah. Moreover, there were more than two groups that told the stories. Along the way we will meet other Torah storytellers. Even in the Noah stories the P source may be retelling a story from an older source (called "E" because that source used the name *Elohim* for God). It may seem confusing at first, but it will become clear soon enough.

The Rainbow

At the end of the P story God makes a covenant with Noah, promising never to destroy the world again and choosing the rainbow to be the sign of the covenant. P stories are always careful to tell us that God is interested in making covenants, agreements with human beings. We will discover more about that as we continue.

Mysterious Differences

P stories are careful about time: exactly when the flood started, exactly when the flood ended. P stories are careful about measurements: exactly how big and how many stories high to make the ark, exactly what wood to use ("gopher wood"), and exactly how to cover it with tar. P stories are careful about places: exactly which mountain the ark landed on. And P stories are careful about families: exactly how old Noah was, the names of Noah's sons, and so on. At the end of this P story there is the same message given as in the P story of creation: "Be plentiful and multiply, and fill the earth."

J stories speak of Adonai as God, yet they picture Adonai as like us and near us. J stories ask, How does Adonai feel about things? Why is Adonai upset by human beings? What pleases Adonai? and so on. At the end of this J story it is Adonai who learns a lesson from the flood: people will always do bad things from time to time, but it is not good to destroy the world just because some people are evil. After all, people also do good things, just as Noah did when he built the altar and sent a pleasant aroma into the heavens for Adonai to enjoy.

In other words, the moral of the stories—the reason for telling them—is different in each case. The P-teller's story concludes that human violence is evil, and evil must always be punished. After the evil is punished, the world can go on and multiply and be plentiful again. The J-teller's story explains how Adonai discovered that people will always be both good and evil.

The Tower of Babel

The famous tale of the Tower of Babel is also told in this portion. The J source tells the tale in just nine verses:

> Everyone on earth had one language and used the same words. As they migrated from the east they found a valley in the land of Shinar and settled there. They said to one another, "Come, let us make bricks and bake them hard." Brick was their stone, and bitumen was their mortar. And

they said, "Come, let us build us a city, and a tower with its top in heaven, to make a name for ourselves—otherwise, we shall be scattered across the face of the earth." Adonai came down to see the city and tower that the humans had built, and Adonai said, "Behold, they are one people with one language, and this is what they have started to do, and now nothing that they decide to do will be too difficult for them. Let us go down, then, and scramble their language, so that one shall not understand the language of another." Then Adonai scattered them from there over the face of the whole earth; and they stopped building the city. That is why it was called Babel ["babble"], because there Adonai scrambled the language of the whole earth; and from there Adonai scattered them over the face of the whole earth.

Clearly, the J teller is using the Tower story to explain more about the beginnings of the world as we know it: where the people of Babylon (Shinar) originated (the East), why their cities included huge towers (today we know that the ancient Mesopotamians built these "towers" or ziggurats as bases for their temples, feeling that houses for the gods should be close to the heavens), how the people came to speak many languages instead of one, and why human beings are "scattered across the face of the earth." The J teller also explains to the readers of the Torah (who must be living in Canaan) that towers and cities in Mesopotamia are made of baked bricks joined with bitumen (tar). This is a bit strange to readers who use stone for their important buildings and place mortar between the stones. Lastly, the J teller pokes fun at the Israelites' ancient enemy, Babylon (Babel), by saying that Adonai caused the Babylonians to babble at one another (to this day we still use the word "babble" for words or sounds without meaning).

The Ziggurat of Babylon

Below: Bible scholars think the Tower story was based on the ziggurat of Babylon, a pyramid of many levels with a temple at its top. We have located the ruins of at least twenty ziggurats in ancient Mesopotamia. This sketch shows how one may have looked.

The Discovery

So there are two stories of Noah! How odd. And a story about how people came to be scattered and speak many languages. How interesting! You can see from this portion that the Torah is not a straightforward history book, putting one fact after another. You can also see that the Torah has little interest in science or history, at least as we know them. Then what exactly is the Torah? We are now well on our way to finding out.

Haftarah: Isaiah 54:1-55:5

The Rabbis connect the flood that destroyed all creation with the punishment Israel suffered in the destruction of the Temple, the Promised Land, and the Kingdom of Judah by the Babylonians, as told in the Book of Isaiah. In both cases God saved a small group of people to make a new start. In the Book of Isaiah, God says,

> This is like the days of Noah to Me, when I promised never again to cover the earth with vast floods. Now, I promise never again to be so angry with you [Israel] or to punish you so harshly.

In three parts, the haftarah tells the Israelites that the time for return to the Promised Land is near. (1) It is time to prepare, for even if you have been sad, "great shall be the happiness of your children."

(2) You can trust God to protect you from any enemies:

> No weapon designed to hurt you can succeed. You shall defeat any who rise against you. This is the inheritance of Adonai's servants.

And (3) If you have faith, God will provide all you need:

> Come buy food without money, wine and milk at no cost. ... Why spend your earnings for what does not satisfy? ... Heed Me and you shall eat what is good; your souls will overflow with delight.

The food our souls really crave is the everlasting covenant, God's true love. If you seek this, other nations will seek you out to discover the glory of Adonai your God.

Abram, Abraham; Sarai, Sarah

Twin Stories

The Torah has many twice-told stories about Abraham and Sarah. In one story God promises to give Abraham a son. A little later, God again promises Abraham a son. In one place Abraham tells a king that Sarah is his sister and, a little later, does the same thing in a second story, but with a different king. And there are also different stories about how Isaac got his name.

The first book of the Torah is named *Bereishit*, "beginnings". The stories we have met thus far are mostly about beginnings: how the world was created, how the snake came to crawl, why Adonai created the rainbow, and so on. When it came time to put *Bereishit* together, to tell about beginnings, there were many popular stories to include. They were like the little pieces inside the box of a large puzzle. It took a real puzzle-solver to fit the pieces together in a way that would make sense.

There were also many lists—lists of the generations from Adam to Noah, from Noah to Abraham, and onward. Each list recorded the names of important people and the names of their parents and children. The puzzle-solver used these lists as a guide, fitting stories about the people neatly into the lists wherever they seemed to make sense.

In this portion, *Lech-Lecha*, "You must leave", the puzzle-solver begins the work of piecing together the many stories of Abraham and Sarah. When the tale of Abraham begins, he is still called by the name his father and mother gave him: Abram. And his wife is called by the name she was given at birth, Sarai.

Fitting the Pieces

When it came to two or more tales that were very much alike, the puzzle-solver had some difficult choices to make. If the stories were not too much alike, one was put right after the other, as with the two stories of creation. If the stories were almost exactly the same, as with the story of the flood, the puzzle-solver fitted them together into a single story. And sometimes the puzzle-solver just scattered the stories to make it seem that they happened at different times.

Quote to Remember

לֶךְ־לְךָ מֵאַרְצְךָ וּמִמּוֹלַדְתְּךָ
וּמִבֵּית אָבִיךָ אֶל־הָאָרֶץ
אֲשֶׁר אַרְאֶךָּ.

You must leave your country, your homeland, your father's house; and go to the land that I will show you.

The Call of Abram

Adonai said to Abram, "You must leave your country, your homeland, your father's house; and go to the land that I will show you. And I will make you a great nation and I will bless you; I will make your name known, and you will be a blessing. I will bless those who bless you; whoever curses you, I will curse. And all the families of the earth will be blessed through you." ... Abraham was seventy-five years old when he set out from Haran. He took his wife Sarai, his nephew Lot, their possessions that belonged to them, the people that they had gotten in Haran, and they went out to leave for the land of Canaan. And they came to the land of Canaan. And Abram passed through the land....

Already Seventy-Five Years Old!

We know very little about Abram before Adonai called on him. We know even less about Abram's father Terach (except for names of people in his family and the fact that he lived 205 years). Abram was born in Ur of the Chaldees. The word *Ur* means "city", and just as now, many places were called "city"—for example, Oklahoma City, Kansas City, or New York City—so the Torah tells us that Abram was born in "Chaldee City".

It was in Chaldee City that Abram married Sarai. They had no children. Abram's father Terach wanted to move the whole family to Canaan, but when they reached the city of Haran they settled there. Abram's brother (Lot's father) was named Haran (which is spelled the same way as the name of the city in English but not in Hebrew). They lived in Haran a long time. Terach died. Then Adonai spoke to Abram, commanding him to leave.

The Torah does not say why Adonai called on Abram. Nor do we know why Lot decided to go with Abram. The Torah does not tell us how Abram and Lot made their living in the city of Haran. It's a mystery. Yet we are told that they had possessions to take to Canaan and also people who somehow "belonged" to them. What would Abram and Lot do for a living in Canaan? For now, that is also a mystery.

Down to Egypt

As Abram traveled through Canaan a time of famine came. Abram went "down to Egypt, to live there for a while." Abram told Sarai,

> I know what a beautiful woman you are. When the Egyptians see you, they will say, "This is his wife." Then they will kill me and let you live. Say you are my sister, so that I will be treated well for your sake and my life will be spared because of you.

Pharaoh heard how beautiful Sarai was, and he had her brought into his palace. He gave Abram "sheep and cattle, male and female donkeys, male and female servants, and camels." He thought that Sarai was Abram's sister, so he treated Abram well. But Adonai brought serious diseases (plagues) on Pharaoh and all Pharaoh's household. Then Pharaoh called Abram, asking, "What have you done to me? Why didn't you tell me she was your wife? … Take her and go!" And Pharaoh told his people to send Abram away with his wife and all the things he owned. So, the Torah says, "Abram had become very wealthy in herds and in silver and gold." Abram and Sarai went back to Beth-El in Canaan, where Abram called on Adonai at the altar he built.

Did Abram lie to Pharaoh? Was it a trick? Did Abram "sell" Sarai to Pharaoh, knowing that Adonai would rescue her and Abram and Sarai would become wealthy? Why should the puzzle-solver want a story like this to be a part of the jigsaw puzzle of Abram's life?

Let's imagine for a moment that Abram and Sarai are a bit like Adam and Eve. When the Torah tells the tale of Adam and Eve, it teaches us about how things began. When the Torah speaks here about Abram and Sarai, it is to account for how the Jewish people began. Abram and Sarai were the first Hebrews, just as Adam and Eve were the first humans.

Now let's look at the story again. Abram and Sarai passed through the land of Canaan, and when there was a famine they went down to Egypt; that's just what later happened to the tribes of Israel. Pharaoh thought Sarai was

Altars

The Torah tells us that as Abram journeyed from place to place in Canaan he set up altars to Adonai. What exactly does that mean? From what the Torah says a little later, setting up an altar seems to mean choosing a large stone and setting it upright (and maybe pouring water or oil on it) and declaring this to be an altar sacred to Adonai. Abram's altars marked places where Adonai gave some message to Abram or where Abram said something to Adonai. For example, at the great tree of Mamre near Shechem, Adonai appeared to Abram and said, "I will give this land to your offspring." Abram set up an altar. Near Beth-El Abram called on Adonai by name. Abram set up another altar.

Canaanite Stone Markers

Below: Stone markers from the Canaanite city of Gezer. Archaeologists found them fallen in various places and placed them upright and side by side for display. Abraham's "altars" probably looked like these stone markers.

Hebrews

In this story Abram is called "Abram the Hebrew" for the first time. The word for "Hebrew" is *ivri*, which means "[one who] crossed over" or "[one who] passed through." We have already seen that Adonai commanded Abram to "pass through" or "cross over" the land of Canaan, so the name may mean "Abram the Wanderer" or "Abram Who Crossed Over" into Canaan. In any case, the first name for the Jewish people was *Ivrim*, "Hebrews".

beautiful, so he took her for his own; the tribes of Israel were good laborers, so Pharaoh took them for his own, forcing them into slavery. To rescue Sarai, Adonai brought plagues on Pharaoh and his household; to rescue the tribes of Israel, Adonai brought plagues on Pharaoh and Egypt. Abram left Egypt a wealthy man; so too, when the tribes of Israel left Egypt, they also had more than when they came—more people, more livestock, even more silver and gold. When Pharaoh calls Abram to speak with him, it reminds us of how Pharaoh called Moses to tell him to take the tribes and leave! The Torah may be using this story of Abram and Sarai to remind us of the story of our people.

Many Torah stories work this way. Sometimes a story about Abram and Sarai is about what happened to two people, but at other times it is about what happened to the *entire* people. This seems to be a story to teach us a lesson about the *entire* people, the Hebrews. The lesson is: No matter where we go, God looks after us and protect us.

Rescuing Lot

Abram and Lot had so much livestock that their shepherds quarreled over water and land. So Abram told Lot to choose where he would go, whether east or west, and they would separate. Lot went east toward the Dead Sea (in those days, the Torah says, the land there was as beautiful as the Garden of Eden).

Adonai visited Abram and told him to look in all directions, for all the land of Canaan would be his, and his offspring would be "like the dust of the earth, so that if anyone could count the dust, then your offspring could be counted."

Unfortunately, things did not go well for Lot. Four kings joined their armies to conquer the city of Sodom, and they carried off Lot as a captive. Abram called out his 318 soldiers (in this story it seems that he was very wealthy and had many followers). They chased after the kings far to the north, catching up with them near Damascus. Abram and his troops defeated the kings and returned with Lot and with everything that the kings had taken from Sodom.

Another Covenant Story

Adonai's word came to Abram in a vision, "Do not be afraid, Abram, I am your shield, your very great reward." But Abram was worried; he and Sarai still had no child. Adonai told Abram to try to count the stars and said "So shall your off-spring be." Then Abram trusted in Adonai, but he asked, How can I know this will happen? God told Abram to sacrifice a cow, a goat, a ram, a dove, and a young pigeon. In a dream, Adonai told Abram that his descendants would be enslaved for four hundred years, then God would punish the people who enslaved them, and they would come out of slavery with great wealth. Then Adonai made another covenant saying how much land Abram would have.

There were many covenant stories about Abram, each with its own wonderful image. One asks Abram to count the dust, and another asks Abram to count the stars. And there were at least two stories about Abram and things that would happen to the tribes of Israel when they went to Egypt. There was the story about Pharaoh and Abram and this story about the sacrifice. Putting the puzzle together was a big task. The pieces of the jigsaw had to be placed carefully, so that each well-known story would have its own place.

Ishmael

Abram and Sarai decided to adopt a child. In those days, this meant that Abram would have a child with Sarai's maid, an Egyptian woman named Hagar. The child of Sarai's maid would be Sarai's child, as Sarai says, "I can build a family through her." Hagar soon became pregnant, but neither Sarai nor Hagar was happy about this adoption arrangement. So Hagar ran away, taking her child. But an angel of Adonai came and told Hagar to return to Abram's household. "Your descendants," the angel told her, "will be too numerous to count." The angel said that her baby would be a boy, and she should name him Ishmael. But a verse or two later the Torah says that it was Abram who chose the name: "So Hagar bore Abram a son, and Abram gave the name Ishmael to the son she had borne. Abram was eighty-six years old when Hagar bore him Ishmael."

A King and a Priest

Abram returned to Sodom in victory. Malchizedek, king of Sodom, came out to welcome and thank him. Mysteriously, the Torah tells us that Malchizedek was a *kohen*, a priest, of God Most High (*El Elyon*). We still use this name for our God. Malchizedek blessed Abram. For his part, Abram gave Malchizedek one-tenth of everything he had won. In this way the Torah teaches that when we come to a priest we should not come empty-handed. We should be like Abram and give a tenth of everything to the priest. This tenth is called a "tithe", and giving it is called "tithing", and tithing is commanded by the Torah. People reading this story of Abram and Malchizedek would say, "So that is how tithing began!" It is hard to know if that is truly how it began or if tithing was so common that the story was told to explain its origin, sort of like a story about how the kangaroo got its pouch or how the camel got its hump.

To Consider

What did Adonai mean by saying to Abram, "I am your shield, your very great reward"?

An Angel of Adonai

Adonai appears and speaks to Abram directly many times in the Torah, but when Hagar is visited it is by "an angel of Adonai" instead. Hagar, an Egyptian woman, is probably a believer in many gods. Nevertheless, Hagar claims that she has seen God's face.

The Sign of Circumcision

Why should there be a "sign" to help us remember a covenant with God? What does the rainbow have in common with circumcision? If the sign of circumcision is only on males, how do female Jews share in the sign? (Hint: Think about the ceremony of circumcision, the *brit milah*. Who is there to take part in it?)

Name Changes and More

When Abram was ninety-nine years old, Adonai appeared to him ....

And God said to him, "... You will be the father of many nations. No longer will you be called Abram, your name will be Abraham, for I have made you a father of many nations...." Then God said to Abraham, "This is my covenant .... Every male among you shall be circumcised. You will be circumcised and it will be the sign of the covenant between Me and you. Through the generations, every male of eight days must be circumcised...."

God also said to Abraham, "As for Sarai your wife, you will no longer call her Sarai. Her name will be Sarah. I will bless her and certainly give you a son by her. ... She will be the mother of nations; kings of people will come from her."

Abraham fell face down. He laughed (*va-yitzchak*) and said to himself, "Will a son be born to a man a hundred years old? Will Sarah bear a child at the age of ninety?" ... God said, "But your wife Sarah will bear you a son, and you will call him Isaac (*Yitzchak*)...."

Abraham was ninety-nine years old when we was circumcised, and his son Ishmael was thirteen. Abraham and his son Ishmael were both circumcised on that day. And every male in Abraham's household ... was circumcised with him.

New Names

The story of Hagar and Ishmael tells us how the Arab nations began and how they are related to the Hebrews. *Ishmael* means "God hears". At first the Torah says that an angel gave Ishmael his name. Later the Torah says that Abram gave Ishmael his name. Abram also receives a new name, *Avraham*, and the Torah says it means "father of many nations." Sarai's new name is *Sarah*, which means "princess", since she will be "the mother of nations." God promises a son to Abraham and Sarah. When Abraham laughs to himself, God seems to know this, so God tells Abraham to call the new son *Yitzchak*, meaning "laughter". This is one story about how Isaac got his name. Another one is coming later. All these are stories of *Bereishit*, "beginnings".

Haftarah: Isaiah 40:27-41:16

The Rabbis connect God's choice of Abraham to Isaiah's words about God's choice of the people of Israel. As God's promise to Abraham came true, so will Israel's faith be rewarded. The haftarah has one message for us: God has not forgotten Israel. Even though they are in a strange land (Babylonia), help is on the way.

> Why do you say, [O Israel], "My way is hidden from Adonai, my punishment is ignored by my God?" Do you not realize? ... All who trust in Adonai renew their strength. Like eagles, they soar on wings. They run and never tire of running. They march and never grow weary.

Only those who do not know God will waste their time making idols. They are fools! But Israel is God's "chosen one". God has "chosen you and not rejected you."

> Have no fear, for I am with you; do not be frightened for I am your God. I will give you strength. I will help you. ... I, Adonai your God, hold you by your hand.

As God's servants, the Israelites should not be afraid of the future. You may think of yourselves as worms today—weak, small, and oppressed. But one day, God says, you will look around and you will discover that it is not you but your enemies who have vanished.

Here is My promise, says Adonai: "I, your Rescuer, the Holy One of Israel—I will help you."

וירא
Vayeira
Genesis 18:1–22:24

Testing God; Testing Abraham

Combining Stories

This portion, *Vayeira*, begins with two stories woven into one—the same way the two Noah stories were. Before they were combined, one story told of Adonai visiting Abraham at Mamre. The other story told of three men who visited Abraham at Mamre. It seems that both stories were well known, popular, and beloved; and since both took place at Mamre, it made sense to combine them. This time we look at the story just as it is found in the Torah. First the Torah says, "Adonai appeared...," then "three men standing...." Abraham says, "My lord..." as if speaking to Adonai (or one person); then Abraham continues, "All of you..." as if speaking to the three men. If you read the combined story quickly, you might hardly notice these changes—like so many people who read the Torah, you might think you were reading only one story!

Nothing Is Too Difficult

Adonai appeared to Abraham at the great trees of Mamre as Abraham was sitting in the heat of the day by the tent entrance. [Abraham] looked up and saw, behold, three men standing nearby him. He ... rushed ... to greet them, and he bowed down toward the ground. He said, "My lord, if I have found favor in your eyes, do not pass your servant by. Let a little water be brought. All of you can wash your feet and rest beneath this tree."

Abraham runs to Sarah and asks her to bake some bread. Next he runs to get a fine calf. He tells a servant to hurry to cook it. Then he brings yogurt, milk, and meat to the visitors and stands under a tree while they eat.

"Where is your wife Sarah?" they asked him. "There in the tent," he said. Then one said, "I shall surely return to you next springtime, and your wife Sarah will have a son."

Now Sarah was listening... Abraham and Sarah were old ... and Sarah was past the age of child-bearing. So Sarah laughed inside, as if to say, "After I am worn out and my husband is old, will I now have this pleasure?"

Adonai said to Abraham, "Why did Sarah laugh? ... Is anything too difficult for Adonai to do? ..." Then Sarah was afraid. She lied, saying, "I did not laugh." And [Adonai] said, "Yes, you did so laugh!"

This is the second tale that promises the birth of Isaac and tells why he will be named *Yitzhak*, "laughter". In the first, Abraham laughed to himself and Adonai knew it. In this one, Sarah laughed inside and Adonai knew it. Adonai is there by the tent. How do we know? Because Sarah is afraid and lies—she must be lying *to* Adonai, since she speaks her lie out loud. And Adonai is right there to say, "Yes, you did so laugh!" The story contains two lessons: Adonai knows our thoughts, and nothing is too difficult for Adonai to do.

The Bargain

When the men got up to leave they looked down toward Sodom. Abraham walked along with them to see them on their way.

Adonai was thinking, "Shall I hide from Abraham what I am about to do? Abraham will surely become a great and powerful nation .... I have chosen him ... to keep the way of Adonai by doing what is right and just...."

Then Adonai said, "The screams of Sodom and Gomorrah are so great and their sin is so heavy! Now I will go down and see if what they have done is as bad as the scream that has reached me. If not, I will know." The men turned away and went toward Sodom, but Abraham remained standing before Adonai.

Abraham came closer and said, "Will you sweep away the righteous with the wicked? What if there are fifty righteous people in the city? Will you ... not forgive the place for [their] sake ...? Far be it from You to do such a thing—to kill the righteous with the wicked ... Will not the Judge of all the earth do what is just?" Adonai said, "If I find fifty righteous people in the city of Sodom, I will forgive the whole place for their sake."

Abraham answered, saying, "Behold, I was bold to speak to my Master, though I am nothing but dust and ashes. What if the righteous people number five less than fifty? Will you destroy the whole city because of five?" [Adonai] said, "If I find forty-five there, I will not destroy it." Again, he spoke to [Adonai], "What if there are only forty?" [Adonai] said, "For the sake of the forty, I will not do it." [Abraham] said, "Let not my Master be angry, but

Quote to Remember

הֲשֹׁפֵט כָּל־הָאָרֶץ לֹא יַעֲשֶׂה מִשְׁפָּט:

Will not the Judge of all the earth do what is just?

Now I Will Go Down

We usually imagine that God is omniscient, able to see and know all things. But according to the story of Sodom and Gomorrah, Adonai does not see everything from heaven. That is why Adonai said, "I will go down and see if what [Sodom and Gomorrah] have done is as bad as the scream that has reached me."

Speaking to God

Abraham speaks with Adonai here as you might speak with a parent—a powerful parent, of course. Before the conversation begins, Adonai wonders whether or not to "hide" the destruction of Sodom and Gomorrah from Abraham. Abraham was standing in front of Adonai, and then Abraham "came closer." Later on, the Torah will say that no one ever saw Adonai face-to-face as Moses did. But the stories in *Bereishit* are very old—and in these stories Adonai enters the world and speaks directly to Adam and Eve, to Noah, and to Abraham.

To Consider

How did Adonai destroy the cities of Sodom and Gomorrah? Read Genesis 19:27-28. From what Abraham saw, how do you think the cities were destroyed?

let me speak: What if only thirty can be found there?" [Adonai] said, "I will not do it if I find thirty there." Abraham said, "Behold, I was bold to speak to my Master: What if twenty were found there?" [Adonai] said, "For the sake of twenty, I will not destroy it." And he said, "Let my Master not be angry and let me speak just this once: What if only ten can be found there?" [Adonai] said, "For the sake of ten, I will not destroy it."

And Adonai departed when [Adonai] was finished speaking with Abraham. And Abraham returned to his home.

The End of Sodom and Gomorrah

This marvelous story holds us spellbound because Adonai has not yet decided whether the cities should be destroyed. Abraham is respectful but bold: "Will not the Judge of all the earth do what is just?" In the end, Adonai agrees not to destroy Sodom if ten righteous people can be found there.

As the story continues, it is not Adonai, but two angels who arrive in Sodom to see if the city is wicked. In fact, the people are very wicked; they even try to harm the angels. The only righteous folk in Sodom are Lot and his family.

The angels inform Lot that Sodom and Gomorrah will be destroyed. Lot and his family should flee and never look back. But Lot's wife *does* turn to look back, and she is transformed into a pillar of salt. This is definitely not science and definitely not history. People can't turn into salt except in a Torah story where anything can happen: where serpents can talk and angels can go on inspection tours! Before there was television and before there was radio, there was the Torah with stories that could entertain and teach at one and the same time.

Midrash

At least two tales (and probably more) were combined to make the story of the visit and the destruction of Sodom. But by now you are beginning to understand how the Torah works its magic. For example, you often hear people say that "the Rabbis" told this story, then "the Rabbis" told an-other story, or "Rabbi So-and-So" said this and "Rabbi Thus-and-Such" said that. The Rabbis taught over a period of several hundred years. They did not all live at the same place or in the same time. Their teachings were just col-lected and set side by side, like a conversation—very much the same way that the Torah was built.

For example, the Rabbis noticed that we know almost nothing about Abraham's father, Terach. One rabbi sug-gested that Terach must have been an idol-worshiper. An-other suggested that Terach might even have been a maker of idols. He told a story about how young Abram was left in charge of Terach's idol shop one day. Abram took a broom-stick and broke all the idols but one—the largest. Abram put the broomstick in the hands of the large idol. Of course, when Terach returned, he was angry with Abram for break-ing the idols. But Abram said, "I did not break the idols. The big idol broke all the smaller ones!" Terach said, "Idols are just wood and clay. They can't break one another." And Abram said something like, "If they are useless, why should people worship them?"

This is a *midrash*—a story that teaches a lesson by fill-ing in missing details with imagination—a "teaching story". And we know that the Rabbis loved to create midrash to teach their lessons. But there was midrash a long time be-fore there were rabbis. Torah stories come from a time when such tales were already popular, when generations of storytellers knew and told stories about the beginnings of things, including the beginnings of the Jewish people.

Two More "Repeated" Stories

Back at the Torah, Abraham moves south and sets up his tent in Gerar, where he tells people that Sarah "is my sister." Abimelech, the king of Gerar, takes Sarah, planning to make her his wife. But God visits Abimelech in a dream and says, "You are as good as dead because of the woman you have taken, for she is a married woman." Abimelech replies that he is innocent. He thought Sarah was Abraham's sister, and anyway, he has not touched her. Still in the dream, God

Making the Pieces Fit

The Torah is fitting pieces to-gether. It tells the stories of Adonai, the three men, and the two angels as if they were one story. But looking closely, we can see that once there were sepa-rate stories about how Isaac got his name, about Abraham dis-cussing Sodom and Gomorrah with Adonai, and about Lot and the two angels in Sodom. The Torah combines all these to make its puzzle seem more like one picture.

To Discuss

When a lot of people tell stories or teach lessons in the same way, we sometimes call them "a school of thought." For example, among the Rabbis we sometimes think of two "schools" of sages who thought differently—the Academy of Shammai and the Academy of Hillel. Each school of thought had many rabbis in it, and different schools taught at the same time. The Torah has "schools of thought", too. As we have seen, they teach in different ways. The J source is one. The P source is another. And there are more. Can you name some schools of thought that exist to-day? (Here's a hint: Think about elections.)

Wife-Sister Stories

This is the second story in which Abraham claims that Sarah is his sister. Here the Torah wants us to know that Abraham really is a truthful person, so it says that Abraham was not lying—Sarah really was his half-sister. Just as in the story about Abraham and the Pharaoh, Abimelech needs Abraham's blessing to make things right because Abraham "is a prophet." The Torah fit both stories into the jigsaw puzzle of Abraham's life.

Hagar-Ishmael Stories

This is the second story about Hagar and Ishmael leaving the camp of Abraham. Both stories speak of the beginnings of the cousins of the Hebrews, the Arab peoples, who were also "children of Abraham" (as the Hebrews were). In both, an angel speaks to Hagar. This may be the reason for *Ishmael's* name, which means "God hears".

instructs Abimelech to return Sarah to Abraham, "for he is a prophet, and he will pray for you, and you will live."

Early the next morning Abimelech spoke to Abraham, saying, "What have you done to us? … What was your reason for doing this?" Abraham answered that he had believed there was no fear of God in Gerar and that people might kill him to get Sarah. "Besides," he adds, "Sarah really is my sister, the daughter of my father though not of my mother, and she became my wife." According to this story, long ago, before they left Haran, Abraham told Sarah, "This is how you can show your love for me: Everywhere we go, say of me: 'He is my brother.'" Hearing this, Abimelech gave Abraham goats and sheep and silver for Sarah. He invited Abraham to live anywhere in Gerar. In return, Abraham prayed to God, and God healed Abimelech, his wife, and his slave girls so that they could have children again. The very last line explains: "For Adonai had closed up every womb in Abimelech's household because of Abraham's wife Sarah."

There is also a "repeated" story about Hagar and Ishmael in this portion. This time Sarah tells Abraham to send Hagar and her child away. God tells Abraham to do as Sarah wishes. Abraham gives Hagar and Ishmael some food and water and tells them to go. When they use up the water, Hagar puts baby Ishmael under a bush and walks on a little way, thinking, "I cannot watch the boy die." God hears her sobbing, and the angel of God calls to her from heaven, saying, "Do not be afraid. … Lift the boy up … for I will make him into a great nation." Then God opens Hagar's eyes, and she sees a well of water. They are saved. And "God was with [Ishmael] as he grew up. He lived in the desert and became an archer." In the meanwhile, Isaac was born.

Isaac

A while passed, the Torah says, and then came the time for Abraham's test. God tells Abraham to take his beloved son Isaac to a mountain and sacrifice him there. Abraham, his servants, and Isaac travel by donkey to a mountain three days' distance. The servants stay with the donkeys. Abraham and Isaac climb the mountain. Isaac (who is carrying the wood) says, "The fire and the wood are here, but where is the lamb for the sacrifice?" Abraham answers, "God will provide the lamb for the sacrifice, my son."

When they reach the right place, Abraham builds an altar (this time Abraham probably gathered many stones, rather than just setting one stone upright), puts the wood on it, and then ties up Isaac and lays him on the altar, on top of the wood. "Then he reached out his hand and took the knife to slay his son." All this is told by one storyteller. Now a second story is woven in:

> But the angel of Adonai called to him from the heavens, saying, "Abraham, Abraham!" And he answered, "I am here." And [the angel of Adonai] said, "Do not lay your hand on the boy and do nothing to him."

The first story returns: "Now I know that you fear God for you have not withheld from me your son, your only son." Then the second story says:

> Abraham looked up and there in a thicket, he saw a ram caught by its horns. He … took the ram and sacrificed it as a burnt offering instead of his son. So Abraham named that place, "Adonai will provide." And to this day it is said, "On the mountain of Adonai things will be provided."

> The angel of Adonai called to Abraham from heaven a second time, saying, "I swear by Myself, declares Adonai, since you have done this and not withheld your son, your only son, I will surely bless you and make your offspring as numerous as the stars in the sky and as the sand on the seashore. … And through your offspring all nations will be blessed, because you have obeyed Me."

Then someone—perhaps the puzzle-solver who combined the stories—finishes the tale by saying: "Then Abraham returned to his servants, and they set off together for Beersheba. And Abraham dwelled in Beersheba."

The Mystery of the Binding of Isaac

From one telling it seems that Isaac actually was sacrificed on the mountain. In the second telling Isaac is saved be-

Isaac's Name

Just before the story of Hagar and Ishmael, the Torah says that Isaac was born to Sarah because "Adonai was gracious … and Adonai did for Sarah" what Adonai had promised. "Abraham gave the name Isaac to the son Sarah bore him." Isaac was circumcised at the age of eight days and "Abraham was a hundred years old when … Isaac was born to him." The Torah adds that Sarah gave the name Isaac to her son because "God has brought me laughter, and everyone who hears about this will laugh with me"—because she was so old when Isaac was born. (Notice how many tales we have heard about how Isaac got his name.)

Two Stories of the Test

How do we know there is more than one story here? Just as in the stories of creation, the two stories here use different names for God. One uses *Elohim* ("God") and the other uses *YHVH* ("Adonai"). If you read the story looking for where the names of God change, you can see there really are two stories.

The Ram in the Thicket?

Below right: Archaeologist Sir Leonard Woolley (1880-1960) was very excited to find a beautiful statuette that he called "the ram in the thicket." He found it in a town he thought was Ur and connected the statuette to the story of Abraham. Later it was found that the "ram" was really a goat reaching for leaves to nibble; and today we know that there is no proof that the town he excavated was Abraham's Ur. Nevertheless, the statuette is a fine work of art.

cause Adonai "provides" a ram for the sacrifice. Either way, at the end of the story Abraham returns to the servants without Isaac. Of course, we know that there are more stories about Isaac to come. So this is a Bible mystery. All we can say is that however the stories used to end, what we have now is a combined story that provides a major lesson: Adonai tests human beings, but Adonai does not want human beings to sacrifice other human beings.

Haftarah: 2 Kings 4:1-37

In *Vayeira* Sarah is promised a son even though her husband is old. The Rabbis connect this with the story of how the prophet Elisha promised a son to a Shunammite woman who also had an aged husband.

The haftarah contains stories about the prophet Elisha, the chief disciple of Elijah. In the first story the widow of a prophet asks Elisha for help. Her husband died owing money, and the creditors want to take her house away. All she has is a small jar of oil. Elisha tells her to get as many jars as she can and to pour oil in them. As often as she pours from her little jar, the other jars keep filling until no more jars can be found. Then Elisha says, "Sell the oil and pay your debt; you and your children can live on what is left over."

In another story Elisha is given a room by a couple in Shunem (in the valley of Jezreel). He asks the

woman what he can do to repay her. She asks for a son, though her husband seems too old. But Elisha promises her a son. And she has one.

The son grows up, but one day he cries out, "My head, my head!" and dies. His mother lays him on the bed that Elisha slept in and calls for Elisha. She says, "You gave me a son, but now he has died. It was all a lie." But Elisha prays to God, then stretches himself out over the boy. The boy sneezes seven times and comes back to life.

What are the lessons here? Wisdom is like the jar of oil; it can be poured into many jars without ever running out. And the son of the Shunammite woman is like the people of Israel. Though the people may seem dead to others, their prayers and faith in God can always restore them to life.

A Cave and a Wife

חיי שרה
Chayei Sarah
Genesis 23:1–25:18

History and Facts

Everyone who writes history is a storyteller. What facts need to be told? What facts can be left out? Every history is a story. And every storyteller wants to say something important. Even today, when two or more people take hold of the same story they tell it differently. For example, a Mexican storyteller will tell the history of the battle of the Alamo very differently from a Texan storyteller. In the same way, the storytellers of the Torah often take hold of the same story but tell it very differently.

The priests speak of the One God (*Elohim*) as commanding all, creating all, knowing all, and controlling all. The priests would say that if Persia defeated Babylon, it was because *Elohim* sent the Persians to defeat Babylon. God is in command, and God's special servants—people like Abraham and Sarah—are righteous and can do no wrong.

The J-tellers believe that Adonai (*YHVH*) is near to us, helps with human problems, and is particularly concerned for good people like Abraham and Sarah. They especially like stories about how things came to be. How did the first murder happen? How did Abraham become rich? Where did the Arab people come from? And so on.

The Torah brings stories from many tellers together to make one history of our people and the peoples around us.

The Death of Sarah

Sarah died at the age of one hundred and twenty-seven. The Torah says, "Sarah died in Kiriath-arba—which is now Hebron—in the land of Canaan; and Abraham mourned for Sarah and bewailed her."

There is a small clue in these words. When is "now"? For example, you may know that the space center in Florida was originally named the Cape Canaveral Space Center. Today it is named the Kennedy Space Center. It is the same place;

Knowing Who Told the Stories

We already know that some Torah stories were told by priests (the P-source) and some by a group that spoke of *YHVH* (the J-source). We have also seen some stories that come from tellers who always used the name *Elohim* for God and who are called the E-source. It is interesting but not too important to know who told the stories. In some cases, not even the experts can tell for certain. What is most important to us is what the stories say and why they say things differently.

Archaeology

In the past people often explained Torah stories through
midrash—new stories that added
ideas. Later they also explained
the stories through Bible criti-
cism, learning who told them and
when. Today we have more tools
to help us. We can now read
many of the languages spoken in
Bible times, and by digging up the
places of the past we have discovered many ancient documents
that help us understand the Bible
better. This is the work of archaeologists. But the archaeologists not only dig up ancient
documents; they also uncover
facts from the buildings and objects they discover buried in the
earth.

only the name has changed. Imagine that you are doing a
report on the space shuttle. You find an old story that says,
"The space shuttle was launched from Cape Canaveral, in
the State of Florida." You write in your report, "The space
shuttle was launched from Cape Canaveral—which is now
the Kennedy Space Center—in the State of Florida." This
shows us (1) that you are writing your story *after* the place
was renamed and (2) that you want to help people *now* and
in the future to recognize the place you are writing about. In
the same way, the Torah verse above tells us that (1) someone was telling the story *after* Kiriath-arba was renamed
Hebron and (2) that someone wanted people *now* and in the
future to be able to find the place. Clearly, your report is not
the original telling, but a re-telling of the story. So is the report we have here about Sarah's death. Sentences like
"Kiriath-arba—which is now Hebron" are one way we know
that the stories in the Torah were retold many times by
many different people.

Let's return to the story: Sarah died. Abraham wanted to
bury her, but he owned no land. So he bought the field of
Machpelah, near Mamre. And he buried Sarah in the cave
that was in that field.

Now Isaac was old enough to have a wife, but Abraham
did not want Isaac to take a Canaanite wife. Instead Abraham told his most trusted servant to find a wife for Isaac
back in the "homeland", the place from which Abraham and
Lot had come. The servant took ten camels and part of
Abraham's treasure and traveled to the city of Nahor. He
made the camels kneel down by the well at the time when
the women of the city usually came to draw water for their
families.

Rebecca at the Well

And [the servant] said, "Adonai, God of my master
Abraham, give me good fortune today and grant
mercy for my master Abraham. Here I stand by
the spring as the daughters of the townspeople
come out to draw water. Let it be the maiden to
whom I say, 'Please, lower your jar that I may
drink,' and who answers, 'Drink, and I will also

give water to your camels'—let her be the one whom You have decreed for Your servant Isaac. By this, I shall know that You have granted kindness to my master."

He had hardly finished speaking when Rebecca … came out with her jar on her shoulder. The maiden was very beautiful …. She went down to the spring, filled her jar, and came up. The servant ran toward her, saying, "Please, let me sip a little water from your jar." "Drink, my master," she said, and she quickly lowered her jar to her hand and let him drink. When she had let him drink his fill, she said, "I will also draw water for your camels, until they finish drinking." Quickly emptying the jar into the trough, she ran back to the well to draw, and she drew [water] for all his camels.

Abraham's servant gave Rebecca gifts: a gold nose-ring weighing a *beqa* and two gold armbands, ten *shekels* in weight. He asked, "Whose daughter are you?" When Rebecca said she was the daughter of Bethuel of the family of Nahor, the servant knew he had found a family of Abraham's relatives. He asked if there was room at her father's house for him and his camels to spend the night. She invited him to stay.

The man bowed low in thankfulness to Adonai, saying, "Blessed be Adonai, the God of my master

Quote to Remember

וַתֹּאמֶר גַּם לִגְמַלֶּיךָ אֶשְׁאָב עַד אִם־כִּלּוּ לִשְׁתֹּת.

She said, "I will also draw water for your camels, until they finish drinking."

Gifts for Rebecca

Archaeologists often uncover weights used in ancient times to measure things like gold. A small weight is sometimes marked as a *beqa*—the weight of the nose-ring that the servant gave to Rebecca at the well. Larger weights are labeled *shekel*, the weight of the armbands that Rebecca received as a gift. The weights do not prove that the story actually happened, but they do prove that the Torah tells things in factual ways.

Left: Dome-shaped limestone weights from around the time of King Hezekiah (728-699 B.C.E.). The smallest is marked as one *shekel*, the next is two *shekels*, and the last is four. Weights like these were placed in one side of a scale and whatever was being measured was placed in the other side.

To Discuss

What were Abraham's reasons for wanting a wife for Isaac? Why did he want Isaac to marry a wife from among his relatives back home instead of a wife from among the Canaanites who were close by? The Torah does not answer these questions, so you are free to use your imagination—you can create your own midrash.

O Sister

Ancient clay tablets tell us how the oldest brother became the head of the household after his father died. That could be why Laban is the one who welcomes the servant of Abraham and arranges the marriage of his sister Rebecca. But the story mentions Bethuel, father of Laban and Rebecca, as if he is still alive. If so, why does her brother arrange the marriage and not her father? Some archaeologists think that Bethuel has died and Laban is taking his father's place in the story. They point to where the family bids goodbye to Rebecca by saying, "O sister!" If Bethuel had been alive, they say, we might have heard "O daughter!" instead.

Abraham …. For I have been guided on my errand by Adonai, to the house of my master's relatives."

Rebecca ran ahead to tell her family all that had happened. Her brother Laban went out to greet the man. The camels were unloaded and fed; and food was brought for Abraham's servant. But the servant refused to eat until he had explained his mission.

"I am Abraham's servant," he began. "Adonai has greatly blessed my master, and he has become rich …. Sarah, my master's wife, gave my master a son in her old age, and [Abraham] has given [Isaac] everything he owns. Now my master made me swear, saying, 'You shall [go] to my relatives, and get a wife for my son.' And I said to my master, 'What if the woman does not follow me?' He answered me, 'Adonai, whose ways I have followed, will send an angel of Adonai with you and make your errand successful….'"

Then the servant told how he had prayed to Adonai and set up a test for the right woman, and how Rebecca passed the test, allowing him to drink from her jar and also giving drink to the camels until they had finished (which, for ten thirsty camels, means fetching an enormous amount of water from the well—a great labor indeed).

When the servant finished telling his story, he said, "Now, if you mean to treat my master with true kindness, tell me; and, if not, tell me that also, so that I might turn either right or left."

Then Laban and Bethuel answered, "The matter was decreed by Adonai. We cannot discuss with you whether it is bad or good. Behold, Rebecca is before you. Take her and go. As Adonai has spoken, let her be the wife of your master's son." When Abraham's servant heard their words, he bent low to Adonai.

The servant brought out items of silver and gold, and garments, and presented them to Rebecca. He gave presents to her brother and her mother. Then he and the men with him ate and drank, and they spent the night. When they arose the next morning, he said, "Allow me to return to my master." But her brother and her mother said, "Let the maiden remain with us some days or ten days, afterwards you shall go." He said, "Do not delay me now that Adonai made my errand successful. Give me leave to return to my master." They said, "Let us call the girl and ask for her reply."

They called Rebecca and said to her, "Will you go with this man?" And she said, "I will go." So they sent off their sister Rebecca and her nurse along with Abraham's servant and his men. They blessed Rebecca, saying, "O sister! May you grow into thousands of ten thousands, and may your offspring seize the gates of their enemies!" Then Rebecca and her maids rose and mounted the camels and followed the man. …

And Isaac went out walking in the field at dusk and, raising his eyes, he saw camels coming. And Rebecca raised her eyes; and she saw Isaac. She got down from the camel. She said to the servant, "Who is that man walking in the field to greet us?" And the servant said, "That is my master." So she took her veil and covered herself.

The servant told Isaac everything he had done. Isaac then brought [Rebecca] into the tent of his mother Sarah. He took Rebecca as his wife. He loved her, and so Isaac was comforted after his mother's death.

True or Not

The servant of Abraham sets up a kind of test for "Adonai, God of my master Abraham." As he finishes speaking, Rebecca appears. She behaves just as the servant prayed. The servant rewards her even before he knows that she is related to Abraham. But is this "history"? Probably not. The story of Rebecca at the well teaches about kindness and hospitality, the kind of lessons that the Torah delights to tell.

The story may not be history, but it is surely true in another way. In 1925 archaeologists discovered the main city

To Consider

The Torah says that Abraham "mourned" for Sarah. It does not tell us exactly how Isaac felt when his mother died. Where do we find out how Isaac felt about the death of his mother? How did Isaac's marrying Rebecca help?

Apiru

Tablets from Nuzi speak of people called the *apiru*, a word we now think may mean "refugee". The *apiru* had special rights. They could travel freely, buying and selling, but they were forbidden to own any real estate. According to the Torah, this was how Abraham and Sarah lived—traveling through Canaan, not owning any land. This may be why the purchase of the cave and the field near Mamre was so important—this was the first time that Abraham owned any land. Some archaeologists even think that the name "Hebrew" may come from the word *apiru*, and that the early Hebrew tribes were "refugees" or "wanderers".

of an ancient kingdom called Nuzi. It is likely that the Hebrew tribes once came from this area, and this was close to where the Bible says that Abraham's servant went to find a wife for Isaac. In Nuzi the archaeologists found nearly 4,000 clay tablets containing written contracts, legal documents, ancestor lists, and stories—enough to give us a lot of information about life in Torah times.

Archaeology may never find proof that Rebecca or Isaac or Abraham ever lived. But it has already proven that their stories are "true to life." The tellers of the Torah wanted their tales to be believable, even if they were not exactly historical. And today, in books or movies, we try to make the details real so that our stories will seem "true" to us even though we know that they are imaginary. Storytellers do not tell stories to lie to us, but rather to entertain us and teach us lessons about ourselves and about our lives. Think about it: Wouldn't the world be a better place if all of us were as kind as Rebecca?

Haftarah: 1 Kings 1:1-31

When Sarah died, Abraham sent his servant to seek a wife for his son. The Rabbis connect this with the way Solomon was chosen to be the next king even while King David was still alive. In both cases, the important thing was to make sure that the future of the family (the kingdom) would be in good hands.

As the story in the haftarah begins, King David is old. He has ruled for forty years (from about 1010 B.C.E.). His son Adonijah raised an army of chariots and behaved as if he were taking over the kingdom. But David's most loyal followers, including the prophet Nathan, refused to bow to Adonijah.

Nathan advised Bathsheba to save her son Solomon, saying, "Go at once to King David and have Solomon made king, as David promised." Bathsheba went to David, saying, "Adonijah is acting

like a king, but you promised to make Solomon the next king."

Nathan came to King David and said, "Look, the people are already shouting 'Long live King Adonijah!' Did you command this?" Then David took an oath to Bathsheba:

> As Adonai lives—the One who rescued me from every disaster—and as I once swore to you by Adonai, God of Israel, that your son Solomon would be king after me and sit on my throne, I will make it so this very day!"

Bathsheba bowed and said, "May my lord King David live forever."

Our future always depends on our keeping the promises we made in the past. Because Abraham kept his promises, and King David kept his, the future of Israel was secured.

The Twins

A Difficult Birth

These are the generations of Isaac the son of Abraham: … Isaac was forty years old when he took Rebecca … to be his wife. And Isaac prayed to Adonai … because [Rebecca] was barren, and Adonai accepted his prayer, and [she] became pregnant. The children struggled in her womb, and she said, "If such, why am I thus?" And she went to inquire of Adonai. Adonai said to her, "Two nations are in your womb, and two peoples from within you will separate; one people will become stronger than the other, and the older will serve the younger." When the time came for her to give birth, behold, there were twins in her womb. The first one to come out was red, he was altogether like a coat of hair; so they named him Esau. After this, his brother came out, with his hand grasping Esau's heel (*eikev*), so he was named Jacob (*Ya'akov*). Now Isaac was sixty years old when she gave birth to them.

The story of Isaac and Rebecca is very much like the story of Abraham and Sarah. Both couples share great difficulty in having a child. Sarah and Abraham grew old waiting. Finally Adonai promised them Isaac, and Isaac was born. At first Rebecca, too, could not have a child. Only after Isaac prayed to Adonai did Rebecca become pregnant.

God promised both Abraham and Sarah and Isaac and Rebecca that each of their children would become a mighty nation. Abraham's first son, Ishmael, became the ancestor of the Arab nations. Abraham's son Isaac became the second father or "patriarch" of the Hebrews. Likewise, in this story, Esau is born first, and he becomes the ancestor of the Edomites—neighbors of the Hebrews who lived in the Hills of Edom. Jacob becomes the third patriarch or "father" of the Hebrews.

Three to Make a Child

The Hebrews believed that it took three partners to make a child—a mother, a father, and God. No matter how much a mother and father wanted a child, no child would arrive until God decided that the time was right. Even today, with all our science, people still know that having a child is a kind of miracle and that God plays a part in it.

Esau's Names

We think that the name *Esav* or Esau actually means "hairy", which explains why the Torah says "he was altogether like a coat of hair." But the Torah also says "the first one to come out was red." *Edom* means "red". When the sun strikes the Hills of Edom you can see that they are truly the "Red Hills". So the Torah is explaining how the boy and the hills and the nation came to have the name *Edom*, "Red". Sometimes the Torah actually calls Esau "Edom", perhaps to remind us that Esau sold his birthright for a pot of "red red" lentil stew.

The Younger Son

When Sarah commanded Abraham to send Hagar and Ishmael away, God told Abraham to do as Sarah commanded. In this way God agreed with Sarah in the choice of Isaac (see *Vayeira*). In one place the Torah actually calls Isaac Abraham's "only son", which could either mean his "only *true* son" or his "*precious* son".

And we notice something else about the Torah: The younger son usually becomes God's favorite. Just as Isaac was the younger brother; now Jacob is the younger brother.

The Red Stew

The young men grew up. Esau became a skillful hunter, a man of the open country. But Jacob was a quiet fellow, staying close by the tents. Isaac (who had a taste for wild game) loved Esau; but Rebecca loved Jacob.

Once Jacob cooked some stew. Esau came from the field, and he was very hungry. Esau said to Jacob, "Quick! let me have some of that *red red* stuff! For I am famished!"—and it was because of this that he was called "Red" (*Edom*).

Jacob said, "First sell me your birthright."

And Esau said, "Look, I am about to die. What good is the birthright to me?"

But Jacob said, "Swear it to me this day!" So [Esau] swore to him, selling his birthright to Jacob. Then Jacob gave Esau bread and the lentil stew, and he ate and drank; then he rose and left. In this way Esau scorned his birthright.

In Bible times—even today, in many places—the oldest son would receive most of the family wealth after his father's death. The oldest son's share is called the *bechorah* or "birthright" (since it is based on the order of birth). Sarah arranged for Isaac to receive the birthright of the older son. She commanded Abraham to send Hagar and Ishmael (Isaac's older half-brother) away so that the birthright would go to Isaac and not to Ishmael. It was Sarah, not Abraham, who decided that the younger son would become the next leader or "patriarch" of the Hebrews.

In this portion Rebecca takes the place of Sarah. It is Rebecca who chooses the next patriarch of the Hebrews. Rebecca seems wiser and stronger than her husband Isaac. The Torah explains that Isaac loves his older son best not because Esau is a good person or a great leader, but because Isaac likes the taste of the animals that Esau hunts.

And the Torah says Esau does not deserve to be the next chieftain of the Hebrews, since Esau cares more for a delicious meal of "red red" meat than for his birthright. Esau is the kind of person who only cares about what is important now, this minute, and thinks nothing about what is important in the long run. He sells his birthright to Jacob because he is hungry *now*.

My Wife Is My Sister

Just then there was a famine in the land of Canaan, like the time of hunger when Abraham and Sarah went down to Egypt. But Adonai commands Isaac, "Do not go down to Egypt. Live in the land that I tell you." In time, Adonai says, the land will belong to Isaac and to his children. Adonai promises to keep the covenant that was made with Abraham, so that Isaac's tribe will grow as "numerous as the stars." And Adonai adds, "Through your children all nations on earth will be blessed because Abraham heard My voice and kept My requirements, My commands, My laws, and My teachings." So Isaac stayed in Gerar, in Canaan.

> When the people of that place asked him about his wife, [Isaac] said, "She is my sister," because he was afraid to say, "She is my wife." He thought, "The men of this place might kill me on account of Rebecca, for she is beautiful to look upon." And when they had been there a long time, King Abimelech of the Philistines, looking from the window, saw Isaac caressing his wife Rebecca. Then Abimelech summoned Isaac and said, "What is this? She is your wife! Why did you say, 'She is my sister'?" Isaac answered, "Because I thought, perhaps I will die because of her."

King Abimelech is upset by Isaac's answer. He sends an order to all his people, saying, "Anyone who harms this man or his wife shall surely be put to death." Now that Isaac is living under the king's protection, he plants crops and reaps a rich harvest. He becomes so wealthy that the Philistines grow jealous of him. They have been forbidden by their king to harm him, but they find a way to keep Isaac from growing any richer. They fill in all the water wells dug by the Hebrews.

Birthright and Blessing

The birthright (*bechorah*), the wealth of Isaac, is only half of what Jacob needs to become the next leader of the Hebrews. Now that he has the birthright, he also needs Isaac's *berachah* or "blessing". And that's a story that comes later in this portion.

Do Not Go Down to Egypt

Some Bible scholars believe that the story of Isaac may also be a tradition explaining why a certain group of Hebrews never left the land of Canaan and were never slaves to Pharaoh in Egypt.

Quote to Remember

וְהִתְבָּרְכוּ בְזַרְעֲךָ כֹּל גּוֹיֵי הָאָרֶץ.

Through your children all nations on earth will be blessed.

Isaac and King Abimelech

Why is the story about Isaac and Rebecca told? Isn't it almost the same as the two wife-sister tales that we read about Abraham and Sarah? Why does the Torah tell this story at all? Here are some possible reasons: (1) to let us know that Rebecca was just as beautiful as Sarah; (2) to show that Isaac thought a lot like Abraham did; (3) to show how Isaac became rich and powerful; or (4) because there were very few stories about Isaac to choose from. Yet this is not a flattering story. We know that Rebecca is not Isaac's sister, so Isaac must be playing a trick on King Abimelech. But that could be an important clue to what is about to happen in Isaac's own family—indeed, "playing tricks" will be featured in many of the stories soon to come.

King Abimelech advises Isaac to move away: "For you have become too powerful for us."

For now, Isaac's servants again dig up the wells that the Philistines closed up. Soon after, Adonai appears to Isaac a second time and promises to make him into a great nation, so Isaac sets up an altar and calls "on the name of Adonai." Meanwhile, King Abimelech comes to make a treaty with Isaac. Abimelech says, "We saw clearly that Adonai was on your side." Isaac gives a feast, and the next morning, before Abimelech leaves, the Hebrews and the Philistines swear to live peacefully side by side.

Suddenly a servant of Isaac appears to say that they found water while digging a new well. This was good news indeed! Water was the most precious thing to find in Canaan. So much so that every well deserved its own name. And Isaac calls this well *Sheba* (the word can mean either "oath" or "seven"—but the Torah wants us to think that the well is named after the oath that Isaac and King Abimelech just swore). "To this day," the story ends, "the name of the town has been Beersheba."

Okay! You picked up that sentence right away. If the Torah says "to this day," then it must mean that the story was told long after it happened. And you probably also noticed the Torah telling how things came to be the way they are: why Isaac moved away from the better lands near the sea (where the Philistines were), and how he found water in the Negev (even though the name *Negev* means "Dryness"), and how the town of Beersheba (which can mean "well of the oath") got its name. If you noticed all these, you are becoming a "Torah detective", skilled at catching the clues.

Before the next story begins, the Torah pauses to tell us that when Esau was forty years old he took two wives, both Hittite women, and "The women brought bitterness to Isaac and Rebecca."

The Blessing

As Isaac grew old his eyes weakened, becoming so dim that he could not see. Isaac told Esau that he might soon die. He asked Esau to hunt an animal for his last meal. Then, said

Isaac, before he died, he would give the blessing to Esau. Rebecca heard all this, and she hurried to prevent it.

Rebecca told Jacob to take two goats from the flock and bring them to her. When Jacob brought the goats, his mother cooked them in the tasty way that Isaac loved. Then she dressed Jacob in Esau's best clothes and covered his hands and the smooth part of his neck with hairy pieces of goatskin. She told Jacob to pretend to be Esau: to take the stew in to his father and receive Isaac's blessing. The trick was ready to be played.

> [Jacob] came to his father, and said, "My father." [Isaac] answered, "Here am I, my son. Which one are you?" Jacob said, "I am Esau, your firstborn. … Please sit up. Eat of my wild meat, then give me your innermost blessing." Isaac asked, "How did you find it so quickly, my son?" And he answered, "Adonai, your God, gave me success."

> Isaac said to Jacob, "Now come closer, that I may feel you, my son. Are you really my son Esau or not?" Jacob came closer to his father Isaac. He felt him and said, "The voice is the voice of Jacob, but the hands are the hands of Esau." He did not recognize [Jacob] since his hands were hairy like his brother Esau's hands ….

Curse and Blessing

Rebecca was ready to help Jacob trick Isaac. But Jacob was scared. I have smooth skin, he said to his mother, but Esau is hairy. What if my father touches me? What if he discovers that I am Jacob? If he knows I am tricking him, he will curse me, not bless me. Rebecca answered, "Let the curse be on me. Just do as I say."

What Would Esau Hunt?

Hunters in ancient Canaan had many choices for game to hunt— from the famous lion of Judah (pictured *left* from a mosaic floor at Beit Guvrin) to the lowly hare. Since Rebecca told Jacob to take two goats for his father's meal, Esau was probably hunting for wild goat, ibex, or gazelle. But he could also have chosen to hunt bison, wild ox, bear, leopard, cheetah, or ostrich. Almost all of these were once common in Canaan, though many of them have been hunted to extinction. The last lions disappeared in the fourteenth century, and the last ostriches were hunted down in the early years of the twentieth century.

To Consider

It seems that the life of Isaac and Rebecca is filled with one struggle after another. What were the problems that they faced? What happens when parents play favorites with their children? Should a parent love one child more than another? Should a child obey one parent and not the other? How do you feel about parents playing favorites?

The Blessing of the Firstborn

It is Isaac who tells us that once the blessing of the firstborn is given, it cannot be taken back. He also blesses Esau, but not with the important blessing that Esau wanted. The blessing of the first-born decides who will be the next leader of the tribes of the Hebrews. So Jacob has succeeded in (1) getting Isaac's wealth when Isaac dies (the *bechorah*) and (2) becoming the next leader of the Hebrew nation (the *berachah*).

[Isaac] said, "Bring it nearer to me. I will eat my son's game that I may give you my innermost blessing." And he brought it nearer, and he ate; and [Jacob] brought him wine, and he drank. And his father Isaac said to him, "Come near now, and kiss me, my son." And [Jacob] came near, and kissed him; and [Isaac] smelled his clothes and blessed him, saying, "See, the smell of my son is like the smell of a field that Adonai has blessed. Let God grant you the dew of heaven and the fat of the earth, lots of new grain and wine. Let peoples serve you and nations bow down to you. Be master over your brothers and let your mother's sons bow to you. May those who curse you be cursed, and those who bless you be blessed."

Just as Isaac finished blessing Jacob—and Jacob left his father Isaac's presence—his brother Esau came from his hunt. … Isaac his father said to him, "Who are you?" And he said, "I am your son … Esau." And Isaac was seized with trembling, saying, "Who came before you, hunted the game, brought it to me, and I have eaten it all? I have blessed him! Indeed, he shall remain blessed."

When Esau heard his father's words, he burst into wild and bitter sobbing, saying, "Bless me—me too, my father." But [Isaac] answered, "Your brother came with trickery. He took away your blessing." And [Esau] said, "He is truly named *Jacob*[, the 'heel-grabber']. For he has grabbed me by trickery these two times—he took my birthright; and, see, now he has taken away my blessing.…" And Esau held a grudge against Jacob because of the blessing which his father had given him. Esau said to himself, "[After the death of my father and after the days of mourning for him are done]—then I will kill my brother Jacob."

The Tricksters of the Bible

All of us love stories about great tricksters, and the stories in this portion are full of tricksters. Jacob tricks Esau into selling him the birthright. Isaac and Rebecca trick Abimelech into thinking that Rebecca is Isaac's sister. And Rebecca coaches Jacob in how to trick Isaac into giving him the blessing of the firstborn son. Jacob succeeds.

But Jacob does not succeed alone. Isaac is surely not the most important Hebrew of his time. Rebecca is. She chooses the right person to be the next leader of the Hebrew people. And now that Jacob will be the next leader of the Hebrews, she tells Isaac to send Jacob to her family to find a wife among her relatives.

Esau is not a bad person. When he understands that the two women he married are not pleasing to his father, he takes a third wife, one of the daughters of Ishmael. He really does try to please his dad. But we know that he is always just a little too late. We even feel kind of sorry for him. He should have paid closer attention to his sneaky brother and his crafty mother.

To Consider

Where is Adonai in these Torah stories? Look back at the very beginning of the chapter. What was Adonai's promise to Rebecca? How did Rebecca know that she was doing the right thing in helping Jacob? Does Adonai play only a small part in this portion? Or is the Torah saying that all this was Adonai's plan right from the start?

Haftarah: Malachi 1:1-2:7

The Rabbis connected the fate of the Edomites (children of Esau) in the time of Malachi with the troubles between Esau and Jacob that began while they were still in their mother's womb. The prophet's name, Malachi, means, "My Messenger". Whoever he was, Malachi preached in Israel in the early years of the return, before Ezra and Nehemiah arrived.

The tribes of Edom and Israel were close relatives and started out as friendly neighbors. They became enemies when the Edomites rejoiced in the fall of Jerusalem and looted the city. When the Judeans returned to rebuild the Temple and resettle the Promised Land, the Edomites made their lives difficult and dangerous.

Now Malachi preaches that God "loved Jacob and hated Esau" (though the Torah only said that God

preferred Jacob over Esau). And Malachi compares the Edomites to the Israelites, stating that if Edom said "We shall rebuild," God would answer: "They may build, but I will tear down."

In the haftarah Malachi also speaks to the Israelites, saying that their Temple services are corrupt and unclean. People bring stolen and sickly animals to offer as sacrifices, but Adonai, "the God of the armies of heaven; My name is feared among the nations," deserves better.

Malachi preaches: Command the priests to keep Adonai's covenant with Levi, or else Adonai will curse them.

> Give honor to My Name ... for a priest's lips should speak knowledge so that people look to the priest for wisdom—for the priest is a messenger of Adonai....

The Great Dream

Quote to Remember

אָכֵן יֵשׁ יְהֹוָה בַּמָּקוֹם הַזֶּה
וְאָנֹכִי לֹא יָדָעְתִּי.

Surely Adonai is here in this place, and I did not know it.

Jacob's Ladder

For centuries, people who speak English thought of the stairway in Jacob's dream as a ladder. That is how the Hebrew word *sulam* was translated in the King James Bible. There *were* ladders in ancient times, but try to imagine angels going up and down at the same time on a ladder—it doesn't make good sense. Recently, as we discovered letters and stories in other ancient languages, we learned that *sulam* more often meant a "ramp" or "stairway". This makes better sense. On a ramp or stairway, angels could easily be going up and down at the same time.

A Stairway to Heaven

Jacob left Beersheba, going toward Haran. He came to a certain place and stopped there for the night, for the sun had set. Taking one of the stones of the place, he put it under his head and lay down in that place.

He had a dream; behold! a stairway was set on the ground and its top reached to the sky, and behold! angels of God were going up and down on it. And behold! Adonai was standing beside him, saying, "I am Adonai, the God of your father Abraham and the God of Isaac: the ground on which you are lying I will assign to you and to your children. Your descendants shall be as the dust of the earth; you shall spread out west and east, north and south. All the families of the earth shall bless themselves by you and your descendants. Remember, I am with you: I will protect you wherever you go and will bring you back to this land. I will not leave you until I have done what I promised you."

Jacob awoke from his sleep, and he said, "Surely Adonai is here in this place, and I did not know it." Shaken, he said, "How awesome is this place! This is none other than the house of God, and that is the gateway to heaven." Early in the morning Jacob arose and took the stone that he had put under his head and he set it up as a pillar and poured oil on the top of it. He named the place Beth-El, but before the name of the city had been Luz.

Dreaming

The Bible tells of many dreams. This dream is the most famous. Yet like all dreams, this one is mysterious. Here are just a few of its mysteries.

Why are the angels going first up and then down? If these are angels, why don't they come down from heaven first? The answer may be in the words *malachei elohim*, "angels of God". Actually, the word for "angel" here (and everywhere in the Torah) simply means "messenger". So instead of "angels of God" we could say "God's messengers".

This leads to an interesting possibility, one that our ancestors probably knew. In Mesopotamia (where Haran is located) there was a kind of stairway intended to "connect" heaven and earth. It was the staircase on a kind of pyramid called a *ziggurat*. Unlike the pyramids of ancient Egypt, which were tombs for the Pharaohs, the ziggurats of Mesopotamia were temples for the gods. In fact, each ziggurat had a small house at the top called a *beit el*, a "house of the god". And archaeologists tell us of a gateway on the steps leading up to the top. This was known as the "gate of heaven". On holy days and festivals the priests would climb the stairway of the ziggurat to worship their god. Afterward, they would come down again. So if "God's messengers" is a way of saying "priests", then they would surely begin climbing from the bottom, as the "angels" do in the dream.

You might also have noticed that Adonai says to Jacob, "I am Adonai, the God of your father Abraham…." But we know that Jacob was the son of Isaac, not Abraham. What happened here may also be easy to understand. In ancient times, books were rare. Each copy had to be made by a scribe. This was tedious work. The scribe always tried to copy each book exactly, but sometimes a scribe made a mistake—not through carelessness, but through being intelligent! A scribe might come to this sentence and see "the God of your father Isaac and the God of Abraham." But the scribe, being intelligent, knew that Abraham came before Isaac, so the scribe automatically put the names in that order, accidentally making it seem as if Jacob were the son of Abraham. Little problems like this are found throughout the Torah. Many times they are just caused by scribes who tried

Dreaming of Haran

Before the dream, we are told, Jacob is "going toward Haran." He had probably heard of the great ziggurat pyramids of Mesopotamia, one of which was in Haran. So it is not hard to imagine that he would stop to dream of it along the way.

The Ziggurat

See the portion of *Noach* for more about ziggurats and an artist's sketch of one ziggurat (on page 17) based on archaeological evidence.

To Consider

Jacob's dream of the staircase tells us that Jacob believed there is a connection between heaven and earth. How does the dream story show that God is concerned with what happens on earth? Jews still believe that God is concerned with what happens on earth. Are there ways in which we can tell that this so?

Beth-El

Jacob calls this place Beth-El, "the house of God". But Abraham already set up an altar at a place he named "Beth-El", and they seem to be the same place. Later on Jacob sets up another altar at Beth-El and names the city again. Why is Beth-El so important that there are three stories about how it got its name? And why does the Torah add that "before the name of the city had been Luz"? For this we need a little history. After King Solomon, the Hebrew kingdom split in two, north and south. The Temple of Solomon was in the south, in Jerusalem. Not to be outdone, the northern kingdom officially used *two* temples: one at Dan and another at Beth-El. *Bereishit* is all about beginnings, so here it explains how Beth-El came to be a holy place. (And surely the story was written long after Jacob's time, since the Torah reminds us that "before" it was called Luz.)

to make corrections, sometimes in places where no corrections were needed.

In this dream Adonai repeats for Jacob the promises that were made to Abraham and Isaac. In this way we learn that Adonai is happy with the choice of Rebecca, that Jacob will be the next great leader of the Hebrew nation. Adonai also promises to go with Jacob and protect him wherever he travels. In return, Jacob promises to give to Adonai a tenth of everything. We remember this idea of "tithing" from the story in which Abraham gave a tenth of everything his army had won to the priest of *El Elyon*. Here the lesson of *tzedakah*, "righteous charity", is repeated.

Jacob and Two Wives

When Jacob arrived in Haran, he found a well covered by a large stone. He asked the shepherds there if they knew where he might find his uncle Laban. They pointed to a young shepherd lady just coming to the well and said, "That is Rachel, the daughter of Laban." So Jacob rolled the heavy stone away from the well and watered the flocks of Rachel. (Of course, this reminds us of how his mother Rebecca watered the camels at this same well.) Jacob is welcomed into Laban's home. At the end of a month Laban asks what Jacob would like as his wages for working.

> Now Laban had two daughters; the name of the older one was Leah, and the name of the younger was Rachel. Leah had weak eyes; Rachel was shapely and beautiful. Jacob loved Rachel; so he answered, "I will serve you seven years for your younger daughter Rachel." Laban said, "Better that I give her to you, than that I should give her to an outsider. Stay with me." So Jacob served seven years for Rachel and they seemed to him but a few days because of his love for her.

At the end of seven years Jacob asked for his wife. But Laban tricked him and gave him Leah instead of Rachel. When Jacob asked why, Laban answered, "It is not our way to marry off the younger before the older. Wait until the bridal week of this one is over, and we will give you that one, too, provided you serve me another seven years." Because of Laban's trick, Jacob married two wives and served Laban fourteen years instead of seven! Jacob and Leah had many sons before Rachel and Jacob had Joseph.

A Little Bit of Magic

After Joseph was born, Jacob asked Laban for permission to take his wives and his children and return to his home. But Laban answered, "I have learned through divination that Adonai has blessed me because of you." Divination is another word for "fortune telling". Superstitious folk believe that our fortunes can be read in the stars, in crystal balls, in tea leaves in a cup, and in a thousand other ways. The Torah does not tell us which way Laban used; it just says that he did not want Jacob to leave because he believed that Adonai was being good to him as long as Jacob remained. Laban tells Jacob to stay and to name a price for his work.

So Jacob works a trick of his own. The Torah story is a bit confusing, but the idea is simple. Jacob says that he will keep only the sheep and goats that are spotted or speckled, and Laban will keep the rest (most sheep are born white). Laban agrees. Jacob then places sticks of white and speckled sticks near the flocks. He puts the white sticks in front of the goats, and many goats are born white. In front of the much more valuable sheep he puts the speckled sticks, so that they gave birth to many speckled sheep. In this way Jacob gains large, valuable flocks while Laban's flocks are smaller and less valuable. By magic, the Torah says, Jacob becomes rich.

Now Laban's sons grow angry, believing that Jacob is stealing from their father. So Jacob holds a secret meeting with Rachel and Leah in the fields where no one can hear them. He tells them that he had a dream. An angel of God said to him, "I am the God of Beth-El, where you anointed a pillar and made a vow to Me. Now … leave this land and return to your native land." His wives agree to go, and the next time that Laban is away from home, out shearing the sheep, Jacob and his wives escape with all their servants, all their flocks, and all that Jacob owns.

Just as they are leaving, though, Rachel pauses to steal her father's "household idols". Household idols were doll-

God and Children

Once again in this story the idea that God controls who will have children is important. Jacob loved Rachel more than Leah (which reminds us of how Isaac and Rebecca played favorites with their sons). The Torah says that "Adonai saw that Leah was unloved," so Adonai blessed Leah with children. Jacob had many sons before Rachel finally was "remembered" by God. Only then did Rachel gave birth to Joseph.

Magic Sticks

Today we know that speckled and white sticks do not make any difference to the color of animals being born. In ancient times, though, people believed in magic, and the story was told to show how Jacob could use magic to be an even greater trickster than Laban.

To Consider

Toward the end of the portion, Laban says that, if Jacob had told him he was leaving, Laban would have made a feast with dancing and song to send him off. In the end, Jacob shared a meal with Laban and his relatives on the Height. In what way does sharing a meal and making a feast bring us closer together? Can you think of an example of how Jews share a meal to bring us all closer together?

sized statues used by idol-worshipers as a kind of insurance policy. They were supposed to protect the home against any evil. Rachel must have wanted them to protect her household, and that is why she stole them.

The Showdown with Laban

Three days later Laban discovered that Jacob had fled. The chase was on. Laban saddled up his fastest camels and rode out after Jacob. He and his men caught up with Jacob in the hills of Gilead. But that night, before he could ride into Jacob's camp, God appeared to Laban in a dream, saying, "Beware of attempting anything with Jacob, good or bad." (The Torah reminds us: God promised to protect Jacob.)

Laban set up his tents on one hill while Jacob had his family and his tents on the Height (a higher hill). Laban visited Jacob and said, Why were you so sneaky? If you had just said you were leaving, I would have made a big feast with music and dancing to send you off. Now I could hurt you, but your God warned me not to harm you. Okay, you can leave, but why did you steal my gods?

But Jacob did not know that Rachel had stolen the idols. Jacob said to Laban, I have only taken what belongs to me. If you find that someone in my camp has stolen your household gods, let that person be put to death!

So Laban went into Jacob's tent and Leah's tent and the tents of the two maidservants; but he did not find [the household gods]. Leaving Leah's tent, he entered Rachel's tent. Rachel, meanwhile, had taken the idols and placed them in the camel cushion and sat on them; and Laban rummaged through the tent without finding them.

Rachel told her father that she had to keep sitting on that spot because she was not well. Finally Laban gave up looking for his household idols. Now Jacob complained, Why do you treat me like a thief? You found nothing belonging to you here! I served you for twenty years, and I have always been honest. If God was not protecting me, you would send me away empty-handed, without my wife and children, and without my servants and my flocks. "But God took notice of my plight and the toil of my hands, and God gave judgment last night [in your dream]."

Laban said, You know that everything in your camp, except for your sons and daughters, really belongs to me. But what can I do? So Laban gathered stones and made a pile of them, and Jacob set up a stone as a pillar. Then Laban said,

> Here is this mound [of stones] and here the pillar which I have set up between you and me: this mound shall be witness and this pillar shall be witness that I am not to cross to you in anger past this mound, and that you are not to cross to me [in anger] past this mound and this pillar. May the God of Abraham [Jacob's God] and the god of Nahor [Laban's god] … judge between us.

Then Jacob sacrificed an animal and invited his relatives to feast with him. After the meal they spent the night together on the Height. The next morning Laban kissed his daughters and left to go home. "Jacob went on his way. And suddenly angels of God met him. When he saw them, Jacob said, 'This is God's camp.' He named that place Machanayim." And so the story of Jacob and Laban ends.

From Beginning to End

The story of Jacob is full of dreams. The dream of the stairway where God promises to protect Jacob. The dream of an angel of God saying it is time to leave Laban. Laban's dream when God warns him not to harm Jacob.

And the story is filled with reminders. Jacob watering the flocks of Rachel, just as his mother Rebecca watered the flocks of Abraham's servant. Leah's weak eyes, like Isaac's eyes that were "too dim to see." Jacob's loving Rachel more than Leah, just as his mother loved him more than Esau and his father loved Esau more than him.

And the story is full of tricks: Laban tricking Jacob into marrying the younger daughter Leah first, just as Rebecca tricked Isaac into giving the younger Jacob his blessing. Laban tricking Jacob into staying six extra years. Jacob tricking Laban with the magic sticks. Rachel tricking her father by sitting on the household idols.

What Belongs to Whom?

Jacob believed that his wives and all his wages (sheep and goats) rightfully belonged to him, since he had worked for them. But even after tricking Jacob into staying six extra years (after the fourteen that he served for his two wives), Laban believed that everything Jacob owned really belonged to him because Jacob was part of Laban's household. In different ways, they were both right.

To Consider

Machanayim means "two camps". Does Jacob name the place Machanayim because of the two camps of Laban and Jacob? Does he call it that because his is one camp and the angels of God are a second camp? The Torah gives no answer. What do you think?

Boundary Stones

All around the world, since ancient times, people have used stones to mark boundaries. Some were simple—a pile of stones (like the one *far right*) might mark the end of one field and the beginning of another. Some were highly decorated. This one (*right*) comes from the time of Nebuchadnezzar (1125-1104 B.C.E.). The text on the back calls on nine gods to "bear witness" to the boundary. The carvings show twenty Babylonian divine symbols.

But the portion ends as it began. At its start Jacob saw angels of God on the staircase and at its end Jacob meets angels of God along the way. And now that you know that the word for an "angel" in the Torah is the same as the word for "messenger", what kinds of messages do you find in this Torah portion that is so full of dreams, magic, and wonder?

Haftarah: Hosea 12:13-14:10

The first two verses of this haftarah speak about the years Jacob spent as a shepherd to earn his wives Leah and Rachel. Even though the rest of the prophet's words are about other matters, the Rabbis used these verses to connect this reading with *Vayeitzei,* the story of Jacob in Aram.

Hosea tells of the sins of the tribe of Ephraim. "They added sin to sin," he says, making idols and worshiping Baal. (The tribe of Ephraim stands for the northern Kingdom of Israel.) Now, God says, Israel will be destroyed "like a lion I will devour."

But the people of Israel can be saved, God says

> Return, O Israel, to Adonai your God, for you have stumbled in your sinning. Bring words with you and return to Adonai and say, "For-

give all sins and accept the good and we shall offer the fruit of our lips."

If they turn back to Me, God says,

> I will love them freely ... I will be like dew to Israel. They shall blossom like the lily and grow roots like [the trees of] Lebanon. ...

> The wise shall understand these things and the thinkers shall know, that Adonai's ways are straight for the righteous, causing [only] sinners to stumble.

The last part of the haftarah beginning with "Return" (*shuvah*) is also read as part of the haftarah on the Sabbath between the High Holy Days. It is called *Shabbat Shuvah* ("The Sabbath of Returning").

WRESTLING

Messages and Messengers

The Jacob story includes many angels. This is confusing since, as you now know, the word for "angel" in Hebrew (*malach*) is the same as the word for "messenger". So, when the Torah says "angel" it may mean a half-human, half-spirit being, or it may just mean a person carrying a message from here to there.

In the last Torah portion Jacob was met by "angels of God". Seeing them, Jacob said, "This is God's camp." He named the place "Two Camps" (*Machanayim*, in Hebrew). As this story begins Jacob sends "messengers" to his brother Esau. Long ago Esau had vowed to kill Jacob. But Jacob's men behave more like scouts than messengers. They return with grim news for Jacob. Esau is headed this way, and he has four hundred men with him.

> Jacob was greatly frightened; in his fear, he divided the people with him, and the flocks and herds and camels into two camps, thinking, "If Esau comes to the one camp and attacks it, the other camp may yet escape."

Jacob then speaks a prayer to God. He (1) reminds God that God promised to protect him; (2) says that he does not deserve God's kindness, but is grateful for it; (3) asks God to defend him against Esau; and (4) reminds God of God's promise to make Jacob's descendants "as the sands of the seas, which are too numerous to count."

The next morning Jacob divided his servants into groups, giving each group goats, sheep, rams, camels, cows, bulls, and donkeys—550 animals in all! He told the groups to march toward Esau while keeping a distance between one group and the next. Jacob gave the same message to each group: "Tell Esau these animals are gifts from his brother Jacob."

Wrestling with Torah

The Bible is a library of books gathered over many centuries. When the Torah—the first five books of the Bible—was complete, the prophets came on the scene to teach the meaning of the Torah. When the books of the prophets were complete, the Rabbis created midrash—stories to teach it. Today we try to explain the Bible by reading other ancient texts and by digging up the places of the past. Through the ages Jews have also wrestled with Bible through "commentary". At times a commentator may tell a new story, but usually he or she just adds a wise comment, a bright idea, a sort of "Post-it note" to explain what's happening in the Bible.

Three Commentators

The greatest Bible commentator of all time was **R**abbi **Sh**lomo ben **I**saac of France (c. 1040-1105). He is known by the nickname *Rashi* (based on his initials). Rashi usually starts with a question and shows how the Bible answers it. In Rashi's time women often went untaught, but Rashi educated his daughters well. The two daughters of Rashi became famous as Bible scholars.

Rashbam (**R**abbi **Sh**muel ben **M**eir, 1085-1174) was a grandson and student of Rashi. His notes often explain what Rashi said and sometimes add new ideas, too.

Moshe ben Nachman (1194-1270) was the leading rabbi of Spain. He is best known by the name, "Nachmanides", which means "son of Nachman". In his commentary he seeks mystic secrets: hidden messages that he believes God planted in the Bible for us to find.

For [Jacob] thought, "If I please [Esau] with many gifts in advance, and then face him, perhaps he will be kind to me." And so the gifts went on ahead, while [Jacob] remained in camp that night.

Commentators Say

In other portions we turned to what archaeologists found or modern scholars learned. But for this portion (and many others) the questions are, What is Jacob doing and why? These are human questions, food for thought, the very best subjects for commentary. Here is what three commentators say.

Rashi believes that the first messengers Jacob sent to Esau were actually angels from "God's camp". Rashi also points out that Jacob chose carefully the best gifts for Esau—Jacob knew how much his brother loved animals, for animals were the riches of the ancient world. And, Rashi says, giving the gifts all at once would be less pleasing than sending them in groups the way Jacob did—making them seem like many gifts instead of one.

Rashbam suggests that Jacob sent the gifts in separate groups for a different reason: to force Esau and his four hundred men to slow down. As soon as Esau accepted the first gift, he and his men were no longer just soldiers; they also had to serve as shepherds, driving the animals in front of them. Every gift slowed them down a little more. As Esau gained animals, Jacob gained time to gather his camp and flee. But, says Rashbam, God did not want Jacob to flee.

Nachmanides sees a mystic or hidden meaning in this story: It shows how we should behave when we know we are in danger. Like Jacob, we should trust that God will send an angel to save us. But also like Jacob, we should not wait to be saved. Jacob went into action, thinking, "God will help me, but only if I also help myself." If we use this story as a model when we are faced with danger, we learn to (1) pray, (2) send gifts to soften our enemy's heart, and (3) prepare to make war (as Jacob did when he divided his camp).

These are hints from just three commentators. Actually, there are hundreds of commentaries we could read. As you think about Bible texts, you too may see things in a unique way—you may begin building your own commentary.

Wrestling the Stranger

Jacob took his family across the Jabbok river, then crossed back over to be on the side closer to Esau.

> Jacob was left alone. And a man wrestled with him until the break of dawn. When [the man] saw that he had not bested [Jacob], he injured Jacob's hip at its socket, so that the socket of his hip was strained as he wrestled with him. Then [the man] said, "Let me go, for dawn is breaking." But [Jacob] answered, "I will not let you go unless you bless me." Said the other, "What is your name?" He replied, "Jacob." Said he, "Your name shall no longer be Jacob, but Israel, for you have wrestled with beings divine and human, and have bested them." Jacob asked, "Please tell me your name." But he said, "You must not ask my name!" And he left him there. So Jacob named the place Peniel, meaning "I have seen a divine being face to face, yet my life has been preserved." The sun rose upon him as he passed Penuel, limping on his hip. That is why the children of Israel to this day do not eat the thigh muscle that is on the socket of the hip, since Jacob's hip socket was wrenched at the thigh muscle.

The Torah does not say that the stranger who wrestled with Jacob was an angel. This idea was taught by the sages in Midrash. Rashi agreed, saying that the stranger was actually Esau's guardian angel. Why did the angel not wish to give his name? Rashi explains: Angels do not have a single name—their names change each time God gives them a new message to deliver. Why did the angel have to depart before dawn? Rashi answers that angels must be in heaven to praise God for each new morning. The angel says, "Your name shall no longer be Jacob, but Israel, for you have wrestled with beings divine and human, and have bested them." Who are the "beings divine and human"? Rashi says that "divine" means the angel and "human" refers to Esau

A Mystery for All Times

We will never know the answer to this mystery. The Torah says "Jacob was left alone. And a man wrestled with him until the break of dawn." Modern scholars think this may be a story told by the E-teller, but that does not help explain what is happening. Archaeology has no tools for explaining how a person can be alone and wrestle with someone else. Nor have we found any similar ancient story to help us explain it. So this mystery forces us to think for ourselves, which is exactly what commentators do.

To Consider

You be the commentator. After reading these different commentaries explaining the mysterious stranger who wrestled with Jacob until dawn, who do you think the stranger was?

and Laban. Jacob has wrestled with all of them and won out against them all.

Rashbam thinks that this angel was sent to wrestle with Jacob to keep Jacob from fleeing for his life. God wanted Jacob to stay, to witness how God would protect him. If Jacob made a quick getaway, he would miss his lesson. When Jacob's hip was hurt, Rashbam says, it was to punish Jacob for not trusting God to save him.

Another well-known commentator, Obadiah ben Jacob Sforno (c. 1475-1550), thinks that the angel had to somehow weaken Jacob before he could hurt Jacob's hip. How did the angel weaken Jacob? By telling Jacob all the sins that future leaders of the Israelites would commit. Sforno believes that the angel could not give a name because no human can understand the language of the angels. Lastly, Sforno explains, the rising of the sun immediately healed Jacob's wounds, for the sun is the source of all healing.

Modern commentators and thinkers continue to add suggestions. Julian Morgenstern (1881–1977) said that Jacob's struggle actually takes place in a dream. This makes sense, since many important things in Jacob's life happen in dreams. And of course, a dream is something that would surely have to leave at dawn when Jacob awakens.

Psychologists who study dreams talk about a "shadow" that often appears to dreamers. The shadow is a dark, frightening, faceless figure. When you dream of the shadow, they say, it is really a part of you that you are either struggling against or trying to befriend. Perhaps Jacob is wrestling his "shadow".

Mythologists studying myths (legends) from around the world remind us of a widespread belief that every river has its own demon spirit. This idea may arise from the dangers of rivers—people often lost their lives in river crossings. So every river crossing could be like a struggle against a demon. Was Jacob here wrestling against the demon of the Jabbok river?

An angel, a demon, a shadow, the guardian spirit of Esau—all of these make some sense. All of these are possibilities. In commentary, nothing is final; everything is open to discussion.

What's in a Name?

We have seen the importance of names in the Bible, and Jacob's new name is vital to us. We still call ourselves "the people of Israel" or "the children of Israel" or just "Israel". Rashi (and many others) comment that the new name "Israel" is meant to take the place of the old name "Jacob". But why a new name at all?

According to the Torah, Jacob got the name *Ya-akov* by grabbing at the heel (*eikev*) of his twin Esau as he was born. *Ya-akov* can also mean "the tripper"—one who is always playing tricks on other people to make them stumble—or "the place-taker"—one who takes the rightful place of another person (the way Jacob did when he pretended to be Esau to gain his father's blessing). In all of these meanings the name *Ya-akov* recalls Jacob's past.

Yisrael is a name for Jacob's future. The Torah tells us that Jacob is named "Israel, for you [Jacob] have wrestled with beings divine and human." This points to the two parts of the name: *ysr,* meaning "to wrestle", and *el,* meaning "God". But some think the first part of the name may actually come from another word: *yashar* ("straight"). If so, the name means, "the one who shows that God is true." The first part could also come from the word *sar* ("prince"). If so, the new name could mean, "prince of God".

The name Israel fits the Jewish people well, though. We Jews have always thought of ourselves as the people that "wrestles" with God. Like wrestlers, who cling together even as they struggle, we have always tried to attach ourselves to God, even though at times we find it difficult to understand why God seems to punish us or allow others to harm us. Nevertheless, we keep wrestling with our idea of God.

Meeting Esau

The Torah says that dawn came and the man who wrestled with Jacob disappeared. "Looking up, Jacob saw Esau coming, along with four hundred men." Jacob left the women and children behind him. He went forward and bowed low seven times as he drew closer to his brother. But Esau ran

To Consider

Going back in history, one of the two kingdoms that arose after the death of King Solomon called itself the "Kingdom of Israel"; the other called itself the "Kingdom of Judah". In 1948, when it came time to name the new Jewish state in the Middle East, the founders decided to call it "The State of Israel". What reasons could they give for choosing this name?

The Man in the Moon

People have always thought that they could see the image of a man in the moon. Early Jewish legends claimed that Jacob was the "perfect" man and that God placed Jacob's image in the moon. Now that we have walked on the moon, we know it isn't so. But imagination is powerful stuff. See what you can imagine in the moon photo from NASA *below*.

Quote to Remember

עַל-כֵּן רָאִיתִי פָנֶיךָ כִּרְאֹת
פְּנֵי אֱלֹהִים.

For to see your face is like seeing the face of God.

To Consider

You be the commentator. What did Jacob mean when he said that seeing the face of Esau was like seeing the face of God? Could that have anything to do with the mysterious stranger who wrestled with Jacob?

up to greet him. Esau "embraced" Jacob and kissed his neck, "and they wept."

Esau was glad to greet the wives and children of Jacob. But why did you send me these gifts? he asked Jacob. Don't you know that I am already a rich man? You can take your gifts back. But Jacob said, Please keep the gifts, "for to see your face is like seeing the face of God."

After spending the day together, Jacob and Esau went their separate ways. Jacob led his household to Sukkot, where he "built a house for himself and stalls for his camels; that is why the place was called Sukkot." Sukkot means "booths" or "temporary houses". Of course, you know that, since Jews celebrate the holiday of Sukkot every year.

Haftarah: Hosea 11:7-12:12

The Rabbis connected Jacob wrestling a stranger with the way Hosea used that story to show that the Kingdom of Israel had gone astray and must return to God. Hosea calls the northern kingdom Ephraim because its first king, Jeroboam, was from the tribe of Ephraim. God mourns:

How can I give you up, Ephraim?
How can I let you go, O Israel?

God is disappointed with Israel: "Ephraim surrounds Me with lies ... while Judah even now stands firm with God." The kingdom called itself "Israel", naming itself after Jacob; but Jacob was worthy of God's love, and the kingdom is not.

Jacob seized his brother's heel in birth, and when he was grown he "wrestled with a divine being." The haftarah says it was an angel that Jacob wrestled (though the Torah calls the "stranger" a person, not an angel). Then God explains,

... With us [Jacob] spoke, Adonai *Tzeva'ot* ("of the armies of heaven"), who is called Adonai.

Like Jacob, the kingdom of Israel must turn back to God. "Hold fast to steady love and justice, and wait constantly for your God." Give up cheating in business and thinking that the kingdom of Israel has become rich on its own.

I, Adonai, have been your God since Egypt, I can make you live in tents again ... I spoke to the prophets ... and through the prophets I gave parables.

Thus Hosea completes the parable that compares Jacob to the kingdom of Israel.

The Interpreter of Dreams

A Coat and Two Dreams

At seventeen years of age, Joseph tended the flocks with his brothers…. And Joseph brought bad reports of them to their father.

Now Israel loved Joseph best of all his sons, for [Joseph] was the child of his old age; and he made him a coat of many colors. And when his brothers saw that their father loved him more than any of his brothers, they hated him so that they could not speak a friendly word to him.

Once Joseph had a dream, which he told to his brothers; and they hated him even more. He said to them, "Hear this dream which I dreamed: There we were binding sheaves [of grain] in the field, when suddenly my sheaf stood up and stayed standing; then your sheaves gathered around and bowed low to my sheaf." His brothers answered, "Do you mean to reign over us? Do you mean to rule over us?" And they hated him even more for his talk about dreams.

He dreamed another dream and told it to his brothers, saying, "Look, I have had another dream: And this time the sun, the moon, and eleven stars were bowing down to me." And when he told it to his father and brothers, his father scolded him. "What," he said to [Joseph], "is this dream you have dreamed? Are we to come, I and your mother and your brothers, and bow low to you to the ground?" So his brothers were angry with him. But his father kept the matter in mind.

The Coat of Many Colors

In Hebrew, the famous "coat of many colors" is two words: *ketonet passim*. Sometimes these words are translated as the "coat with ornaments". We know that *ketonet* means "tunic"—a kind of judge's robe or uniform coat. Joseph's coat was not meant to keep him warm, but to make him special. But no one is quite sure what the Hebrew word *passim* means. One guess is that the word and the tunic point to Egypt, where Joseph's future lies. Egyptologists (archaeologists who study ancient Egypt) tell us that only princes and pharaohs were allowed to wear a *striped* tunic. They say we should probably translate *ketonet passim* as a "striped tunic" and not as a "coat of many colors".

Repeated Dreams

From ancient times onward people have believed that when a dreamer was visited by the same dream more than once, it would surely come true. So when Joseph dreams almost exactly the same thing twice, this is a way of telling us that his dream will no doubt come true. Perhaps that is why his father Jacob "kept the matter in mind."

Twenty Pieces of Silver

Egyptologists tell us that "twenty pieces of silver" was the price actually being paid for slaves around the time of Joseph. People may differ on whether the tale of Joseph being sold into slavery is true or false, but archaeological evidence tells us that the Torah certainly got the price right!

Young Joseph

Young Joseph is not very likable. At age seventeen he is his father's favorite son. And he behaves like a spoiled child. He is a tattletale. He shows off a special coat that his father gave him. He tells his brothers a dream that makes them angry and jealous. Then he tells them a second dream that makes them hate him even more—a dream that surprises even his father.

The Pit

One day Jacob sent Joseph out to where his brothers were tending the flocks. "Bring back word about how they are doing," Jacob said. Joseph went off, ready to be a tattletale again. But his brothers saw him coming. They said to one another,

> Here comes that dreamer! Come now, let us kill him and throw him into one of the pits; and we can say, "A savage beast has eaten him." We shall see what becomes of his dreams!

When Reuben heard what his brothers had in mind, he said, Let's not murder him. Just throw him into the empty water pit. (Reuben, it seems, planned to return later and rescue Joseph.) When Joseph arrived, the brothers stripped off his fancy coat and threw him into the pit. As they were eating, they saw an Ishmaelite camel caravan passing by. Judah said, "Instead of killing Joseph and having his murder on our hands, let us sell him to the Ishmaelites." They pulled Joseph up from the pit when the Midianites came near and sold him for twenty pieces of silver to the Ishmaelites, who took Joseph down to Egypt.

Reuben returned after that and saw that Joseph was gone. "What shall I do?" he asked his brothers. So they took Joseph's coat and dipped it in goat's blood. They took the coat to their father and said, "We found this. Please look at it carefully. Is it your son's coat or not?" Jacob recognized the coat at once. "Joseph was mauled by a beast!" he cried. He tore his clothing, put on rough sackcloth, and mourned for Joseph for many days. His children tried to comfort him, but he refused to be comforted. He said, "No, I will go down into Sheol still mourning for my son."

The Midianites, meanwhile, sold Joseph into slavery in Egypt. Joseph was sold to Potiphar, a member of the royal court and the chief steward of Pharaoh.

You know this story, but the way it is told in the Torah is a little confusing. Was it Reuben or Judah who planned to save Joseph's life? Was it a caravan of Ishmaelites (of the family of Ishmael) or of Midianites (from the land of Midian)? As you can guess, two stories seem to be joined together here. One story was probably told by the tribe of Reuben, and their ancestor Reuben was the hero. Another may have been told by the tribe of Judah, with Judah as its hero. One story spoke of Ishmaelites. The other spoke of Midianites. The Torah tells the stories as if they were always one.

Joseph in Potiphar's House

Potiphar put Joseph in charge of his whole household. The Torah says that Adonai blessed the household of Potiphar as long as Joseph was there. Joseph was very handsome, and the wife of Potiphar wanted him for her own. Once, when no one else was in the house, she grabbed Joseph by his coat and begged him to love her as she loved him. But Joseph was loyal to his master Potiphar, and he fled from Potiphar's wife. Unfortunately, as he escaped the tunic he was wearing came off in her hand. When Potiphar returned home, his wife held up Joseph's tunic and claimed that Joseph had left it behind when he came to beg for her love. It was a lie, but Potiphar believed it. He was so angry that he threw Joseph into Pharaoh's prison.

Two Coats; Two Pits

It seems as if tunics brought Joseph nothing but bad luck. His brothers hated his striped coat and used it to convince Jacob that Joseph was dead. They threw Joseph into a pit. Later, in Egypt, Potiphar's wife grabbed Joseph's tunic and used it when she lied about Joseph. And Potiphar threw him in prison. Two coats; two pits.

The Baker and the Wine Steward

The Torah tells us that even in prison, Adonai was with Joseph. Joseph befriended the head jailer, and the head jailer gave Joseph a great honor. He allowed Joseph to look after two of Pharaoh's servants—a baker and a cupbearer. Both had displeased Pharaoh and both had been sent to prison.

Quote to Remember

הֲלוֹא לֵאלֹהִים פִּתְרֹנִים,
סַפְּרוּ־נָא לִי.

Surely God can interpret! Tell me [your dreams].

A Speaking God of Egypt

Egyptians worshiped almost every living thing, from beetles to cats to hippopatami. Gods like the sphinx were often pictured as half-animal, half-human. The god Horus was sometimes drawn as a man with the head of a falcon and sometimes as just a falcon. One unique statuette of Horus (*below*) was designed with hollow tubes inside (*below, left*). Strings were placed in the tubes to make the beak move so that Horus could "speak"—with a little help from a priest. Most idols were silent, even though they were brightly painted and sometimes even dressed up for special occasions.

Joseph served meals to the baker and the cupbearer for a whole season. Then, they "dreamed in the same night, each his own dream and each dream with its own meaning."

When Joseph came to them in the morning, he saw that they were upset. He asked Pharaoh's officers … "Why do you appear downcast today?" And they said to him, "We had dreams, and there is no one to interpret them." So Joseph said to them, "Surely God can interpret! Tell me [your dreams]."

Pharaoh's cupbearer went first. He told his dream about preparing wine for Pharaoh. First he spoke about three vines, then the grapes, then the pressing of the wine, then pouring, then placing the cup in Pharaoh's hand. Joseph said, "In three days Pharaoh will free you from prison and give you back your job as cupbearer. Please remember me and speak about me to Pharaoh. For truly, I was kidnaped from the land of the Hebrews, and I have done nothing wrong here in Egypt, and [I do not belong] in this pit."

The chief baker liked the way Joseph interpreted the dream of the cupbearer, so he, too, shared his dream with Joseph. In his dream the baker saw three baskets on his head, the top one filled with all the kinds of food that bakers prepare for Pharaoh; and birds were eating from the basket above his head. Joseph said, "It means that in three days Pharaoh will cut off your head and put it on a pole so that birds will come to peck at it."

On the third day—his birthday—Pharaoh made a banquet for all his officials, and singled out his chief cupbearer and his chief baker…. He restored the chief cupbearer to his cupbearing, and [the cupbearer] placed the cup in Pharaoh's hand; but the chief baker he impaled—just as Joseph had interpreted to them. Yet the chief cupbearer did not think of Joseph; he forgot him.

Joseph in Egypt

Egyptologists can help us understand the Joseph story. For example, they explain the jobs of the cupbearer and the baker at Pharaoh's court. The chief cupbearer not only gave wine to Pharaoh; he was also in charge of all wine-making. He watched over planting the vines, harvesting the grapes, pressing the grapes into juice, and fermenting the juice into wine. No wonder the cupbearer dreams about wine-making! Also, Egyptian cupbearers had one other job: Pharaohs always worried that someone might poison their wine. It was the cupbearer's duty to sip from the cup before placing it in Pharaoh's hand. That is why the cupbearer was often at Pharaoh's side.

The chief baker was another high official. He was in charge of preparing at least fifty-seven different kinds of bread and thirty-eight different types of cake nearly every day. No wonder the baker dreamed of "all kinds of food for Pharaoh." Of course, the chief baker would visit Pharaoh or the royal family regularly to plan menus, so the chief baker was also an important part of Pharaoh's inner circle.

The Torah does not say why the Pharaoh was angry with his cupbearer and baker, or why Pharaoh chose to forgive the cupbearer and to punish the baker. The Torah just shows us that Joseph could tell the future from dreams.

Interpreting the Dreams

Egyptologists have solved another mystery in this portion. When young Joseph dreams two dreams, he tells them to his family. His family understands them at once. But when the cupbearer and the baker dream their dreams, they are downcast because, as they say, "there is no one to interpret them." People everywhere dream. But in ancient Egypt, interpreting dreams was the work of special priests—the same priests who were in charge of Egypt's religious magic. The baker and the cupbearer only wish there was a priest nearby to explain the meaning of their dreams to them.

Joseph does not claim to be a magician or a priest. He does not even say that he is an interpreter of dreams. He just says, "Surely God can interpret! Tell me [your dreams]."

We know that dreams played a special role in the story of Jacob, Joseph's father. You might say that Jacob is the Torah's great dreamer. In this portion dreams play a great role in the story of Joseph. You might say that Joseph is the Torah's greatest interpreter of dreams. But Joseph might

Getting It Right

Slaves were bought and sold in ancient Egypt, just as the Torah tells. Slaves could become managers of households, just as Joseph did. There was a royal prison where officials who displeased the Pharaoh received special treatment. Pharaoh's court did include a chief baker and a chief cupbearer, and they were surely high officials. Checking the Torah story against the history of Egypt, we can see that whoever first told this story knew Egypt and Pharaoh's court very well indeed.

To Discuss

What details in the story might lead you to believe that Joseph was a real person and that the story might be true? What details might lead you to think that it is like many other early stories of the Torah—a story that helps us learn what to think and how to act?

To Consider

Do you remember your dreams? Do you like to tell them to other people so that they can help you understand them better? That is what the cupbearer and the baker wanted to do. In ancient Egypt, telling the meaning of a dream was thought to be great magic—so much so that it was part of Egyptian religion, and priests were taught how to interpret dreams. Do you think that rabbis today should be trained to help us understand our dreams? What might Joseph say about that?

not agree. Joseph might say something like "Hebrews do not need dream interpreters because God is the greatest interpreter of dreams. Just tell me a dream, and God will tell me what it means."

Of course, Joseph says that God knows what dreams mean, but Joseph also says, "Tell me [your dreams]." Perhaps Joseph thinks that God is whispering the meaning in his ears, or perhaps Joseph thinks that God has given him this special talent. Egyptologists can help us to know that interpreting dreams was a religious ritual in ancient Egypt. They cannot, however, tell us what Joseph believed about his power to tell the meaning of dreams. That remains a mystery—one that continues right into the next portion.

Haftarah: Amos 2:6-3:8

Vayeishev tells how Joseph was sold into slavery by his brothers, and the Rabbis connected that to the first verse of the haftarah. Amos accuses the Israelites of selling the righteous for silver. They even sell "the needy for a pair of sandals," he says.

Adonai has done much for them, Amos says—destroying the Amorites, taking them out of Egypt, leading them in the wilderness, giving them prophets and Nazirites (see *Naso*)—but the Israelites rejected God.

> You made the Nazirites drink wine and forbade the prophets from speaking prophecy. Behold, I will make you unsteady, as a wagon is unsteady under a full load of freshly cut grain.

On that day, Adonai says, "even the bravest of soldiers shall flee away naked." Even Judah will be punished—everyone who came out of Egypt. "You alone have I known from among all the families of earth, therefore I will punish you for your sins."

To everything there is a purpose: Do two walk together without agreeing? Does the lion roar when there is no prey? Does a bird fall in a trap that has no bait? God has a purpose, too, and tells it to the prophets. So listen and beware.

> The lion has roared, who will not fear? Adonai God has spoken, who can keep from speaking prophecy?

Amos' message is that turning back to God means turning back to justice. The Israelites must learn to act as God acts—they must act in the image of God.

Joseph and Pharaoh

Pharaoh's Dream

Pharaoh had a dream. Seven good-looking, healthy cows came out of the Nile River and grazed in the reeds nearby. From behind came seven ugly, skinny cows. The ugly, skinny cows swallowed the healthy ones. Pharaoh awoke. When he fell back to sleep he had a second dream. Seven lovely ears of grain grew from one stalk. But close behind were seven thin ears of grain, scorched by the wind. The thin ears of grain gobbled up the lovely grain. Pharaoh awoke a second time. He knew it was a dream.

> Next morning [Pharaoh's] spirit was troubled, and he sent for all the magicians of Egypt, and all its wise men; and Pharaoh told them his dreams, but none could interpret them for Pharaoh.

> The chief cupbearer said to Pharaoh, I apologize. When I was in Pharaoh's prison with the chief baker, we each had dreams the same night. A Hebrew youth interpreted our dreams. "Just as he interpreted for us, so it came to pass."

> Thereupon Pharaoh sent for Joseph. [Joseph] was rushed from the dungeon. He had his hair cut and was given new clothes, and he appeared before Pharaoh. And Pharaoh said to Joseph, "I have had a dream, but no one can interpret it. Now I have heard it said of you, that for you to hear a dream is to tell its meaning."

> Joseph answered Pharaoh, saying, "Not I! God will see to Pharaoh's welfare."

Joseph listened as Pharaoh repeated the two dreams. Pharaoh said, "I have told my magicians, but none can tell me the meaning." Then Joseph spoke, saying, "Pharaoh's dreams are one and the same. God has told Pharaoh what God is about to do." Joseph explained: The seven healthy cows and the seven lovely ears of grain mean that there will be seven years of good harvest. But the seven ugly cows and

A Midrash

The Rabbis asked, "How did the magicians of Egypt explain Pharaoh's dreams?" They answered with a midrash: The magicians said the seven healthy cows meant Pharaoh would soon have seven new daughters. The seven ugly cows meant that seven of Pharaoh's daughters would soon die. Since Pharaoh had many wives, children were constantly being born, and in those days, many died even at birth. When it came to the dream about grain, the magicians explained that Pharaoh's armies would conquer seven lands, and afterward, seven lands would be lost. Since the armies of Egypt were always at war somewhere, they were always winning and losing cities and lands. Of course, this is a midrash. The Torah just states that the magicians failed to explain the dreams.

Wisdom

The magicians of ancient Egypt were actually priests celebrated for their wisdom. One Bible commentator, Sforno, suggested that the magicians failed this time because they thought Pharaoh's two dreams were *different*. Pharaoh did not agree. And one midrash asks, "Doesn't everyone dream?" "True," it answers, "but the dreams of a king concern the whole world." When the magicians failed, Joseph succeeded in telling Pharaoh the true meaning of his dreams. The Torah is teaching that God's wisdom is greater than the wisdom of the Egyptians. The same kind of contest takes place again when Moses and Aaron come face-to-face with the magicians of Egypt.

the seven thin ears of grain mean that afterward there will be seven terrible years of famine. "As for Pharaoh having had the same dream twice, it means that the matter has been decided by God, and that God will soon carry it out."

Joseph gave Pharaoh a plan: "Find a wise person to watch over the land of Egypt. Collect food in the seven good years, save it in Pharaoh's store cities, and then there will be food when the seven bad years come." Pharaoh liked the plan. He said to his court, "Can we find another like [Joseph], a person in whom is the spirit of God?"

God and Joseph

To learn the meaning of his dreams Pharaoh called on his wise men, his magicians. Egyptologists tell us that "magicians" and "wise men" were both words used to speak about the priests of Egypt. Wisdom was the heart of the religion of ancient Egypt.

Even though he was a foreigner, Joseph seemed wiser than the magician-priests. First, Joseph was sure that both Pharaoh's dreams had one meaning. Second, Joseph believed that Pharaoh's dreams were about Egypt—in fact, about the whole world. And Pharaoh thought Joseph was wise when Joseph explained that the dream came twice, meaning that God would definitely bring the seven good years and the seven lean years soon. And—here is something to notice—Pharaoh used religious words to speak of Joseph's wisdom. Pharaoh said that Joseph had "the spirit of God" in him.

Almost at once Pharaoh came down from his throne, took the ring from his finger, and placed it on Joseph's finger. "From now on," he told Joseph, "I give you power over everything in Egypt, everything except me." Pharaoh dressed Joseph in fine linen (the costume of royalty). Pharaoh put a gold chain around Joseph's neck. And Pharaoh ordered that Joseph would ride in a chariot right behind his own. And wonder of wonders, Egyptologists have found ancient tomb paintings and writings in Egypt showing us that this is precisely how people were honored by a Pharaoh. Once more, the story of Joseph is true in its details!

Joseph Sees His Brothers Again

Pharaoh gave Joseph an Egyptian name, calling him *Zaphenath-paneah*, and he chose a wife for Joseph. Her name was Asenath, daughter of Poti-phera, the priest of On. Joseph was thirty years old, and soon he had two sons. He named the first son Manasseh, meaning "God has made me forget my hardship and my childhood." He named the second Ephraim, meaning "God has made me prosper in the land where I suffered." For seven years Joseph traveled through the land of Egypt buying grain and storing it.

Then came the seven terrible years. There was hunger everywhere, just as Joseph had predicted. The Torah says "All the world came to Egypt to buy food, for the famine had become severe throughout the world."

Back in Canaan, Jacob heard there was food in Egypt. He told his sons, "Go down and get food for us there, that we may live and not die." He sent ten of Joseph's brothers to Egypt. But he kept his youngest son, Joseph's brother Benjamin, at home. The ten brothers came before Joseph to buy food. Joseph knew them at once, but the brothers did not recognize Joseph because he was dressed like Egyptian royalty and behaved like a stranger to them. Joseph accused them of being spies. He said they were lying about needing grain for their family. At last Joseph let nine of the brothers go home with grain, but he kept Simeon as a hos-

Honored by Pharaoh

Left: An Egyptian tomb painting of the dressing ceremony, as a Pharaoh raises a man named Paser to the rank of Vizier of Egypt. Just as in the Torah, the new clothing given by the Pharaoh becomes a symbol of power over Egypt. Paser is also given a staff like Pharaoh's and a feather rod. If you look closely, you will see the falcon god Horus above Pharaoh's head. Horus was the great protector of Egypt's rulers.

A New Name

Jacob received the new name "Israel" in his wrestling match. Now his son Joseph is given a new name by Pharaoh. This reminds us that names held deep meaning for our ancestors, even as they do for us today. Joseph's new name is also the start of a new tradition. When Jews live outside the land of Israel, they often have two names—a Hebrew name and a name in the language of the land in which they are living. Can you imagine good reasons for having two names?

Quote to Remember

הֲנִמְצָא כָזֶה אִישׁ אֲשֶׁר
רוּחַ אֱלֹהִים בּוֹ.

Can we find another like this one, a person in whom is the spirit of God?

tage, saying, "Return to me with your youngest brother; else, I will know you truly are spies."

Joseph played another trick on them, too. When his brothers paid gold for their sacks of grain, Joseph's servants put the gold back in the sacks. That night, after they left, they discovered the gold in their grain sacks, and they were afraid. They asked, "What has God done to us?" They wondered if God was punishing them for selling their brother into slavery long ago. When they reached home they told their father everything. "Now," they said, "we must return to Egypt with Benjamin in order to rescue Simeon." But Jacob said, "Joseph is no more and Simeon is no more, and now you would take away Benjamin. These things always happen to me!" And he would not let them return to Egypt.

In time, though, the famine grew worse until Jacob had no choice. Judah said, "Trust me with Benjamin. On my life, I promise nothing will happen to him." So Jacob sent his sons back to Egypt and gave them gifts for the Egyptian governor (not knowing that it was Joseph). And he sent double the gold with them, so they could pay for the new grain and also for the grain that they had taken before.

When Joseph heard that his brothers were in Egypt, he ordered his servant to prepare a feast. He told the servant to bring them into his house, but the brothers were afraid, thinking that the governor might trap and enslave them. They confessed to the servant about finding the gold in their bags of grain. "We brought the money for that grain and more money for more grain, too," they said. But Joseph's servant said, "Your God, the God of your father, must have put treasure in your bags for you. I got your payment."

When Joseph came home for lunch the brothers gave him gifts from their father Jacob—spices and honey, almonds and pistachio nuts. They bowed before him. Joseph greeted them, asking, "How is your aged father? Is he still in good health?" They said Jacob was well. Then Joseph saw Benjamin, his only brother born of his mother Rachel.

Suddenly Joseph hurried out of the room. He was about to cry, and he did not wish his brothers to see him weeping. After a while Joseph washed his face and returned. "Serve the meal," he ordered. Then he made the brothers sit, telling each one exactly where to sit. And he sat them in order, from the oldest to the youngest. The brothers were puzzled. How could the governor of Egypt know who was oldest and who was youngest?

True to Life

Joseph has one more trick to play, but before he plays it, let's look at the facts. The Torah knows just the gifts that would be sent from Canaan to Egypt—even in a time of famine there would still be spices and honey, almonds and pistachio nuts to send. And when it comes to seating everyone for lunch, Joseph sits alone (which is what the governor of Egypt would do), the brothers sit together, and (the Torah says) the Egyptians who were there sat separately, "for Egyptians could not dine with the Hebrews, for that would be displeasing to them." And that is exactly right, too!

The ancient Egyptians were a proud people and their customs were different from the customs of the Hebrews. In Egypt, because of the awful heat, people shaved the hair from their faces and heads. Of course, members of the royal court—like Pharaoh and Joseph—would wear wigs over their shaven heads and dangle false beards from their ears. Hebrews, however, let their hair grow and sported real beards. Egyptians also bathed often, but Hebrews seldom bathed because water was precious and pools of water were rare in Canaan. So the Egyptians looked upon the Hebrews as savages. They would not sit near Hebrews at a meal.

The Last Trick

After the meal Joseph told his servants to give his brothers as much grain as they could carry. But he said, "Put each one's money in the mouth of his bag, and put my silver goblet in the bag of the youngest one, along with his money."

With the first light of morning, the men were sent off … They had … not gone far, when Joseph said to his servant, "Up, go after the men! And when you overtake them, say to them, 'Why did you repay good with evil? [The goblet you have stolen] is the very one from which my master drinks and

An Egyptian Feast

There was no sitting at a table during an Egyptian meal. Each person had a chair or a couch, but food and wine was piled on small tables. Servants brought food on platters to each person. The Torah story paints this picture, saying, "Portions were served to [the brothers] from Joseph's table…." And that is exactly how feasts were conducted in Egypt.

The Silver Goblet

Later on the Torah forbids Jews from practicing magic; and in time Jews were disappointed to hear that Joseph used his silver goblet for magic. Some Bible commentators tried to excuse Joseph by saying that he only *pretended* to use his goblet when he spoke the word of God. He did this to impress the Egyptians, who were used to the ways that their priests worked magic.

To Consider

The magic of Egypt that the Bible talks about was not the kind that you see when a modern magician makes things appear and disappear. In Egypt, as the chapter says, people believed that wisdom was magical. Priests were trained to perform magical acts. And since most Egyptians could not read or write, reading and (especially) writing were also thought to be magical arts. Do you agree with the Egyptian idea that wisdom is a kind of magic?

which he uses to seek the word of God. It was a wicked thing for you to do!'"

He overtook them and spoke those words to them. And they said to him, "Why does my lord say these words? Far be it from your servants to do anything of the kind! … Whichever of your servants [the goblet] is found with shall die; the rest of us, moreover, shall become slaves to my lord." [The servant] replied, "… Only the one with whom [the goblet] is found shall be a slave, the rest of you shall go free."

Of course, the goblet was found in Benjamin's sack of grain. The brothers tore their clothes as if someone had died, for they knew that their father Jacob would truly die if Benjamin was enslaved in Egypt. So all the brothers returned to Joseph's house. Joseph said to them, "What is this deed that you have done? Do you not know that a man like me practices divination [to seek God's word]?"

Judah answered. He said that the brothers were all guilty, and all of them were ready to be slaves to the governor. But Joseph said, "No. Only Benjamin shall be my slave, for the cup was found in his sack. The rest of you return in peace to your father."

Joseph's Silver Goblet

Divination (from the word "divine") means seeking the word of God through magic. You may be surprised to hear that Joseph used a silver goblet to seek the word of God. Joseph did not need a goblet to tell the baker or the cupbearer what their dreams meant. And Joseph did not need a goblet to tell Pharaoh the meaning of his dreams. Why does Joseph now claim that he needs his silver goblet to receive God's word?

Egyptologists think the answer has to do with Joseph's wife, who was the daughter of Poti-phera, priest of On. The famous city of On was the center of sun worship in Egypt; and Pharaoh, who was a god in Egypt, was called "the child of the sun". In other words, Joseph's father-in-law, Poti-phera, was Pharaoh's head priest and the chief magician of the greatest academy of magic, wisdom, and priesthood in all of Egypt. Could it be that, as governor of Egypt, Joseph studied Egyptian magic with his father-in-law?

This is not hard to imagine. In Canaan the Hebrews had learned to set up pillars and anoint them. This was an ancient practice of the Canaanites long before the Hebrews arrived. Of course, when Abraham, Isaac, and Jacob set up altars, their altars were dedicated to Adonai, and not to the gods of the Canaanites. Joseph lived among the Egyptians. When Egyptian priests used a goblet for divination, they sought wisdom from the god of the sun. Joseph may have learned to concentrate by looking at the surface of the wine in his goblet, just as the Egyptian magicians did, but when Joseph did it, he sought wisdom from God.

Wherever Jews have lived we have adopted some of the ways of the people we live among, but we have never abandoned the One God. We have always kept a little Jewish island deep inside of us.

Haftarah: 1 Kings 3:15-28; 4:1

The Rabbis connect the dreams in *Mikeitz* to the dream of Solomon in the Book of Kings. Both Joseph and Solomon were young. Joseph was taken from prison to interpret Pharaoh's dream. Solomon had just become king, and his dream is told just before the haftarah begins. In that dream God asked Solomon to choose any gift, and Solomon asked for wisdom. God granted him wisdom, along with wealth and glory. As the haftarah begins, "Solomon awoke: It was a dream!" He brought gifts of thanks to the altar at the Ark of the Covenant.

Two women come to Solomon for judgment. One says, "I had a baby, and three days later she had one. Hers died, and one night she took mine, leaving me the dead child. But when I looked close, I saw it was her dead child." The other woman said, "No, this living child is mine." King Solomon said, "Bring me a sword."

Cut the living child in two, and give half to the one and half to the other.

The real mother cried, "Please, my lord, give the living child to her. Don't kill it, whatever you do." The other said, "Cut it in two. It shall be neither yours nor mine."

Then Solomon knew the real mother and gave the child to her. And when the Israelites heard of his decision, they knew that he had "divine wisdom to do justice." "And King Solomon was now king over all Israel."

Thus the Book of Kings shows how Solomon's dream was a true message from God and wise leaders like Solomon and Joseph are true gifts of God.

Joseph and Jacob

Joseph Tells His Brothers

This portion begins at a very intense moment in the story of Joseph and his brothers. The silver goblet was found in Benjamin's sack. His brothers are worried and nervous. They promised Jacob that they would let nothing happen to Benjamin. Now all depends on what the governor of Egypt will do. And they still do not know that the governor is really Joseph, the brother they sold into slavery long ago.

Joseph commanded that Benjamin stay in Egypt as his servant. The rest of the brothers, he said, were free to return home. But Judah begged, saying:

> "Our father will die if we return without his youngest son. For our father Jacob said, 'One son is already gone from me, torn apart by a wild beast! And I have not seen him since. If you take Benjamin also, and he does not return, I shall surely die.' So I promised to bring Benjamin back safely. Therefore, keep me as your servant, but let Benjamin return to his father."

> Joseph could no longer control himself …. [He] said to his brothers, "Come forward to me." When they came forward, he said, "I am your brother Joseph, the one you sold into Egypt. Now do not be distressed or angry with yourselves because you sold me to this place. It was to save life that God sent me ahead of you. … It was not you who sent me here, but God; and God has made me like a father to Pharaoh, master of all [Pharaoh's] household, and governor over the whole land of Egypt."

His brothers stood in surprise and shock, but Joseph told them to hurry home to Jacob. "There are five more years of famine to come," he said. "But you can come down to Egypt and live near me, in the region of Goshen. I will provide food for you and your children, for your grandchildren, your flocks and herds, and all that is yours." He said, "Tell all this to my father and tell him how I have become governor of Egypt. Then bring my father here with all speed!"

Joseph hugged and kissed Benjamin, and both of them wept. He kissed all his brothers, weeping with every touch. And Joseph and his brothers began speaking all at once, as families often do.

The news reached Pharaoh's palace: "Joseph's brothers have come." Pharaoh and his officials were pleased. Pharaoh said to Joseph, "Say to your brothers, 'Do this: Load your beasts, and go at once to Canaan. Take your father and your households and come to me … And never mind your belongings, for the best of all the land of Egypt shall be yours.'"

Testing the Brothers

There is a mystery in the Torah story: Why did Joseph force the brothers to bring Benjamin to Egypt? And why did Joseph threaten to keep Benjamin as his slave? Perhaps it was all a test. Joseph wanted to know if the ten brothers would let another son of Rachel be enslaved. He wanted know if they had learned their lesson in the years that had passed since they sold him. Would they protect Benjamin or abandon him and tell another lie to their father?

It was only when Judah offered himself in place of Benjamin that Joseph knew the brothers were truly sorry for what they had done to him. It was then that he revealed to them that he was their brother Joseph.

The brothers were shocked, startled, and confused. How could this Egyptian, the governor of all Egypt, be Joseph? (They only remembered Joseph as a boy.) The Bible commentator Sforno explains: Before they were sure that it was their brother, Joseph had to remind them how they had sold him into slavery. This was a family secret—one that only Joseph and the brothers could possibly know.

Pharaoh Hears the News

There are no secrets in a royal court. Before speaking to his brothers, Joseph sent all the Egyptians out of the room. But his sobs were so loud that they heard him crying. Even before Joseph could finish talking to the brothers, Pharaoh had already heard what was happening. Just as Pharaoh had promised, all the land of Egypt was in Joseph's hands, so Pharaoh sent word to Joseph. He welcomed Joseph's family to Egypt with open arms.

Egyptian Comfort

Archaeology makes it easy to imagine what life was like in ancient times. For instance, if Pharaoh was resting when the news about Joseph's brothers came to him, he might have been lying on a high couch like this one from the tomb of Rameses III (below). The steps were to help him climb onto the couch, and he would have placed his head on the ivory headrest (which was usually turned sideways at the head of the couch). Egyptians used headrests instead of pillows.

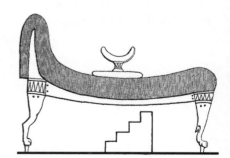

On Lying

Our sages said that the story of Jacob's brothers teaches us why lying is a bad choice. When the brothers told Jacob that his son Joseph had been eaten by a wild beast, they were lying, but Jacob believed them. Now, when they told Jacob that his son Joseph was still alive and was governor of Egypt, Jacob did not believe them. It is always this way, the Rabbis said. When liars tell the truth, no one believes them.

Jacob Dreams Again

A "vision by night" is another way of saying a "dream". This dream of Jacob's reminds us of the stairway dream, when God promised to go with Jacob to Haran. Jacob is now headed for Egypt, but God makes the same promise. Rashi said that God repeated Jacob's name twice as a sign of great love. Nachmanides noted that God called him Jacob (not Israel) because the children of Jacob would struggle as slaves before they finally became a nation. While struggling like a wrestler, Jacob was called by his old name, but later the freed nation would surely be called Israel.

Jacob's Journey to Egypt

… [The brothers] came to their father Jacob in the land of Canaan. And they told him, "Joseph is still alive; yes, he is governor over all the whole land of Egypt." And Jacob's heart went numb, for he did not believe them. But they told him all that Joseph had said to them …. "Enough!" said Israel. "My son Joseph is still alive! I must go and see him before I die."

Jacob set out for Egypt. He was anxious to see his son Joseph. When he came to Beersheba he stopped and "offered sacrifices to the God of his father Isaac."

God called to Israel in a vision by night: "Jacob! Jacob!" He answered, "I am here." And God said, "I am God, the God of your father. Fear not to go down to Egypt, for I will make you there into a great nation. I Myself will go down with you to Egypt, and I Myself will also bring you back; and Joseph's hand shall close your eyes."

So Jacob set out from Beersheba. The sons of Israel put their father Jacob and their children and their wives in the wagons that Pharaoh had sent for carrying [them]; and they took their livestock and the wealth they had gained in the land of Canaan. Thus Jacob and all his children with him came to Egypt….

The Torah names all those who journeyed with Jacob to Egypt.

All the persons belonging to Jacob who came to Egypt—his children and grandchildren, not counting his daughters-in-law—numbered sixty-six. And Joseph's sons who were born to him in Egypt were two in number. Thus the total of Jacob's household [counting Jacob and Joseph] who came to Egypt was seventy persons.

Judah rode on ahead to point the way and tell Joseph that they were coming. Joseph went on his chariot to meet his father. When he came before Jacob he wept for quite a while. Then Israel said, "Now I can die, for I have seen for myself that you are still alive."

Next Joseph brought Jacob to the Pharaoh. Pharaoh asked Jacob, "How old are you?" Jacob answered, "The years of my journey on this earth are one hundred and thirty. My life has been hard, and my years are fewer than those of my father and grandfather."

When the meeting with Pharaoh was over, Joseph settled his family in the best land of Egypt, in the region of Rameses called Goshen, as Pharaoh had ordered. And Joseph provided everything for his father and his brothers and all those who were with them.

The years of hunger continued. The people of Egypt came to Joseph for grain. To buy the food they needed, they sold their farms and fields to Pharaoh—Joseph bought the whole land of Egypt for Pharaoh. Then Joseph gave seed to the people of Egypt and told them to sow the land.

> And [the Egyptians] said, "You have saved our lives! We are grateful to [you], and we shall be servants to Pharaoh." And Joseph commanded a land law in Egypt, which is still true, that a fifth [of everything] should be Pharaoh's; only the land belonging to the priests did not become Pharaoh's.

> Thus [the people of] Israel settled in the country of Egypt, in the region of Goshen; they got holdings in it, and had many children, and increased greatly.

The Dangers of Egypt

Philo (c. 20 B.C.E.-50 C.E.), a Jew from Alexandria, was a great Egyptian writer. In his book *On the Creation* he wrote that Jacob had good reason to fear going to Egypt. Folks who live in foreign lands, Philo said, adopt foreign ways. Jacob was afraid that this would be especially true in the land of Egypt, a land where people were blind to the true God and where they turned everything around them into gods. Egyptians worshiped the sun and moon, stars, rivers, beetles, birds, hippopotami, crocodiles, and even cats. They built temples and made sacrifices to any and all of these. Jacob worried that his children might be tempted to take on the

To Consider

Even though Joseph is the governor of the whole land of Egypt, he does not wait in his royal home for his father to arrive. He mounts his chariot and rides out to greet Jacob. Why is the way we greet our parents so important? Is it just as important on a daily basis as it is when we have not seen a mother or father for a long time?

The Land Law

Through many dynasties and many centuries very little about life in Egypt ever changed. Life was as regular as the Nile River itself. The Torah credits Joseph with one of the greatest changes that ever took place in Egyptian life. When Joseph directed that a fifth of everything in Egypt belonged to Egypt, the people accepted his law in return for the grain that they needed to live. The pharaohs were much richer and much more powerful after the time of Joseph. And the Torah adds that this is "still true".

To Consider

There is a lot of weeping and sobbing in this story. Normally we think of crying as something that happens when we are particularly sad. But there are times when sadness and gladness get mixed up in crying. Look back at the times that Joseph and his brothers weep in the story. What are the glad things that make them weep? What are the sad things that make them weep?

ways of the Egyptians. It was for this reason that God visited Jacob in a dream, telling him not to be afraid to take his household to Egypt. God promised, "I Myself with go with you." And God promised, "I Myself will also bring you back."

Haftarah: Ezekiel 37:15-28

The Rabbis connect the story of Joseph being re-united with his brothers in *Vayigash* with a prophecy mentioning Joseph. Adonai told Ezekiel to take two sticks. On one he was to write "For Judah and the [tribes of] Israel that belong to it." On the other he was to write "Joseph's—Ephraim's—stick and all the House of Israel that belongs to it."

Adonai told Ezekiel to bring the sticks together—the one for the southern kingdom (Judah) with the one for the northern kingdom of Israel (Ephraim). When people ask, "What are you doing?" Ezekiel should say: Adonai God is making two sticks into one.

> Thus says Adonai God: Behold, I am about to take the people of Israel from where they went among the nations. I will gather them

from all around and bring them back to their soil. There, on the hills of Israel, I will make them into a single nation with a single king to rule them. Never again shall they be two nations; never again shall they divide into two kingdoms.

God will grant the tribes of Israel a "covenant of peace" (see *Pinchas*), an everlasting covenant.

> My dwelling will be among them: I will be their God and they shall be My people. … The nations shall know that I am Adonai who sanctifies Israel.

Thus Ezekiel used the sticks to act out the hopes of the people that a time would come when the twelve tribes would be united again.

Israel in Egypt

וִיחִי
Vayechi
Genesis 47:28-50:26

Jacob Blesses Ephraim and Manasseh

After seventeen years in Egypt, at the age of one hundred and forty-seven, Jacob knew he had little time left to live. He said to Joseph, "Promise that you will not bury me in Egypt. When I lie down with my fathers, take me up from Egypt and bury me in their burial-place." Joseph promised. A short time later, Joseph was told, "Your father is ill." He and his sons, Manasseh and Ephraim, came to Jacob's room. Jacob was very weak, but he forced himself to sit up in bed.

Jacob said to Joseph, "*El Shaddai* appeared to me at Luz in the land of Canaan, and blessed me, and said to me, "I will make you fruitful and numerous ... and I will assign this land to your offspring to come for an everlasting possession. Now, your two sons ... born to you in Egypt ... Ephraim and Manasseh shall be mine no less than Reuben and Simeon."

Jacob's eyes were dim with age, and he could hardly see, and he said, "Bring them close to me so that I may bless them." Joseph brought his sons up close, and Jacob hugged and kissed them. Jacob put his hands on the boys' heads to bless them. He placed his right hand on Ephraim's head and his left hand on Manasseh's head. Jacob blessed Joseph, saying,

"The God in whose ways my fathers Abraham and Isaac walked, the God who has been my shepherd from my birth to this day—the Angel who has saved me from all harm—bless the lads."

When Joseph saw that Jacob's right hand was on Ephraim's head he thought his father had made a mistake. "Not so," Joseph said to his father, "Manasseh was my first-born. You should place your right hand on his head." He took hold of his father's hand to move it. But his father said, "I know, my son, I know. Manasseh will also become a great people,

Jacob's Special Blessing

In this portion Jacob blesses all his sons. But Joseph receives the special blessing. Of course, Joseph is not the youngest son of Jacob; Benjamin was born after him. So Jacob plays one last trick. Instead of blessing Joseph directly, Jacob "adopts" Joseph's sons, saying they are his as much as Reuben and Simeon are. So Ephraim and Manasseh become his "youngest" sons, with Ephraim the very youngest. Jacob places his hands on the heads of the two boys, but the Torah states "Jacob blessed Joseph."

יְשִׂמְךָ אֱלֹהִים כְּאֶפְרַיִם
וְכִמְנַשֶּׁה.

God make you like Ephraim and Manasseh.

but his younger brother shall be greater than he and will become nations." So Jacob blessed them, saying, "All Israel will bless their children in your names. They will say, 'God, make you like Ephraim and Manasseh.'" In this way Jacob put the youngest son of Joseph, Ephraim, first.

Then Jacob made three promises to Joseph. God would look after him. God would bring him back to the promised land. And Joseph would be given an extra portion of the land—more than his brothers would receive.

The Younger Son

All the stories in Genesis echo this idea: The younger son is favored over the older. Isaac is born after Ishmael, yet Isaac is chosen to lead the Hebrews. Jacob is born after Esau, yet Jacob is chosen to lead the Hebrews. And now, though Ephraim is younger than Manasseh, Ephraim receives Jacob's greater blessing. Even in the case of Jacob's wives, Rachel is born after Leah, yet Jacob always places Rachel and her sons, Joseph and Benjamin, first.

This was not normal in ancient times. The blessing and the birthright (the largest portion) usually was given to the oldest son in a family. Why are things reversed in the early stories of our people? Why does the younger child always seem to be favored? We can guess the reason.

Our people are not the oldest, and have never been the largest, of nations. Even in the days of David and Solomon our kingdom was never as great or rich as Babylon or Egypt. Among nations we have always been like a younger child. Yet we believed that we received God's special blessing, that one day we would be greater than the older kingdoms. Each time a younger child in Genesis receives the special blessing it reminds us that even the small and young can be the most treasured, the most blessed.

The Death of Jacob

Now Jacob gathered all his sons. He wanted to bless them, but also to tell them what would happen to each of them. Some sons had angered or disappointed Jacob in the past. He foretold that they might suffer in the days to come. Others had pleased Jacob. He foretold great things for them. He gave each of his twelve sons a parting word to fit that son. Then he told them all,

> "Bury me with my fathers in the cave that is in … the field of Machpelah … the field that Abraham bought from Ephron the Hittite for a burial site— there Abraham and his wife Sarah were buried; there Isaac and his wife Rebecca were buried; and there I buried Leah…." When Jacob finished his instructions to his sons he drew his feet into the bed and, breathing his last, he was gathered to his people.

Telling Our History

The stories of the patriarchs were written down long after the time of Abraham, Isaac, and Jacob. The stories came from many different parts of Canaan, from the different tribes and clans of Israel. If one story came from the northern kingdom of Israel, where it was remembered by the tribe of Ephraim, another story might come from the southern kingdom of Judah, where it was remembered by the tribe of Judah. Kingdoms and tribes were important then, just as states or regions are important to us now—folks thought of themselves as Ephraimites or Judahites they way people today think of themselves as Texans or New Yorkers.

In order to create one history that would include Californians, Virginians, Pennsylvanians, and so on, we could collect their many stories and create one book about the United States. In the same way, the stories of the twelve tribes were gathered into one history of the Hebrews in the Book of Genesis. So when we read about Judah or Reuben doing something, these stories were originally told by or about the tribes of Judah or Reuben. These were local stories. But the stories of Abraham, Isaac, and Jacob are more like a history of the United States. They are our *national* story. When Jacob died, the Torah's history of the patriarchs ended and the history of the tribes of Israel—the story of how separate tribes became one nation—began.

The Last Patriarch

In our prayers today we speak of "the God of Abraham, the God of Isaac, and the God of Jacob". When we think of the beginnings of our people we think of our three patriarchs or "fathers"— Abraham, Isaac, and Jacob; and of our four matriarchs or "mothers"—Sarah, Rebecca, Rachel and Leah. After the death of Jacob we speak about "the children of Israel" or the "tribes of Israel". But after Jacob we never had another patriarch.

The Map of Our People

Abraham and Jacob traveled the map of our people. Both lived for a while in Mesopotamia, then went down into Egypt, then returned to the Promised Land. This was the route our people traveled, too. At some time in the distant past family groups or clans of Hebrews came from the land of Mesopotamia and settled in Canaan. At some time clans of Hebrews probably went down into Egypt (though some clans, as in the story Isaac, may never have left Canaan). And some time later clans of Hebrews came out of Egypt to return to the Promised Land. So we can see how the travels of the three patriarchs—Abraham, Isaac, and Jacob—are linked to the travels of the Hebrew nation.

A Caravan to Bury Jacob

When Jacob died, Joseph wept over him and gave him a last kiss. Joseph told the Egyptians to embalm his father. The Torah story is correct when it notes that "It required forty days, for such is the full period of embalming." The Egyptians joined Joseph in mourning for seventy days. Then, the Torah says, "Joseph spoke to Pharaoh's court...."

Joseph told the court of Pharaoh that he had promised to bury his father in the land of Canaan. When Pharaoh heard, he instructed Joseph to go up to Canaan to bury Jacob and then to return. But Joseph did not go alone. Instead it was a great and colorful caravan that took the body of Jacob back to the old burial cave. All of Pharaoh's officials walked with Joseph, along with all Joseph's household, his brothers, and his father's household. There were even chariots and horsemen marching beside Joseph. Only the children and the flocks were left behind in Egypt.

In Canaan Joseph and his brothers mourned Jacob for another seven days. Then they buried their father Jacob in the cave in the field of Machpelah near Mamre, in the field that Abraham had purchased so many years before. Afterward the whole caravan returned to Egypt.

Will Joseph Take Revenge?

Joseph's brothers were worried. Now that their father was dead, would Joseph want to take revenge for the evil they did to him? Long ago they had hated Joseph enough to want to kill him. Did Joseph still bear a grudge?

> His brothers went to [Joseph], flung themselves before him, and said, "We are ready to be your slaves." But Joseph said, "Have no fear! Am I a substitute for God? Although you tried to harm me, God meant it for good, to bring the present result: the survival of many people. And so, fear not. I will provide for you and your children." Thus he reassured them, speaking kindly to them.

The Torah states that Joseph lived a long life. When he felt his end was near, he told his brothers,

"I am about to die. God will surely take notice of you, and bring you up from this land to the land that God promised on oath to Abraham, to Isaac, and to Jacob." So Joseph made the sons of Israel swear, saying, "When God remembers you, you shall carry up my bones from here."

Joseph died at the age of one hundred and ten years; and he was embalmed, and placed in a coffin in Egypt.

The Story of Joseph

The story of Joseph is lovely both because of what it teaches us and because the story is told in a beautiful way. As we have noted, the story often rings true. When they die, both Jacob and Joseph are embalmed—meaning their bodies are prepared and wrapped in linen as mummies. Jacob was buried in Canaan soon after the forty days that it took for his mummy to be completed, so his body did not require a coffin. But Joseph's mummy would remain in Egypt until the children of Israel left, so it was placed in a coffin. It is all so true to life that it would not surprise us if one day Egyptologists discovered a tomb with hieroglyphs telling that "in this place the coffin of Joseph once rested to wait for its return to the land of Canaan."

The Torah, though, is less interested in facts than in truths we can learn. What does the tale of Joseph say about how we should act and what we should believe? Through Joseph we see how even a spoiled child can grow up to be a fine person. We see how a child treated badly by his family can learn to love his family and care for them, so that they learn to love him in return. And we see how a person who trusts in God can be filled with noble spirit, so that even a Pharaoh could say, "Can we find another like [Joseph], a person in whom is the spirit of God?"

Completing the Book of Genesis

You have now heard the whole Book of Genesis (*Bereishit*). When we finish reading a book of the Torah we Jews have the custom of saying, *Hazak! Hazak! V'Nithazek!* "Be strong!

Mourning the Dead

The Torah gives us the exact details of how Jacob was mourned and buried. When it comes to Joseph, the Torah simply says, "He was embalmed, and placed in a coffin in Egypt." All the same, we learn a lot about Jewish mourning and burial from this portion. In what ways can you compare it with the way Jews mourn loved ones today?

Yuya's Tomb

A man named Yuya once became commander of chariots for Pharaoh Amenhotep III. Archaeologists found his tomb untouched and filled with riches. His mummy was inside a coffin carved in his image (*below, left*), and the case was then placed in a carved sarcophagus (*below, right*). The tomb hieroglyphs tell the story of his life. Oddly enough, like Joseph, Yuya was a Semite who began as a simple worker and rose to high office in Egypt.

Joseph and God

The Torah says that God often spoke to Jacob in dreams. Joseph, however, did not seem to hear the voice of God in his dreams. And when Joseph helped others to understand their dreams, the Torah does not say that Joseph was "listening" to God's voice. Looking back at the whole story of Joseph, is there a way that we could say, "God spoke to Joseph"? In what way is God present in the Joseph story?

Be strong! And may you be strengthened!" It's our way of saying, "Congratulations on finishing the study of a book of the Torah. Prepare yourself! You will need all your strength! For the study of Torah never ends!" Now that you know the custom, you can celebrate by saying the words out loud, with strength: *Hazak! Hazak! V'Nithazek.*

חֲזַק חֲזַק וְנִתְחַזֵּק!

Haftarah: I Kings 2:1-12

About to die, David gives some final instructions to Solomon. The Rabbis chose this short haftarah from the Book of Kings because *Vayechi* includes the final instructions of the dying Jacob to his sons.

David tells Solomon, "I am going the way of all the earth. You must be strong now; prove yourself a man."

> Keep faith with Adonai your God. Walk in God's ways. Carry out the laws, commandments, judgments, and instructions of God that are recorded in the Torah of Moses, in order that you shall succeed in all that you attempt, in whatever direction you turn.

David says that if Solomon is faithful, then Adonai will keep the promise made to David:

> If your children take care in how they live, if they walk before Me faithfully with all their heart and all their soul, there will never be a time when one of yours is cut off from the throne of Israel.

David makes a few last-minute requests. Solomon should take revenge on two enemies of David and reward one who helped David. The Bible seems to be saying that kings do not forget or forgive, even on their deathbeds.

David died and was buried in Jerusalem (the City of David).

> Now Solomon sat on the throne of his father David, and his rule was strong and secure.

The Baby and the Bush

שמות
Shemot
Exodus 1:1-6:1

Names

These are the names [*shemot*] of the children of Israel who came to Egypt with Jacob, each coming with his household: Reuben, Simeon, Levi, and Judah; Issachar, Zebulun, and Benjamin; Dan and Naphtali, Gad and Asher. ... Joseph died and all his brothers of that generation. But the Israelites ... multiplied and increased very greatly, so that the land was filled with them. And a new king arose over Egypt who did not know Joseph.

The second book of the Torah is Exodus, from the Greek word for "going out". In Hebrew it is called *Shemot* or "Names". It starts by listing the names of Jacob's sons, the tribes of Israel. Joseph had died, the Hebrews had many children, and in time there was a Pharaoh who did not remember the good Joseph had done for Egypt.

All Egyptians "belonged" to Pharaoh—everyone was Pharaoh's servant. But the new Pharaoh uses the Israelites as if they were captured enemies. He does not want their tribes to grow larger. "In case of war," he says, "they may join our enemies in fighting against us." Pharaoh forces the Hebrews to serve on labor gangs, building the cities of Raamses and Pithom. He puts taskmasters over them "to oppress them" and treat them harshly. All this, the Torah says, was because the Egyptians were afraid of the Israelites.

The Midwives

The king of Egypt spoke to the Hebrew midwives, one of whom was named Shifrah and the other Puah, saying, "When you deliver [the babies of] the Hebrew women ... if it is a boy, kill him; if it is a girl, let her live." The midwives, fearing God, did not do as the king of Egypt had told them; they let the boys live. ... And God did good for the mid-

Remembering and Forgetting

Remembering and forgetting are important road signs in the Torah. Good things happen when God and human beings remember promises and vows. But bad things happen when people forget promises and vows. Joseph's Pharaoh remembered. He lived up to all the promises he made to Joseph. In this portion we read about a new king who forgot Joseph and forgot all the promises made to Joseph. Bad things began to happen.

Shifra and Puah

Shifra and Puah play a small part in the Torah. We meet them this once and never again. So it seems odd that we remember their names. Of course, there are many stories about women in the Bible—important women like Rebecca, Sarah, Hagar, and Rachel. But the story of Shifrah and Puah reminds us that God is not only interested in important people. Because these two women believed in God and refused to kill babies, the Torah says, God did good for them.

wives; and the people multiplied and increased greatly. ... Then Pharaoh charged all his people, saying, "Every boy that is born you shall throw in the Nile, but let every girl live."

Midwives are nurses who help women with childbirth. But saying there are only two Hebrew midwives for all the thousands of Hebrews is like saying that there are only two doctors in Chicago. The Bible commentator Abraham ibn Ezra (1089-1164) suggested that these two midwives were actually in charge of all the Hebrew midwives in Egypt.

The Basket in the Nile

Pharaoh demanded that every Hebrew baby boy should be thrown into the Nile River, but baby Moses was saved by the Nile River. Moses is born to parents from the tribe of Levi. He is a beautiful baby, and his mother hides him for three months. Then she covers a basket with pitch and bitumen to make a floating nest. She sets Moses afloat on the Nile, telling his sister to watch carefully what happens. We know what happens. Pharaoh's daughter is out bathing in the river. She takes pity on the baby, saying, "This must be a Hebrew child." Moses' sister steps up to the princess and says, "Shall I go and find a Hebrew nurse to feed the child for you?" The princess agrees. So the sister goes and brings back her mother. The princess says, "Take this child and feed it for me, and I will pay your wages." The mother and sister take baby Moses home and care for him.

> When the child grew up, [the mother] brought him to Pharaoh's daughter, who made him her son. She named him Moses, explaining, "I drew him out of the water."

Even today, when a new mother is forced, for some reason, to separate from her baby, she may place it where it is safe and can easily be found—beside a hospital door, on the steps of a church, and so on. Yet there is also a rule here: Folk tales are told about almost all great people in history, and most include how, as a baby, he or she narrowly escaped death. The story of baby Moses is unique because his little ark is found by a daughter of the same Pharaoh who wanted to kill Hebrew babies; he is nursed by his own mother; he is given to the princess when he is a lad; and he grows up as a prince in the palace, under Pharaoh's nose.

The Name Moses

This portion is called *Shemot,* "names", and one interesting name is "Moses". By the time the story was written down, few Israelites could speak the Egyptian language. So the Torah explained the name with a word-play, saying that *Mosheh* came from the Hebrew word *mashach,* meaning "take out from". The two words are different, but they sounded alike enough to make this a very popular little pun.

Still, the Egyptian princess who named Moses probably knew less Hebrew than you do, so Moses was surely not a Hebrew name. In Egyptian, "moses" means "child of" and is normally joined to the name of an Egyptian god to make a complete name. For instance, "Tut*mose(s)*" means "child of [the god] Tut" and "Ra*meses*" means "child of [the god] Ra". So something is definitely missing in Moses' name! Where is the name of a god that it should begin with? Perhaps it was meant to be this way: the name Moses may mean "child of [the invisible God]". Giving Moses a half-name that points to the God of the Hebrews may even have been a way of poking fun at the gods of the Egyptians.

The Murder and Midian

Some time after that, when Moses had grown up, he went out to his people and witnessed their labors. He saw an Egyptian beating a Hebrew, one of his people. He turned this way and that and, seeing no one about, he struck down the Egyptian and hid him in the sand. ... When Pharaoh learned of the matter, he sought to kill Moses; but Moses fled from Pharaoh. He settled in the land of Midian and sat down beside a well.

Reuel, the priest of Midian, had seven daughters. One day the daughters went to the well to draw water for their father's flock. Shepherds came and tried to chase them away. Seeing this, Moses drove off the shepherds and watered the

Babies in the River

One Bible scholar counted thirty-two stories from the ancient Near East, all of them about famous babies who were saved by being placed where they would easily be found. In Egypt there was a story that the god Horus as a baby was saved by being floated on the Nile. In Mesopotamia the baby who later became King Sargon (2334-2279 B.C.E.) was saved in the same way. Sargon tells how his mother "set me in a basket of rushes, with bitumen she sealed my lid. She cast me into the river which ... carried me to Akki [who took me] as his son."

To Discuss

In Pharaoh's palace all the princes went to lessons taught by the priests of Egypt. Moses probably went, too. What kinds of subjects do you think Moses studied? What might he have learned that would help him later to become a masterful leader of his people?

Moses and the Murder

When the Torah says that Moses "went out to his people," it means that Moses knew he was a Hebrew. He was upset because "one of his people" was being beaten. What he did next was no accident. He first checked to see if any Egyptians were nearby; then he murdered the Egyptian. Of course, there were Hebrews nearby, and they whispered to one another how the prince slew the taskmaster. Moses knew the news would soon reach Pharaoh. Even a prince would be put to death for murder. So Moses hurried out of Egypt into the wilderness. When he reached Midian he felt safe enough to settle down by a well.

Quote to Remember

וַיַּרְא וְהִנֵּה הַסְּנֶה בֹּעֵר
בָּאֵשׁ וְהַסְּנֶה אֵינֶנּוּ אֻכָּל.

He gazed and there was a bush all aflame, yet the bush was not consumed.

flock for the girls. The grateful Reuel invited Moses to join his household. He gave Moses his daughter Zipporah as a wife. Soon Moses and Zipporah had a son they named Gershom, "a stranger there", for Moses said, "I have been a stranger in a foreign land."

A long time after that, the king of Egypt died. The Israelites were groaning under the bondage and cried out; and their cry for help ... rose up to God. God heard their moaning, and God remembered the covenant with Abraham and Isaac and Jacob. God looked upon the Israelites, and God took notice of them.

The Burning Bush and God's Name

Now Moses, tending the flock of his father-in-law Jethro, the priest of Midian, drove the flock into the wilderness, and came to Horeb, the mountain of God. An angel of Adonai appeared to him in a blazing fire out of a bush. He gazed and there was a bush all aflame, yet the bush was not consumed. Moses said, "I must turn aside to look at this marvelous sight; why doesn't the bush burn up?" When Adonai saw that he turned aside to look, God called to him out of the bush: "Moses! Moses!" He answered, "Here am I." ... And Adonai [said], "I have marked the plight of My people in Egypt ... I have come down to rescue them from the Egyptians and to bring them out of that land to a ... land flowing with milk and honey. ... I will send you to Pharaoh, and you shall free My people, the Israelites, from Egypt."

But Moses said to God, "Who am I that I should go to Pharaoh and free the Israelites from Egypt?" And God said, "I will be with you; that shall be your sign ... When you have freed the people from Egypt, you shall worship God at this mountain."

Moses said to God, "When I come to the Israelites ... and they ask me, 'What is God's name?' what shall I say to them?" And God said to Moses,

"Ehyeh-Asher-Ehyeh." God continued, "Thus you shall speak to the Israelites, 'Ehyeh sent me to you." And God said further to Moses, "Thus shall you speak to the Israelites, 'Adonai [*YHVH*], God of your fathers, the God of Abraham, the God of Isaac, and the God of Jacob, has sent me to you: This shall be My name forever, for all eternity."

Before the burning bush story, some Torah stories use only the names *El* or *Elohim* (we translate both as "God"). Other stories use only the name *YHVH* (which we translate as "Adonai"). Only once, in one creation story, God's name was given as *YHVH-Elohim*. After the burning bush story the names—*El*, *Elohim* and *YHVH*—are used together, anywhere and any time.

There are many ideas about why this happens. One idea is that only some of the Hebrew tribes were slaves in Egypt. Leaving Egypt, they entered Sinai and wandered in the wilderness until they joined with the Hebrew tribes that had never left Canaan. The tribes in Canaan knew many stories of Abraham, Isaac, and Jacob—they knew their God by the name *El* or *Elohim*. The tribes coming from Egypt knew their God by the name *YHVH*. The Torah uses the story of the burning bush to inform all the tribes—the ones who were in Egypt and the ones who stayed in Canaan—that *El*, *Elohim*, and *YHVH* are all names of the One God. Another idea is that our Torah stories are based on even older stories. One of these old stories—the one about the bush—explains how God came to have many names: *YHVH*, *El*, and *Elohim*.

At the Bush

At the burning bush Moses asks, What shall I do if the Israelites refuse to believe that Adonai has sent me? Adonai tells him to throw his walking stick on the ground. Moses does this, and the rod becomes a snake, scaring Moses. Adonai says, "Put out your hand and grasp it by the tail." Moses does this, and the snake turns back into a rod.

Adonai then tells Moses to put his hand into his clothing. When Moses pulls out his hand, it is crusted with white scales! When he puts his hand back in his clothing and pulls it out again, it is magically healed. Adonai says that if these

Three Names for God

God reveals the name "Ehyeh-Asher-Ehyeh". In English this might mean "I Am What I Am" or "I Will Be What I Will Be". Then God tells Moses to say, "Ehyeh sent me." This could mean "*I Am* sent me" or "*I Will Be* sent me". Then God says to tell the Israelites "YHVH ... has sent me ... This shall be My name forever." God has really given Moses three names, not one! They all come from the Hebrew word that means "to be" or "to exist". YHVH—the name we use today—must mean something like "[God] Is" or "[God] Exists". This is not the kind of name a person would have, but that may be exactly why it is our sacred name for God.

To Discuss

It is fitting that the book we are now studying is called "Names" (*Shemot* in Hebrew). It was said that the greatest magic in ancient times was to know the "secret" or "true" name of a person or thing. People thought that if you could discover a "true" name, you could force a person or thing to do whatever you wanted. But Adonai does not seem worried that Moses will be able to control God by knowing God's "true" name. Why is this?

A Great Magic Trick

The burning bush catches Moses' eye, and Moses turns aside to look at it. It was a small thing. A bush, not a tree. Other people might have passed without noticing it—so the Rabbis said. Like all Egyptians, though, Moses loved magic, and the burning bush was like a great magic trick. So he paused to pay attention. It seems that Adonai knew that the Egyptians would be impressed by magic. And the Israelites, who had lived among the Egyptians for four hundred years, would be impressed by it, too.

two signs are not enough to convince the Israelites, Moses should take some water from the Nile and throw it on the ground. The water will turn to blood.

But Moses complains, saying, "I am slow of speech and slow of tongue." Adonai asks, "Who gives speech to human beings? Who causes people to be dumb or deaf, seeing or blind? ... I will be with you as you speak and I will instruct you what to say." But Moses begs, "Please, Adonai, send someone else." Adonai is angry at Moses. Adonai says, "There is your brother Aaron the Levite. ... I will speak to you and you will tell him what to say. He will be your spokesman, with you playing the role of god to him. And take with you this rod, with which you shall perform the signs."

> Adonai said to Moses in Midian, "Go back to Egypt for all the men who sought to kill you are dead." So Moses took his wife and sons ... and went back to the land of Egypt; and Moses took the rod of God with him. And Adonai said to Moses, "When you return to Egypt, see that you perform before Pharaoh all the marvels that I have put within your power. I, however, will stiffen his heart so that he will not let the people go."

Adonai commanded Aaron to meet Moses in the wilderness. When the brothers met Moses told Aaron all that had happened. Together they went to the chieftains of the Israelites, and Moses performed the wonders that God had taught him and repeated the words that Adonai had told him. The Israelites accepted Moses as their leader. Then Moses and Aaron went to Pharaoh, saying, "The God of the Hebrews has appeared to us. Let us go a distance of three days into the wilderness to worship Adonai."

But Pharaoh sent them away, saying, "Why do you distract the Israelites from their labor?" Then Pharaoh told the taskmasters to stop giving the Israelites straw for making bricks. They would gather their own straw from now on— and still make the same number of bricks each day. The Israelites complained, but Pharaoh made their jobs harder. On top of that, the taskmasters grew angry. Now the Israelites complained to Moses, saying he had made their life worse now than before. So Moses complained to Adonai, "Why did You send me? Ever since I came to Pharaoh to

speak in Your name, he has dealt worse with this people; and still You have not delivered Your people."

> Adonai said to Moses, "You shall soon see what I will do to Pharaoh: he shall let them go because of a greater might; indeed, because of a greater might he shall drive them out from his land."

Why the Magic Lesson?

The story of Joseph helped us understand how Egyptians felt about magic. It was central to their religion. Their priests were trained as magicians. We will hear about these magician priests again when we come to the ten plagues. For now, look closely at the first meeting between Adonai and Moses. It begins with magic: a bush that burns without being harmed. And magic is what Adonai gives to Moses—the kind of magic that Egyptians adore—three "wonders" to perform. Even as Moses leaves the bush, Adonai reminds him to take the "rod of God" with him. We could think of it as his "magic wand". He will use it again and again.

It might be a little surprising to think that this great moment, when Moses stands before Adonai for the first time, centers on magic tricks and marvels. Yet these are the tools Moses needs. Moses does not need an army or a secret weapon. Moses does not need money or fine clothing to impress Pharaoh. And even though Moses is speaking to the One God, the creator of the universe, Moses does not need the answers to big questions like Why are we alive? Why do we die? What happens to us after death? Why do bad things sometimes happen to good people? Adonai will do the real work of freeing the Israelites from Pharaoh. What Moses

Making Bricks

Painted on the tomb wall of the chief brick maker of Pharaoh Tutmose III, the drawings above show how bricks were made in ancient Egypt. *Bottom left*: Mud is measured and carried. *Top middle*: An Egyptian overseer sits and watches the laborers pour mud into wood forms. At this point, straw or broken pottery pieces might be added to the mud to give it greater strength. *Top left*: The forms are stacked to dry in the desert heat. *Bottom middle*: Bricks are stacked and measured and evened out. *Top right*: Bricks are carried to the building site. *Far right*: An Egyptian taskmaster raises his rod to warn a worker to keep up the speed. The text above the drawings tells us that these workers are Nubians and Semites.

Store Cities

The Torah says that the Israelites were slaving to make bricks in order to build the store cities of Pithom and Raamses. Archaeologists still do not know exactly where these two cities for storing the grain, wine, beer, and other goods of the Pharaoh were located. But the photo of another ruined store city (*right*) shows what they were like and how the bricks were used.

needs now is a few magical wonders to impress the Israelites and the Egyptians.

In time, though, Adonai will teach Moses and the Israelites that there is a kind of religion that is more wonderful than magic, a religion that does not depend on magic or miracles.

Haftarah: Isaiah 27:6-28:13; 29:22-23

Shemot tells how the Israelites were made slaves in Egypt and God sent Moses to rescue them. The Rabbis connect that slavery with the troubles of the kingdoms of Israel and Judah described in the prophecies of Isaiah.

God was forced to destroy the kingdom of Israel, to send the ten tribes into exile. It was God who punished them, and a day would come, Isaiah says, when "a great shofar will be sounded" and the tribes will return from Assyria and from Egypt to "worship Adonai on the holy mountain in Jerusalem." (Of course, that day never came for the "ten lost tribes".)

Even those who will be saved from destruction will turn back to evil ways. Like children, they need to be taught "little by little, one command and then the next, a little here and a little there."

Adonai tells the prophet to speak to them "slowly and with simple words." Even then they may refuse to listen. They may slide backward, and the prophet will have to repeat the lesson again, "little by little, one command and then the next, a little here and a little there."

The haftarah speaks of the drunks of the tribe of Ephraim, but it may not mean that they were drinking too much. It most likely means that the people of Ephraim were not thinking straight, the way those who take too much liquor cannot think straight. So they fell into sin.

These words of Isaiah were so depressing that the Rabbis added two upbeat verses from Chapter 29 at the end, to say, "Adonai, who saved Abraham, tells the House of Jacob, no more shall Jacob be put to shame … when his children [the Israelites] see what I am doing for them, they shall make My name holy…."

Let My People Go

ואוא
Va'eirah
Exodus 6:2-9:35

Pharaoh's Heart

Adonai said to Moses, "See, I place you in the role
of God to Pharaoh, with your brother Aaron as
your prophet. ... I will harden Pharaoh's heart,
that I may multiply My signs and marvels in the
land of Egypt. ... And the Egyptians shall know
that I am Adonai, when I stretch out My hand over
Egypt and bring out the Israelites....

Moses was eighty years old and Aaron eighty-
three when they ... came before Pharaoh. ...
Aaron cast down his rod ... and [the rod] turned
into a serpent. Then Pharaoh, for his part, summoned the wise men and the sorcerers; and the
Egyptian magicians, in turn, did the same with
their spells, each cast down his rod, and [the
rods] turned into serpents. But Aaron's rod swallowed their rods. Yet Pharaoh's heart stiffened and
he did not heed them, as Adonai had said.

The contest of the Ten Plagues begins. Pharaoh challenged
Adonai (in Exodus 5:2), saying: "Who is this Adonai ...? I do
not know Adonai, nor will I let Israel go." Now Adonai in-
tends to prove to the Pharaoh and the Egyptians that "I am
Adonai" and that no Pharaoh or Egyptian god is equal to
Adonai.

The Torah states that Pharaoh himself is stubborn from
the outset. Pharaoh continues to be stubborn, and also to lie
about letting Israel go, until the sixth plague. Afterward—
from the sixth plague to the tenth—God "hardens Pharaoh's
heart." Maimonides, the Spanish-Jewish philosopher, says
that this shows the Torah's way of thinking about behavior.
If we are stubborn and evil, then God soon helps us to continue to be stubborn and evil, until we finally learn that being stubborn and evil is the wrong way to behave.

Serpents

"Serpent" was most likely the
Hebrew word for "crocodile". In
the days of the Pharaohs, crocodiles were plentiful in the Nile
(though they were unknown in
Canaan). The story of the first
contest between Pharaoh's magicians and Moses' brother Aaron
is more exciting if we picture the
rods turning into crocodiles. It is
more gruesome, too, to imagine
Aaron's crocodile ripping and
chewing on the crocodiles of the
Egyptian magicians.

To Consider

You have learned a lot about Egypt, religion, and magic. Aaron is the wonder-worker in the first three plagues. Why do you think the Torah describes these plagues as a contest between Aaron and the magicians of Egypt?

Magic Rods

Egyptologists have found many "magic rods" used by the priests of Egypt. The rods are square and hollow, with small figures of various animals attached to them. The magician-priests probably thought that the rods gave them special power over these animals. With the rod *below* the magician might try to control lions, crocodiles, frogs, and turtles.

The First Three Plagues

And Adonai said to Moses, "Pharaoh is stubborn; he refuses to let the people go. Go to Pharaoh in the morning, as he is coming out to the water …, taking with you the rod that turned into a serpent. And say to him, 'Adonai, the God of the Hebrews, sent me to you to say, "Let my people go that they may worship Me in the wilderness." But you have paid no heed until now. Thus says Adonai, "By this you shall know that I am Adonai." See, I shall strike the water in the Nile with the rod that is in my hand, and it will be turned to blood….'"

And Adonai said to Moses, "Say to Aaron, Take your rod and hold out your arm over the waters of Egypt … that they may turn to blood…. Moses and Aaron did just as Adonai commanded: he lifted up the rod and struck the water in the Nile in the sight of Pharaoh and his court, and all the water in the Nile was turned to blood and the fish … died. The Nile stank so the Egyptians could not drink of the water from the Nile; and there was blood throughout the land of Egypt. But when the magicians of Egypt did the same with their spells, Pharaoh's heart stiffened….

When seven days had passed … Adonai said to Moses, "Go to Pharaoh, and say to him… 'Let my people go… If you refuse to let them go, then I will plague your whole country with frogs….'" Aaron held out his arm over the waters of Egypt, and the frogs came up and covered the land of

Egypt. But the magicians did the same with their spells, and brought frogs upon the land of Egypt.

Then Pharaoh summoned Moses and Aaron and said, "Plead with Adonai to remove the frogs … and I will let the people go to sacrifice to Adonai." … The frogs died …. And [the Egyptians] piled them together upon heaps, till the land stank. But when Pharaoh saw that there was relief, he became stubborn…, as Adonai had spoken.

Adonai said to Moses, "Say to Aaron: Hold out your rod, and strike the dust of the earth, and it shall turn to lice throughout the land of Egypt. And they did so. … and vermin came upon man and beast; all the dust of the earth turned to lice throughout the land of Egypt. The magicians tried the like with their spells to produce lice, but they could not. … And the magicians said to Pharaoh, "This is the finger of God!" But Pharaoh's heart stiffened and he would not heed them, as Adonai had spoken.

The first three plagues are a contest between Aaron's magic and the magic of the Egyptian sorcerers. When the magicians of Egypt cannot produce lice, they realize that the plagues are "the finger of God". They have lost the contest. But Pharaoh continues to be stubborn. And the plagues continue to multiply.

The Second Three Plagues

And Adonai said to Moses, "Early in the morning present yourself to Pharaoh, as he is coming out to the water … and say to him, 'Thus says Adonai, "Let my people go, that they may worship Me. For, if you will not let My people go, I will let loose swarms of insects …. But on that day I will set apart the land of Goshen, where My people dwell, so that no swarms of insects shall be there, that you may know that I Adonai am in the midst of the land…."'"

Where's the Water?

It is clear that the accounts of the plagues are exaggerations. Aaron's rod turns all the waters of Egypt into blood. But if so, where do the Egyptian magicians find water to repeat the marvel by turning all the waters to blood again? And if frogs are everywhere, how could the Egyptian magicians also produce frogs everywhere? It's not quite realistic—it's a little larger than life—but it works every time we hear the story, because it draws pictures that are vivid and memorable.

Many Plagues, Many Stories

The Ten Plagues probably came together out of many stories. This may be why some of the plagues come directly from God, some are the work of Moses, and some are the work of Aaron. Psalm 78 (verses 44-51) lists eleven "wonders" that Adonai worked on the Egyptians, but only lists seven of the plagues that we know. Psalm 105 (verses 28-36) lists ten "wonders" performed by Moses and Aaron but also only includes seven of the plagues we know. The Torah settled on exactly ten plagues—arranged as three, three, three, and one. Since we can count to ten on our fingers, ten is a good number for memorizing things— things like the Ten Plagues or the Ten Commandments.

And Adonai did so. ... the land was ruined because of the swarm of insects. Then Pharaoh summoned Moses and Aaron and said, "Go and sacrifice to your God ... Plead for me." And Moses said, "... I will plead with Adonai that the swarms of insects depart ... but let not Pharaoh again act deceitfully, not letting the people go to sacrifice to Adonai." ... But Pharaoh became stubborn this time also, and would not let the people go.

Adonai said to Moses, "Go to Pharaoh and say to him, 'Thus says Adonai, the God of the Hebrews: "Let my people go to worship Me. For if you refuse to let them go, and continue to hold them, then the hand of Adonai will strike your cattle in the fields—the horses, the asses, the camels, the oxen, and the sheep—with a very severe disease. But ... [no cattle] shall die of all that belongs to the Israelites.'" ..." And Adonai did so the next day; all the cattle of the Egyptians died... When Pharaoh inquired, he was told that not a head of the cattle of Israel had died; yet Pharaoh remained stubborn, and he would not let the people go.

Then Adonai said to Moses and Aaron, "Each of you take handfuls of soot from the kiln, and let Moses throw it toward the sky in the sight of Pharaoh. It shall become a fine dust all over the land of Egypt, and cause ... boils on man and beast.... So they took soot of the kiln, and appeared before Pharaoh. Moses threw it toward the sky, and it caused ... boils on man and beast.

The magicians were unable to confront Moses because of the boils; for the boils afflicted the magicians, as well as all the other Egyptians. But Adonai hardened the heart of Pharaoh, and he would not heed [Moses and Aaron], just as Adonai had told Moses.

Why do the magicians of Egypt appear again in the sixth plague, when they were not mentioned at all in the fourth or fifth plague? One reason may be that plagues four and five come directly from Adonai, without the help of any magic from Moses or Aaron. When Moses and Aaron return to work the sixth plague, the Egyptian magicians are mentioned again, even though it is only to say that they were helpless.

The Seventh Plague

Adonai said to Moses, "Early in the morning, present yourself to Pharaoh, and say to him, 'Thus says Adonai, the God of the Hebrews: Let My people go to worship Me. For this time I will send ... My plagues ... in order that you may know that there is none like Me in all the world. I could have stretched forth My hand ... and you would have been erased from the earth. Nevertheless, I have spared you for this purpose: that My fame may resound throughout the world....'"

Adonai said to Moses, "Hold out your arm toward the sky that hail may fall on all the land of Egypt, upon man and beast, and all the grasses of the field in the land of Egypt." So Moses held out his rod toward the sky, and Adonai sent thunder and hail, and fire streamed down to the ground... The hail was very heavy—fire flashing in the midst of the hail—such as had not fallen on the land of Egypt since it became a nation. Throughout the land of Egypt the hail struck down all that were in the open, both man and beast; the hail also struck down all the grasses of the field and shattered all the trees of the field. Only in the region of Goshen, where the Israelites dwelled, there was no hail.

Thereupon Pharaoh sent for Moses and Aaron, and said to them, "I stand guilty this time. Adonai is in the right, and I and my people are in the wrong. Plead with Adonai that there may be an end of God's thunder and of hail. I will let you go...."

Leaving Pharaoh, Moses went outside the city and spread out his hands to Adonai: the thunder and the hail ceased, and no rain came pouring down

Quote to Remember

כֹּה־אָמַר יְהֹוָה אֱלֹהֵי הָעִבְרִים שַׁלַּח אֶת־עַמִּי וְיַעַבְדֻנִי.

Thus says Adonai, the God of the Hebrews: Let My people go to worship Me.

To Consider

How can we tell that the plagues were divided three-three-three and one? Look for the way that the first, fourth, and seventh plagues begin. What does God tell Moses to do before each of them? And for "extra credit", see if you can find the different reasons Adonai gives for the first three, the second three, and the seventh plagues.

on the earth. But when Pharaoh saw that the rain and the hail and the thunder had ceased, he became stubborn and reverted to his guilty ways, as did his courtiers. So Pharaoh's heart was hardened and he would not let the Israelites go, just as Adonai had foretold through Moses.

This portion, *Va'eirah* ("I appeared"), ends with the seventh plague—the hail. Plagues eight, nine, and ten are in the next portion.

Explaining the Plagues

People have tried to explain the plagues in many ways. In the midrash, the Rabbis suggested one idea that became very popular. Each plague, they said, tells how Adonai defeated one of the Egyptian gods. The Egyptians worshiped the Nile River as a god. In the first plague Adonai defeats the Nile by turning its water to blood. Frogs were worshiped by Egyptians. In the second plague Adonai defeats the frogs by controlling them. And so on. This is an interesting idea, but the Torah never mentions the gods of Egypt.

Scientists tell us that nine of the plagues—all but the last—are natural events that occur in Egypt from time to time. An ancient Egyptian text tells of a time when the Nile waters ran as red as blood. The scientists say that when the Nile waters were bad, fish died and frogs infested the land looking for fresh water. When the frogs died of thirst, their rotting bodies gave rise to lice. The lice led to skin diseases like boils. Likewise, there were years when terrible hailstorms destroyed crops, killing people and animals who were caught outdoors.

But even if all of these were natural, it is hard to imagine all of them occurring together at just the right time for Moses and Pharaoh. And archaeologists remind us that we have never found any mention of a major disaster like the Torah's plagues in any of the ancient Egyptian texts.

We examine more ideas about the plagues in the next portion. For now we can note that the story of the Ten Plagues may exaggerate the truth by saying that the blood was *everywhere* in Egypt for seven days, by saying that the hail destroyed the *all* the crops, that the swarms of insects were *everywhere but where the Hebrews lived*, and so on; but there is a kernel of truth in the tale, too, because most of the punishments the Torah speaks of are the kind that can happen in the land of Egypt.

Haftarah: Ezekiel 28:25-29:21

The Rabbis connect the plagues brought on the Egyptians in the time of Moses with the punishment that Ezekiel predicts for Egypt if the Egyptians refuse to help Judah against the Babylonians as they had promised.

Egypt had made a treaty with the Kingdom of Judah, but when Jerusalem was first attacked by Babylonia, the Egyptians never came. The city was conquered, and Ezekiel was among the prisoners taken. He preached six sermons against Egypt; the first two are in this haftarah.

In the first sermon he speaks out against Egypt's empty promises, warning the Israelites never to trust Egypt again.

> Thus says Adonai God: I am against you, Pharaoh, king of Egypt, for you are a great croco-

dile, lurking in the [Nile] River's edges, thinking, "My River is mine…." But I will put hooks through your jaws [and] throw you out into the wilderness … on dry ground.

Because you thought the River was yours, God says, Egypt will be a ruin. Never again will Israel trust you. "They will know that I am Adonai."

In the second sermon Ezekiel preaches that God will send King Nebuchadnezzar of Babylon against Egypt. He "shall carry off its riches, ruin it, and plunder it" to give his armies their wages. All this because they wronged the Israelites.

> That day, I will make the House of Israel strong, and I will give you the courage to speak to them. They will know that I am Adonai.

Adonai and Pharaoh

Moses' Rod

"So Moses held out his rod …." We could ask the question, Why did Adonai command Moses to use a rod at all? Couldn't Adonai bring the plagues without Moses waving his rod? Of course. But look at any statue, coffin, or painting of an Egyptian Pharaoh, and you will notice that the Pharaohs always held a shepherd's crook or rod as an important symbol of power over Egypt. It is for this reason that Adonai commands Moses and Aaron to use shepherd's crooks or rods—to show that the real power is not in the rod but in the works of Adonai. Pharaoh's rod of power is useless against the rod of God.

Locusts and Darkness

Then Adonai said to Moses, "Go to Pharaoh. For I have hardened his heart and the heart of his courtiers, that I may display these My signs among them, and that you may recount in the hearing of your children, and of your children's children, how I made a mockery of the Egyptians … in order that you may know that I am Adonai." So Moses and Aaron went to Pharaoh and said to him, "Thus says Adonai, the God of the Hebrews, 'How long will you refuse to humble yourself before Me? Let My people go that they may worship Me. For if you refuse to let My people go, tomorrow I will bring locusts on your territory. …'" With that he turned, and left Pharaoh's presence.

Pharaoh's courtiers said to him, "…Let the men go to worship Adonai their God! Are you not aware that Egypt is lost?"

Pharaoh called Moses and Aaron to return to the palace. He said, "Go and worship your God, but who will be going?" Moses answered, "We will take our young and our old, our sons and our daughters, our flocks and our herds." But Pharaoh said, "You are up to mischief! Only take the men." And Pharaoh sent them away again.

Then Adonai said to Moses, "Hold out your arm over the land of Egypt for the locusts, that they may come upon the land of Egypt and eat up all the grasses in the land, whatever the hail has left." So Moses held out his rod … and Adonai drove an east wind [that] brought the locusts. … Never before had there been so many, nor will there ever be so many again. They hid all the land from view, and the land was darkened … they ate [until] nothing green was left, of tree or grass of the field, in all the land of Egypt.

Now Pharaoh called Moses and Aaron and asked them to plead with Adonai to stop the locusts; but when the locusts were all gone, God hardened Pharaoh's heart, and he refused to let the people go.

Then Adonai said to Moses, "Hold out your arm toward the sky that there may be darkness upon the land of Egypt, a darkness that can be touched." Moses held out his arm toward the sky and thick darkness descended upon all the land of Egypt three days ... but all the Israelites enjoyed light in their dwellings.

Now Pharaoh said, "Take your people and go." Moses said, "Only if you give us animals for our sacrifices." But Adonai hardened Pharaoh's heart. Pharaoh told Moses, "Go away and never see me again!" Moses said, "You speak well. I will never see your face again." Then Moses told Pharaoh:

Thus says Adonai, "Toward midnight I will go forth ... and every first-born in the land of Egypt shall die, from the first-born of Pharaoh ... to the first-born of the cattle."

Then Moses left. He was terrible in his anger. But again Adonai promised that the Israelites would be safe.

Passover

Adonai said to Moses and Aaron ...: This month shall ... be the first month of the year to you. Speak to the whole community of Israel and say that on the tenth of this month each of them shall take a lamb ... from the sheep or the goats. You shall keep watch over it until the fourteenth day of this month and ... slaughter it at twilight. They shall take some of the blood and put it on the two doorposts and on the lintel of the houses in which they are to eat it. They shall eat the meat that same night ... roasted over the fire, with unleavened bread and bitter herbs. ... You shall not leave any of it over until morning; if any of it is left

Was Adonai Fair to Pharaoh?

The people of Egypt worshiped Pharaoh as their god. The real contest in the plagues was not between magicians and Aaron or between Moses and Pharaoh. It was a contest between Adonai, God of the Hebrews, and the false man-god called Pharaoh. When Adonai "hardens" Pharaoh's heart, it is to show how weak the god of Egypt is. To make the point of the plagues very clear, Adonai says that in time to come "you may recount in the hearing of your children, and of your children's children, how I made a mockery of the Egyptians and how I displayed My signs among them—in order that you [the Israelites] may know that I am Adonai." Was it fair for Adonai to "harden" Pharaoh's heart? It was not only fair, it was absolutely necessary.

Quote to Remember

וּפָסַחְתִּי עֲלֵכֶם וְלֹא־יִהְיֶה
בָכֶם נֶגֶף לְמַשְׁחִית בְּהַכֹּתִי
בְּאֶרֶץ מִצְרָיִם.

I will pass over you, so that no plague will destroy you when I strike the land of Egypt.

To Consider

Scholars believe that the stories of the plagues may be exaggerated but the details of life in Egypt ring true. The plagues seem to be a memory of something real and not just stories made up hundreds of years later. Did you ever tell a true story, but tell it in an exaggerated way to impress someone?

until morning you shall burn it. This is how you shall eat it: your loins girded, your sandals on your feet, and your staff in your hand; and you shall eat it hurriedly: it is a Passover offering to Adonai. For that night I will go through the land of Egypt and strike down every first-born ... and I will mete out punishments to all the gods of Egypt, I Adonai. And the blood on the houses where you are staying shall be a sign for you: when I see the blood, I will pass over you, so that no plague will destroy you when I strike the land of Egypt.

Adonai commanded a week of remembrance, telling the Israelites to keep it for all time, saying, "Seven days shall you eat unleavened bread." The first and last day of this week should be holy, and Israelites should not work on these days, except to prepare food. This is the feast of "unleavened bread" to remember that "on this very day I brought your folk out of the land of Egypt." Then Moses repeated the commands of Adonai to the elders of the Israelites, adding, "No one should go outside this night."

And when your children ask you, "What do you mean by this ceremony?" you shall say, "It is the Passover sacrifice to Adonai who passed over the houses of the Israelites in Egypt, smiting the Egyptians, but saving our houses." The people then bowed low .... And the Israelites [did just] as Adonai had commanded Moses and Aaron, so they did.

The New Year

There are three strange items in this portion called *Bo* ("Go"). First, the Torah states that Passover comes in *Aviv* ("spring"), the first month of the year. But we know that the Jewish new year (Rosh Hashanah) comes in the fall.

Second, Adonai commands that the Passover lamb be roasted and eaten along with unleavened bread (*matzah*) and that the Israelites obey God's commands. But later the Torah states that matzah was first baked when the Israelites hurried out of Egypt and did not wait for their bread dough to rise.

Third, Adonai gives laws about remembering the first-born (later the Torah states that the lamb of the eighth day must be a first-born lamb). Adonai commands that matzah be eaten with the roasted meat.

Bible scholars explain that long before the Exodus, Egyptian and Canaanite farmers celebrated a spring festival—a time for finishing the old grain before eating the grain of the new harvest. Any remaining old grain was burned; the new grain was eaten as matzah, unleavened bread. This was the new year for them. Israelite farmers adopted this old festival, adding the story of the plagues and the Exodus to explain its beginnings.

Israelite shepherds adopted a different festival. For shepherds, new lambs and kids were born in the spring, so the springtime began their new year. Their feast offered the first-born of their flocks to Adonai. They added the story of the plagues and the Exodus to explain their festival of the first-born.

As the Israelite tribes became one nation, the two festivals—which came at almost the same time—and the two celebrations—of matzah and the first-born—were joined together to make Passover as we know it now. Later the New Year would move to the fall. But the idea that the world of nature begins anew every spring never faded, and we continue to celebrate the Exodus on Passover to this very day.

The First Month

For farmers and shepherds, the time of *aviv* ("spring") started the new year with crops and new births. For the priests, the sound of the *shofar* ("horn") on Rosh Hashanah and the sacrifices of atonement on Yom Kippur were more important. Much later in our history, as more and more Jews lived in cities, as synagogues replaced the destroyed Temple, and as new prayers and practices were added to Rosh Hashanah and Yom Kippur, the fall holidays grew more serious and intense. The month of Passover (now called *Nisan*) remained the first month of the year; but now the High Holy Days, in the seventh month of the year, were fixed as the "official" Jewish new year.

The Death of the First-Born

In the middle of the night Adonai struck down all the first-born in the land of Egypt, from the first-born of Pharaoh who sat on the throne to the first-born of the captive who was in the dungeon, and all the first-born of the cattle. And Pharaoh arose in the night … because there was a loud cry in Egypt; for there was no house where there was not someone dead.

That very night Pharaoh called Moses and Aaron and told them to gather their people and get out of Egypt.

The Egyptians urged the [Israelites] on … for they said, "[If you stay,] we shall all be dead." So the [Israelites] took their dough before it was leav-

Torah and Haggadah

Take a look at the way the contest of the plagues is told in the Passover *Haggadah*. What differences do you see between the way the *Haggadah* tells the plagues and the way the contest is told by the Torah?

A Mighty Hand

The Torah tells how Adonai rescued the Israelites with a *yad hazakah* ("mighty hand") and a *zeroa netuyah* ("outstretched arm"). The Egyptians used the same words when they told how a Pharaoh conquered his enemies through a "strong arm"; or that a Pharaoh "extended" or "sent forth" his arm, meaning that his armies went out to meet his enemies. At Tell el-Amarna Egyptologists found a letter from a man named Abdu-Heba of Jerusalem. The letter was sent to the Pharaoh and used the word *zu-ru-uch* (an Egyptian spelling of *zeroa*) to mean "the strong arm [of the Pharaoh]". So the Torah not only tells us how Adonai overcame the Pharaoh and all the gods of Egypt; it even uses the words of the Egyptians themselves.

ened…. The Israelites had done Moses' bidding and borrowed from the Egyptians objects of silver and gold, and clothing. … Thus [with the help of Adonai] they stripped the Egyptians [of wealth].

Leaving Egypt

The Israelites journeyed from Raamses to Sukkot, about six hundred thousand men on foot, aside from children. Moreover, many non-Hebrews ["a mixed multitude"] went up with them, and very much livestock, both flocks and herds. And they baked unleavened cakes of the dough that they had taken out of Egypt, for it was not leavened, since they had been driven out of Egypt, and could not delay…

The length of time that the Israelites lived in Egypt was four hundred and thirty years; at the end of the four hundred and thirtieth year, to the very day, all the ranks of Adonai departed from the land of Egypt. That was for Adonai a night of vigil to bring them out of the land of Egypt; that same night is Adonai's, one of vigil for all the children of Israel throughout the ages. … That very day Adonai freed the Israelites from the land of Egypt, troop by troop.

Adonai spoke further to Moses, saying, "Consecrate to Me every first-born, man and beast …." And Moses said to the people, "Remember this day … in the month Aviv. So when Adonai has brought you into the land of the Canaanites, the Hittites, the Amorites, the Hivites, and the Jebusites, which [Adonai] swore to your fathers to give you, a land flowing with milk and honey, you shall observe in this month the following practice: Seven days you shall eat unleavened bread, and on the seventh day there shall be a festival of Adonai. … And you shall explain to your child on that day, 'It is because of what Adonai did for me when I went free from Egypt.' And this shall serve you as a sign on your hand and as a reminder on

your forehead—in order that the Teaching of Adonai may be in your mouth—that with a mighty hand Adonai freed you from Egypt.

Are We All Pharaohs?

Why does the Torah mention the idea of wearing something on our hands and on our foreheads? You probably think of the *tefillin*—one for the head (*tefillin shel rosh)* and one for the arm (*tefillin shel yad*). These leather boxes tied to the body with straps have been used in daily prayer by some Jews since ancient times. The Rabbis of the Talmud thought they came from Egypt. They said this is why they are mentioned as ways of remembering the Exodus.

It may be true that *tefillin* began to be used about the time that the Israelites left Egypt, but there is another reason they became a symbol of the Exodus. If you look at statues and paintings of ancient Egypt, you will see that the Pharaohs wore a lot of gold and silver jewelry. Most Pharaohs wore a circlet of gold or silver—a crown shaped like a snake with its head sticking upward—on their foreheads. And on their arms they often wore an armband. In Egypt, common Egyptians and slaves were always forbidden to

A Little More Magic

Everything a Pharaoh wore had special meaning. *Top left:* The mask of Pharaoh Psusennes I, showing the spitting cobra (called the *uraeus* in Greek). The cobra protected the king at all times and gave fright to his enemies. *Bottom left:* One of the gold and lapis armbands Psusennes wore. Each band weighs nearly four pounds. There is no writing on the outside of the bands. But hidden inside, the king's name is carved, along with a blessing that guarantees him a place in the afterlife. *Above:* Pharaoh Seti I offers incense in a scene from his tomb. He is also wearing armbands and the *uraeus*.

wear any clothing like that of Pharaoh. But when the Israelites were set free by Adonai, they were commanded to remember the wonder of their Exodus by wearing "a sign" on their hand and a "reminder" on their forehead. Perhaps this was Adonai's final way of saying: Pharaoh is conquered. Every person in Israel is equal to Pharaoh now, and we should always remember that!

Haftarah: Jeremiah 46:13-28

The Rabbis connect Pharaoh's struggle with Adonai to the struggle between Egypt and Babylonia in the time of Jeremiah. Pharaoh Necho of Egypt invaded Judah in 609 B.C.E. and killed Josiah at the battle of Megiddo (see *VaYeilech*). Babylonia would come to punish Egypt, Jeremiah said, and four years later, in 605, Necho was defeated by Nebuchadnezzar at the battle of Carchemish. After that Egypt was a second-rate power for generations to come.

The haftarah begins as Jeremiah warns Egypt, saying, "Take your stand and be prepared, for the sword is devouring all around you." Egypt is like a cow (the cow was worshiped in Egypt) that is ripe for slaughter. She is like a snake hissing when she is attacked by axes. The Babylonian armies will "outnumber the locusts", and they "cannot be counted".

Fair Egypt shall be put to shame, given over to a northern people. Adonai *Tzeva'ot* ("of Armies"), the God of Israel, says, Behold, I will punish [the god] Amon of No and Pharaoh and Egypt and all her gods and her kings....

But Israel should not fear, though its people are scattered. For Adonai promises to save Israel "from that distant place" and to bring them back to the Promised Land, so that "none shall make [them] afraid."

Have no fear, O My servant Jacob, for I am with you, says Adonai.

So the prophet states that Adonai is not just the God of Israel, but in control of the fate every nation.

Miracles, Song, Dance, and War

בשלח
B'Shalach
Exodus 13:17-17:16

Who Was This Pharaoh?

The Torah calls the king of Egypt *Pharaoh,* but all Egyptian kings had names. For centuries Bible scholars have tried to uncover the name of the Pharaoh of the Exodus. The Bible itself gives a few clues. The Book of Kings says that the Exodus took place 480 years before "the fourth year of Solomon's rule over Israel." Solomon became king around 966 B.C.E. So one date for Exodus is around 1446 B.C.E. The Pharaoh then was Amenhotep II, son of Tutmose III. But this answer does not solve all the problems. For example, in the days of Tutmose and Amenhotep, the king of Egypt was not yet called "Pharaoh" by the Egyptians.

Then, too, the Torah says that the Hebrew slaves helped build the store cities of Pithom and Raamses, so many scholars think that the Pharaoh of the Exodus was Rameses the Great (Rameses II, c. 1301-1234 B.C.E.), son of Seti I. If so, the Jews would have left Egypt around 1250 B.C.E.

Or perhaps it was Ramases the Great who died while Moses was in Midian. In that case, the Pharaoh of the Exodus would have been Merneptah, and the Exodus would have happened around 1230 B.C.E. Merneptah would seem a good choice, but there is a factual problem. In his list of victories over his enemies in Canaan Merneptah mentions the people "Israel". His is the first mention of Israel outside of the Bible, but it would mean that Israel was already living in Canaan by Merneptah's time. If so, he could not have been the Pharaoh of the Exodus.

Of course, there would be no mystery if the Torah had only named the Pharaoh. Why is his name missing? One reason may be that by the time the Torah was put in writing, no one remembered the Pharaoh's name. Another reason may be the old custom of never mentioning the name of a hated enemy. The Torah remembers and names two minor

Pharaoh

The word *Pharaoh* actually means the "Great House"—that is, the palace of the king. Calling the king of Egypt "Pharaoh" is like calling the president of the United States "White House". Of course, we do just that. Newspapers, radio, and television often state that "the White House said …" or "the White House announced…." Perhaps it began this way in Egypt, too. Following the time of Rameses, the king of Egypt was officially called "Pharaoh".

Another Clue

The mention of the Philistines is another clue that the Exodus may have taken place around the time of Rameses II. The Philistines were among the Sea Peoples who invaded Canaan around this time. They were such fierce warriors that Rameses II even paid some of them to join his army. Years later, in the time of Rameses III, the Philistines were defeated when they tried to invade Egypt. But when God said, "The people may ... see war, and return to Egypt," the "war" may have been the early invasion of the Sea Peoples.

characters—the Hebrew midwives, Shifrah and Puah—but only calls the king of Egypt Pharaoh.

We may never know the name of the Pharaoh of the Exodus, but this is clear: The Torah is much more interested in Israelites than in Egyptians, much more interested in names of God than in names of Pharaohs, and much more interested in beliefs than in history.

The Cloud and the Fire

Now when Pharaoh let the people go, God did not lead them by way of the land of the Philistines, although it was near, for God said, "The people may ... see war, and return to Egypt." So God led the people roundabout, by way of the Wilderness at the Sea of Reeds. Now the Israelites went up armed out of the land of Egypt. Moses took with him the bones of Joseph.... They set out from Sukkot, and encamped at Etham, at the edge of the Wilderness. Adonai went before them in a pillar of cloud by day, to guide them along the way, and in a pillar of fire by night, to give them light, that they might travel day and night: The pillar of cloud by day and the pillar of fire by night did not depart from before the people.

Some modern Bible scholars think that the Torah's "pillar of cloud" and "pillar of fire" are really memories of Solomon's Temple. Two large wooden pillars stood at the door of this Temple, each with an open furnace at the bottom where fires were kept burning. During the day it looked as if pillars of smoke rose to cover the wooden pillars. At night the smoke was lit red by the fires below and looked like pillars of fire. These pillars "protected" the House of God. The Torah may have them in mind.

Or there may be a simpler explanation: When many people move across dry land together in daytime, the dust rising up may look like a pillar of smoke. When they move by torchlight at night, the pillar of smoke may look like a pillar of fire. Or, even simpler: In the middle ages the commentator Abraham ibn Ezra suggested that the pillars were imaginary—just a way of highlighting God's protection.

Israel at the Sea of Reeds

Meanwhile, Pharaoh probably still thought that the Israelites had only left Egypt to worship Adonai for three days. So Adonai told Moses to trick the Egyptians by turning the people back toward Egypt. Pharaoh would think the Israelites were lost, unwilling or unable to cross the Wilderness. Adonai said, "I will stiffen Pharaoh's heart and he will pursue [the Israelites], that I may gain glory through Pharaoh and his host; and the Egyptians shall know that I am Adonai." Pharaoh's spies told him that the Israelites were not worshiping, but fleeing, so he gathered all his chariots to chase them. The chariots caught up with them near the Sea of Reeds.

When the Israelites saw the army of Pharaoh driving toward them, they were very frightened. There was nowhere for them to go but into the sea. They said to Moses, "Were there no graves in Egypt? Why did you bring us to the Wilderness to die? We were better off as slaves in Egypt!" But Moses said, "Be silent. Don't be afraid. Adonai will deliver you this day." Then Moses began to pray.

> Adonai said to Moses, "Why do you cry out to Me? Tell the Israelites to go forward. Lift up your rod and hold out your arm over the sea and split it; so that the Israelites may march into the sea on dry ground. I will stiffen the hearts of the Egyptians so that they go in after them...." The angel of God ... now moved ... behind them; and the pillar of cloud shifted from in front of them and took up a place behind them, and it came between the army of the Egyptians and the army of Israel ... all through the night.
>
> Then Moses held out his arm over the sea and Adonai drove back the sea with a strong east wind all the night .... The waters were split, and the Israelites went into the sea on dry ground, the waters forming a wall for them on their right and on their left. The Egyptians came in pursuit after them into the sea, all of Pharaoh's horses, chariots, and horsemen.
>
> At the morning watch, Adonai looked down upon the Egyptian army from a pillar of fire and cloud,

To Pray or to Do?

Adonai said to Moses, "Why do you cry out to Me? Tell the Israelites to go forward." Rashi explains that Moses was upset when the people complained, so he stopped to pray to Adonai. But Adonai reminded Moses that when people are in trouble, that is no time for prayer. Other Bible commentators say that Adonai was not speaking to Moses, but to all the Israelites, because half were complaining and the other half were praying. But Adonai said, "Why do you [Israelites] pray now? Now is the time for doing something!" It was then that Adonai gave Moses instructions to hold out his arm and split the sea.

The Chariots of Egypt

Above: A sketch from the carvings of the temple at Abu Simbel showing Rameses and his chariots and armies in battle. These were the kind of chariots that frightened Israel before Adonai defeated them with wind and water!

Total Victory

Many have tried to explain how the Sea of Reeds split. Some say the "sea" was a muddy swamp that people could cross, but not chariots. Some say rains caused a dry riverbed to look like a sea, that separated, then returned. Probably explaining is not so important. It is enough to just enjoy the story.

and threw the Egyptian army into panic. [Adonai] locked the wheels of their chariots so that they moved forward with difficulty. The Egyptians said, "Let us flee from the Israelites, for Adonai is fighting for them against Egypt."

Then Adonai said to Moses, "Hold out your arm over the sea, that the waters may come back upon the Egyptians upon their chariots and upon their horsemen." Moses held out his arm over the sea, and at daybreak the sea returned to its normal state, and the Egyptians fled at its approach. But Adonai hurled the Egyptians into the sea. The waters turned back and covered the chariots and the horsemen—Pharaoh's entire army that followed them into the sea; not one of them remained. But the Israelites had marched through the sea on dry ground…

Thus Adonai delivered Israel that day from the Egyptians. Israel saw the Egyptians dead on the shore of the sea. And when Israel saw the wondrous power which Adonai had wielded against the Egyptians, the people feared Adonai; they had faith in Adonai and in [Adonai's] servant Moses.

The Song at the Sea

Then Moses and the Israelites sang this song to Adonai. They chanted:

I will sing to Adonai
For [Adonai] has triumphed gloriously,
Horse and driver [Adonai] hurled into the sea.
[Adonai] is my strength and might ....
Adonai, the Warrior—Adonai is [God's] name!
Pharaoh's chariots and his army
[Adonai] cast into the sea....

Who is like You, Adonai, among the gods;
Who is like You, majestic in holiness
Awesome in splendor, working wonders!

Then Miriam the prophetess, Aaron's sister, took a timbrel in her hand, and all the women went out after her in dance with timbrels. And Miriam chanted for them, "Sing to Adonai, for [God] has triumphed gloriously; horse and driver [God] has hurled into the sea."

The Rabbis of the Talmud believed this poem called "The Song of the Sea" was written by Moses himself. Rabbi Judah the Prince translated the introduction as "Moses ... will sing this song to Adonai," saying that Moses sang it first at the sea, but at the end of days Moses will sing it again. In the Midrash the Rabbis noted that many in the Bible had been rescued before—Isaac by the ram, Jacob from the stranger, Jacob from Esau, and more—but this was the first time that the rescued sang a song of praise to God. When God heard the Israelites singing, God said, "I have been waiting for them."

Many modern scholars think this poem was written either in the days of David and Solomon, or even much later when the Jews were in Babylon. But it could be much older. In the library of the ancient Canaanite city of Ugarit we discovered a poem very much like this that dates all the way back to the time of Moses.

Quote to Remember

אָשִׁירָה לַיהוָה כִּי־גָאֹה גָּאָה,
סוּס וְרֹכְבוֹ רָמָה בַיָּם.

I will sing to Adonai for [Adonai] has triumphed gloriously,
Horse and driver [Adonai] hurled into the sea.

Mi Chamocha

The Song at the Sea is such a powerful poem that we recite it in our regular prayer services as we say *Mi chamocha*, "Who is like You, Adonai, among the gods!" Today, of course, we understand this to mean "There is no god but Adonai!" but the Torah may have meant just what it says: that Adonai is the greatest of all the gods people worship.

To Consider

Do you think it was right for Moses and Miriam and the Israelites to rejoice at the Sea of Reeds while the armies of Pharaoh were dying? Why or why not?

Science Explains

Bedouin Arabs who live in the Sinai wilderness still collect a sweet-tasting, wafer-like substance they call *manna*. It appears on tamarisk trees, usually in June, but only if the rain has been plentiful. Scientists explain that this manna is not produced by the dew or the tree, but by two insects that live on tamarisk trees. Scientists also say that certain kinds of wood will actually turn bitter water into sweet water. So the two miracles seem to have explanations. Perhaps. Actually, there is never enough natural manna for people to live on—it is more a candy than a food. And it would take a great amount of tree and time to turn water sweet for a thousands of people. The best explanation is that the Torah wove its miracle tales around some very scientific facts.

Water and Food

Three days into the Wilderness, at Marah ("bitterness"), the Israelites found the water too bitter to drink and they complained to Moses. Adonai showed Moses a piece of wood. When Moses threw the wood in the water, it turned sweet. Through Moses, Adonai told the Israelites: "If you heed Adonai carefully, doing what is right in My sight, then I will not bring on you any of the diseases that I brought on the Egyptians, for I Adonai am your healer."

The Israelites made camp at Elim, with its many springs of water and its seventy date-palm trees. From there, they journeyed to the Wilderness of Sin. Now there was no food. The people complained to Moses and Aaron: "We had plenty of bread in Egypt." Adonai told Moses, "I will rain down food from heaven. Every day people can gather a portion, but on Friday their portion will become two portions. This evening the people shall have meat and tomorrow morning, bread. Then you will know I am Adonai."

That evening flocks of quail appeared and the people had meat. The next morning when the dew lifted it left behind a strange flaky powder. The Israelites said, "What is it?" Moses said, "That is the bread which Adonai has given you to eat. …" The people each gathered an *omer* of it each day, twice as much on Friday. Moses said, "Six days shall you gather it; on the … Sabbath there will be none."

> The house of Israel named it *manna*; it was like coriander seed, white, and it tasted like wafers in honey. … And the Israelites ate manna for forty years … until they came to the border of the land of Canaan. The *omer* is a tenth of an *ephah*.

God commanded Moses to tell Aaron to set aside one *omer* of manna to be kept forever, so that Israel would always remember the bread of the Wilderness. Aaron put a portion into a pottery jar and placed the jar in front of the covenant between Adonai and Israel.

The Midrash says that manna tasted different to every person who ate it. It tasted like every person's favorite food. Adonai gave them a single food that everyone liked—that's quite a miracle, too!

The Idea of Shabbat

In the creation story God rested on the seventh day. But in the instructions for gathering manna, the command for a holy Sabbath day is given to Israel, God's people. The idea of a week of seven days is otherwise unknown. There was no division of time into seven-day segments in Egypt, Canaan, or Mesopotamia. Today we take the week for granted, but this story and the story of Creation seem to tell how the week first came to be. Perhaps the Torah is tying the sweetness of Sabbath rest to the sweetness of the manna.

Another Water Emergency and a War

At the next camp, Rephidim, there was food but no water. The people complained. Moses feared they might grow angry enough to stone him to death. Adonai said, "I will stand before you on the rock at Horeb. Take the rod you used to strike the Nile. Strike the rock and water will come from it." Moses did as Adonai commanded. The place was named Massah and Meribah because the people tested Adonai there, saying, "Is Adonai present among us or not?"

While the Israelites were camped the Amalekites attacked them. Moses sent Joshua forward with an army. He took the rod of Adonai and climbed to the top of a hill, along with Aaron and a man named Hur. While Moses held the rod high, raising both his arms, the army of Israel did well. But when Moses' arms tired the Amalekites fought fiercely. So Aaron and Hur stood on either side of Moses and held his arms high until the sun set. In this way Joshua and the army of Israel defeated the Amalekites.

> Adonai said to Moses, "Write this in a document as a reminder … I will utterly blot out the memory of Amalek from under heaven." And Moses built an altar and named it Adonai-nissi ["Adonai is my miracle"]. He said, "It means 'Hand upon the throne of Adonai!' Adonai will be at war with Amalek throughout the ages."

To Consider

Even when Adonai was working miracle after miracle for the Israelites—after the plagues, the parting of the Sea of Reeds, the pillars of cloud and fire, the quail and the water—the Israelites continued to complain to Moses and even asked the question "Is Adonai present among us or not?" What is the Torah trying to tell us about human beings?

Eternal War

The Amalekites attacked just when the people had challenged God by asking "Is Adonai present among us or not?" Bible commentators have often said that Israel's victory over the Amalekites and Adonai's promise to join Israel in an eternal war against the Amalekites was an answer to this question.

Amalek

The Amalekites seem to have been a tribe, or group of tribes, of nomads. Archaeologists have found no trace of them. This is not surprising, since they had no cities and were often on the move. Later the Torah tells us that the Amalekites attacked Israel from the rear in a surprise attack that especially angered Adonai and the Israelites. In the time of Samuel and Saul the Amalekites returned to make war with Israel, and in the days of King Hezekiah the Amalekites were defeated. After that they just disappeared from history. Nevertheless, in the Book of Esther Haman is said to be from the tribe of Amalek. And throughout Jewish history, any tyrant who threatened our survival has been called an "Amalekite".

To our ears it seems very harsh that Adonai should vow to make an eternal war on the Amalekites, but to the Israelites—as we can see very well in this portion of the Torah—Adonai was a warrior god fighting on the side of Israel. And that image of God is still a great comfort to us in dangerous times.

Haftarah: Judges 4:4-5:31

The parashah *B'shalach* includes the crossing of the Sea of Reeds, the final defeat of the Egyptians by Adonai, Moses' "Song at the Sea", and the war with Amalek. War and a song of victory are at the heart of this haftarah, too. But this time the hero is a woman who is a judge, a prophet, and a warrior.

Deborah sat beneath a certain palm tree between Ramah and Beth El (in the hills of Ephraim). People came to her from all Israel to seek wisdom and justice. Once she sent for Barak, telling him to take an army of ten thousand to Mount Tabor. She would bring the Canaanite army to him, and Barak would defeat them. But Barak sent back word: "I will go only if you come with me." She went.

The Canaanites had nine hundred iron chariots and an army —all led by Sisera, the warrior chief of King Jabin. They came to Mount Tabor to face the army of Deborah. And Adonai gave victory to Israel. No Canaanite soldier escaped the sword, but Sisera fled on foot. He sought safety at the tent of Jael, a Kenite woman, but she murdered him in his sleep, driving a tent peg into his head. The Israelites kept fighting until Jabin was destroyed. On that day Deborah and Barak sang:

> Rouse yourself Deborah, arouse! Arise Barak … take your captives! … Heaven itself fought, the stars … opposed Sisera. … Most blessed of all women be Jael. … Let all your enemies, Adonai, end like that; but let those who love You be like the sun rising in its might!

This is the "Song of Deborah", who led the Israelites to victory and gave them forty years of peace.

Law and Order

Jethro

Jethro, Moses' father-in-law, came to the mountain of God where the Israelites were camped. He brought Moses' sons and wife. "Blessed be Adonai," Jethro said, "who is greater than all gods." And Jethro brought sacrifices for God; and Aaron and the elders of Israel made a feast before God.

The next day Jethro watched as Moses sat as a judge from morning to night, listening to people argue before him and deciding who was right, teaching God's laws.

> [Jethro] said to him, "The thing you are doing is not right; you will surely wear yourself out, and these people as well. For the task is too heavy for you; you cannot do it alone. Now listen to me. I will give you advice, and may God be with you!"

Jethro advised Moses to choose trusted people to be the chiefs (judges) of thousands, others to be chiefs of hundreds, others to be chiefs of fifties, and others to be chiefs of ten. If a question or dispute was small, it would be judged by these chiefs. Only the hardest problems would come to Moses for judgment. Moses took Jethro's advice. Then, the Torah says, Jethro left.

Jethro had given good advice. The Israelite tribes already had "chiefs", those who had been elders in Egypt. But Jethro told Moses to choose trustworthy people as judges. The result was a system of government headed by people loyal to Moses. In this new system the people became one nation, no longer separate tribes. Egyptologists tell us that just before the time of Moses there was a Pharaoh who reorganized Egypt by appointing new judges in this same way. Maybe Jethro knew this. Or maybe Moses studied it when he was growing up in the palace of the Pharaoh. It is also possible that the new system of chiefs was based on the Egyptian reform. If so, it would be easier for the Israelites to accept if their new system was based on advice from Jethro.

The Wise Jethro

The Torah's stories about the wise Jethro must be very old. By the days of Saul, David, and Solomon, the Midianites were bitter enemies of the Israelites. It is unlikely that anyone living then would make up a story about a wise Jethro or would be proud to say that Moses was married to a Midianite woman. So this story must have been told for a long time before being written down.

To Consider

The Torah makes it clear that Moses could speak directly to God and ask any question he liked. But Moses listened to the good advice of Jethro. Why is it important to listen to advice from other people? How do you know when their advice is good and when it is not?

The Temples at Timnah

Around the time of Jethro the Midianites worked in the copper mines of the Egyptians. These mines were located at Timnah, near present-day Eilat. Archaeologists discovered an old Egyptian temple dedicated to the goddess Hathor at Timnah. Hathor is pictured and worshiped by the Egyptians in many different ways. Sometimes she is a cow (which reminds us of the golden calf). At other times she is shown as the cobra or snake who coils around the head of the sun-god Re (and the crown of Pharaoh). The Egyptian Temple at Timnah was destroyed by an earthquake. The Midianites then built a temple on the same spot; and in the ark of that Midianite temple, archaeologists found only one object: a copper snake with a golden head (see *Chukkat*).

The Mountain

We know that Moses saw the burning bush while tending the flocks of Jethro in the land of the Midianites. We were told that the bush was on the holy mountain of Adonai. Now Moses and the people stand at Mount Sinai. But where is it? The Torah draws no map. Local folklore claimed it was in southern Sinai, at the mountain called *Jebul Musa*, "the Mountain of Moses" (about 7,500 feet in height). The early Christians built a monastery there; and tourists still visit to climb to where they think Moses once stood. Modern scholars, however, think that Mount Sinai had to be closer to the Mediterranean Sea, possibly at *Jebul Hilal* (about 3,000 feet high). This mountain is only thirty miles from Kadesh-Barnea, where the Torah says the Israelites settled for many years.

The Midianites, though, were settled near Timnah in northern Sinai, and there are tall cliffs rising from the desert there (the *Amudei Shlomo* or "Pillars of Solomon"). We know that the Midianites built a sanctuary there with an altar for sacrifices. The story of Jethro and his sacrifice feast may be based on a memory of a treaty between the Midianites and the Israelites. If so, the location of Mount Sinai might be there, too, since the very next story is about how Moses went up the mountain to receive Adonai's covenant.

In fact, the next story begins with the Israelites arriving at the mountain. So the stories seem mixed up in time. The Rabbis—and almost all Bible commentators since then—noticed this and explained it in different ways. Some say the story of Jethro came after the story of the sneak attack of the Amalekites to show that while some non-Jews could be cruel, other non-Jews could be kind to Israelites. Some thought that Jethro spent a long time with Moses and was in the Israelite camp even later when Moses spoke the words of the covenant. Modern scholars think that when the stories were collected they were pieced together in the same jigsaw-puzzle way that we remember from the Book of Genesis.

The Covenant

… Moses went up to God. Adonai called to him from the mountain, saying, "Thus shall you say to the house of Jacob and declare to the children of Israel: 'You have seen what I did to the Egyptians, how I bore you on eagles' wings, and brought you to Me. Now then, if you will obey Me faithfully and keep My covenant, you shall be My treasured possession among all the peoples. Indeed, all the earth is Mine, but you shall be to Me a kingdom of priests and a holy nation.' …"

Moses … put before [the elders] all that Adonai had commanded him. All the people answered as one, saying, "All that Adonai has spoken we will do!"

On the third day, at dawn, there was thunder and lightning and a cloud on the mountain. There was a shrill blast of the shofar, and the people trembled. Moses led them out of camp, and they stood at the foot of the mountain.

Now Mount Sinai was all in smoke, for Adonai had come down upon it in fire … and the whole mountain trembled violently. The blare of the shofar grew louder and louder. As Moses spoke, God answered him in thunder. Adonai came down upon Mount Sinai, on the top of the mountain, and Adonai called Moses to the top of the mountain and Moses went up.

Commandments

God spoke all these words, saying:

I Adonai am your God who brought you out of the land of Egypt, the house of bondage: You shall have no other gods besides me.

You shall not make for you a sculptured image, or any likeness of what is in the heavens above, or on the earth below, or in the waters under the earth. You shall not bow down to them or serve them. …

Quote to Remember

וִהְיִיתֶם לִי סְגֻלָּה מִכָּל־הָעַמִּים.

You shall be My treasured possession among all the peoples.

My Treasured Possession

Adonai begins making the covenant three days before the people come to the foot of Mount Sinai. And the people of Israel agree to the covenant even before they learn what laws Adonai will place on them. Bible scholars tell us that this kind of agreement was usually reached between kings when one king was much more powerful than the other. In addition, we have discovered other ancient treaties in which the idea of a "treasured possession" is mentioned. What makes the covenant in the Torah unique is that it is an agreement between Adonai and *all* the people of Israel.

The "Words"

Today we know these as the Ten Commandments. But the word "commandment" is not used for these laws in the Torah. The Torah calls them *devarim*, "words"— "God spoke all these words ...." In Hebrew, they have always been called *aseret ha-dibbrot*, "The Ten Words". Greek-speaking Jews called them "ten" (*deka*) and "words" (*logoi*) and to this day we also refer to them by that Greek name, *Decalogue*. Still, we think of them as ten commands. But the Torah also does not say anything here about "ten". In fact, Jews and Christians have always disagreed on how to divide these words to form ten commands. Even Jews do not always agree with one another. One Jewish commentator divided the words into *thirteen* commands!

You shall not swear falsely by the name of Adonai your God; for Adonai will not clear one who swears falsely by [Adonai's] name.

Remember the Sabbath day and keep it holy. Six days you shall labor and do all your work, but the seventh day is a Sabbath of Adonai your God: you shall not do any work—you, your son or daughter, your male or female slave, or your cattle, or the stranger who is within your settlements. For in six days Adonai made heaven and earth and sea, and all that is in them, and rested on the seventh day; therefore Adonai blessed the Sabbath day and hallowed it.

Honor your father and your mother, that you may long endure on the land that Adonai your God is assigning you.

You shall not murder.

You shall not commit adultery.

You shall not steal.

You shall not bear false witness against your neighbor.

You shall not set your heart on your neighbor's house; you shall not set your heart on your neighbor's wife, or his male or female slave, or his ox or his donkey, or anything that belongs to your neighbor.

Stories about the Ten Commandments

The Rabbis noticed that the first two commands are spoken by Adonai in the first person (using the word "I"). The rest speak to the people, but about Adonai. The Rabbis suggested that God spoke only the first two commands to all the Israelites. The others were given to Moses, who later gave them to the people. The Rabbis also created other midrashic stories about the covenant. They said that at the moment that God spoke to the people, the world was absolutely quiet. There was a great stillness; not even a bird chirped. So the words came like a whisper on a wind. One rabbi imagined that the people only heard the first three words of the first command—*Anochi Adonai Elohecha*, "I Adonai am your God." Another rabbi says that the people only heard God's voice in the first letter of the first word, the letter *aleph*, which, as we know, is a silent letter.

One rabbi said that God gave the commandments in the wilderness to show that these words belong to every nation, not just to the Israelites. Another said that Adonai held the mountain over the heads of the Israelites and said, "Will you accept My commands? If not, I will drop this mountain on you." Of course, the Israelites chose to accept the commands.

And one rabbi told how God first offered the commandments to every nation in the world, starting with the biggest nations. Each nation asked, "What is in them?" and when they heard, they refused to accept them. Finally God came to the tiny nation of Israel and asked, "Will you accept My commands?" The Israelites said, "All that Adonai speaks we will do!" Then God took Israel as a "treasured possession", "a kingdom of priests and a holy people", and made the covenant with the Israelites.

A Few More Words

All the people witnessed the thunder and lightning, the blare of the shofar and the mountain smoking; and when the people saw it they fell back and stood at a distance. "You speak to us," they said to Moses, "and we will obey; but let not God speak to us, lest we die." …

Adonai said to Moses: Thus you shall say to the Israelites: You yourselves saw that I spoke to you from the very heavens. … You shall not make any gods of silver, nor shall you make for yourselves any gods of gold. Make for Me an altar of earth and sacrifice on it your burnt offerings and your sacrifices of well-being, your sheep and your oxen; in every place where I cause My name to be mentioned I will come to you and bless you.

And if you make for Me an altar of stones, do not build it of hewn stones; for by striking your tool upon them you have profaned them. …

Are These Laws Different?

There are some differences between the Ten Commandments and the laws of other ancient nations. Rulers did not often worry about what ordinary people "set their heart on" or about setting aside a day of rest each week. Yet most of the ten commands were well known before they were given to the Israelites. Many are similar to laws inscribed on a stone tablet by Hammurabi, king of Babylon, five hundred years before the time of Moses. The top of the tablet (*below*) shows Hammurabi (*standing*) receiving a rod and ring of power from his god Shamash (*seated*). Here again, as with the story of the plagues, it is not because the ten commands of God were new that they are special to us, but because they are gathered together in a grand way, given to all the people and not just to a king—and they are easy to remember.

To Consider

Aaron is only mentioned once in this portion (when he shares a meal with Moses, Jethro, and the elders). What special role does Moses play in the giving of the Ten Commandments? How is Moses special to Adonai? How is Moses special to the Israelites?

Adonai adds to the covenant: (1) forbidding silver or gold idols, (2) saying a simple altar can be made of earth, (3) saying altars can be built anywhere—Adonai "will come to you and bless you," and saying (4) an altar can be built of stones, but tools cannot be used to cut the stones.

It was said that King David did not build an altar because David had been a warrior. The altar should remind us of peace, not war. So it was Solomon who built the Temple and the altar. The Rabbis asked, "If the stones were not cut with tools, how did they fit so well?" They answered with a tale about a worm called the *shamir* that could eat stone. They said that God prepared this worm even before the creation of the world, just so that Solomon could use the worm to shape the stones of the altar for the Holy Temple.

Haftarah: Isaiah 6:1-7:6; 9:5-6

The Rabbis connect the Israelites' accepting the covenant at Sinai with Isaiah's accepting the task of prophecy in a vision. Isaiah saw the throne of Adonai surrounded by angels calling to one another: "Holy, holy, holy is Adonai *Tzeva'ot* ("of Multitudes"). The Presence [of God] fills the whole earth!"

One angel touched Isaiah's lips with a fiery coal, saying, "Now your guilt is gone; your sin is wiped away." Then Isaiah heard the voice of God asking, "Whom shall I send?" And Isaiah said *Hineni*, "Here am I. Send me." (*Hineni* was the word used by Moses at the burning bush and by Samuel who heard God's call in a dream.)

God said: Go tell the people, Listen again and again (but they will not understand); Look again and again (but they will not see)—as with Pharaoh,

God would send the message, but the heart of the listeners would be hardened so that the message would be ignored. God said: You will preach until their cities are destroyed.

It seems the tribes of the northern kingdom were planning to attack Judah and conquer it, to make one kingdom again. But God sent Isaiah to King Ahaz of Judah with the message "Be calm," no harm will come even though they are plotting against you.

The Rabbis added two verses at the end that promise Judah a new king who will lead them based on "justice and right, now and forever". Christians later said these verses referred to Jesus, but the Rabbis said that Isaiah was predicting the birth of Hezekiah (see *VaYeilech*), a king who tried to restore the glory of Adonai in the land of Judah.

Rules

Rules and Laws

"These are the *mishpatim* that you shall set before them."

Mishpatim are "rulings" or "rules"—decisions made by rulers (like Moses) or by judges (like those Moses appointed). Each decision becomes a "rule" to be followed by other judges. So the first line says "These are the *rules* you shall set before them." Who is "them"?

Moses appointed judges—judges over thousands, hundreds, fifties, and tens. Judges need rules to make even simple decisions. The Ten Words are laws, but they do not set rules about how to punish people or what should be done when people harm one another. So the "rules" are for "them"—for the judges of Israel.

For life among the Israelites to be fair and just, equal for everyone—whether a person came from the largest or the smallest tribe—there had to be only one set of rules for everyone. The Torah teaches that all the laws were given by Adonai to Moses at Sinai, and repeated by Moses to the people at Sinai, and written down by Moses in the book of the covenant at Sinai. Later it will even say that the whole Torah—all Five Books of Moses—was given by Adonai to Moses at Sinai and written down by Moses at Sinai. This is just a way of saying that Israel is one people with one God. The rules are for "them"—for all Israelites.

History and Sense

This is not good history. We know that there are many rules and laws in the Torah that were written after Sinai, just as the Torah itself was completed after Sinai. But the Torah is not really a history. And, anyway, we do the same thing today. Every new law in the United States, for example, has to follow the root law of our one nation, the covenant we call "the Constitution". Of course, the people who wrote the

From Many Tribes to One People

In Egypt the children of Israel were many tribes, and each tribe had its own rules. The moment that Adonai spoke to the Israelites—not to one tribe, but to the people all together—everything changed. Sure, Israelites would still be loyal to their families and tribes. But now they put Adonai above families, above tribes. The Torah is saying there is only one Adonai, only one covenant with Adonai, and only one Moses to speak for Adonai.

Laws from Many Times and Places

There was no slavery among the Israelites in the Wilderness, but the first rules in *Mishpatim* are about slavery. These rules were not used in the days of Moses. They may have come from the time when the Israelites in Canaan were led by judges, priests, and prophets. Or they may have been used later, when the Israelites lived under kings. Rules in the Torah come from different times and places. But they are set down side by side, one group after another, no matter when or where they came from.

Constitution could not know that one day we would need rules about automobiles stopping at red lights, but rules like this still work because they keep "the spirit of the Constitution".

Sometimes a new rule or law is so important that we "amend" the Constitution. We add the rule to the Constitution. Whenever the Constitution is printed out after that, the new rule is part of it. And we act as if it were always part of the Constitution. The Torah grew in the same way. Important rules and laws were added to the story of Sinai so that we would act as if they were given to Moses by Adonai. So Sinai is the beginning, not the end, of our covenant with Adonai. When we say that the Torah was written by Moses at Sinai, we are saying that all the laws and rules of the Israelites should be obeyed as if they came directly from Adonai. This may not be history, but it made sense then, and it makes sense now.

God's Rules for Slavery

The portion *Mishpatim* ("rules") opens with laws about slavery. Adonai commands that a slave will serve for "six years; and in the seventh year, he shall go free, without payment."

> But if the slave declares, "I … do not wish to go free," his master shall take him before the judges. [Then, the slave] shall be brought to the door or the door post, and his master shall pierce his ear with an awl; and he shall remain his slave for life.

The laws for a female slave are given next. When a girl or woman became a slave, she did not go free after six years. She became part of her new "family," often a wife for the master of the house or the son of the master. But she still had to be treated fairly. If her new family was unhappy with her, she could be bought back by her real family. If her new family mistreated her, "she shall go free, without payment."

Slavery was part of life in ancient times. Though there was no slavery among the Israelites standing at Sinai, there was plenty of slavery once they settled in Canaan. Anyone who could not repay a debt might become a slave. A poor couple with many daughters might have to "sell" a daughter. The people and the judges needed rules: How should slaves be treated? How could slavery be made "fair"? Should slavery be permanent, the way it was in Egypt? These rules answered real questions. Because we were slaves in Egypt, Israelites never loved slavery. These rules tried to make slavery as fair as possible for the slaves.

Eye for Eye, Tooth for Tooth

Next come rules about murder and how murderers should be punished. People who commit murder "shall be put to death." But if you kill someone by accident, you can flee to a special place. The Torah says that if you strike your mother or father or insult them in public, you can be put to death. A kidnapper must be put to death. If you injure someone, you have to pay for their doctors and medicines and also for the time that they cannot work. And so on. Then the Torah gives judges one general rule about all kinds of harm:

> The penalty shall be life for life, eye for eye, tooth for tooth, hand for hand, foot for foot, burn for burn, wound for wound, bruise for bruise.

Whoa! This famous law, followed by many nations, is so cruel that we gave it the name *lex talionis*, "the law of the talon". A "talon" is a claw—like the claw of a lion or a vulture. In other words, this rule is purposely cruel, even as beasts may be. If you wound someone, it says, you should be wounded in the same place. If you knock out someone's teeth, the judge should have your teeth knocked out.

Commentators point out that this rule was intended to stop "blood feuds". Without this rule, if a person from one tribe was killed, his or her relatives tried to kill the murderer. Then the relatives of the murderer tried to kill the one who took revenge. This went on and on until whole tribes would go to war. The *lex talionis* actually put an end to this kind of feud. It said that only one person should be punished.

Hundreds of years later the Rabbis of the Talmud (who were also judges) taught that "life for life, eye for eye" was an unfair rule. They gave many examples of why it never gives equal justice. "What if the eye of one person is big and the other's eye is small?" "What if a dwarf murders a giant, or a giant murders a dwarf?" The Rabbis said the Torah rule re-

נֶפֶשׁ תַּחַת נָפֶשׁ. עַיִן תַּחַת עַיִן שֵׁן תַּחַת שֵׁן יָד תַּחַת יָד רֶגֶל תַּחַת רֶגֶל.

Life for life, eye for eye, tooth for tooth, hand for hand, foot for foot...

Is the Torah Always Right?

How could the Rabbis change a law that Moses said came from Adonai? The answer is that the Rabbis always knew that some laws in the Torah are far from perfect. True, the Torah said that Adonai "gave them." But of course, the rules were set down by humans, and humans are not perfect. Even Moses did not always "get it right." If a rule like the *lex talionis* needed fixing, the rabbis fixed it. Even today, when a Torah law needs to be "fixed" or "amended", we Jews—from Orthodox to Reform—try to find ways to make it fair for all.

ally should mean that a fair amount of money or cattle should be paid to an injured person. Everyone agreed. The *lex talionis* stayed in the Torah, but Israelites did not use it.

Damages: Hurtful Things

The Torah turns to a group of laws about "damages": what to do when people or property gets hurt—if someone's ox gores a man or woman, if someone's ox hurts someone else's ox, if someone opens a pit and another person accidentally falls into it. There are also laws about thieves and thievery. If a thief still has whatever was stolen, then the thief has to pay back double the amount. If a thief can't give back what was stolen, the thief can be sold as a slave to pay it back. Two rules tell what to do if a thief accidentally gets stuck in a wall while trying to break in. And there are rules about being a good neighbor. You have to pay if your cattle grazes in someone else's field or if you set fire to someone's field or grain. If you borrow from a neighbor, whatever you borrow must be returned unhurt. All these rules seem like court cases: if such and such happens, such and such is the punishment.

Another Kind of Law

The next group of rules clearly comes from some other time or place. They have little to do with judges. Today we call such rules, "ethics", right rules for living. Most are about matters of the heart and the conscience. We follow laws like these not because we fear punishment, but because we believe they are fair and right.

It is a little strange that the first rule in this group commands us to put witches to death. But in ancient times, as now, people said there were two kinds of magic: the good or "white" magic of a Joseph or Moses and the "black" magic of witches who tried to harm others. This law was aimed at witches and sorcerers who practiced "black" magic.

> You shall not wrong a stranger or oppress [a stranger], for you were strangers in the land of Egypt. You shall not ill-treat any widow or orphan.... If you lend money to My people, to the

poor among you ... [take] no interest [on the money—take back only the amount you lent].

If you take your neighbor's *simlah* [garment] in pledge, you must return it ... before the sun sets; it is [your neighbor's] only covering ... In what else shall [your neighbor] sleep? Therefore, if [your neighbor] cries out to Me, I will pay heed; for I am compassionate.

More Examples

Here are a more examples of rules from this portion: "You shall neither side with the mighty to do wrong ... nor shall you show favor to a poor person in a dispute." Simply said, "Don't take sides based on who people are." The rich and powerful are not always right; and neither are the poor and needy. Always seek the truth.

"Six years you shall sow your land ... but in the seventh year you shall let it rest .... Let the needy among your people eat of it .... Six days you shall do your work, but on the seventh day you shall cease from labor, in order that your [animals] may rest, and that your [slave] and the stranger [working for you] may be refreshed." Here, the law of the Sabbath is repeated with kindness in mind. The land should rest in the seventh year. Anything that grows wild in that year provides food for the needy, just as the weekly Sabbath provides rest for slaves and workers, both human and animal.

Along with these rules, Adonai commands us to keep three festivals. "Three times a year all your males shall appear before the Ruler, Adonai." We know these three—the "Feast of Unleavened Bread" (Pesach), the "Feast of the Harvest" (Shavuot), and the "Feast of the Ingathering at the end of the year" (Sukkot). We call these "pilgrimage festivals", the *shalosh regalim* (the "three times of going by foot").

Many of the rules in this group are mainly for farmers and shepherds. Even the rules of the three festivals are about bringing part of the harvest or the flock to share with Adonai. Scholars noted the festival rules were based on an old Israelite farmers' calendar, when Pesach was the first holiday of the year and Sukkot was the last. Today, as we know, Sukkot comes near the beginning of the Jewish year.

The Case of the Simlah

A *simlah* was a square of cloth that could be worn as a cape during the day and used as a blanket at night. At an Israelite fortress at Yavneh-yam archaeologists found a letter of complaint from the seventh century B.C.E. A poor man who was hired to work the fields of an officer was writing to complain. The officer took his *simlah* to hold until the work was done, but now the officer refused to return it. This letter of complaint from 2,600 years ago tells us why the Torah includes a rule about a *simlah*. If a person was poor, the *simlah* might be his or her only possession, so it was cruel to hold on to it overnight, even if it was given as a pledge.

To Consider

We sometimes give things to be held as a pledge. At a swim club or bowling alley you may be asked to leave something you own in exchange for towels or bowling shoes. When you return the towels or give back the shoes, your card is returned. In what ways is this like the case of the *simlah*? How does it feel to have to leave something personal behind? Why is the rule about returning the *simlah* important enough to be in the Torah?

A Plague on the Canaanites

Adonai promised, "I will drive [the Canaanites] out before you little by little ..." Adonai would send a plague on the Canaanites. Some scholars believe that the word for "plague" here, *tzirah*, could mean a plague of "hornets". Other scholars think it is a play on the word *mitzrayim*, "Egypt", meaning that Adonai will send the Egyptians against the Canaanites time and again to weaken them. That is what happened: Egyptian attacks against Canaanite cities made it easier for the Israelites to settle in Canaan. *Below:* Bronze plaque from the city of Hazor showing a Canaanite, possibly a priest or high official.

An Angel or a Messenger?

For now, Adonai promises to send "an angel before you to guard you ... and to bring you to [Canaan]." Scholars and commentators remind us that the word for "angel" also means "messenger". The "angel" may even be Moses or Joshua. If the Israelites obey the "angel", Adonai will send a "plague" on the Canaanites to destroy them a little at a time. Adonai adds, "Make no covenant with [the Canaanites] and their gods. [If] you serve their gods ... it will prove a snare to you."

Back to the Mountain

Adonai told Moses to come up to the mountain. When Moses returned he told the people Adonai's rules. The people answered with one voice, saying, "All the things that Adonai has commanded we will do!" The Torah says that Moses then wrote down the rules.

Afterward Moses built an altar at the foot of the mountain, setting up twelve pillars, one for each tribe. Young people brought sacrifices of oxen. Moses sprinkled half the blood of the sacrifices on the altar. The other half he collected in pots. Moses read "the book of the covenant" to the people, who swore again, "All that Adonai has spoken we will faithfully do!" Moses then took the pots and threw the blood on the people, saying, "This is the blood of the covenant...."

> Then Moses, and Aaron [with his sons], and seventy elders of Israel ascended; and they saw the God of Israel: under [God's] feet was what seemed like a pavement of sapphire, like the very sky for purity. Yet [God] did not [harm them]; they beheld God, and they ate and drank.

> Adonai said to Moses, "Come up to Me on the mountain and wait there; and I will give you the stone tablets with the teachings and commandments which I have inscribed to instruct them." ... So Moses and his attendant Joshua arose ... [Moses said to the elders,] "Wait here ...." When Moses had ascended the mountain, the cloud covered the mountain. ... Now the Presence of

Adonai seemed to the Israelites like a consuming fire on the top of the mountain. Moses went into the cloud … and Moses remained on the mountain forty days and forty nights.

The story of the Israelites at the mountain of God is so important that many stories were included. One told how God came down on the mountain. One told how Aaron and his sons ate a feast on the mountain. One told the part Joshua played. All the stories were fit together by someone that Bible critics often call "R", the "Redactor" or final editor.

In fitting the stories together the R-teller imagined the mountain to be very much like the Temple of Solomon. R divided the mountain into three "rooms" or "zones". The people could stand at the foot of the mountain, but no closer. The elders, Aaron and his sons, and Joshua could go up partway on the mountain, but no closer. Only Moses could go to the top of the mountain and enter the cloud to meet with God. In the same way, the ancient Temple had a courtyard for the people, an inner chamber (called "the Holy") only for priests, and a final inner chamber (the "Holy of Holies") that only the High Priest could enter. Looking back at all the stories about the mountain, it is easy to see this arrangement. Looking forward, we will soon see it again.

To Consider

In the Temple, blood was sprinkled on the altar. But in the story of Sinai, half the blood of the sacrifices was sprinkled on the altar, and the other half was thrown on the Israelites! If you were commenting on the Torah, how would you explain this? (Hint: Think of "blood brothers".)

"R"—The Redactor

The Jewish philosopher, Franz Rosenzweig (1886–1929), said that "R" could also stand for *rabbenu*, "our teacher"—a name that tradition reserved for Moses, calling him *Moshe Rabbenu*, "Our Teacher Moses". Rosenzweig did not think the R-teller was Moses, only that the final editor of Torah was a great teacher, perhaps as great as Moses.

Haftarah: Jeremiah 34:8-22; 33:25-26

Mishpatim begins with the commandments about releasing slaves. The haftarah tells how the people of Judah betrayed their Hebrew slaves in the time of Jeremiah.

King Zedekiah made a covenant with the people of Israel to set free all Hebrew slaves, hoping that God would grant mercy and save the kingdom of Judah from the Babylonians attacking Jerusalem (589 B.C.E.). A year later the Babylonians suddenly retreated, and the former slave owners canceled the release and took back their slaves.

Adonai's word came to Jeremiah, and he prophesied, saying, God ordered that every seven years Hebrew slaves would be set free. But your ancestors ignored this command. Then you "did the right thing… You made a covenant in My presence, in the house that bears My name." But you broke your word.

> Therefore, says Adonai … I will declare a liberty for you—of the word, of plague, and of hunger. I will make you a horror before the kingdoms of the world! … I will give the leaders of Judah and Jerusalem, the officials, and all the people of the land who [made the covenant] to their enemies, their mortal foes. Their dead bodies shall be food for the birds of the sky and the beasts of the earth.

The Rabbis added two verses at the end to soften the message. In these verses Adonai promises to bring a king who will renew the throne of David. Adonai declares, "I will restore their fortunes and take them back in love."

Gifts

Where would the Israelites get all the wonderful things that they needed to build God's sanctuary? The Torah does not say. Were all these jewels and fabrics and riches what the Israelites "borrowed" from their Egyptian neighbors? Would their neighbors have been that rich? The commentators say that the sanctuary built in the wilderness became the model for the Temple built by Solomon. Modern Bible scholars think it may be just the opposite. The portrait of the sanctuary of the wilderness was based on the rich and beautiful Temple built by Solomon.

Gifts from the Heart

> Adonai spoke to Moses, saying: Tell the Israelite people to bring Me gifts; you shall accept gifts for Me from every person whose heart is moved [to give].

Adonai asks for gifts "from every person whose heart is moved" to give. The gifts are for the building of a sanctuary. Franz Rosenzweig commented that in Egypt the Israelites were slaves, forced to build cities for Pharaoh. But Adonai does not force them to build the sanctuary. Adonai tells Moses to accept gifts—gold, silver, and copper; fine yarns dyed blue, purple, and crimson; animal skins and fish skins; fine oil and spices; precious stones and gemstones; and time, labor, and skill—but only from those who wish to help and want to give. Slaves are forced to do things. Free people do things because they choose to.

The story of Adonai's sanctuary gives exact measurements and many details. Like other parts of the Torah, it seems to be a single tale until we look closer. Sometimes the portable sanctuary built in the wilderness is called the Tabernacle (*Mishkan*, in Hebrew). Sometimes it is called the Tent (*Ohel*, in Hebrew). At times both words seem to point to the same thing, and at times they seem to specify two different places. It is marvelous how the tellers wove the stories together into one precise tale. They constructed a message about giving freely, about giving your best to God.

Let Them Make Me a Sanctuary

Adonai tells Moses, "And let [the people] make Me a sanctuary (*mikdash*) that I may dwell among them." The Israelites will build a sanctuary for Adonai—not a house (a *bayit*, in Hebrew), but a *mikdash* (from the word for "holy", *kadosh*), a "holy place". And Adonai does not say "so that I can dwell in it," meaning inside the sanctuary. Adonai says "so that I can dwell among them," meaning among the Israelites.

The "Throne" of Adonai

> They shall make an ark of acacia wood, two and a half cubits long, a cubit and a half wide, and a cubit and a half high. Overlay it with pure gold—overlay it inside and out—and make upon it a gold molding round about. ...

Adonai starts with the heart of the *mikdash*, the Ark. Inside the Ark Moses will place the tablets of the Law (the Ten Commandments). The ark is made with poles to carry it from place to place. It is made of wood covered everywhere with gold. And it is shaped like a platform with a kind of throne on its top. Here is what the "throne" looks like:

> Make two cherubim of gold ... one cherub at one end and the other cherub on the other end .... The cherubim shall have their wings spread out above [to make the seat of the throne] ... the faces of the cherubim being turned toward the cover. Place the cover on top of the Ark, after depositing the covenant inside the Ark .... There I will meet with you, and I will pass on to you—from above the cover, from between the two cherubim that are on top of the Ark ... all that I will command you concerning the Israelite people.

Adonai would speak from between the two cherubim ("sphinxes"), as a king or queen speaks from a throne. And at the feet of Adonai, close to Moses, would be the tablets of the covenant that tie together heaven and earth. Like a throne, the Ark with its "chair" made by the cherubim, with their wings forming the seat, was bound to be a place of great power.

Two Holy Objects

Adonai gives Moses instructions for making "a table of acacia wood" coated with gold to hold the "bread of display" that should always be set out as a gift to Adonai. The com-

Dwelling among Them

The Israelites, dwelling at the foot of the mountain of Adonai, felt close to God. Yet, as the commentator Umberto Cassuto (1883–1951) said, they knew that they were bound to leave the mountain and thought this might mean leaving Adonai, too. The *Mishkan* is being built as a way of keeping the thought of Adonai with them at all times, so they will know that God is dwelling "among them."

To Discuss

Cassuto thought the reason for building the *Mishkan* was so the Israelites would always feel near Adonai wherever they traveled. Can you give other reasons why the Israelites would want to build the *Mishkan*?

Seen an Angel Lately?

Cherubim were popular everywhere in the ancient world as "sphinxes", imaginary creatures with animal bodies, wings, and human heads. The cherub you surely know best is the Great Sphinx of Egypt (*below*). It has the body of a lion and the head of a Pharaoh.

The Israelites did not go out and buy presents for Adonai; they gave gifts from what they owned. When we give gifts from the things that are precious to us we are saying something important about ourselves. Is it hard to give up things that are precious to you? Do you think it might have been harder for the Israelites? Why or why not?

mentator Abrabanel thought that the idea that gods need to be fed daily came from Egypt and other ancient cultures. The Israelites, he said, needed to believe that they were doing as much for Adonai as other peoples did for their gods. This was the reason for the table for the bread and the bread of display (sometimes called "shew bread").

And Adonai gives Moses instructions for the golden *Menorah*, or lampstand. It should be shaped like a tree and decorated with flowers, petals, and cups shaped liked almond blossoms (to hold oil for burning). It should have a single straight branch in the center (like a tree trunk, but the size of a branch) with three branches coming from each side of it. From the time of Solomon's Temple the Menorah became a visual symbol of the Jewish people.

The Tabernacle

The Ark would be in a space called the *Kodesh HaKadoshim*, the "Holy of Holies". A tent would cover the Holy of Holies, the Table for bread, and the Menorah. This tent was called *HaKodesh*, the "Holy". An embroidered curtain would separate the Holy from the Holy of Holies. The Mishkan itself, with everything in it, would be a wooden rectangle twice the size, covered with a tent of ram and dolphin skins.

In the front part of the Mishkan would be an altar made of acacia wood covered with copper. The altar would have four horns—one at each corner. It would be used for offering sacrifices, so it had to have pails for removing the ashes of burnt animals, basins for collecting blood, flesh hooks, and pans for holding the burning coals used to set the fires. All of these tools were made of copper.

Everything—the Ark and the Holy of Holies; the Table and the Menorah and the tent of the Holy; the copper altar and the large tent of the Mishkan—would be fitted with rings and clasps and poles so it could all be broken apart and carried from place to place.

Gold, Silver and Copper; Blue, Purple, and Crimson

At Mount Sinai the people could go as far as the foot of the mountain, the priests and the elders could go partway up the mountain, and only Moses could go to the top. In the Mishkan the people would be able to go into the Tabernacle, the priests into the Holy, and only Moses or the High Priest into the Holy of Holies.

All the holiest things—the Table, the Ark, and the Menorah—would be made of gold or of wood covered in gold. Many parts of the Holy would be of silver. And most everything used in the outer Mishkan would be made of copper (though this probably means a mixture of copper and tin known as bronze, since pure copper is very soft).

The hangings and curtains for the Holy of Holies would be dyed blue, the most precious color and the most expensive dye known in ancient times. The blue dye came from seashells, and it took enormous numbers of shells, carefully prepared, to make this special blue color. In the Holy the hangings would be purple, a color made from a more plentiful kind of seashell. Even the crimson color to be used in the rest of the Mishkan was precious, though it probably came from an insect and was more easily made.

All these things were arranged in threes, from the most precious to the least precious—from the Holy of Holies to the Holy to the Mishkan itself.

Ancient Temples

Ancient temples were often constructed in this three-part way. In Egypt, for instance, people could only come as far as the courtyard outside the temple, priests could go into the temple, and only the Pharaoh or the High Priest could go into the holiest chamber where statues of the gods were kept. The most precious metals and gifts were kept in the innermost holy chamber, less precious gifts were in the temple, and statues and other gifts were kept out in the courtyard where people could see them. So the Mishkan was very much like Egyptian temples.

Models of the Mishkan

Experts have tried making models of the Mishkan. Most now agree that, given the way it is described in the Torah, it would have been much too heavy to be carried through the wilderness. Surely it was a large construction, very much like a wooden building covered by a tent. In fact, the Torah makes it seem like a smaller-sized copy of the First Temple in almost every way, except for its tent top.

Quote to Remember

וְעָשׂוּ לִי מִקְדָּשׁ וְשָׁכַנְתִּי
בְּתוֹכָם.

Let them make Me a sanctuary that I may dwell among them.

But it was unlike those temples in a very important way. In Egyptian temples there were thrones for the gods, but there were also beds for the gods to rest on. In the Mishkan there was no place for Adonai to take a nap, because the Israelites did not think of Adonai as needing sleep like a human. The Egyptians set aside beer and wine and bread in enormous quantities every day for their gods to eat, but the Israelites only placed bread on display to show that they connected Adonai with the blessing of food. The Mishkan would not be built as a place to keep Adonai in, but as a reminder that wherever we settle, Adonai dwells among us. Just as Adonai had commanded Moses "Let them make Me a sanctuary that I may dwell among them."

Haftarah: I Kings 5:26-6:13

Adonai commanded, "Let them make Me a sanctuary that I may dwell among them." The building of the *Mikdash*—the sanctuary in the wilderness—in *Terumah* is connected by the Rabbis with the building of the Temple in Jerusalem in this haftarah.

Solomon came to the throne around 970 B.C.E. and soon began building the Temple.

> Adonai gave Solomon wisdom as [Adonai] had promised. There was peace between Hiram [King of Tyre] and Solomon. The two made a treaty.

Much of the work was done in Lebanon, north of Israel, Hiram's territory. Solomon sent thousands of workers to quarry ashlars, huge stones shaped to fit one another exactly. Along with the stones the workers cut timber. All was brought to Jerusalem by Solomon's forced laborers.

"No hammer or axe or any iron tool was heard in the Temple while it was being built," so that Adonai's peace would not be disturbed. And when all was complete, in the fourth year of Solomon's reign, the word of Adonai came to Solomon:

> About this Temple ... if you obey My laws and My judgments and take care to keep all My commandments, I will keep My promise that I made to your father David. I will dwell among the children of Israel, and never forsake My people Israel.

The Mishkan was designed for temporary use; Solomon's Temple would serve the people for almost four hundred years.

Mishkan and Temple

You can use these two floor plans to compare the way the Torah describes the Mishkan with the way that other books of the Bible describe the First Temple built by Solomon. Should you need to build a Temple some day, here is how

Don't Be Fooled by Size

Actually, the Mishkan was far smaller than Solomon's Temple. The diagram of the Mishkan is enlarged here to make it possible to show everything in it.

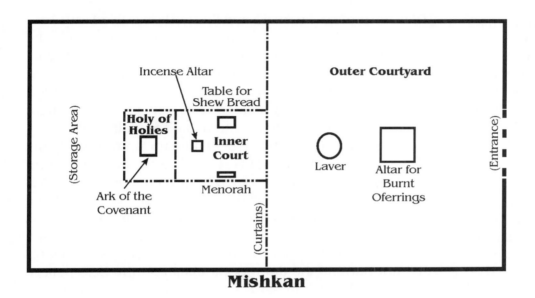

Mishkan

Solomon's Temple

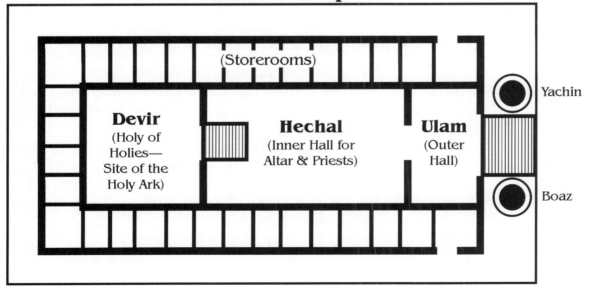

Instructions

A Missing Moses

Adonai gives instructions in this portion. In the last portion, though, Adonai's commands were given Moses to be told to the people. In this portion the instructions still seem to be given to Moses, but the name of Moses does not occur even once.

To Consider

We think of the ner tamid today as the "eternal light". But if it is electric, we know the bulb burns out; and if it is gas, we know there are times that the gas is turned off. So the word "eternal" is not actually true. What is the difference between an idea and something that is the symbol of a idea?

Instructions

Titzaveh means "instruct", and this portion is filled with Adonai's instructions. The portion begins with lamps for the Tent of Meeting and ends with incense. In between Adonai appoints Aaron and his sons as priests for all time, giving instructions for dressing the priests—especially the High Priest—and for how to make priests holy to Adonai. There are also instructions for how to make the altar holy.

First come instructions for setting up lamps outside the Holy of Holies. Aaron and his sons will tend the lamps "from evening to morning" so they will burn as a *ner tamid. Ner* means "lamp" and *tamid* means "regular". Of course, we Jews today use the name ner tamid for the lamp that burns above our synagogue arks. In English we call the ner tamid, the "eternal light". But the lamps in the Mishkan probably did not burn all the time. Both Rashi and Ibn Ezra believe that since the Torah says "from evening to morning", the original ner tamid lamps were lit each evening to burn through the night. They were "regular" but not "eternal".

Clothing for the Priests

> You shall bring forward your brother Aaron, with his sons … to serve Me as priests…. Make [holy] garments for your brother Aaron, for dignity and adornment.

Adonai instructs that talented tailors be found to make clothing for the priests. The special garments for the High Priest include a breastplate, an *ephod*, a robe, a fringed tunic, a headdress, and a sash. Adonai begins with the most important piece, the ephod.

Ephod

The ephod is a bit of a mystery. The historian Josephus, who was a priest in the days of the Second Temple, said it looked like the upper part of a woman's outer robe, with shoulder straps and sleeves. Some scholars think the ephod was more like an apron. But archaeologists have found the word *ephod* in several ancient languages including Ugaritic, Assyrian, and Akkadian, and it always means an expensive coat.

The Torah says that on each shoulder strap of Aaron's ephod there was a large stone of lapis in a gold setting. The stones were engraved with the names of Jacob's sons—six on each stone. So the High Priest wore the names of the twelve tribes of Israel on his shoulders.

The Breastplate of Decision

Adonai next gives directions for making "the breastplate of decision". This was a kind of pouch or pocket decorated with twelve different gemstones. Each gemstone was set in gold, and each had the name of one tribe carved into it. The breastplate was not a "plate" at all. It was made of fabric and attached to the ephod with gold fittings. Adonai instructed: "Aaron shall carry the names of the sons of Israel on the breastplate of decision over his heart, when he enters the sanctuary…."

> Inside the breastplate of decision, you shall place the Urim and Tummim, so they are over Aaron's heart when he comes before Adonai. Thus, Aaron shall carry the instrument of decision for the Israelites over his heart before Adonai at all times.

Adonai said to "place" the Urim and Tummim in the breastplate, not to "make" them, so the Urim and Tummim were not something new to the Israelites. But what were they? Since Adonai does not tell Moses how to make them, we only know what they were like from how they were used. Important questions were brought to the High Priest. The High Priest took the Urim and Tummim from the breastplate of decision and asked the question. The Urim and Tummim gave Adonai's answer to the question.

Gideon's Ephod

In the Torah the ephod seems to be a coat. In the Book of Judges, though, Gideon made an ephod out of gold, and the people "worshiped" Gideon's ephod like an idol. We know that Egyptians and other ancient peoples would dress their idols in fine clothes on special occasions. Maybe Gideon's ephod was used to dress an idol or else set up to look like an idol. You can find the story of Gideon's ephod in chapter eight of the Book of Judges.

More about Urim

The Urim and Tummim are sometimes called just *Urim*. In Hebrew they could be a noun phrase standing for one thing and not two. The word Urim begins with *alef*, א, the first letter of the Hebrew alphabet. The word Tummim (spelled "thummim" in English dictionaries) begins with the letter *tav*, ת, the last letter of the alphabet. The idea may be that Urim and Tummim could answer any question "from A to Z". as we would say. The word *urim* may mean "lights" and the word *tummim* may mean "completions" or "perfections". Since light was the first thing created by God and perfection is our final goal, this may be another way of saying that Urim and Tummim can answer all things from beginning to end.

Urim and Yale

The official seal of Yale University (*above*) includes the Hebrew for Urim and Tummim and translates the words into Latin as *Lux et Veritas*, "Light and Truth", the university's motto.

Bells

This idea of bells on the robe of the High Priest may come from a popular superstition. The great scholar of folklore Sir James Frazer (1854-1941) told how people in Europe, Asia, and Africa believed that the noise of bells would drive away demons and evil spirits. Towns and villages would ring bells at dangerous times, as darkness fell, or on days they thought were evil. Even today bells are still found in churches—of course, now it is said that the bells ring to call people to prayer, but in the Middle Ages many churchgoers and priests still believed that the ringing of the bells kept demons away.

What can archaeology tell us about the breastplate of decision and the Urim and Tummim? Well, we know there were breastplates: Archaeologists found one just like the one described in the Torah in a king's tomb in Phoenicia. We also know of an ancient legend that tells how the hero Marduk took the "tablets of destiny" from his dead enemy and put them on his own chest—this, too, must have been a kind of breastplate. On the other hand, we have never found anything like the Urim and Tummim, but this could be because we have no idea what to look for. Also, the Hebrew does not say "the" Urim and "the" Tummim, so Urim and Tummim could be common items like gems or stones.

The Robe and Headdress

Adonai instructed that the robe the High Priest would wear under the ephod would be pure blue. It had a hole in its center so it could be pulled over the head. All around the hem at the bottom of the robe there were gold bells and gold pomegranates. Adonai said the gold bells would save Aaron from death when Aaron went in and out of the sanctuary.

Adonai instructed that Aaron's headdress should be of linen with a band of gold around it. The gold band was engraved with the words "Holy to Adonai". It was attached to the headdress with a blue cord. Aaron was to wear the gold band on his forehead at all times. This reminds us of the head piece of the *tefillin,* and the two-part headgear also reminds us of the two-part crown worn by the Pharaohs of Egypt. Other priests wore headdresses something like turbans, it seems. In Bible times most men wore nothing on their heads, so the headdresses of the priests helped set them apart and mark them as holy.

The Rest of Aaron's Outfit

Adonai instructed that the High Priest's tunic (remember the loose coat worn by Joseph?) would be a fringed garment made of fine linen. It would be held on top of the robe, the ephod, and the breastplate with an embroidered sash, a kind of fabric belt. Other priests also wore tunics and sashes "for dignity and adornment". Adonai instructed,

Put these [garments] on your brother Aaron and on his sons, as well; anoint them [with oil], ordain them and consecrate them to serve Me as priests.

Adonai instructed the priests to wear one more garment: short linen pants. These pants, or "breeches", went from the waist to just above the knee to cover "their nakedness". Israelite men did not wear pants under their robes, only a kind of underwear. But priests were constantly bending as they worked at the altar, and since they were doing holy work, it would be undignified for them to be accidentally showing their underwear!

Making the Priests Holy

Adonai instructed that the priests should be made holy through sacrifices: a bull and a ram. Blood from the sacrifices would be sprinkled on each priest's ear, thumb, and toe. Here, the Torah mentions other special sacrifices, too: wave offerings, heave offerings, and sin offerings. "Wave offerings" were waved by the priests, just as we shake the *lulav* on Sukkot. "Heave offerings" were raised or "heaved" on high before being sacrificed. Adonai instructed that an offering of one bull had to be made daily as a sin offering for all of Israel. Then Adonai said the ritual for making priests holy would last seven days. Afterward the altar would be made holy in the same way, also for seven days.

All this—clothing, sacrifices, altar, and lamps—helped to make a special place, a holy place. And Adonai promised,

I will dwell among the Israelites, and I will be their God. And they shall know that I Adonai am their God, who brought them out from the land of Egypt that I might dwell among them, I Adonai am their God.

An Altar for Incense

Lastly Adonai instructed that a special small altar of wood be made and covered with gold. At the top, on each corner, a piece of wood covered with gold would jut out like a horn. The altar would be placed in front of the curtain in front of the Ark. Aaron would burn incense on it every morning and

Quote to Remember

וְקִדַּשְׁתִּי אֶת־אֹהֶל מוֹעֵד וְאֶת־הַמִּזְבֵּחַ וְאֶת־אַהֲרֹן וְאֶת־בָּנָיו אֲקַדֵּשׁ לְכַהֵן לִי.

I will make holy the Tent of Meeting and the altar, and I will make holy Aaron and his sons to serve Me as priests.

A Horned Altar

Below: Archaeologists have found several incense altars like this one among the remains of Canaanite cities. The sharp rises at the four corners are the "horns" of the altar. The Torah tells us that the Israelite's incense altar was covered in gold.

To Consider

After the Second Temple was destroyed, no more incense was burned by Jews. Today the only thing like incense in Jewish practice is the smelling of spices during the service of Havdalah, which separates Sabbath from the rest of the week. Do you think that modern synagogues should go back to the practice of burning incense?

every evening. Once a year the horns of this altar would be purified with the blood of a sin offering.

Some commentators thought that burning incense in the sanctuary was meant to remind the Israelites of God's pillar of cloud. One commentator, though, thought it was meant to add to God's mystery.

To a large degree, all the instructions about the sanctuary (sometimes called "the Tent of Meeting") and all the instructions about the High Priest, the priests, and the costumes of the priests add to the mysterious feeling we call "holiness".

Haftarah: Ezekiel 43:10-27

The Rabbis connect the incense altar in *Titzaveh* with Ezekiel's vision of the altar in a new Temple to be built in the future to replace the Temple of Solomon. Adonai says,

> Describe the Temple to the House of Israel … show them the plan of the Temple … all its rules and instructions. Write it [down] as they watch, so that they can follow and care for all its plans and rules.

Ezekiel explains that the entire area of the Temple is "most holy". He describes the design and laws of the altar. He says that Adonai has chosen the priests of the family of Zadok (High Priest under Solomon, of the family of Aaron) to serve the new altar.

Ezekiel gives the rules for dedicating the altar. The rituals must be done every day for seven days. If all is done properly, then the altar will be holy to Adonai.

> After those days, from the eighth day on, the priests shall present your burnt offerings and your offerings of well-being on the altar, and I will show you favor, says Adonai.

Ezekiel had predicted that the Temple of Solomon would be destroyed. He was still alive when this happened. With this prophecy, though, he gave the people hope that Adonai was already planning a new Temple.

Indeed, within a few years after Ezekiel's death the Israelites returned to Jerusalem and began building a new Temple. They did not use Ezekiel's plans, and later commentators said that this was because the prophet's plans were really for a third Temple that would be built in the time of the messiah.

A Golden Bull Calf

כי תשׂה
Ki Tisah
Exodus 30:11-34:35

Counting and Collecting

"When you take a census [to count the people]," Adonai said to Moses, have each male of twenty years or older pay a half-shekel. "The rich shall not pay more and the poor shall not pay less than a half-shekel."

The reason for taking the census and collecting the money now is not clear. Once the Torah calls it a "ransom". Then it is called an "atonement" for sin. And then it is said to be for the Tent of Meeting. In ancient times people thought that any time a census was taken was dangerous—the words "ransom" and "atonement" carry this idea of danger. Scholars remind us that counting was usually done before a war (at twenty years, a man became a soldier) or before a new tax. Even today we think of such times as dangerous. In the end, the Torah says, the silver collected was to be used for making the Tent.

Bezalel and Ohaliab

A few more items were needed for the sanctuary. Adonai tells Moses to make a copper washstand for the priests. They would wash their hands and feet there before entering the Tent and going to the altar "to use fire to turn an offering [sacrifice] for Adonai into smoke." Adonai also gives Moses instructions for making special oil and incense for the sanctuary. These must be mixed by skilled perfumers. And the exact formulas must be guarded, holy, and used only for the service of Adonai. Then comes one last instruction about making all the things for the sanctuary:

> Adonai spoke to Moses: See, I have singled out by
> name Bezalel ... of the tribe of Judah. I have
> [given] him ... a divine spirit of skill, ability, and
> knowledge in every kind of craft .... Moreover, I
> have assigned to him Oholiab ... of the tribe of
> Dan; and I have also granted skill to all who are

The Sancutary Weight

The half-shekel was originally a weight, not a coin, and the Torah states that it is equal to twenty *gerah*s "by the sanctuary weight". Archaeologists have found many stone weights marked "shekel" (*see Chayei Sarah*). But not all are the same kind of weight. In the time of the kingdoms of Israel and Judah the shekel came in three weights. One was the shekel used by priests, "the sanctuary weight". Another, "the going weight", was used in business and trading; and a third, "the royal weight", was used by the government. Since the Torah speaks here of the "sanctuary weight"— which did not exist until the time of the kings—the story must have been set down in writing at least three hundred years after Moses.

Quote to Remember

וְשָׁמְרוּ בְנֵי־יִשְׂרָאֵל אֶת־
הַשַּׁבָּת לַעֲשׂוֹת אֶת־הַשַּׁבָּת
לְדֹרֹתָם בְּרִית עוֹלָם.

The Israelite people shall keep the Sabbath, observing the Sabbath throughout the ages as a covenant for all time.

The Finger of God

Does God have a finger? Or do the words "inscribed with the finger of God" mean something else? Rashi said that the words could mean that God personally carved the tablets or else that the Torah is just saying that the tablets contained the work of heaven. Maimonides rejected the idea that God was human in any way. He imagined that the tablets were prepared by God during the days of creation. We can put this in a more modern way. The words on the tablets were so important that no matter who carved them on the stone, they would forever be remembered as the work of God. The Talmud often says about the Torah, "The ideas are the ideas of God, the words are human words."

skillful, that they may make everything that I have commanded you.... Just as I have commanded you, they shall do.

In ancient times artists were thought to be godly folk: They built temples and carved statues of the gods, they cut stone and crafted jewelry. For this reason we still know the names of many ancient artists. On Mount Sinai Adonai personally appointed the main artists for the sanctuary, Bezalel and his assistant, Oholiab. The Torah says that Bezalel has a "divine spirit" of skill and that Adonai has given skill to others to help him. Surely Bezalel must have been a great artist. Adonai filled him with *ruach Elohim*, "God's spirit", talent that is like wisdom. As Rabbi Yohanan says in the Talmud, "The Holy One grants wisdom only to a person who already has it." Even today, when we see the work of great artists or hear the wisdom of great sages, we thank God for giving them *ruach Elohim*, "divine spirit".

V'Shamru and the Tablets

Adonai commands Moses that the people should rest on the Sabbath, even during the time they are building the sanctuary. Here we find the words of one of our favorite Sabbath prayers, *V'shamru*, "They shall keep".

The message of Sinai was complete. Moses had been on the mountain forty days and forty nights.

When [Adonai] finished speaking with him on Mount Sinai, [Adonai] gave Moses the two tablets of the covenant, stone tablets inscribed with the finger of God.

A Golden Bull

When the people saw that Moses was so long in coming down from the mountain, the people gathered against Aaron and said to him, "Come, make us a god who shall go before us; for that man Moses, who brought us from the land of Egypt—we do not know what has happened to him." Aaron said to them, "Take off the gold rings that are on the ears of your wives, your sons, and your daughters, and bring them to me." And all the people took off the gold rings that were in their ears and brought them to Aaron. This he took from them and cast in a mold, and made it into a molten calf. And they exclaimed, "These are your gods, O Israel, who brought you out of the land of Egypt!" When Aaron saw this, he built an altar before it; and Aaron announced: "Tomorrow shall be a festival of Adonai." Early next day, the people … brought sacrifices …; they sat down to eat and drink, and then rose to dance.

What a story! Worried people! A golden calf! Made by Aaron! What does this mean, and why is it here? Let's take the story apart and see what is really happening.

(1) "The people gathered against Aaron"—When people gather "against" someone they become a mob, and mobs can be dangerous. The story shows why Moses was a great leader and Aaron was not. When the Israelites complained to Moses, Moses turned to Adonai for help. But when the Israelites gathered against Aaron, they said, "Make us a god," and Aaron did just that.

(2) "That man Moses"—People speak about someone as "that person, so-and-so" when they are criticizing. The Midrash says that Moses promised to return after forty days and forty nights but forgot to mention the time it would take to come down the mountain. When the time was up, the people thought "Maybe *that* god has taken *that* man and left us here without a leader and without even a god."

(3) "A molten calf"—The Hebrew word used for "calf" really means a "young bull". A calf would be a weak symbol, not a god for warriors. Calves do not lead people, and people do not respect or fear calves. But people do fear strong young bulls! And this bull was pure gold! Archaeologists have found evidence of bull worship among the Canaanites and even among the Israelites. You can picture the story more realistically if you can change the image you used to carry in your mind of "a golden calf" into the much stronger image of "a young golden bull".

Gold Earrings

It is hard to imagine that the Israelites, who were servants to Pharaoh in Egypt, wore solid gold jewelry and had enough earrings to melt down to make a golden bull. This is just one of the reasons that modern scholars think the story about the golden calf comes from a much later time.

Jeroboam's Plan

The people in the Kingdom of Judah imagined Adonai sitting on a small throne—made of the two sphinxes with the Ark as a footstool—in the little chamber of the Holy of Holies. But in the Kingdom of Israel Jeroboam wanted his people to imagine Adonai standing with one foot on the gold bull at Beth-El near Jerusalem and the other foot on the gold bull in the farthest north at Dan. Jeroboam hoped that the Ten Tribes would imagine Adonai guarding the whole Kingdom of Israel, from one end to the other.

The Real Thing

Did you ever imagine that you would see the golden calf? The bronze zebu bull *below* was found at Tel Dan, in the far north of Israel. It is like another found at Hazor, also in the north. Both are statuettes. Yet they tell us that bulls were used to represent God (*El* or *Elohim*) throughout the north, probably by Canaanites as well as by Israelites. It's not the golden calf, but it's close enough.

"These Are Your Gods, O Israel"

Aaron made only one golden bull. Why do the people cry out, "*These* are your *gods*, O Israel"? The mystery may be solved in another Bible story. When King Solomon died (around 928 B.C.E.) the Israelite nation split into two kingdoms. The two southern tribes became the Kingdom of Judah. They took Solomon's son Rehoboam as their king, kept Jerusalem as their capital, and kept the Temple as their religious center. The ten northern tribes formed the new Kingdom of Israel. They took Jeroboam as their king and made Schechem their capital.

Jeroboam thought, "If my people go to the Temple in Jerusalem to worship Adonai, then my kingdom will be lost!" He knew that the sphinxes on the Ark in the Temple were thought to be Adonai's throne and that the people loved Adonai. They took gifts and made pilgrimages to the Temple. The Book of Kings explains what Jeroboam did:

> And the king [Jeroboam] … made two golden bulls. He said to [the people], "You have been going up to Jerusalem long enough. These are your gods, O Israel, who brought you up out of the land of Egypt." And he set one [bull] in Beth-El, and the other he placed in Dan.

Jeroboam's plan was clever. Canaanites and Israelites shared the idea of a bull being the "pedestal" or footstool of a god. The Canaanites often made idols showing their god Baal standing on a bull. And archaeologists have found a statue of just the bull (with no god standing on it) in an old Israelite temple. Jeroboam made two bulls so that Adonai could be worshiped in two places in his kingdom. To celebrate, Jeroboam declared a new festival to Adonai.

The Kingdom of Israel lasted two hundred years. It was conquered by the Assyrians in 722 B.C.E. The Assyrians exiled the Israelites to distant lands. Some northerners fled to the south, but the Ten Tribes were lost forever. The priests in the Kingdom of Judah asked, "Why did God allow Israel to be destroyed and the Ten Tribes to be lost?" They decided it must have been because of great sins. And what were the great sins of the Ten Tribes? Here is how the Book of Kings describes the two great sins:

[Setting up the two golden bulls] proved to be a cause of guilt; for the people went to worship [the calf at Beth-El and] the one at Dan. [Jeroboam] also made [altars in other] places and appointed priests … who were not Levites.

Back to Sinai

When the people at Mount Sinai cry out, "These are your gods, O Israel!" they are using the exact words that Jeroboam used. When Aaron announces: "Tomorrow shall be a festival of Adonai," he does exactly what Jeroboam did when Jeroboam created a new festival for Adonai "of his own mind". Many modern scholars and some earlier commentators believe that these two tales are too much alike to be different stories. After the Kingdom of Judah was destroyed in 586 B.C.E., people asked, "Why did God allow Judah to be destroyed?" The priests again answered, "It must have been because of a great sin." But what sin? So the story of the great sin of the Kingdom of Israel was told in the Torah as if it happened at Mount Sinai. But in the Torah it was told about the whole people—everyone together at the foot of the mountain—all worshiping *one* golden bull and making a sinful festival to Adonai.

> Adonai spoke to Moses, "Hurry down; for your people, whom you brought out of the land of Egypt, have … been quick to turn aside from [My] way …. They have made themselves a molten [bull] and bowed low to it and sacrificed to it, saying, "These are your gods, O Israel, who brought you out of the land of Egypt."

Adonai threatened to destroy the Israelites and start a new people, with Moses as their father. But Moses reminded Adonai of the promises made to Abraham, Isaac, and Jacob. And the Torah says, "Adonai renounced the punishment [Adonai] had planned to bring upon [the Israelites]."

Just one more thing: The story of the sin of Jeroboam and the story of the golden bull-calf were surely told by priests from the southern kingdom. Northern priests of the time of Jeroboam would not have thought of the two bull statues as idols. They would have said that the statues were

The Ten Lost Tribes

Many legends grew up around the Ten Tribes who were taken out of Israel as prisoners of the Assyrians. Even today people look for them everywhere in the world. In the time of the Rabbis it was said that they lived beyond an imaginary river called the Sambatyon. Six days a week the river rushed so fiercely that it could not be crossed. On the Sabbath the river rested. But the tribes could not cross it then because of the laws forbidding travel on Shabbat. You can find many more stories about the Ten Lost Tribes in an encyclopedia or on the Internet. Most scholars agree, though, that the people taken from Israel soon married into the peoples among whom they were settled and faded from history forever.

To Consider

Moses asked Aaron, "Why did you bring such great sin upon the people by making this golden bull?" Aaron gave two excuses. First he said, "this people is bent on evil." Then he said, "I threw the gold into the fire, and out came out this calf!" When we do something wrong, we often make excuses the way Aaron did. What was wrong with Aaron's excuses? Who did Aaron forget to blame?

just like the carvings of sphinxes in the Holy of Holies in the Temple in Jerusalem—a platform or throne of God.

Breaking the Tablets

Moses went down the mountain carrying the two tablets.

> As soon as Moses came near the camp and saw the calf, and the dancing, he became enraged; and he hurled the tablets from his hands and shattered them at the foot of the mountain. He took the calf … and burned it; he ground it to powder and strewed it upon the water and so made the Israelites drink it.

> Moses said to Aaron, "What did this people do to you that you have brought such great sin upon them?" Aaron said, "Let not [Moses] be enraged. You know that this people is bent on evil. They said to me, 'Make us gods ….' They gave [gold]. I hurled it into the fire, and out came out this calf!"

Moses stood in the camp gate, calling, "Whoever is for Adonai, come here!" When the Levites (his tribe) came to his side, Moses told them to kill the leaders of the mob. They killed three thousand people that day. Then Moses returned to Adonai and said, "Forgive the people or else erase me from Your plans." Adonai promised to punish only guilty people. "Adonai sent a plague on the people, for what they did with the calf that Aaron made." Of course, a plague does not kill everyone, so the Torah must mean that Adonai's plague killed only the guilty Israelites.

The Tent of Meeting

Moses set up the Tent of Meeting outside the camp and met with Adonai there "face to face, as one person speaks with another." While Adonai was with Moses a pillar of cloud stood at the entrance to the Tent. Then the people would come to the openings of their tents and bow low to Adonai. Afterward Moses would return to the camp, but Joshua stayed to guard the Tent of Meeting.

Let Me See You

Then Moses asks Adonai a personal favor, saying, "Oh, let me behold Your Presence!" Adonai says, "I will make all My goodness pass before you .... But you cannot see My face, for no one may see Me and live."

> And Adonai said, "See, there is a place near Me. Station yourself on the rock and, as My Presence passes by, I will put you in a cleft of the rock and shield you with My hand until I have passed by. Then I will take My hand away and you will see My back; but My face must not be seen."

Afterward Adonai told Moses to carve two tablets of stone like the first two and to bring them up the mountain. Then, the Torah says, Adonai made a new covenant for the people, giving them ten commands.

The Ten Commands

The Ten Commands in this story are different from "The Words" that we now call "The Ten Commandments" (see *Yitro*). The commands given here are (1) You must not make a covenant with the Canaanites, and you must tear down their pillars and holy places. (2) You must not make molten gods. (3) You must observe the Feast of *Matzot* to remember leaving Egypt. (4) Every first-born animal or son belongs to Adonai—it must either be brought as a sacrifice or redeemed with silver or gold. (5) Anyone coming to Adonai's holy place must bring some kind of sacrifice. (6) You must rest on the Sabbath. (7) You must observe Shavuot and Sukkot, coming three times a year to worship before Adonai. (8) You must not offer the Passover sacrifice with anything but matzah, and you must eat it all before morning comes. (9) You must bring the best of the first fruits of the harvest to the house of Adonai. And (10) You shall not boil a kid in its mother's milk.

Adonai told Moses to "Write down these commandments [as] a covenant...."

> And [Moses] was there with Adonai forty days and forty nights; he ate no bread and drank no water;

You Cannot See My Face

The Torah says that Adonai's "face" must not be seen. Of course, the Torah includes stories about Adonai speaking with Adam and Abraham face to face. But the idea here is that looking directly at Adonai would be too powerful. In one midrash a Roman emperor demanded that a rabbi show him God. The rabbi told the emperor to look at the sun when it is strong. The emperor said, "I cannot." The rabbi replied, "If you cannot stare into the sun, which is just one of God's servants, how can you expect to see God and live?" So the Torah says that Adonai passed by Moses, showing Moses some of Adonai's glory. Like Moses, we can see some of Adonai's glory every day if only we pause to pay attention to the marvels in the world that God created.

To Consider

Which commandments were written on the stone tablets? Were the same commandments on the first set of tablets as on the second set? Putting the two different lists of ten commandments side by side, which of them do you think has more of the *ruach Elohim*, the "divine spirit"?

and he wrote down on the tablets the terms of the covenant, the Ten Commandments.

Here is a great mystery. The Torah calls these "the Ten Commands". We can imagine the Torah's final editor, the R-teller (see *Mishpatim*), faced with the problem of having two different lists of ten commands, both traditional and well known. To fit them neatly into the puzzle the R-teller placed the list called the "Ten Words" before the story of the Golden Calf and the list called the "Ten Commands" after it. Which list was actually carved on the tablets that Moses brought down from Sinai? That is a mystery no one can solve.

Haftarah: I Kings 18:1-39

The Rabbis connect the golden calf event, when the people betrayed Adonai, with the people's worship of Canaanite gods in the time of the prophet Elijah. The haftarah tells the exciting story.

In the third year of a drought Adonai told Elijah to go to King Ahab and tell him that rain was coming. Elijah knew that Ahab hated him, so he went first to Obadiah, a man close to Ahab who showed he was loyal to Adonai by saving a hundred prophets when Jezebel, the king's wife, had tried to kill them all. Obadiah sent the king out to meet Elijah.

The king saw the prophet and asked, "Is this you, the troubler of Israel?" But Elijah answered, You are the troubler of Israel, for you turned "away from the commands of Adonai by worshiping the idols of Baal."

Elijah tells the king to set up a contest. Elijah alone will face the 450 prophets of Baal and the 400

prophets of Asherah that Jezebel supports. Ahab then brings everyone together at Mount Carmel. Elijah asked the people,

> How long will you hop between two opinions? If Adonai is God, follow Adonai. If Baal is God, follow Baal!

In a dramatic duel Elijah proves that the prophets of Baal have no powers, while Adonai can send fire from heaven to consume a sacrifice on the altar.

> When they saw this, all the people threw themselves to the ground and cried out: "Adonai is God: Adonai is God."

Elijah the prophet became a hero of Jewish legend. It was even claimed that he never really died. He was transported to heaven in God's own fiery chariot.

Too Much

Assembling the People

Moses then assembled the whole Israelite community and said to them:

These are the things that Adonai has commanded you to do: On six days work may be done, but on the seventh day you shall have a Sabbath of complete rest, holy to Adonai; whoever does any work on it shall be put to death. You shall kindle no fire throughout your settlements on the Sabbath day.

In giving Moses the instructions on Mount Sinai, Adonai's final command was that the Israelites should continue to observe Shabbat even as they built the Tabernacle. Now Moses assembles the people to repeat Adonai's instructions to them. Moses starts where God ended, with the command to observe Shabbat.

This time, however, Moses adds, "You shall kindle no fire throughout your settlements on the Sabbath day." The sages of the Talmud pointed to the words "throughout your settlements" and said this means "for all time and wherever you may live". So Jewish law did not permit fire to be lit on the Sabbath. But the Torah commanded the people to use fire on the altar in the Temple on the Sabbath and holy days to honor God. The sages said this law does not mean that fire cannot be used on Shabbat—Jews can use fire in their homes on the Sabbath provided that the fires are lit before the Sabbath begins.

Around the time that the sages were discussing this, Judaism was being challenged by two sects or groups, Samaritans and Karaites. Both of these sects claimed to follow the laws of the Torah—in fact, they claimed that they were even more Jewish than the Jews themselves. They lit no fire on the Sabbath and unlike the Jews, they used no fire on the seventh day. On the Sabbath they ate only cold foods, sat in darkness when night fell, and suffered when the weather

The Kenites

Some Bible scholars believe that the words "You shall kindle no fire throughout your settlements on the Sabbath day" were added as a special instruction to the Kenites, a nation that helped the Israelites in the Wilderness. The Kenites were blacksmiths who used fire in working metals. The command was to tell them that even fires used for making materials for the sanctuary should not be made on Shabbat. The Kenites are mentioned many times in the Bible as special friends to the Israelites.

The Gift to Teach

Moses explained that Adonai had given Bezalel a special gift: the gift "to give directions." The Bible commentator Ibn Ezra said that this was surely a divine gift, since many artists can design, but not many can teach others to design. He added that likewise there are many who are great scholars, but not every scholar knows how to teach.

To Discuss

Everyone brought some kind of gift. Even the chieftains of the tribes brought gifts—they gave the jewels that Bezalel would work into the clothing for the High Priest. Why was it important for everyone to be involved in the making of the Tabernacle?

turned cold in the winter, believing that this was what God commanded in the Torah.

The sages rejected both groups as being untrue to the Torah. The sages said that God gave the Sabbath to the Jews to be a delight and a celebration. The Sabbath should be a taste of the world-to-come when things would return to the way they were in the time of the Garden of Eden, when work would not even be necessary. Jews, they said, should not suffer on the Sabbath.

Gifts for Adonai

After repeating the command for Sabbath to be observed, Moses tells the Israelites what is needed for making the sanctuary and the clothing for the priests. All that Adonai instructed Moses on the mountain is repeated. It was up to each Israelite how much to bring. Moses just told them the kinds of things that were required:

> Gold, silver, and copper; blue, purple, and crimson yarns, fine linen, and goats' hair; tanned ram skins, dolphin skins, and acacia wood; oil for lighting, spices for the anointing oil and for the aromatic incense; lapis lazuli and other stones for setting....

Moses informed the Israelites that Adonai called Bezalel by name to be the chief designer of the Tabernacle, and named Ohaliab as his assistant. Anyone who had been given a skill by Adonai should come and help them.

The people brought their gifts to Moses, who handed them to Bezalel and Ohaliab. Suddenly it became clear that the people were bringing too much!

> But when [the Israelites] continued to bring free-will offerings to him morning after morning, all the artisans who were engaged in the tasks of the sanctuary came, each from the task upon which he was engaged, and said to Moses, "The people are bringing more than is needed ... in the work that Adonai has commanded." Moses thereupon had this proclamation made throughout the camp: "Let no man nor woman make further ef-

fort toward gifts for the sanctuary!" So the people stopped bringing; their efforts had been more than enough for all the tasks to be done.

All the Things to Be Made

The Torah lists all the things that were made and how they were made. It tells how the Tabernacle and its coverings were crafted and how the inner Tent to cover the Ark was made. Bezalel made the Ark himself, with its cover of pure gold and its two cherubim or sphinxes. Then he made the table for the showbread and the seven-branched Menorah. Afterward he crafted the small altar for incense and the large altar for sacrifices. Next he made a laver or washstand out of copper. And the Torah adds that the copper for the laver was from "the mirrors of the women who performed tasks at the entrance of the Tent of Meeting."

In ancient times mirrors were often made out of metals like gold, silver, or brass. They were polished smooth so you could easily see your reflection in them. Rashi commented that at first Moses did not want to accept the women's mirrors as gifts, since mirrors are used for admiring oneself. It did not seem right to give God things that were used purely for human vanity. But God told Moses to accept the mirrors because the women had used them in Egypt to make themselves beautiful for their husbands so that the Israelites

To Consider

An old Yiddish saying has it that "Too much is no good." Adonai told Moses to take gifts from all who wanted to give them. But the people brought too much! Even the workers complained! Have you ever had too much of a good thing? How can too much of a good thing be bad?

Mirrors

Early humans found reflections in pools of water and soon discovered that they could polish stones and metals to make mirrors. Simple mirrors, like the one *far left*, were made by putting polished brass between two pieces of wood. Makeup was common—it could be mixed from simple ingredients—and every woman wanted a mirror to help her apply color around her eyes and rouge to her lips. Egyptians imported perfumed oils and expensive makeups from the east. Royal ladies placed jewelry or rouge and powders in shallow gold bowls like the elegant one at the *bottom*. And queens might think fine thoughts while gazing in a mirror with a handle bearing the image of the goddess Bat with her cow's ears and horns, and her promise of fertility (*left*). It was a real sacrifice when the Hebrew women offered their mirrors to Moses.

Quote to Remember

מַרְבִּים הָעָם לְהָבִיא מִדֵּי הָעֲבֹדָה לַמְּלָאכָה אֲשֶׁר־צִוָּה יְהֹוָה לַעֲשֹׂת אֹתָהּ.

The people are bringing more than is needed for the tasks in the work that Adonai has commanded.

would love one another and have many children. And that, surely, was a good thing.

The Tabernacle

Bezalel and the craftspeople made the enclosure for the Tabernacle. The greatest part of their labor was complete. Adonai had said, "Let them make Me a sanctuary so that I may dwell among them," and Moses, Bezalel, Ohaliab, and the people had made a portable sanctuary for God. Wherever they would go in their wanderings, the presence of Adonai would go with them.

Haftarah: I Kings 7:40-50

In building the sanctuary in the wilderness, Bezalel served as the chief architect for Moses. To build the Temple in Jerusalem, Solomon hired Hiram of Tyre to serve as his chief architect. This Hiram had the same name as the king of Tyre, but he was the child of an intermarriage between a man from Tyre and an Israelite mother.

The lines of the haftarah come from official records that probably were kept in the royal library. Every small detail is recorded by the scribes. It begins:

> Hiram made the pots, the shovels, and the basins to complete all the work he was doing for Solomon in the House of Adonai.

Different metals were used: bronze for objects that would be used near the Temple and gold for objects that stood close to the Holy of Holies and so had to be "more holy". In addition, Solomon ordered that the doors to the large hall of the Temple be covered with gold. So many objects were created that the scribes either lost count of them or had difficulty counting them, so Solomon decided to leave them unweighed.

The haftarah tells a small piece of the work of creating the Temple. Other pieces are found in the *haftarot* for *Terumah* and *Pikudei*. The records given here are repeated almost word for word in the Book of Second Chronicles (4:11-18).

Serving Adonai with articles of beauty has always been important to Jews. Jewish artists still lavish their greatest care on objects for our synagogues, especially those things nearest to the ark that

Creating God's Place

פְּקוּדֵי
Pikudei
Exodus 38:21-40:38

These Are the Records

Pikudei begins, "These are the records of the Tabernacle, the Tabernacle of the Covenant." Moses appointed Aaron's son Ithamar to be the accountant. His job was to check on everything that Bezalel and Oholiab had made. The record includes the gold, the silver, and the copper—how much was used in each part of the sanctuary. Ithamar also tallies up the weight of all the half-shekels collected in the census, given by each male over twenty years of age. Weighing all the silver they gave, Ithamar reports that there are 603,550 households in the community.

Ithamar accounts for everything used to make the special clothing or vestments of Aaron and the other priests—the yarn; the ephod with two large jewels engraved with the names of the tribes; the breastplate and its twelve jewels, each engraved with the name of a tribe; the robe with its hem decorated with bells and pomegranates; the tunics; the headdress of the High Priest; the turbans of the other priests; the linen pants or breeches; the sashes; and the gold circlet made for Aaron, engraved with the words "Holy to Adonai". All this, Ithamar says after each item on the list, was done exactly "as Adonai had commanded Moses."

> Thus was completed all the work of the Tabernacle of the Tent of Meeting. The Israelites did so; just as Adonai had commanded Moses, so they did.

Presenting the Tabernacle to Moses

When everything was complete, Bezalel and Oholiab, all the designers and craftspeople, and all the Israelites presented the pieces of the Tabernacle to Moses for his inspection. From the biggest piece, the Tent of Meeting, to the smallest pieces, the poles and pegs; from objects of gold like the Ark of the Covenant to things like the bread for display, the in-

To Discuss

From ancient to modern times, accountants have been important to every society. Ithamar's records listed everything used in making the Tabernacle. Because of his careful record, everyone in Israel could point and say, "I brought gold, so my donation is right here in the Tabernacle"; or "I brought jewels, so my gift is right here in Aaron's uniform"; or "My silver is right here in the Tabernacle." Everyone could be sure that his or her gifts were used—nothing stolen or set aside—and everyone's gift was important. Without every gift there would be no Tabernacle. Look around your own synagogue. Are there ways that we still keep records of everything that is given?

Blessing the People

In Ithamar's list he repeats the words "as Adonai had commanded Moses" seven times. The commentators therefor compare the work of making the Tabernacle with the work of God's creation of the world. And just as God blessed the world as soon as it was completed, so Moses blessed the people of Israel as soon as the work of the Tabernacle was completed.

cense for burning, and the oil for lighting the lamps—they brought it all to Moses. "When Moses saw that they had performed all the tasks … Moses blessed them."

Setting Up the Tabernacle

> And Adonai spoke to Moses, saying: On the first day of the first month you shall set up the Tabernacle of the Tent of Meeting.

Some commentators believe that God's command was for Moses to set up the Tabernacle on the day we now call Rosh HaShanah, when we celebrate the birth of the world. The making of the Tabernacle, they say, is like another story of creation. But many Bible scholars believe that the day the Torah calls "the first day of the first month" really means the first day of the month Aviv ("spring") according to an old calendar based on farming. For farmers the new year came in the month of nature's rebirth. Either way, the idea is the same. The completion of the Tabernacle marks a new beginning for the people of Israel.

An Everlasting Priesthood

> You shall bring Aaron and his sons forward to the entrance of the Tent of Meeting and wash them with the water. Put the sacred vestments on Aaron, and anoint him and consecrate him, that he may serve Me as priest. Then bring his sons forward, put tunics on them, and anoint them as you have anointed their father, that they may serve Me as priests. This their anointing shall serve them for everlasting priesthood throughout the ages. This Moses did; just as Adonai had commanded him, so he did.

Most Bible scholars believe that this part of the story of Sinai—the making of the Tabernacle, the making of the uniforms of the priests, and the anointing (blessing with oil) of the priests—is told by the P (Priestly) source. The priests from the family of Aaron (Aaronides) wanted people to know how they became an "everlasting priesthood throughout the ages." They were chosen "just as Adonai had commanded" Moses at Sinai.

There was a time when not everyone would have agreed with this statement (see *Korach*). Scholars note that in Bible times, there were other priestly families. In addition to the Aaronide priests there were Mushite priests (called this because they came from the family of Moses) and Levite priests (from other families in the tribe of Levi). In the time of David two of these families served as priests in Jerusalem. But Solomon sent away one of the families and placed the Temple in the hands of the Aaronide priests. Hundreds of years after Sinai, when the Torah was finalized in writing, the P source included this story to say "this is how it was at Sinai, and this is how it is should be, now and forever."

Setting Up the Tabernacle

Moses sets up the whole Tabernacle and the Tent of Meeting. The lines about setting up the Tabernacle sound like a prayer or poem, constantly repeating the refrain "as Adonai had commanded Moses."

> He took the covenant and placed it in the ark… and brought the ark inside the Tabernacle ….— just as Adonai had commanded Moses.

> He placed the table in the Tent of Meeting …. He laid out the setting of bread before Adonai—as Adonai had commanded Moses.

> He placed the lampstand in the Tent of Meeting …. He lit the lamps before Adonai—as Adonai had commanded Moses.

> He placed the altar of gold in the Tent of Meeting …. He burned aromatic incense—as Adonai had commanded Moses.

> … At the entrance … he placed the altar of burnt offering …. He offered up the … offering—as Adonai had commanded Moses.

> He placed the laver … and put water in it for washing. …—as Adonai had commanded Moses.

Quote to Remember

כַּאֲשֶׁר צִוָּה יְהוָה אֶת־מֹשֶׁה.

Just as Adonai had commanded Moses.

Architects

The first pyramid, its temples, and its courtyards were designed by the Egyptian architect Imhotep (see sketch *below*). This extraordinary man was also a scribe, a healer, a sage. Pharaoh Djoser made Imhotep his vizier and honored him. Moses was already a sage and a scribe, and he would also be a healer. In directing the building of the Mishkan Moses became an architect. But there were important differences. The pyramid was built to improve Pharaoh's life after death. The Mishkan was built to improve the people's life in this world. Imhotep was made a god and worshiped by the Egyptians, but Moses was pleased to remain the humble servant of the One God.

The Way the Priests Tell It

When the P source tells the story in the Torah, the Tabernacle and the Tent of Meeting are combined. The Tent of Meeting is the Holy of Holies at the center of the Tabernacle, and Moses cannot go in—only the High Priest (a member of Aaron's family) can enter it. This is the way things were at the Temple in Jerusalem. Other Torah stories say the Tent of Meeting is outside the camp, and Joshua guards it. In these stories Moses can go into the Tent to speak with Adonai at any time even when the cloud covers it (see *Naso*.)

To Consider

We do not usually think of clouds as a wonderful thing. Cloudy days are not the best. Clouds block the light and warmth of the sun. Clouds bring rain. Are there good things about clouds? Why would the Israelite people feel good when they saw the cloud above the Tent of Meeting?

God Enters the Tabernacle

When Moses had finished the work, the cloud covered the Tent of Meeting, and the Presence of Adonai filled the Tabernacle. Moses could not enter the Tent of Meeting, because the cloud settled upon it, and the Presence of Adonai filled the Tabernacle. When the cloud lifted from the Tabernacle, the Israelites would set out, on their various journeys; but if the cloud did not lift, they would not set out until such time as it did lift. For over the Tabernacle a cloud of Adonai rested by day, and fire would appear in it by night, in the view of all the house of Israel throughout their journeys.

W. Gunther Plaut (1912-), a modern commentator, says, "We doubtless have before us a mixture of tradition and imagination, of ancient memories and records …" Elsewhere in the Torah we find different pictures of the Tabernacle and the Tent of Meeting. Sometimes the Torah speaks of the Tent of Meeting being "outside the camp" while the Tabernacle is said to be "in the center of the camp" (see *Naso*).

How can we explain the cloud by day and fire by night? Scientifically, it is not difficult. We only need to remember the altar for incense and the Menorah for light. The burning incense sent a great cloud of smoke rising above the Tabernacle. All day long the Israelites saw the cloud of smoke. All night long the priests kept the Menorah lamps burning. The red light on the cloud of burning incense looked just like a pillar of fire. Of course, when it was time to travel the priests stopped burning incense because they had to pack everything up to move. Now everyone in the camp could look and see that there was no more cloud above the Tabernacle, and they would know that it was time to journey on.

It is easy to explain how it looked. But we can only imagine how it felt. God had commanded, "Let them make Me a sanctuary so that I may dwell among them." The Israelites had joined together to create one sanctuary, just as God had created the world in the beginning. And now it truly felt that God was dwelling with them. All the scientific reasons in the world cannot match that special feeling of being close to God.

Completing the Book of Exodus

You have now surveyed the Book of Exodus (*Shemot* in Hebrew). Our way of saying "Congratulations on finishing the study of a book of the Torah" is to remind ourselves that we need strength to continue our studies. So we say *Hazak! Hazak! V'Nithazek!* "Be strong! Be strong! And may you be strengthened!" The study of Torah never ends. So *Hazak! Hazak! V'Nithazek!* and on to the Book of Leviticus!

חֲזַק חֲזַק וְנִתְחַזֵּק!

Explaining

If we can easily explain the cloud and the fire, it is possible that there really was some kind of portable Tabernacle built at Sinai. It may not be the one pictured in this portion—more likely, it was just a single Tent containing an Ark—but the Torah always combines history with mystery in wonderful ways.

Haftarah: I Kings 7:51-8:21

Pikudei tells of the completion of the Mishkan, the wilderness Tabernacle, while its haftarah tells of the completion of Solomon's Temple in Jerusalem. Solomon deposited all the objects that King David had made for the Temple inside it. Then, on Sukkot, he called the people to assemble.

While countless sacrifices were offered, the Ark of the Covenant was brought up from the city to the Temple mount. The Ark was placed in the Holy of Holies beneath the outspread wings of the cherubim (sphinxes). The poles used to carry the Ark were so long that, the Bible says, they can be seen above the cherubim "to this day".

All that was in the Ark were the two stone tablets that Moses placed there at Horeb [Sinai], where Adonai made a covenant with the Israelites…. As soon as the priests left the [inner] sanctuary, the cloud filled the House of Adonai and the priests could not stand to do their service. The Presence of Adonai filled the House of Adonai.

Solomon prayed "Now I have built for You a royal palace, a place You may dwell in forever." Solomon recalled how God promised his father David the kingship over Israel. David "set his heart" on building a Temple, but God said, "Not you, but your son … will build that House for My Presence." Solomon said, "See now, that promise has been kept!"

I made there a place for the Ark that holds the covenant that Adonai made with our ancestors in leading them out of Egypt.

Offerings

Codes

Books filled with laws are often known as "code books" (or just "codes") because they state things briefly. If you have played with secret codes (like alphabets where letters reverse: "z" stands for "a," "y" stands for "b," and so on), you know that you can write a whole book in a secret code. All the same, the code itself may be simple (once you discover its "key"). The law codes in Leviticus are not secret codes. With a little work, anyone can understand them.

The Book of Leviticus

The third book of the Torah is called *Vayikra* in Hebrew. The Hebrew name, like most names for books and portions, is the first important word in the first sentence. *Vayikra* means "called" or "summoned".

> Adonai called to Moses and spoke to him from the Tent of Meeting, saying, Speak to the Israelite people, and say to them: When any of you presents an offering of cattle to Adonai, you shall choose your offering from the herd or from the flock.

In Greek the book was named *Leviticus* because it collects laws or codes of law for the priests, and the Torah says that the priests were from the tribe of Levi. This makes Leviticus a very unusual book.

In ancient religions, priests were thought to have magic power because they kept their laws and rituals secret from the people. But, in Leviticus Adonai commands Moses, "Speak to the Israelite people...." The priestly codes are given to all of us. As part of our covenant with Adonai (as stated in *Yitro* in the Book of Exodus), we Israelites are a "kingdom of priests and a holy people". So the laws—even laws for priests—are not kept hidden or secret from us.

The World of Sacrifice

Many nations believed that the spirits of the dead, gods, and demons required food. One Babylonian tablet says that gods must be fed an evening meal, a main morning meal, and a second morning meal. In Egypt and Mesopotamia, vast amounts of food were brought to their temples every day (and more on festival days). The food was placed before the statues of the gods. Most of it was later removed before it spoiled, to be eaten by either the priests or the king. Bernard Bamberger (1904–1980), a modern commentator, notes that ancient people thought the gods lived not by eating the food, but by inhaling it. We find a trace of this, he says, when the Torah often repeats that the priest

> shall turn the sacrifice into smoke on the altar …
> an offering by fire of pleasing odor to Adonai.

In any case, the Torah never claims that Adonai needed to be fed like other gods. Most Israelite sacrifices were divided, with large parts going to the priests and their families and other parts going to feed the poor. And some sacrifices, like the Passover sacrifice, were returned to the person who gave them so that his or her family could "share a meal with Adonai." Usually only a small amount of the sacrificed animal or grain or bird was burned to produce the "pleasing odor".

The Burnt-Offering

In this portion the Torah gives five groups of laws for five different kinds of sacrifices. Four groups begin with the word "if". They start this way: "If your offering is *[this kind of sacrifice]*, then …" followed by how the sacrifice should be made. Only one group begins with the word "when" instead of "if".

S. David Sperling (1941-), a modern scholar, explains that the way the groups of laws begin indicates that at least four of the kinds of sacrifices were already well known to the Israelites. The codes here do not teach new kinds of sacrifice, only the proper way to offer sacrifices to Adonai.

The first group of laws begins by saying:

> If his offering is a burnt offering … bring it to the
> entrance of the Tent of Meeting, for acceptance …
> before Adonai.

In Hebrew, the burnt-offering is called *olah*, "what goes up". Israelites often brought burnt-offerings when they thought they had sinned and wanted to atone, so it was usually voluntary. Richer folk brought bulls or rams or he-goats. People who were poorer could bring turtledoves or young pigeons. The person bringing the sacrifice placed a hand on it to show that it was dedicated to Adonai. Then the Israelite or the priest slaughtered it. Blood from the sacrifice was col-

Quote to Remember

אִשֵּׁה רֵיחַ נִיחֹחַ לַיהוָה.

An offering by fire of pleasing odor to Adonai.

Why Sacrifices Began

The Torah tells how sacrifices began soon after creation, in the story of Cain and Abel. But the Torah does not say *why* the brothers decided to bring sacrifices to Adonai. Archaeologists have uncovered evidence of sacrifices made more than 70,000 years ago. Some think that these early sacrifices were made to feed dead ancestors. Some think they were made to please good spirits or bribe evil spirits. From the beginning of history, every ancient nation sacrificed animals, grains, drinks, and sometimes even perfumes and incense.

Much or Little

Comments on Leviticus made by the sages of the Talmud were later collected into a book called *Sifra*. Speaking of the burnt-offering, *Sifra* says, "Whether you offer much [a bull or ram] or little [a pigeon or turtledove] makes no difference, if only your heart is turned toward God."

Minchah

After the destruction of the Second Temple the Rabbis taught that prayer should replace the sacrifices of animals and grain. To remind us that our prayers were now "sacrifices", they called the afternoon prayer service *Minchah*.

To Consider

When leaders—priests or chieftains—sin, even accidentally, they often cause the community to sin, too. In talking about the sin-offering of a leader, the Torah uses the word "when" instead of "if". One medieval commentator said that the word "when" is carefully chosen, since leaders almost always sin. Do you think he was right? Do you think that it is hard to be a leader without "missing the mark" sometimes?

lected in bowls and sprinkled at the corners of the altar (so that some would spray on every side). If the offering was an animal, the hide was removed and given to the priest as payment. The rest of the offering was divided into parts and burned in the flame on the altar.

The Meal-Offering

> When you present to Adonai a meal-offering … it shall be brought to the priest who shall take it up to the altar. The priest shall remove [a small amount] … and turn it into smoke on the altar as an offering by fire, of pleasing odor to Adonai. The rest of the meal-offering shall be for Aaron and his sons, a most holy portion …. No meal-offering for Adonai shall be made with leaven, for no leaven or honey may be turned into smoke as an offering by fire to Adonai.
>
> You shall season your every offering of meal with salt; you shall not omit from your meal offering the salt of your covenant with God; with all your offerings you must offer salt.

The second kind of sacrifice, the meal-offering, is called a *minchah*. This word means "gift" and it is sometimes used to mean any kind of sacrifice. A meal-offering was grain or flour mixed with oil and salt and sometimes sprinkled with frankincense (to make a more pleasant aroma). The Torah teaches two lessons here.

The Torah says that Adonai wishes no leaven on the altar. Leaven is anything like yeast that causes flour to rise. Year in and year out, we eat bread made with leaven. But one week each year, on Passover, we clean all the leaven out of our homes and eat only matzah, unleavened bread. So once a year we make our homes holy the way Adonai's altar is holy, by removing anything made with leaven. In other words, on Pesach we eat as if we were at God's table.

Before refrigerators and freezers—through most of history—salt was used in almost everything that was eaten. Salt helps to preserve foods. In ancient times, sharing a meal was often spoken of as "taking salt together." Several times the Bible speaks of an agreement made through eating together as a "covenant of salt".

The Sacrifice of Well-Being

In Hebrew, the sacrifice of well-being is called *zevach sh'la-mim*, "slaughter for welfare". In another portion of Leviticus we learn that most of this sacrifice was returned to the person who brought it so that a festive meal could be made from it and guests could be invited to share a sacred meal together. In other words, the sacrifice of well-being was used for festive occasions and celebrations.

The Sin-Offering

If people learned or feared that they had sinned by accident, they could bring an offering called the *chatat* or "sin offering". In Hebrew the word *chatat* is related to the word for "bow" as in "bow and arrow". For the Israelites, the idea of sin was "missing the mark" or "not hitting the target." Of course, if a person sinned on purpose, this offering was of no use. A person who sinned on purpose had to accept punishment and repent and offer prayer on Yom Kippur. But the *chatat* could be offered by a priest or a chieftain or by anyone who felt guilty because of some accidental sin, something they had done that had "missed the mark."

The Guilt-Offering

An *asham*, a "guilt-offering" or "penalty-offering", was supposed to be a ram. If someone took property from another person, he or she had to return the property and give an additional twenty percent of its value to the person. Afterward he or she had to bring the ram as an offering to Adonai, and then the "guilt" or *asham* would be forgiven. Of course, if you were poor, you could substitute other things for the ram—a meal offering, a sheep, even a pair of birds.

Salt

Rashi repeats a midrash about the "covenant of salt". When God separated the waters below (the rivers, lakes, and oceans) from the waters above (heaven), the waters below complained that they were far from God and being treated as inferior. God comforted them, saying that one day the Temple would be built and the salt in the waters below would be used in every sacrifice meant to bring heaven and earth closer together.

To Consider

After the Temple was destroyed and sacrifices were no longer offered, some rabbis thought that prayer would replace the sacrifices. Other rabbis said that doing good deeds—particularly doing good for others without any hope of reward for yourself—was a better replacement for sacrifices. What do you think? Which is a better replacement—prayer or good deeds? Why?

A Test Case for the Guilt-Offering

How does the guilt-offering work? Suppose you took a dollar from someone's desk and later felt guilty. You would first have to ask for forgiveness, then pay back $1.20 (or, according to later sages, $1.25) and then bring a sacrifice to the Temple. This might make you think twice about "borrowing" without permission. You might agree that it is better to ask in the first place.

Accidental Sins

All five of these kinds of sacrifices are made when a person sins accidentally. One modern commentator, Jacob Milgrom (1923-), says that putting accidental sins first shows how important they were to the community. When we are careless or insensitive in the way we treat others, we cause God to turn away from us. Then, even as we ask forgiveness from the people we hurt, we also have to ask for God's forgiveness.

The usual Hebrew word for "sacrifice" is *korban,* meaning "approaching" or "drawing closer to". In this word we get a better sense of the reason for sacrifices in ancient Israel. We can understand the idea of sacrifice as a way of "approaching" or "drawing closer to" Adonai.

Haftarah: Isaiah 43:21-44:23

Vayikra begins the Book of Leviticus, which gives the laws of sacrifice. In the haftarah Isaiah reminds the Israelites in Babylonia that they did not keep these laws of sacrifice—and now they cannot keep them—so they must bring offerings of their hearts instead.

In the first part Isaiah speaks of how the Israelites who neglected sacrifice sinned before Adonai. But Adonai will not forget them. "For I am the first, I am the last; there is no God but Me."

The second part speaks of the foolishness of making idols. People make iron and think they are mighty, but a little hunger makes the mighty grow weak. People carve dolls to set up in shrines, but they use the leftover wood to roast their meat and warm themselves. They pray to the statues they made, saying, "You are my god. Save me." They never ask themselves, "Should I ... bow to a block of wood?" They never admit, "I am holding a fake."

The third part is the truth that Isaiah wishes to drive home.

> Remember these things, O Jacob, for You are My servant, O Israel: I formed you. You are My servant, O Israel, do not forget Me!

The idol makers have it all backward: People don't make gods; it is Adonai who "formed you." Gods don't serve people; but "You are My servant, O Israel."

The haftarah ends with words of praise for Adonai who brought Jacob (Israel) out of bondage and who should be glorified by the Israelites.

Memory

צו
Tzav
Leviticus 6:1-8:36

The Torah of Sacrifice

> Adonai spoke to Moses, saying … "This is the to-
> rah of the burnt-offering …."

In this portion, *Tzav* ("command"), the laws of sacrifices begin with "This is the torah of *[this kind of sacrifice]*…" When
we say "Torah" we usually mean the first five books of the Bible, "the Five Books of Moses"; or else we mean the handwritten scroll of these books that we read in the synagogue.
But *torah* does not have either of those meanings here. Old
translations replace the word *torah* here with "law". The new
English translation replaces the word *torah* with "ritual". In
Hebrew and in Jewish tradition, the word *torah* has many
meanings.

Two Torahs

Beginning in the first century B.C.E., the Rabbis taught that
the Torah was given in two parts. They said the *Torah
she-bi'chtav*, the "Torah That Is Written", was mainly set
down by Moses. But, while Adonai was giving Moses the
written Torah, Adonai also taught Moses the *Torah she-bi'al
peh*, the "Torah That Is Memorized", a second Torah that is
"oral" or "spoken". The Rabbis taught,

> Moses received the [Spoken] Torah at Sinai and
> taught it to Joshua, Joshua [taught it] to the El-
> ders, and the Elders [taught it] to the prophets,
> and the prophets [taught it] to the members of
> the Great Sanhedrin. [MISHNAH AVOT 1:1]

The members of the Great Sanhedrin—the assembly of
Israel's greatest scholars and judges—continued to teach
the Spoken Torah, adding their words to it. By the time of
the famous sage Hillel, the Spoken Torah was so large that it
was difficult to remember. Hillel may have been the first to
write down the Spoken Torah, to make it easier for his stu-

Quote to Remember

זאת תוֹרַת הָעֹלָה.

This is the torah of the burnt-offering ….

The Repetition

Why is Rabbi Judah's textbook called the Mishnah, "the repetition"? Because when we recite something we have memorized, we are "repeating" it. Even though the Mishnah is long, everything in it was arranged so that it could be memorized. In those days books had to be copied by hand and few copies were ever available. "A+" students were those who could recite all six divisions—the entire Mishnah—by heart!

dents to memorize. The great sage Rabbi Akiba created the same kind of textbook for his students, as did others. Around the year 200 C.E. Rabbi Judah the Prince, head of the Sanhedrin, brought all the texts together and made one master textbook called the *Mishnah*, "the repetition."

Even then the Spoken Torah continued to grow. More discussions and arguments were collected around the divisions of the Mishnah. These collections were called *gemara*, "completion". Around 400, in the Land of Israel, the Mishnah and *gemara* were combined to form the first *Talmud* or "Teaching". But the Talmud that we usually study today is the Babylonian Talmud, which was completed around the year 600.

Believe it or not, sometimes when we say "the Torah" we mean all of the Written and the Spoken Torah: the Five Books of Moses, the Mishnah, and the two Talmuds.

Even *Your* Torah

But the word "Torah" means more than that, too. It means any "instruction" or "teaching". So we may speak of "the torah of Solomon", meaning everything that the wise King Solomon taught us. Or we may speak of "the torah of science", meaning everything that we learn through science. There is even the idea that everything wise said by any Jew is a part of the Spoken Torah, so we could even speak of *your* "torah" if *you* say something that adds to our learning. In this way, laws are "torah", since they teach us behaviors; and rituals are "torah", too. All this—books, scrolls, instruction, teachings, laws, and rituals—in one Hebrew word.

The P-Teller

The rituals of the burnt-offering, the meal-offering, the sin-offering, the guilt-offering, and the offering of well-being are all repeated in *Tzav* with more details about how the priests should behave. Bible scholars tell us that nearly everything in the entire Book of Leviticus is the work of the "P" or Priestly source. But the laws in *Vayikra*, where each group began with "If your offering is [this kind of sacrifice], then ...," are different from the laws here in *Tzav*, where each group begins "This is the torah of *[this kind of sacrifice]*...." Why doesn't the Torah combine the two groups of instructions to make one code of law for the various kinds of sacrifices? The answer has to do with memorizing.

Remember, there were many priests and very few handwritten copies of any set of rules. So rules were memorized by the priests. If the Torah combined the rules, then priests who had memorized them might no longer recognize them. Priests would have to memorize new rules! So, the Torah includes the rules just as they had been memorized, putting one set of rules after another, losing nothing!

This is what we found in Genesis, too, when there was more than one version of the same story. Some people and some tribes remembered a story one way, and some memorized it another way. Every version was included. The rule used in bringing the Torah together was always the same: Stories and laws from different times and places were set side by side in the Torah. The idea was that what was already memorized was too important to be forgotten.

The Sacrifice of Well-Being

> This is the [torah] ritual of the sacrifice of well-being that one may offer to Adonai: If one offers it for thanksgiving .... [Or if one offers] a votive or a freewill-offering .... The offering to Adonai from a sacrifice of well-being must be presented by that one [personally] ....

The Torah gives three reasons for the sacrifice of well-being. It can be made to give thanks to God (a thanksgiving offering), made because of a vow (a votive offering), or made as a sacrifice freely given from a full heart (a freewill-offering).

Rashi states that it was a custom for people to bring thanksgiving offerings when they returned safely from a sea voyage or a journey through the wilderness, when they were released from prison, or when they recovered from some illness. It might sound strange that he added "released from prison," but in Rashi's time innocent people were often kidnaped and held in prison. They were only released when their friends and relatives collected a ransom and gave it to

To Discuss

The idea of bringing thanksgiving offerings—offerings that were not required as taxes or demanded by God—was unusual in ancient times. Sacrifices were normally only brought when they were required. Now that the days of sacrifice are over, how can we show our appreciation of God?

Assemble the Whole Community

Of course, the entrance to the Tent of Meeting was not a large one, yet God commanded that Moses should assemble "the whole community" there. On this occasion, Rashi says, God miraculously made the community small enough and the entrance to the tent large enough! But Ibn Ezra said "the whole community" actually means the heads of the tribes and the elders. They always represented the whole community.

An Offering

Below: Top of a statuette found on a ziggurat in Mari, Mesopotamia. A man brings a sacrifice to his god.

their captors. What Rashi is saying, then, is that people would bring such sacrifices to thank God for their safety.

Abraham Ibn Ezra noted that it was very common in Bible times for people to make vows in time of trouble or sorrow. A person might say something like "If only Adonai will [*do such and such*], then I will be forever grateful." A person who made such a vow would bring a votive offering in thanks. But a freewill-offering, as Ibn Ezra says, could be made any time a person felt moved to offer it.

Most of the meat of the offering of well-being was returned to the person offering thanks. But it had to be eaten either that day or by the next day. This was a lot of meat. Family and guests—and often even the poor—would be invited to join in the celebration, making a festive meal out of the offering of well-being. In this way people shared their thanks with Adonai, with the priests, with their family, and with the whole community of Israel.

Ordaining the Priests

The Torah now tells us how Moses prepared Aaron and his sons to officially become priests. The ceremony was called "ordination", and it lasted seven days.

Adonai spoke to Moses, saying: Take Aaron along with his sons, and the priestly garments, the anointing oil, the bull of sin-offering, the two rams, and the basket of unleavened bread; and assemble the whole community at the entrance of the Tent of Meeting. Moses did as Adonai commanded him.

Moses dressed Aaron in his special costume. He put a little oil on Aaron's head to anoint him. He dressed the priests in their robes, breeches, and turbans.

He brought forward the ... the ram of ordination. Aaron and his sons laid their hands on the ram's head, and it was slaughtered. Moses took some of its blood and put it on the ridge of Aaron's right ear, and on the thumb of his right hand, and on the big toe of his right foot. Moses then brought forward the sons of Aaron, and put some of the blood on the ridges of their right ears, and on the thumbs of their right hands, and on the big toes of their right feet. The rest of the blood Moses dashed against every side of the altar.

Philo of Alexandria said that the ear, the thumb, and the toe have a lesson to teach us. The priest's whole life had to become holy, "for words are judged by hearing, the hand is the symbol of action, and the foot [is the symbol] of the pilgrimage of life."

To Consider

Rabbis and cantors are still ordained, but we no longer pour oil on their heads or put blood on their ears, their thumbs, and their toes. The ordination of the ancient priests lasted for seven days, but training for ordination today may take many years of study. These are some of the differences. Can you think of some other differences? In what ways do you think that ordination remains the same?

Haftarah: Jeremiah 7:21-8:3; 9:22-23

The Torah speaks of sacrifices, and so does this haftarah; but Jeremiah reminds the people that sacrifices are not enough. They must be joined with a godly way of life.

The haftarah is part of a larger sermon preached by Jeremiah. It is called the "Temple sermon", because the people thought that the Temple and its sacrifices were enough to save them from their sins. But Jeremiah said that true repentance is not bringing sacrifices, but turning away from sinning. Adonai says,

> From the day I brought your ancestors out of Egypt to this moment, I have sent you My servants, the prophets, day after day I sent them.

The people would not listen to the prophets then, and they will not listen to Jeremiah now. Adonai recounts many sins of the Israelites and concludes,

"The day is coming when this valley will no longer be called Tophet ... but the Valley of Slaughter."

The punishment will be severe. There will be too many bodies to bury and none to bury them. The towns will fall silent. There will be no celebrations. Even the bones of those who sinned—leaders and commoners alike—will be spread out under the heavenly bodies they worshiped and consulted, to become fertilizer for the ground. Those that survive will prefer death to life.

The Rabbis added two verses from the next chapter to soften the harsh ending of Jeremiah's sermon. The wise should not be proud of wisdom, nor the rich be proud of their wealth; let them glory in knowing and understanding the ways of Adonai, "for in this do I delight, says Adonai."

Differences

The Presence of God

The priests were ordained in seven days. "On the eighth (*Shemini*) day Moses called Aaron and his sons, and the elders of Israel...." Moses tells the priests they are ready. They should offer the sacrifices as they learned to do. "For today," Moses says, "Adonai will appear to you." When the first sacrifices were performed:

> Aaron lifted his hands toward the people and blessed them; and he stepped down after offering the sin-offering, the burnt-offering, and the offering of well-being. Moses and Aaron then went inside the Tent of Meeting. When they came out, they blessed the people; and the Presence of Adonai appeared to all the people. Fire came forth from before Adonai and consumed the burnt offering and the fat parts on the altar. And all the people saw, and shouted, and fell on their faces.

What does the Torah mean when it says, "the Presence of Adonai appeared to all the people"? In Hebrew, the word for "Presence" is *Kavod*, "glory" or "honor". So the people do not see Adonai directly. What they see is God's "glory". This is a bit easier for us to imagine.

We could say that they see the glory of Adonai in the faces of Moses and Aaron as the two come out of the Holy of Holies in the center of the Tent of Meeting. This reminds us of the poetic idea that Moses wore a veil over his face because his face was so bright with God's light that people could hardly bear to look at him.

Or we could say that "the Presence of Adonai" is like the feeling we get when we stand and open the Holy Ark in our synagogues. When the Ark is open, we feel that we are witnessing something special, something very holy. We feel we are "in the Presence of Adonai".

Bible scholars remind us that Adonai's Presence often appears in a cloud or in a fire. When Moses and Aaron opened the curtain to come out of the inner part of the Tent of Meeting, a cloud of incense probably followed them out, and the reflection of the fire burning inside the tent was caught in the cloud, coloring it. This, too, could be what the Torah means when it says that the people saw "the Presence of Adonai".

Nadab and Abihu

> Now Aaron's sons Nadab and Abihu each took his fire pan, put fire in it, and laid incense on it; and they offered before Adonai alien fire …. And fire came forth from Adonai and consumed them; thus they died …. Then Moses said to Aaron, "This is what Adonai meant when [Adonai] said, "Through those near to Me I show Myself holy, and gain glory before all the people." And Aaron was silent.

Suddenly the same fire that was so glorious as "the Presence of Adonai" kills two of Aaron's sons. Bible commentators throughout time have disagreed about what Nadab and Abihu did to deserve this terrible punishment. Many say that bringing the "alien" or "strange" fire was their sin. Others point to the laws that come right after their deaths—laws forbidding priests to perform sacred duties if they have been drinking. Perhaps Nadab and Abihu were celebrating too much. They may have been punished because they were drunk. Or their drinking may have made them careless. In any case, it was a terrible occurrence.

The Duty of the Priests

Aaron had just lost two of his sons, but he was "silent". In fact, Moses told Aaron and Aaron's younger sons, Eleazar and Ithamar, not to bare their heads or tear their clothes as signs of mourning. It was all right for others in their family to mourn the sad loss of Nadab and Abihu, but not for his father and his two brothers. Nachmanides reminds us that Aaron and his remaining sons were anointed priests. They

The Sons of Aaron

Modern Bible scholar Tikvah Frymer-Kensky (1944-2006) compares priests in ancient Israel with nuclear scientists today. Coming close to holiness, she says, is dangerous, like coming close to atomic energy. In both cases, the slightest mistake could mean instant death. But another modern scholar, Ismar Schorsch (1925-), believes that this story is about "one of the Bible's central themes: the price of being chosen." He points to a similar story that comes much later, in the Book of Samuel, when Eli was the High Priest. Eli's sons, Hophni and Phinehas, were also priests, but they behaved like spoiled children. They took more than their share of things, did not give proper service to God on the altar, and even ignored the warnings of their father. They, too, were both killed on the same day. Schorsch agrees with the commentary in *Sifra* that leaders—priests, prophets, kings, elders—have to be very careful about everything they do because, as Adonai says, "I show Myself holy and gain glory" through "those near to Me."

To Consider

Wine and beer are two of the oldest forms of drink—and often they were safer than water. We have already seen how wine-making made the chief cupbearer a part of Pharaoh's royal court. The art of making wine is ancient (as shown on the wall painting from Thebes, *above*), and the Israelites may have learned it from the Egyptians. By Roman times the Land of Israel was famous for its wine. And making blessings over wine became a part of our religion. In this portion, though, the Torah teaches that there are times when priests are not allowed to drink wine or other alcoholic beverages. When is wine a good drink? When is it bad?

could not pause to mourn because at that moment they were still "on duty".

> And Adonai spoke to Aaron, saying: Drink no wine or other intoxicant, you or your sons, when you enter the Tent of Meeting, that you may not die. This is a law for all time throughout the ages, for you must distinguish (*le-havdil*) between the sacred and the profane, and between the unclean and the clean; and you must teach the Israelites all the laws which Adonai has imparted to them through Moses.

In having Adonai speak directly to Aaron, the Torah goes right to the heart of the meaning of the priesthood in Israel. Priests must always have a clear head to tell the difference between what is holy and what is not holy. They must always have a clear head so that they can teach Adonai's laws to the people of Israel.

Is Aaron Being Punished?

Now the three priests—Aaron and his sons—continue their work. But Moses suddenly grows angry with Eleazar and Ithamar. He tells them that they did not eat the sin offering as they should have. This could mean danger for all of Israel, as Moses says, "For it is most holy, and [Adonai] has given it to you [to eat] to remove the guilt of the community...." But Aaron speaks to Moses and answers for all three of them, saying, Today my eldest sons were taken from me, and I must surely be partly to blame. Adonai would not approve the sin offering for the people if I (or my sons) were the ones to eat it today.

Why should Aaron feel partly to blame for the death of his sons? The Midrash answers that Aaron was never punished for making the golden calf. So when Nadab and Abihu died, Aaron felt that it was partly because Adonai was punishing him for that sin. Aaron could not feel holy right then. And he knew the difference between what is holy and what is not. If he ate the sacrifice that day, the sacrifice would not be holy either. In the Torah, Moses agrees with Aaron; and the first half of the parashah of *Shemini*—the story of what happened on the eighth day—comes to an end.

Clean and Unclean

The second half of the parashah lists animals, fish, birds, and other creatures that are clean or unclean. Those that are clean may be eaten by the Israelites. Those that are unclean are taboo—Israelites are not permitted to eat them.

Generally, the laws allow Israelites to eat animals that have split hooves, chew their cud, and walk on all four legs. Generally, any fish that has both scales and fins is clean and may be eaten. Most birds are clean and may be eaten, but birds like vultures, eagles, and hawks that feed off other animals are not clean and may not be eaten. Insects may not be eaten except for a few like locusts, grasshoppers, and crickets. Animals like moles, mice, lizards, and chameleons are also declared unclean and may not be eaten.

These laws are neatly arranged. They are like a catalog of the animals of the ancient Near East. Visiting the list is a little like visiting a biblical zoo. But the point of the list is to set apart those foods which are clean from those which are unclean. If a person or a utensil (like a cooking pot) touches the dead carcass of an unclean thing, the person or utensil also becomes "unclean" and has to be washed and to wait until the next morning to be "clean" again.

Kashrut

Based on this portion's list and other lists in the Torah, the Rabbis constructed the laws of Jewish eating called *kashrut*, "purity". In the Torah, foods are clean (*tahor*) or unclean (*tamei*). In the laws of kashrut, things are either *kosher*, "pure", or *terefah*, "idolatrous". (Terefah comes from the word for household gods, *terafim*—you may remember the story in *Vayeitzei* about Rachel stealing the household gods of her father Laban.) But even before kashrut came into being, the Torah's laws of clean and unclean were kept by Israelites for a long time. Most Bible scholars believe that these laws are unique to the Israelites.

To Consider

In this parashah we see that things can become unclean in a kind of magnetic way, just by touching something else that is unclean. According to the Torah, things can also become very holy by touching other things that are very holy. People who are leaders are like this, too. If a leader comes too close to something that is "unclean", we stop trusting him or her. Use your imagination. In what ways can our leaders become more holy?

Is Health the Reason?

The philosopher Maimonides was also a physician. He believed that the laws of clean and unclean were given for an important reason. Israelites who obeyed these laws, he said, would be healthier. He set out to prove that all the forbidden animals are actually unhealthy to eat. He may have been somewhat right, of course, but the Torah never gives this reason. In fact, modern science tells us that it is as dangerous for human beings to eat beef as pork. But in the Torah, beef is clean and pork is unclean. So health is probably not the reason for the dietary laws.

To Consider

The dietary laws include many taboos—things that are forbidden for either religious or superstitious reasons. Anthropologists, who study human behavior, tell us that every human group (nation or religion) has taboos that help set it apart from other human groups. Can you think of something (a food or an action) that is "taboo" in your family? In what ways are taboos good for us? In what ways can taboos be harmful to us?

The Purpose of Dietary Laws

Did laws that control what we eat have a purpose? Near the end of the list, the Torah says, "For I Adonai am your God; you shall sanctify yourselves and be holy, for I am holy." This is the reason that the Torah gives for these laws. The list concludes with the words

> These are the instructions concerning animals, birds, all living creatures that move in water, and all creatures that swarm on earth, for distinguishing (*le-havdil*) between the unclean and the clean, between the living things that may be eaten and the living things that may not be eaten.

Philo believed that the laws of clean and unclean foods were given to teach us self-control. In the Garden of Eden, God told Adam and Eve that they could eat of any tree except one. Adam and Eve were forced to leave Eden when they ate fruit from that forbidden tree—that is, when they proved that they could not control themselves. In these laws, Philo says, God gives us a second chance to prove that we are not like the beasts of the jungle, that we human beings can learn to control ourselves.

Most rabbis, even today, teach that the purpose of these laws was to set Israel apart from other nations. This is what we do to make things holy (*kadosh*): We set them apart. Just as Adonai is holy—set apart from all things—so the dietary laws make us holy by setting us apart from unclean food.

Le-Havdil—the Connection

Adonai told Aaron that the work of the priests was *le-havdil*, "to know the difference" between holy and ordinary things, between unclean and clean things. And the word *le-havdil* appears again at the end of the list of forbidden foods, since the list is to help us *le-havdil*, "to make a difference" between clean and unclean foods.

Rabbi Joel Oseran (1949-) reminds us that *lehavdil* has the same root as *Havdalah*, the ceremony that ends each Shabbat. In the *Havdalah* prayer we celebrate differences: between the Sabbath and the six days of creation, between light and darkness, between Israel and the other nations, and also "between that which is holy and that which is un-holy. ... If we can tell the difference," Oseran says, "then we can learn to be more God-like in the ways we behave." As it says in *Shemini*:

> For I Adonai am [the One] who brought you up from the land of Egypt to be your God: you shall be holy, for I am holy.

Haftarah: 2 Samuel 6:1-7:17

The Rabbis connected the tragic deaths of Nadab and Abihu in the Torah with the death of Uzzah in this haftarah. The broad idea is that coming close to holiness can be very dangerous unless you are properly prepared.

David decided to bring the Ark to Jerusalem. (For the first time we hear that the Ark has on it Adonai's name and the words "enthroned on the cherubim [sphinxes]".) They put the Ark on a new cart and began the procession with David and the Israelites dancing before the Ark. But Uzzah tried to stop the Ark from tipping by touching it, and Adonai was so enraged that Uzzah suddenly died.

David stopped the parade and took the Ark to the home of Obed-Edom. It rested there for three months. David was told that it brought much blessing to the house of Obed-Edom. So David went to lead the Ark to Jerusalem. He wore only an ephod (see *Titzaveh*) as he danced with all his might.

As the Ark entered the city, David's wife Michal (daughter of Saul) saw him dancing and "despised him." The Ark was placed in a tent that David had made for it. Later he and Michal had a quarrel about his dancing and the dignity a king should show. The Bible seems to say that Michal was punished for disapproving of David's behavior.

David wanted to build a Temple for the Ark, but the prophet Nathan dreamed the word of Adonai. He told the king that Adonai would make the people (and David) safe from all enemies, but the Temple would be built by David's son and not by David.

> Your house and your kingdom shall always be secure; and your throne shall be established for all time.

Blood

When Adonai accepted Abel's sacrifice, Cain was upset. But Adonai told Cain not to fret. "If you do the right thing," Adonai said, "it lifts up your spirit; but if you do not do the right thing, then sin crouches at your door, waiting for you to do more bad things. Even then," Adonai said, "people can learn to conquer the evil that is in them."

To Consider

We still believe that unclean things can make clean things unclean by touching or contacting them. What are some of the unclean things in the world that can truly hurt us? What are some ways we have of making these unclean things clean again?

Childbirth

Tazria means "[she] brings forth seeds." Of course, women do not really bring forth children the way plants bring forth seeds. But in a way, every child is a seed of the next generation. Here is how *Tazria* begins:

> Adonai spoke to Moses, saying: Speak to the Israelite people thus: When a woman at childbirth bears a male; she shall be unclean seven days … She shall remain in a state of blood purification for thirty-three days; she shall not touch any consecrated thing, nor enter the sanctuary until her time of purification is completed. If she bears a female, she shall be unclean two weeks … and she shall remain in a state of blood purification for sixty-six days.

Blood is the stuff of life, and humans have always known this. In the second story of Creation, the Hebrew word *adam* ("human") is connected to two words: *adamah* ("earth") and *dam* ("blood"). Our "humanness" comes from the earth, and when we die our blood returns to the earth.

The Story of Cain and Abel

Blood is central to the story of Cain and Abel, told in *Bereishit*, the very first parashah. Cain was a farmer. Abel was a shepherd. Both brought offerings to Adonai. Cain brought grain from his field, and Abel brought the finest firstborns from his flock. The Torah says that "Adonai paid heed to Abel and his offering, but to Cain and his offering, [Adonai] paid no heed." One day Cain and Abel were in the field arguing, and Cain killed Abel.

> Adonai said to Cain, "Where is your brother Abel?" And he said, "I do not know. Am I my brother's keeper?" Then [Adonai] said, "What have you

done? Hark, your brother's blood cries out to Me from the ground!"

There are many messages in the tale of Cain and Abel. The one that interests us now is about blood: When *dam* (blood) is spilled, the *dam* cries out from the *adamah* (ground)—and the cries of the *dam* summon Adonai. In other words, the same Adonai who gives us life wants to be sure that the stuff of life (blood) is never wasted. It is a sin for human beings "to spill blood" (to take life).

The Torah says that a murderer is punished by Adonai. Even a murderer put to death by a human court has to answer to Adonai for spilling the blood of another person.

But spilling blood does not apply only to murderers. In a way, we spill blood all the time. We human beings must take life in order to go on living. We must kill the living creations of God—plants and animals—for our food. God understands that. And in the Torah, God provided two ways for ancient Israel to atone—to ask for forgiveness—for having to spill blood.

The first way to atone was through the daily sin-offering made by the priests for all of the Israelite people. By offering an animal to Adonai Israelites shared with God the pain of sacrificing life—animal and plant—as food. We demonstrated that we understood that all life comes from Adonai.

The second way to atone was through the proper treatment of blood, the stuff of life. Blood had to be returned to the earth. When the priests made sacrifices, they threw the blood at the foot of the altar, allowing it to flow back into the earth. When Israelites slaughtered meat at home, they buried the blood, covering it with earth. In fact, one of the worst things the Torah could imagine was a person tearing a limb from a living animal—an animal "with its blood still in it"—for food. That was strictly forbidden.

Blood and Childbirth

When we look back at the first lines of *Tazria*, they are less of a mystery. Blood is present when a child is born. This is natural, and the ancient Israelites accepted that Adonai made things operate this way. But blood that has not been covered by the earth is unclean. And as we learned in the last

To Discuss

Why do we call blood "the stuff of life"? And what is it about blood that tends to frighten us so much?

Quote to Remember

זֹאת תּוֹרַת הַיֹּלֶדֶת לַזָּכָר אוֹ לַנְּקֵבָה.

Such are the rituals concerning her who bears a child, male or female.

Laws of Blood Purity

The rituals around blood and childbirth are very ancient. Some seem superstitious. They may have grown out of the natural fears that all people share about blood. These laws were used in Israel while the priests still made sacrifices at the Temple. The medieval commentator Abraham Ibn Ezra tells us that these laws were *only* meant for Israelites living in the Holy Land, and after the Temple was destroyed, these laws were set aside.

Disease in Egypt

Priests did not act as doctors, but people turned to them when they were ill, looking for "miracle" cures. People expect religion to help them, and they are disappointed when it cannot. In Egypt, they brought gifts to Memphis, to the shrine of the lion-headed goddess Sekhmet (*below left*). She was the powerful daughter of the sun god, Re, and it was said that she could grant healing. For the Israelites, this power rested in the hands of God. Israelite priests could only check to see what God had decided.

portion, anything that touches something unclean also becomes unclean. That is why a woman who gives birth becomes unclean—she is touched by unclean blood. The ancient Israelites believed in the magnetic quality of uncleanness. If an unclean woman touched something holy, then that thing would become unclean, too.

Of course, human beings can become clean again. After giving birth to a male child, the mother waited seven days. Then for thirty-three days she was not to touch anything holy or even to come into the sanctuary. If the child was a daughter, the time was twice as long. (We do not know why—perhaps it was because daughters could also grow up to give birth.) When this time of "blood purification" was over, the mother brought a sin-offering—but not because there was any sin in giving birth! Giving birth was a time of joy. The sin-offering was for the blood spilled in giving birth. The blood of the sin-offering was returned to the earth, and the mother was then clean.

Tzara'at

The rest of the laws given in *Tazria* deal with disease called *tzara'at*. In the past, many translations of the Torah spoke of all the different kinds of tzara'at as "leprosy". Leprosy is the disease we now call Hansen's disease or Hansenitis. Leprosy causes changes of skin color and growths on the skin. People who suffer from it also lose their sense of pain. Over time, if it is not treated, leprosy can cause parts of the body to rot away. Modern medicine can usually stop leprosy from spreading and sometimes even cure it. Before modern times, lepers were feared and mistreated. They were often forced to live outside the community in special "leper colonies". Today, though, we know that leprosy may be an ugly disease, but it is not very contagious.

We also know that the laws in *Tazria* are not mainly about leprosy. Most are about diseases that might clear up in a brief amount of time. If an Israelite noticed a skin problem, he or she would come to a priest. The priest did not act as a doctor or a medicine man. The priest only examined the skin and declared whether the person was clean or unclean. A person who was unclean had to be isolated—separated from other people—not to keep the disease from spreading, but because an unclean person could make other people or things unclean by touching them.

If a skin condition grew serious and did not disappear, even after a second examination made in fourteen days, then the sufferer might be sent to live "outside the camp". (Once the Israelites were settled in Canaan, the diseased were sent to live outside the city walls.) In those days, when not much was known about the causes of skin diseases, some people who suffered from slight problems were probably unjustly treated. Even something as simple as scars caused by burns was examined by the priests for tzara'at. As we said, the priests were not doctors. They just did what they knew how to do—they tried to separate what was clean from what was unclean.

What Is Tzara'at?

The laws of tzara'at speak of common skin ailments like eczema, psoriasis, and impetigo. There are also laws regarding tzara'at of wool, linen, and leather. These were not ailments. They were most probably mildew or fungus that could grow in fabrics or in leathers that had not been carefully treated. For most kinds of tzara'at, people (or fabrics and leathers) were isolated for seven days and then examined again to see if the tzara'at was growing and spreading or if it had disappeared.

Haftarah: 2 Kings 4:42-5:19

Tazria gives the rituals for treating the skin disease the Torah calls "leprosy". The Rabbis connect that with the healing of a skin disease performed by the prophet Elisha. The haftarah actually contains two miracles performed by the prophet.

In the first, a man brought Elisha twenty loaves of barley bread and some "new grain". Elisha said, "Give it to the people to eat." But the man protested that there was not enough there to set before one hundred people. Nevertheless, Elisha said, Adonai says the people will eat and have leftovers, too. And so it came to pass.

The second miracle concerned Naaman, a commander of the Syrian (Aramean) army, who had tzara'at, a skin disease. An Israelite told Naaman about Elisha and his miracles. So the king of Aram wrote to the king of Israel, asking for Naaman to be healed (and sending a reward, too). But the king of Israel asked, "Am I God, with power over life and death?"—for he thought the king of Aram was trying to trick him into a quarrel.

But Elisha heard and told the king of Israel to send Naaman to him, so "he will learn that there is a prophet in Israel!" Naaman waited outside Elisha's home and was told to bathe seven times in the Jordan River to be cured. Naaman was doubtful but finally did what Elisha asked. He was cured. But when he tried to pay Elisha, the prophet refused.

Naaman then promised to worship Adonai forever, even when his master served other gods. Elisha said, "Go in peace."

So Elisha taught that (1) we must have faith in Adonai and (2) we must trust the messages given to us by Adonai's prophets.

From Unclean to Clean

Where We Are

Metzora is the twenty-eighth parashah or weekly reading in the Torah. In most years it is read together with the portion just before it, *Tazria*. Both portions come from the third book of the Torah, Leviticus, a code book made up mainly of laws for the Levites, the priests. The Torah presents all these codes of law as part of the story of the Israelites at Mount Sinai, which begins in Exodus and continues to the Book of Numbers.

Bringing Back the Leper

> Adonai spoke to Moses, saying: This shall be the ritual for a leper (*metzora*) at the time that he is to be cleansed....

A person with almost any skin disease was called a *metzora*, a "leper". Of course, most skin problems were not leprosy. Nevertheless, if the skin disease lasted a while, the metzora was declared "unclean" and sent to live outside the community. Once a person was declared a metzora, the priests were required to come to examine the skin. If the skin had healed, the priests could perform rituals to make the metzora "clean" and bring the person back into the community. The parashah called *Metzora* gives the laws and rituals that guide the priests. But before a person could become "clean" again, the skin had to heal.

How did sufferers heal skin diseases? Some Israelites (and non-Israelites) worked as professional "healers". A metzora might visit one of them the way we visit an allergist. Most medicines were what we would call "home remedies"—the Book of Isaiah tells how pressed figs were applied to the skin. But sunlight was the simplest, and often the strongest, medicine. Priests did not care *how* the skin ailment was healed. Their job was to change the metzora from "unclean before Adonai" to "clean before Adonai".

In lesser cases of "uncleanness" an Israelite had only to bathe in fresh water and wait until evening to be "clean". But once a person was declared a metzora, becoming "clean" became more complex. The priest had to perform two rituals: one on the first day and one on the eighth day.

On the Eighth Day

Let's begin with the ritual of the eighth day, since it is like many we have already met. The metzora brought sacrifices to the entrance of the Tent of Meeting: two lambs, a meal of-fering, and a jar of oil. The priest offered the sacrifices. The only mysterious thing about the ritual of the eighth day was that the metzora was anointed, almost like a priest. Some blood was placed on the metzora's right ear, right thumb, and right big toe. The blood in each place was covered with oil, and the rest of the oil was put on the metzora's head. We can guess why the metzora had to be anointed.

Israel is a "kingdom of priests and a holy people". When the metzora was sent to live outside the community, he or she was separated from the people of Israel. To make the metzora part of the holy, priestly people of Israel again, the metzora had to be anointed almost like a priest. This was done with oil instead of blood. Once it was done and the sacrifices were complete, the metzora was again a part of the "kingdom of priests and [the] holy people" and was de-clared "clean". He or she could go home.

The Ritual of the First Day

The ritual of the first day is more mysterious. Nachmanides tells us that even though a bird was killed in this ritual, the bird was not a sacrifice, since no altar was used—and his statement only deepens the mystery.

Before the metzora could enter the camp (or city) again, here is what was done:

> The priest shall order two live clean birds, cedar wood, crimson [yarn], and hyssop to be brought for him who is to be cleansed. The priest shall or-der one of the birds slaughtered over fresh water in an earthen vessel; and he shall take the live bird, along with the cedar wood, the crimson [yarn], and the hyssop, and dip them together with the live bird in the blood of the bird that was slaughtered over the fresh water. He shall then sprinkle it seven times on [the metzora] ... and he shall set the live bird free in the open country.

The Israelites thought that clean and unclean and holy and unholy were somehow "magnetic". Something clean became unclean just by touching something unclean. Usu-ally this happened by accident. For example, if a priest was

Rich and Poor

If a metzora cannot afford to bring two lambs for the sacrifice on the eighth day, then he or she can bring one lamb instead. The portion repeats all the laws that speak about the ritual of the eighth day twice—once for the rich metzora who can afford two lambs and once for the poor who can only afford one lamb.

To Consider

Jews continue to use the idea of "transference" in many ways. Starting in the ninth century, Jews would "transfer" their sins to a rooster (for the men) or a hen (for the women) on the day before Rosh Hashanah or the day before Yom Kippur. They would then slaughter the fowl and throw its innards to the birds. The fowl itself was usually given to the poor to eat. This ceremony is called *Kaparot*, "atonements". Sometimes sins are "transferred" to money that is given to the poor. Another High Holy Day ceremony, *Tashlich* (from the word "to cast"), "transfers" sins to bits of bread cast into flowing water or to fish swimming in the water.

sprinkling the blood of a "most holy" sacrifice against the altar and a drop or two of blood spilled on his clothes, the clothes became "most holy"—they could not be worn or taken outside until every drop of blood was removed from them.

In the ritual of the first day, the priest used the idea of "magnetism" to send the uncleanness of the metzora away. The first bird was slaughtered over water. Because the blood did not return to the earth, the blood remained unclean. The dead bird and the unclean blood are symbols, they stand for the metzora who has been "dead" outside the community and has been unclean.

Then the priest takes the living bird and dips it into the unclean blood. He adds cedar wood and hyssop—perhaps for their smells—tied together with the crimson yarn—perhaps for its bloody color. When he dips these into the unclean blood, they become unclean, too. The priest "connects" the metzora with all the unclean things by sprinkling some of the water and blood seven times on the metzora. Now the living bird is unclean like the disease, but when it flies away it takes the uncleanness with it. The metzora can return to the camp (or city) and wait seven days to bring sacrifices to the priest.

How It Works

The ancient idea behind this magic ritual is called "transference"—a bad or evil spell can be "transferred" to something or someone else. Nachmanides knew or guessed that it was magic, and that is why he said there was no sacrifice here: There is no altar, and the blood is not returned to the earth in the normal way. *Sifra*, the sages' commentary on Leviticus, tells us that if the bird later returns, it is clean and it may be eaten. How did it become clean again? Since the heavens are the place of Adonai, they are always clean, so when the unclean bird touched the heavens, it became clean again.

This kind of "transfer magic" is far older than the Israelite laws. Yet Jews still use it today. For instance, we are supposed to remove all leavened bread and cereal from our homes to make them kosher for Pesach. An evening or two before Passover begins, we hide some crumbs of leavened bread in the house so that we can perform the ritual called *bedikat chameitz*, "the search for leaven".

Traditional Jews do bedikat chameitz with a candle, a wooden spoon, and feathers. The light of the candle is used to "search" for the bread crumbs, the feathers to sweep them up, and the wooden spoon to collect them. When the crumbs are all gathered, they are placed in a safe place until morning. The head of the household says,

> May all leaven that remains in my possession—
> any I have not seen or searched out and any I might
> have missed—be regarded as not there and be-
> come common property like the dust of the earth.

The next morning comes *bi'ur chameitz*, "the burning of the leaven". Again the head of the household declares that the gathered last bits of leaven stand for any leaven that could make the house unclean for Passover. Once they are burned, any leaven that might have been overlooked is just like the ashes of the burnt leaven—it is "dust of the earth". The house is now fully clean and kosher for Passover.

After the Temple was destroyed, when Jews could no longer make sacrifices at the Temple altar, we made yet another kind of "transference". We substituted prayer services for the daily offerings of the priests. Before, only the priests had prayed each day as part of the ritual of sacrifice. But now all Jews began to pray daily. *Shacharit*, the morning prayer service, took the place of the daily sin offering. *Minchah*, the afternoon prayer service, replaced the afternoon meal offering. Just as the priests in Temple times taught that every sacrifice was essential to the special relationship between Adonai and the Israelites, now daily services became equally vital.

In this way the mysterious ritual for making the metzora clean, the ritual for removing leaven from the household before Passover, and the ritual of substituting prayer services for sacrifices in the absence of the Temple are one and the same. They are all based on the magical idea of transference, a concept that remains very much a part of Jewish religious life today.

To Consider

The morning and afternoon prayer services replaced sacrifices in the Temple, but the evening service, called *Arvit*, did not replace any sacrifice. There was even a debate in the Talmud. Was the *Arvit* service necessary or was it optional? The arguments in favor of praying three times daily were strong. In the end, in most places, the *Arvit* was added to the *Minchah* service so that people could attend the synagogue twice daily but pray all three services. To make a division between the afternoon and evening services, synagogue-goers set aside time for Torah study.

A Plague on the House

The parashah continues by talking about a "plague on a house", a tzara'at that makes the house unclean. The Torah seems to say that this only happens to a house in the Holy Land. Of course, it has nothing at all to do with the Israelites who were at Sinai living in tents, because the plague (probably a fungus or mildew) attacked stones or bricks and the coating or plaster of a house. This is obviously a problem for city folk, not for the Israelites in tents in the wilderness.

If a priest found this tzara'at, any infected stones or bricks would be removed and replaced. If it was in the plaster of the house, the coating would be removed and the walls replastered. If this worked, the priest used the transference ritual of the two birds, the cedar wood, the crimson yarn, and the hyssop to magically make the house clean again. If replacement did not work, then the whole house was destroyed, and all its parts were dumped outside the city. A new house was built.

All the laws for tzara'at are given, but an early statement of the Rabbis says that such a thing never happened to a house in the whole history of the Land of Israel. Perhaps the laws are more ancient than the Israelites. Bible scholar William W. Hallo (1929-) tells us that in ancient Mesopotamia Babylonians would look for omens or signs of the future in the changes that took place in the walls of their houses. Perhaps these laws were placed in the Torah by the P-teller to remind us, "Don't look for the future in a plague on the house, as pagans do. Just repair the house!"

Men and Women

The last part of the parashah speaks of problems and diseases of the sex organs of men and women. It also talks about normal semen and blood that come from our bodies and may turn us unclean for a brief time. Some of these laws are known to be ancient. Some are superstitious. We human beings—male and female—have always been nervous and frightened by anything unusual in the way our sex organs work. And at times there are good reasons. Diseases of the sex organs can be very dangerous.

The Torah, however, is not interested in medical problems. The P-teller includes this group of laws to let us know when we are unclean and should not touch one another, how long we remain unclean and unable to touch one other, and how we should bathe to make ourselves clean again. Most important of all, a person who is unclean may not come near the altar. So the P-teller puts these words in the voice of Adonai: "You shall put the Israelites on guard against their uncleanness, lest they die through their uncleanness by [making unclean] My Tabernacle which is among them."

Jewish tradition states that the Torah was given by God to Moses at Mount Sinai. Yet even the first students of the Torah found problems with this: stories told twice with different details, laws that contradicted one another, and so on. Even the Ten Commandments are given in two or possibly three different versions. In the last two hundred years Bible critics have studied the many "tellers" whose work is included in the Torah. One is the P or Priestly teller. Looking back, we can see how the P-teller collected family lists, laws (especially laws about Levites and kohanim, the priests), and stories about priestly matters. By placing most of the laws—like those found in *Metzora*—into the story of Moses at Mount Sinai, the P-teller was saying that these laws were so important that it was "as if" God gave them at Sinai.

Metzora

Modern folk sometimes say that the parashah of *Metzora* has few lessons to teach us for our everyday lives. Matters of "clean" and "unclean" seem a lot less important than matters of good and evil.

Yet there are many lessons for us in *Metzora*. Some people compare "a plague on the house" to the way evil can spread in a family from parents to children. Others compare "clean and unclean" to "healthy and unhealthy". But one lesson *Metzora* surely teaches is that we can become wiser and better people over time. We do not need to be stuck in old ways of thinking or behaving forever. Jewish law has been changing since its beginning. Even in this one parashah some of the laws are older and some newer; some are su-

Tzara'at and the Rabbis

The Rabbis thought that skin disease (tzara'at) was a punishment sent by God only to those who had spoken evil against other people or were guilty of some other sin. We know from modern medicine that they were mistaken. The wisest of our ancestors did not understand the facts of allergies and skin disease as we do now.

Tzedakah

After the Temple was destroyed, prayer services were substituted for regular sacrifices. The Rabbis also said that "acts of lovingkindness", especially *tzedakah*, charity given because "it is the right thing to do", was the best replacement for the personal sacrifices that used to be offered in the Temple. *Right:* Jewish artists turned their talents through the ages to crafting special tzedakah boxes like this one to be used in synagogues and by rabbis and town officials for collecting charity for the poor.

perstitious, and some are practical; some were actually followed, and some were never used.

In a way, it is up to every generation—right down to you—to decide which of the ancient laws are still "clean" and which of them have become "unclean", which of them remain "holy" and which of them have become "unholy". This is an endless task, and only by studying Torah can we learn to make good decisions.

Haftarah: I Kings 7:3-20

Metzora speaks of "leprosy", and the haftarah speaks of four lepers. Before the story begins, the Aramean armies have encircled Samaria, the capital of the Kingdom of Israel. Inside the walls the Israelites suffer from starvation. Elisha predicts that a miracle will occur, but the king's chief counselor refuses to believe. So Elisha also predicts the death of the counselor. As the story begins, four Israelite lepers are debating what to do. Because they are lepers, they are outside the gates.

The four agree that if they go inside the gates, they will starve. If they remain where they are, they will also die. They may as well face their fate with the Arameans, who will either feed them or put them to death. So they go to the camp of the Arameans.

But Adonai frightened the Arameans so that they ran away, leaving everything. The lepers eat and drink and steal things, but then they decide to tell the Israelites what has happened. The news reaches the king and he sends scouts to check it out. Lo, it is true! Then the people hurry to feast on what the Arameans left behind. In the rush of the crowd, the king's counselor is trampled to death at the gate.

The people eat their fill and have more besides, all from the tents of the Arameans and what they abandoned. All this was as Elisha prophesied. But the dead counselor who doubted the prophet did not live even to the end of the day, nor did he eat even a grain.

This miracle story of Elisha show that we must trust the messages that Adonai sends by the prophets, for Adonai alone can rescue us when our own might fails.

Dangers

אחרי מות
Acharei Mot
Leviticus 16:1-18:30

The Covenant at Sinai

In the books of Genesis and Exodus our P-teller solved a puzzle by setting stories from different times and places into a single picture—starting with Creation and continuing to Mount Sinai. In the Book of Leviticus the P-teller is solving a second puzzle—how to fit many codes of law together. Just as the stories did not always agree, the codes of law did not always agree.

A thousand years had passed since the tribes stood at Sinai. The Israelites were now divided into two kingdoms. In the Kingdom of Israel sacrifices were offered at places like Shiloh, Beth El, and Dan. Priests in these religious centers followed different rituals, the way synagogues follow different practices today. In the Kingdom of Judah there was one main center, the Temple in Jerusalem. It had its own code of priestly laws.

When the Kingdom of Israel was destroyed, some northern priests fled south, bringing their law codes with them. Every code was holy to its priests. The P-teller wanted to create one set of laws for all Israel by showing that *all* codes of law—northern and southern—were commanded by God to Moses at Mount Sinai.

We do the same kind of thing in the United States today. At first there were thirteen colonies, each with its own code of law. To create *one* United States we needed *one* code of law that everyone would accept. It would be too confusing to change the laws that already existed. Instead we created a new Constitution. When our Constitution needs new laws, we do not change the Constitution itself. Instead we add "amendments" to it. We attach new laws to our national covenant, as if the new laws were actually part of the Constitution from the time that it was written. Just as we write new laws into an old constitution, so the P-teller placed all the priestly codes of law together in the covenant, setting them into the laws given at Mount Sinai.

Why Sinai?

At Mount Sinai all Israelites were united by a single agreement, the covenant with Adonai. A thousand years later the story of the giving of the law at Mount Sinai had grown into a legend. No one could say for sure which laws, if any, were actually given to Moses at Mount Sinai. But the P-teller felt free to claim that *all* the codes of law came from Sinai—tying all Israelites, no matter what tribe they came from, into a single nation with a single covenant.

Quote to Remember

וְהָיְתָה־זֹּאת לָכֶם לְחֻקַּת עוֹלָם לְכַפֵּר עַל־בְּנֵי יִשְׂרָאֵל מִכָּל־חַטֹּאתָם...

This shall be to you a law for all time: to make atonement for the Israelites for all their sins...

The Dangerous Place

As the parashah of *Acharei Mot* begins the P-teller reminds us that the people are still at Mount Sinai saying: "Adonai spoke to Moses after the death [*acharei mot*] of the two sons of Aaron who died when they drew too close to the Presence of Adonai."

> Adonai said to Moses: Tell your brother Aaron that he is not to come at will [without careful preparation] into the Shrine behind the curtain, in front of the cover that is upon the ark, lest he die; for I appear in the cloud over the cover.

One law code stated that Moses and Aaron could enter the Shrine (the Holy of Holies) whenever they wished to speak with Adonai. This code allowed the High Priest to enter the Holy of Holies at any time, provided that he followed instructions carefully. The Holy of Holies, the code says, was a dangerous place, even for the High Priest. The spirit of Adonai was concentrated in this place, and the High Priest could die by coming too close or by looking directly at the Presence of Adonai.

Another code probably came from the Temple in Jerusalem. It states that the High Priest could enter the Holy of Holies only once each year. This is the first code to speak of an annual day for Israel to atone for its sins. The day is called *Shabbat Shabbaton*, "the Sabbath of Sabbaths" or "the Sabbath of complete rest". Today we call it Yom Kippur, the Day of Atonement.

> On the tenth day of the seventh month, you shall practice self-denial; and you shall do no manner of work.... For on this day atonement shall be made for you to cleanse you of all your sins; you shall be clean before Adonai. It shall be a Sabbath of complete rest [*Shabbat Shabbaton*] for you.... This shall be to you a law for all time: to make atonement for the Israelites for all their sins once a year.

Combining the two codes, the P-teller created one explanation of what the High Priest was commanded to do on this special day "to make atonement for the Israelites." This combination of laws became the yearly ritual.

The Yearly Ritual

Before entering the Holy of Holies to atone for the people the High Priest had to atone for any sin he himself might have committed during the year. He removed the beautiful clothing that he normally wore, bathed in water, and put on a plain white linen robe and a white linen turban. He brought a bull as a sin offering for himself and his household and two goats as a sin offering for the people.

> Aaron shall take the two he-goats and let them stand before Adonai at the entrance of the Tent of Meeting; and Aaron shall place lots upon the two goats, one marked for Adonai and the other marked for Azazel. Aaron shall bring forward the goat chosen by lot for Adonai, which he is to offer as a sin offering; while the goat chosen by lot for Azazel shall be left standing alive before Adonai, to make atonement with it and to send it off to the wilderness for Azazel.

Now Aaron (the High Priest) offered the sacrifices—his bull, the incense offering, and the goat marked "for Adonai". Blood from the offerings was placed on the horns of the altar and sprinkled all around in the Tabernacle, to clean the altar and Tabernacle of all sin.

> When [Aaron] has finished [all the cleansing] … the live goat [marked "for Azazel"] shall be brought forward. Aaron shall lay both his hands upon the live goat's head and confess over it all the sins and wrongdoings of the Israelites … setting them on the head of the goat; and it shall be sent off to the wilderness …. Thus the goat shall carry on it all their sins … and the goat shall be set free in the wilderness.

Azazel

But who or what is "Azazel"? By the time the codes of law were placed in Leviticus, it seems that no one was quite sure. A few hundred years later some of the Rabbis guessed that Azazel was the name of a place. The *Septuagint*, the first Greek version of the Bible, translated Azazel as "dis-

Lots for the Goats

To choose between the goats Aaron (or the current High Priest) placed two "lots"— probably small stones or pieces of pottery—in a jar or pouch. One was marked "for Adonai" and the other was marked "for Azazel." The High Priest reached in and drew out a lot for the goat on his right side; then he placed the other lot on the goat on his left side. In ancient times the people believed that any decision made by lots was a decision decreed by God.

The Scapegoat

Placing Israel's sins on the goat was a case of "transference." The idea was that all the people's sins were "transferred" to the goat marked "for Azazel." This is the same as the ritual in *Metzora* for bringing the leper back into the camp, when one bird was sacrificed and one bird was set free. This time one goat is slaughtered and one is set free in the wilderness. In English we call the one that was set free the "scapegoat," a word that means "one who bears the sins for others."

The Goat Might Return

Once the sins of the Israelites were placed on the head of the goat marked "for Azazel", the goat was sent into the wilderness. That made the goat dangerous. Anyone or anything touching it would also become unclean. A traveler might accidentally touch it. Or, worse, the goat might wander back into the community. So Rashi tells us that in the days of the Second Temple the goat was pushed backward over a cliff to its death. This was the only way to make certain that the goat would never come back.

To Consider

The Mishnah says it was a good omen if the lot "for Adonai" fell on the goat on Aaron's right. People often look for omens. On Groundhog Day (February 2) we wonder whether the groundhog will see its shadow. If it does, people say there will be six more weeks of winter. Groundhog Day comes from an older festival called Candlemas, which may go back as far back as the fourth century. In England people say that if Candlemas (also February 2) is cloudy and rainy, spring will come soon. When people look for omens—which goat gets the lot "for Adonai" or how long it will be until spring—they are saying that nothing happens by accident; there is a reason for everything.

missal" or "nowhere." Much later Rashi (who thought he knew how the goat was killed in the time of the Second Temple) said that Azazel was "a steep mountain." But these ideas of a place were only one way of explaining Azazel.

Other ancient sources indicate that Azazel was not a "where", but a "who". In some stories Azazel was said to be one of two angels who led a revolt against God. Another legend says that Azazel is a short name for two fallen angels: Uzza and Azza-el. But these popular stories were like the grocery store newspapers and the television shows of ancient times. Most Jews did not seriously believe in angel revolts or "fallen angels" being punished by God.

Modern Bible scholars like Bernard Bamberger tell us that Azazel was the name of a demon, an evil power thought to live deep in the wilderness. Demons have always been a convenient way to explain evil in the world. It was true that people and animals would sometimes disappear "in the wilderness", never to be seen again. Where did they go? What happened to them? They were swallowed by a demon! They went "to Azazel"! So when the Israelites wanted to be rid of their sins forever—never to see them again—they sent the goat carrying all their sins to the demon, "to Azazel".

Goat-Demons

Acharei Mot next commands that all ox, sheep, or goats to be used as food had to be offered to Adonai at the entrance of the Tent of Meeting. The priest would offer part of the animal to Adonai, return the blood to the earth, and give most of the meat to the person who brought the sacrifice. In this way, the law code states, the people will no longer "offer their sacrifices … to the goat-demons after whom they stray. This shall be to them a law for all time, throughout the ages." So it is written, but this never actually became a law "for all times".

It seems that some Israelites had begun to offer sacrifices to "goat-demons"—perhaps imaginary wild goats with human faces like the satyrs of Greek mythology. The law to bring all animals to the sanctuary might have been useful to Israelites in the wilderness, where it was a short walk to the altar. Or it might have been useful to people in Jerusalem or

Dan or Beth El, where an altar was close by. But it could never serve for the whole people of Israel in the Holy Land—most folk lived too far away from Jerusalem to bring every food animal to the Temple just to have it slaughtered.

The Marriage Code

Acharei Mot concludes with a list of forbidden marriages.

> I Adonai am your God. You shall not copy the [marriage] practices of the land of Egypt where you dwelt, or of the land of Canaan…. My rules alone shall you observe, and faithfully follow My laws: I Adonai am your God.

This list forbids the marriage of people who share the same blood or who are closely related. It contains an idea from the story of Creation that when a man and woman marry they become blood relatives. This is not true scientifically, but the ancient codes were based on religious, not scientific, ideas. These laws are what you might expect: a son is forbidden to marry his mother, his aunt, his sister or any of his father's wives (if his father had more than one wife); a father could not marry his son's wife or his granddaughter; and so on. Most of the laws are given from the male point of view, since men were more in control of marriage and household. We meet only a few strange laws here.

One is a commandment forbidding parents from offering up their children to Molech. We once thought that this was a law against sacrificing children. Most scholars now agree that child sacrifice in ancient times was rare. Yet there was a religious group or cult that worshiped a god named Molech ("King," as in *melech*). Members of the group would "pass their children through fire" to dedicate them to Molech. Perhaps the children walked between two fires or perhaps parents lifted babies or young children close to a fire and waved them. But this command simply forbids Israelites from worshiping Molech instead of Adonai.

Other laws in the list forbid homosexuality—sex between men—and bestiality—sex between humans and animals. In biblical times both of these were thought to be sins committed mainly by Canaanites and other peoples who lived near the Israelites. Homosexuality was common in

To Consider

Modern scholars suggest that the law stating that all animals must be brought to the Sanctuary to be slaughtered comes from the time when a small number of Jews had just returned from Babylonia and were all settled in or around Jerusalem. If this is correct, then this code of laws, including the laws against sacrificing to "goat-demons", comes from a time some seven hundred years after Sinai! So you can see how the P-teller tried to include every code of law and to say that all the codes were given at Mount Sinai.

Below: This was how "the goat-demon Azazel" was pictured by an artist in *The Infernal Dictionary*, published in Paris in 1825. In ancient times, though, the Israelites may have imagined goat-demons very differently.

Blood

The law code in *Acharei Mot* repeats many of the ideas about blood that we have already studied. Taking life meant spilling blood. "For the life of the flesh is in the blood," the code says, and pouring out the blood at the foot of the altar atones for our sin in slaughtering animals for food. It was forbidden for anyone to eat the blood spilled when an animal was killed. This was true even for hunters. "If any Israelite or any stranger who resides among them hunts down an animal or a bird that may be eaten, the blood shall be poured out and covered with earth. For the life of all flesh—its blood is its life."

many parts of the ancient world, but it was feared by the ancient priests of Israel in the same way that they feared leprosy. What we read in this law is their fear of things that felt strange to them, things they did not understand.

The marriage code (and its other laws) makes an important connection: sins can cause Adonai's special land to become defiled—that is, unclean. Because the Canaanites sinned in these ways, Adonai was casting them out of the land and giving the land to the Israelites.

> So let not the land spew you out ... as it spewed out the nation that came before you.... You shall keep My charge not to engage in any of [these awful] practices that were carried on before you, and you shall defile not yourselves through them: I Adonai am your God.

Haftarah: Ezekiel 22:1-19

The Rabbis connect the "Marriage Code"—a list of forbidden marriages—in the Torah portion to the sins that Ezekiel lists in the haftarah. Ezekiel denounces the people for two kinds of sin, saying that Jerusalem as a city of blood and of abominable deeds.

> Adonai's word came to me, saying, Now you, mortal, are you ready to accuse the city of blood and to make known her awful deeds?

Ezekiel accused the people of Jerusalem of shedding blood and making idols. The leaders were especially guilty, taking advantage even of strangers, widows, and orphans. "You oppose My holy things and profane My Sabbaths." People slandered one another and ate sacrifices on mountaintops. They married forbidden mates and took heavy interest

from their neighbors, though Adonai forbade these things. Now Adonai says, "I clap my hand...."

> Will your heart stay steady, and your hand be firm, when the time comes for Me to deal with you? I, Adonai, have spoken and I will do it.

The people of Jerusalem will be scattered in foreign lands. When they are punished, they will know "I am Adonai."

The Rabbis included the last two verses to comfort the people and soften the harsh message of destruction. Adonai tells Ezekiel that the people are like metals that can be melted in a furnace. When they are purified in fire, then Adonai will be ready to save them. "Because you all became base metal, I will gather you up to the midst of Jerusalem."

The Heart of the Torah

The Holiness Code

Adonai spoke to Moses, saying: Speak to the whole Israelite community and say to them: You shall be holy [*kedoshim tehiyu*]; for I, Adonai your God, am holy.

All who have studied the Bible from the Rabbis of the Talmud to modern Bible scholars—agree that Chapter 19 of Leviticus is the key to understanding the covenant of ancient Israel. Many modern scholars believe that one priest composed Chapters 18, 19, and 20 of Leviticus. They call these chapters "the Holiness Code", and call the priest the H source. "You shall be holy; for I, Adonai your God, am holy" is the message of the Holiness Code and the beating heart of the Torah.

The Holiness Code repeats all of the Ten Commandments, putting them in a new order and sometimes in new words. It places them beside laws that speak about farming, sacrifice, rituals, and the way we should treat strangers, neighbors, and family. The Holiness Code states that keeping God's commands makes us holy as God is holy.

The Holiness Code stresses that the land of Israel is especially holy to Adonai. In the land of Israel, even strangers are treated like brothers and sisters. In the land of Israel, the code says, Adonai is always near us. In fact, other nations judge our God by the way we behave in the land. We have to behave in holy ways so that all nations will see that our God is holy.

Bible scholars generally agree that the Holiness Code was completed before the destruction of the First Temple in 586 B.C.E. Many scholars think that almost all of the P-teller's work was also done around this time. So when the Holiness Code was written, the Israelites were still living in the land; still harvesting fruit, grapes, olives, dates, and grains; still bringing sacrifices to the Temple; still buying and selling in city markets; still living under kings and holding court in the

Kedoshim

You already know the word *kadosh*, "holy", in many ways. Marriage is *kiddushin*, "a holy partnership". The *kiddush* prayer is recited over wine on Sabbath and festivals. We pray the *kaddish* memorial prayer when a close loved one dies. In the *kedushah* prayer the angels praise God with the words *Kadosh, kadosh, kadosh ...*, "Holy, holy, holy is *Adonai Tzeva'ot*, the whole world is filled with God's Presence." The Holiness Code demands that Israelites should be *kedoshim*, "holy persons", because Adonai is *Kadosh*, "Holy".

The command "Do not ... make molten gods ..." gives scholars a clue to the mystery of when the Holiness Code was written. People in the southern Kingdom of Judah believed that the northern Kingdom of Israel was destroyed because its people worshiped molten gods, the images of two golden bulls set up by their first king, Jeroboam (see *Ki Tisah*). The Kingdom of Israel fell in 722 B.C.E. Many of its people and priests fled to Jerusalem and other parts of the Kingdom of Judah. This makes it likely that the Holiness Code was written sometime in the 136 years between 722 when the northern kingdom fell and 586 when the First Temple was destroyed.

gates of their towns. The Holiness Code speaks about things everyone can understand: everyday life.

Teachings of Holiness

> You shall each honor [your] mother and [your] father, and keep My Sabbaths: I Adonai am your God. Do not turn to idols or make molten gods for yourselves; I Adonai am your God.

Rashi notices that the word "father" comes first in the Ten Commandments, but "mother" is placed first here. He says this teaches that we must treat our mothers and fathers equally—fearing both and honoring both. The words "I Adonai am your God" are repeated to show that obeying each command makes us a little more holy, as Adonai is holy. By learning to fear and obey our parents we learn to fear and obey God. By keeping the Sabbath we learn to rest as God rested. And so on.

> When you reap the harvest of your land, you shall not reap all the way to the edges of your field, or gather the gleanings of your harvest. You shall not pick your vineyard bare, or gather the fallen fruit of your vineyard; you shall leave them for the poor and the stranger: I Adonai am your God.

Holiness demands care for the poor and the stranger—giving them a share of your crops and your fruit, just as you give a share of your crops and fruit to Adonai. This is not *tzedakah* or charity. Of course, charity—giving when you want to give—is also important. But the Holiness Code states here that the poor and the stranger have the *right* to be taken care of by the whole community. Even later, when most Jews were no longer farmers, this law was kept. Jews gave money to the poor fund each week. Food was purchased with the money and given to those who need it.

The Holiness Code continues with laws against stealing, against lying or cheating your neighbor, against taking false oaths using the name of God, against stealing from someone in secret or robbing someone by force, and against making a worker wait for promised wages. All of these we have met before, but the next law is more unusual.

Insulting the Deaf to Not Taking Revenge

You shall not insult the deaf, or place a stumbling block before the blind. You shall fear your God: I am Adonai.

Nachmanides explained that the deaf are singled out because they cannot hear your insult. But the idea is bigger, too: when you insult anyone who is not near enough to hear the insult, that person is also "deaf". The deaf are a good example—but no insults should be given behind a person's back! That helps to explain the second half of the law: not to "place a stumbling block before the blind." Why would anyone be so childishly cruel? But the idea is that all of us are blind some of the time. Imagine that someone offers to trade you a CD for one of yours, and you agree. When you get your new CD home and try to listen to it, you find that it is scratched so badly it will not play. The trade was a cruel trick. You were "blind" when you agreed to the trade, and now you know what a "stumbling block" means.

The Holiness Code reminds judges that the rich are the same as the poor and that decisions must be fair.

The Rabbis said that the next command, "Do not profit by the blood of your [neighbor]," means that when you see your neighbor's life in danger you must help. A modern commentator, Arnold B. Ehrlich (1848–1919), believed the law also means that we should not profit by the death or injury of another person. Likewise, the code says, you should not hate another person in your heart. If you see something wrong happening, you must speak out. And you should not bear a grudge against another person or try to take revenge on another person.

The Golden Rule

Love your neighbor as yourself: I am Adonai.

This commandment of the Holiness Code is called "the Golden Rule". No one can say who first spoke the Golden Rule, but it has been repeated by religious leaders and religious texts in almost every language and time. Sometimes it is spoken in its opposite, as a negative command. Thus when Hillel was asked to sum up everything in the Torah in

Matters of the Heart

Rashi comments that disobeying any of these laws—from insulting the deaf to not taking revenge—are matters of the heart. People know the truth in their hearts, even if they hide it in public. But the words "I am Adonai" are repeated with the laws to remind us that Adonai will judge—because Adonai always knows what is in a person's heart.

Quote to Remember

וְאָהַבְתָּ לְרֵעֲךָ כָּמוֹךָ אֲנִי יְהוָֹה:

Love your neighbor as yourself: I am Adonai.

The Impossible Rule

The medieval commentator Nachmanides believed that the Golden Rule is an exaggeration. It is impossible for us to love our neighbors as much as we love ourselves. This would mean that we would be forced to give our lives for them, which makes no sense. He said the command really means that we should love *good* for others as we love *good* for ourselves. We should always ask, "Would it be good for us?" If the answer is yes, then we should be glad when our neighbor has it or succeeds in it. We should help our neighbor get it.

To Consider

Sforno says that the only cut allowed in Jewish flesh is the circumcision mark made to remind us of the covenant. Rashi says that cutting marks in the flesh includes tattooing with a needle. Tattoos are a good example. When we first get them they may seem very appealing. Later they may become embarrassing to us. But even modern medicine has difficulty removing them. The point is that our bodies are God-like, just as our hearts and minds are God-like. We can treat our bodies with holiness, or we can cut them and mark them as non-believers do. As Rashi says, God knows what is in our hearts.

one rule, he said, "What is hateful to you, do not do to your neighbor." Rabbi Akiba stated that "Love your neighbor as yourself" is "the great principle of the Torah."

The Golden Rule here would not be complete without its second half: "I am Adonai." What makes loving our neighbors a holy way to behave is knowing that Adonai loves all human beings equally. We become holy when we know that all of us are created in the holy image of God. Often it seems that that is not true. Some folk seem so bent on doing evil that loving them hardly seems right. The Talmud teaches this lesson: Rabbi Meir came home one day and told his wife Beruriah that he had been held up by ruffians on the road so many times that he finally prayed to God that the ruffians should die. But Beruriah said, "You should not pray for their death; you should pray that their eyes be opened and that they change their ways." She seems to have understood the Golden Rule very well. The best we can hope for others is the good we want for ourselves, to learn how to be holy by studying the holy ways of God.

More Teachings of Holiness

When a tree is planted, its fruit may not be eaten for three years. In the fourth year the fruit is for rejoicing before Adonai—bringing it to Jerusalem and eating it there. After that the fruit may be eaten freely. The law adds "that [the tree's] yield to you may be increased: I Adonai am your God." Even today, owners of orchards know that taking the blossoms off the trees in the first few years makes trees grow bigger and better fruit afterward. So obeying Adonai's law here showed good sense.

The Holiness Code repeats the law against eating meat with blood, followed by a law against divination or soothsaying—ways of predicting the future. There is a law against the close trimming of a beard or sideburns. The reason seems to be that a knife or razor might cut the skin accidentally. It is followed by a law against cutting marks in flesh or gashing yourself when someone dies.

In other religions, Rashbam tells us, daughters were brought to the temples to serve as official prostitutes, earning money for the temple. This is forbidden by the Holiness

Code. It is also forbidden to ask the dead for help or to seek help from "familiar spirits".

Manners and Business

>You shall rise before the aged and pay respect to the old; you shall fear your God: I am Adonai. … The stranger who lives with you shall be to you as one of your citizens; you shall love [the stranger] as yourself, for you were strangers in the land of Egypt: I Adonai am your God.

These are laws of everyday manners. Rising to give an older person a seat on a bus or train is a sign of respect. Being kind to strangers is a way of reminding ourselves that we were strangers in Egypt and suffered unkindness. To be holy, you should "love [the stranger] as yourself." Remember what Rashi said: God knows what is in your heart.

>You shall not falsify measures of length, weight, or volume. You shall have an honest balance, honest weights, an honest *ephah*, and an honest *hin*.

Honesty in business is also a matter of holiness. We need to be able to trust one another when we buy or trade. If someone says, "I sold you an *ephah* of grain or a *hin* of oil," and hands you a sack or a jar, you have to trust that the weight is correct.

In ancient times, when coins were struck by hammer, they had ragged edges. The value of a coin was in its weight—every silver shekel might be a little different, but it weighed one shekel of silver. "Chiselers" were cheats who chiseled or shaved just a little silver off the edge of a coin and pretended that it still weighed a shekel. Much later, coins were made in perfect shapes. Ridges were added to show where they stopped and to keep chiselers from changing a coin's weight. In ancient Israel people had to trust one another, so honesty was another way of being holy. Chapter 19 of Leviticus ends by reminding us of what we owe God:

>I Adonai am your God who freed you from the land of Egypt. You shall faithfully observe all My laws and all My rules: I am Adonai.

Magic in the Holiness Code

Many of the laws in this group mention blood, and Nachmanides thought that the law against ways of predicting the future pointed to times when people would pour blood in a pit and gather around to see omens of the future in the changes in the blood. Modern archaeologists think he might have guessed right, since they found evidence of this practice in ancient Greece.

Familiar Spirits

Ibn Ezra says that "familiar spirits" are people who claim to know the future. This kind of magic is forbidden for Jews, but Adonai has given us other kinds of magic. Israelites can seek the future through prophets, through the Urim and Tummim, and through dreams.

Below: A shekel coin from Roman times, struck by hammer, with the inscription *Yerushalayim Hakedoshah*, "Holy Jerusalem". The letters and design were as close to the edge as possible to prevent "chiselers" from chipping or shaving the coin.

Adonai Will Punish

Many of the punishments require the community to stone the sinner to death. If the community refuses to do this, Adonai promises "I will set My face against that person…." The Midrash later imagined that what God was saying was: "I will turn away from all My affairs and concern myself only with [punishing] this one person."

The Second Half of *Kedoshim*

The second half of *Kedoshim* repeats many laws found in *Acharei Mot*. It adds punishments for breaking those laws. For example, it states that a person who dedicates a child to the god Molech should be stoned. Death was also the punishment for those who insulted their parents in public and for those who disobeyed nearly any of the laws of incest and forbidden marriages. For a few laws of forbidden marriages, though, the punishment is less than death—instead Adonai promises that the marriage will produce no children.

The end of the Holiness Code is a reminder that other nations are being driven out of the Holy Land because they behave in unholy ways. If Israelites behave like them, the land will also vomit them out. But if we behave in holy ways, Adonai promises:

> You shall possess their land, for I will give it to you … a land flowing with milk and honey. … You shall be holy to Me, for I Adonai am holy, and I have set you apart from other peoples to be Mine.

Haftarah: Amos 9:7-15

Kedoshim speaks the idea that "You shall be holy; because I, Adonai your God, am holy." This haftarah, from the end of the Book of Amos, speaks of a people that behaves in ways that are unholy. The Torah portion is about holiness and the haftarah is about unholiness. But the haftarah ends with the promise of a time when the people will be restored to holiness.

The prophet Amos came from a village near Jerusalem called Tekoa. But he moved north to preach in Samaria and Beth El. He was shocked by the injustices he witnessed in the Kingdom of Israel, and his messages concentrated on justice. Like other prophets of his time, he predicted the end of the northern kingdom and joined his prediction with the idea that Adonai would rescue the Israelite survivors to make a new start.

Speaking for Adonai, Amos asks the Israelites, Are you not like other nations? I destroyed those, and I will destroy you, "though I will not destroy the House of Jacob utterly." God will shake Israel in a sieve (to separate the pure from the impure), yet not a pebble will fall to the ground (since there is nothing pure in Israel). Sinners will die by the sword even though they imagine they are safe.

After the punishment, Adonai will restore the city, repair the breaches in the city walls, and raise up the ruins "as in days of old".

> I will restore the fortunes of My people Israel. They shall rebuild the ruined cities and dwell [in them] … I will plant them on their soil, never again to be uprooted from the ground I gave them, says Adonai, your God.

Priests and Times

אמר
Emor
Leviticus 21:1-24:23

Emor—"Say"

You already know that the name of a portion of the Torah comes from its first important word or group of words. The mystery here is why the word *emor*, "speak", should be so important. The answer may come from grammar—how words fit together to make sense. Usually, when Adonai commands Moses to talk to the people or the priests, the statement is something like: "Adonai said to Moses: Speak [*daber*] to …." But at the beginning of this parashah the statement is made: "Adonai said to Moses: Speak [*emor*] to the priests…." Both *daber* and *emor* mean "speak". But scholars of biblical grammar say there is a difference. *Daber* may also mean "instruct" or "tell" or "command". *Emor* is more often used for talking directly to a particular person or group. The commands given in this parashah are aimed directly at one group of Israelites. This is a code of laws especially for priests—Aaron and his sons.

Levi and Kohen

The priests here are called "Aaron and his sons". But the history of priests in Israel is not so simple.

Long before the P-teller fit the law codes of Leviticus together, the priesthood of Israel underwent many changes. Some changes will always remain a mystery to us because we do not know enough about the beginnings of our priesthood. Our best guesses will have to do. Here is what we guess today.

There was once a tribe called Levi, but it dissolved into the other tribes. Nevertheless, the Tribe of Levi was important for several reasons: (1) Moses, our greatest teacher, was a member of the tribe of Levi. (2) The tribe of Levi might have actually been slaves in Egypt. (3) The tribe of Levi might have been among the group of Israelites who left

The Torah Library

The Torah is a kind of library. You check out a piece of Torah the way you check out a book; but when you do, you leave all the other books or pieces behind. They may say other things than the part you are checking out. How do you know what pieces or books to believe? Often you check the date a book was issued. A book about dinosaurs from 1900 may tell you what people knew up to that time. But knowledge grows and changes. So a book on dinosaurs from the year 2007 would have new things to say—many facts would be different from those in the earlier book. Was the earlier book's author a liar? No. He or she simply set down what was known until 1900. One hundred and seven more years of dinosaur study resulted in many new discoveries and new facts. Books and pieces of the Torah library also come from different dates and have different facts. No one lied. They just created a Torah library.

To Consider

You probably know many people with names like Cohen, Kahn, Cohn, Kahan, and so on. Others have names like Levy, Levi, Levine, and so on. But through history many family bloodlines have blended, and not everyone with these last names is either a kohen or a Levi. All the same, in many synagogues kohanim and Levites are honored. The first reading of each Torah portion is assigned to a kohen (if one is present); the second reading is offered to a Levite (if one is present); and other readings are given to Israelites. (Reform Jews generally do not follow this custom.) Today, of course, the custom only serves to remind us of the past.

Egypt and went to Sinai. And (4) families of the tribe of Levi might have been the first priests of the Israelites.

For these reasons the tribes in the land of Israel used the word Levi or Levite as the title for *any* Israelite priest. Levite priests passed the priesthood from father to son, but sometimes others who were not born Levites also became priests. One of our most famous prophets, Samuel, is a good example. He came from the tribe of Ephraim, but he served the sanctuary at Shiloh and so became a "Levite", a priest. In those days, too, the chief priest at each sanctuary—in Dan, Beth El, Hazor, Megiddo, Shiloh, and other places—was the "high priest" of that sanctuary.

King David appointed two "high priests" for Jerusalem, whereas his son Solomon appointed Zadok to be his only High Priest. When Zadok died, his son took over as High Priest. Later it was said that Zadok and his sons were from the family of Aaron the Levite. By the time of the First Temple, the official priests of Israel were called by a new name: *kohen*, also meaning "priest". (The Arabs used the same word, *kahin* in Arabic, to mean a "seer", someone who could tell the future through omens.) The High Priest was called *kohen ha-gadol*, "the great priest". Other priests, Levites, could still serve in the Temple, but they were always second in rank to the *kohanim*.

The P-teller was not writing a history. The P-teller just gave facts: (1) Levites were from the family of Moses (everyone believed they were, either by birth or by legend). (2) Kohanim were from the family of Aaron and his sons (everyone believed they were, but this was mainly by legend). (3) Both kohanim and Levites came from the Tribe of Levi (and this, too, was mainly legend). And (4) the ruling priests, the family of Zadok, were said to be directly descended from Aaron and his sons. So when the law code speaks to "Aaron and his sons", it is speaking to the priests of the Temple in Jerusalem. The P-teller was not lying about the priesthood or about the code, just stating facts.

Laws for Priests

The code of laws for priests in *Emor* states that a priest must not come into contact with the dead—even the dead body of his own wife. (If no one else could tend to his closest relatives when they died, the priest could take care of it.) Of course, in Egypt, priests spent much time preparing the dead for burial and feeding the dead in tombs. This law sets the Israelite priests apart from Egyptian priests.

Also, nearly all Egyptians shaved their heads bare. Pharaohs and other royalty wore wigs and false beards. But Egyptian priests generally left their bald heads uncovered. Adonai commanded that Israelite priests not shave any part of their heads or make any cuts in their flesh. The idea of not accidentally drawing blood is in this law, but there is also the idea that the Israelite priests should not be like the priests of Egypt.

The code continues: Israelite priests may marry, but not divorced women or women who have bad reputations. The High Priest cannot marry a widow. The daughter of a priest must be put to death if she misbehaves with men, because her actions make her father unclean.

There were also laws about who could eat the sacred gifts meant for the priests. Some donations had to be eaten by the priests in the sanctuary. Most could be taken home for the priests' families. The slave who belonged to a priest could also eat the sacred gifts, but not a worker doing chores for a priest. If a priest became unclean, he could not eat the sacred donations until he bathed and waited until evening to be clean again. If a non-priest accidentally ate some of the sacred donations, he or she had to pay back the amount of money the food would cost, adding a fifth more to the payment.

Animals brought for sacrifices at Adonai's altar had to be without defects. All sacrifice is cruel, of course, but there are also laws here that show kindness toward animals:

> Adonai spoke to Moses, saying: When an ox or a sheep or a goat is born, it shall stay seven days with its mother …. No animal from the herd or from the flock shall be slaughtered on the same day with its young. … You shall faithfully observe My commandments: I am Adonai.

Superstition and Appearance

To serve at the altar, Israelite priests had to be without defects—the blind, the lame, the hunchback, the dwarf, the diseased could not serve. They could still share the food donated to priests, but they could not do the work of the priests. The notion behind this law was that the altar priests should "appear" perfect. It may still seem cruel to us. Through most of human history there has been prejudice against people who seem different. Today we know this is merely superstition. God created us all, and none of us are perfect.

The Gezer Calendar

The earliest Hebrew calendar we know, the Gezer Calendar, was discovered by archaeologists at Tel Gezer. It comes from the tenth century B.C.E. and numbers the months, giving no Hebrew names to them. It was a farmer's calendar, starting with the olive harvest in the fall (our September or October). Then it tells what kind of work had to be done by the farmers month-by month for the rest of the year.

Below: An archaeologist's drawing of the Gezer Calendar stone, showing the lines of ancient Hebrew text in dark ink to make them easier to study.

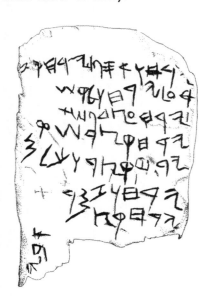

Sacred Times

We take for granted that the Jewish year begins with Rosh Hashanah in the fall, but this was not always the case. In ancient times farmers, priests, and kings each had their own calendar. The Bible includes several calendars, some based on the cycles of the sun, most on the moon. Some holidays mentioned in the Bible are no longer celebrated, some have been joined together (like the holidays of Matzot and Pesach), and even reasons given for celebrating the holidays differ from one calendar to another.

Emor includes the P-teller's calendar. This priestly calendar begins by saying that there shall be a Sabbath every seventh day. Then, on the fourteenth day of the *first* month, we celebrate Pesach by bringing an offering. The fifteenth day begins the feast of Matzot which lasts seven days. So the P-teller's calendar begins in the spring when nature returns to life. The first *omer* or "sheaf" of grain had to be brought to the Temple right after the Shabbat before the new grain could be eaten. The P-teller's calendar is not clear about which Shabbat this means. Later on this caused many arguments, since the "Counting of the *Omer*" for seven weeks also set the time for the next harvest festival, Shavuot.

> From the day on which you bring the sheaf of elevation offering—the day after the Sabbath—you shall count seven weeks. They must be complete: you must count until the day after the seventh week—fifty days; then you shall bring an offering of new grain to Adonai. … On that same day you shall hold a celebration; it shall be a sacred time for you; you shall not work at your occupations. This is a law for all time in all your settlements, throughout the ages.

The P-teller knows about Shavuot but does not give it a name. The P-teller also does not give a name to Rosh Hashanah, only calling it the day of *teruah* ("loud noise"):

> In the seventh month, on the first day of the month, you shall observe complete rest, a sacred occasion commemorated with loud blasts.

The P-teller's calendar repeats the laws for the Day of Atonement from *Acharei Mot*, starting with "Adonai spoke to

Moses, saying: Know that the tenth day of this seventh month is the Day of Atonement." And the P-teller's calendar names the holiday of Sukkot, "booths", telling about it twice.

The first time begins: "On the fifteenth day of this seventh month there shall be the Feast of Booths to Adonai, [to last] seven days." Then the calendar seems to end by saying, "Those are the set times of Adonai ...."

But suddenly the command to observe Sukkot is given a second time. And this time, more details are added:

> Know that on the fifteenth day of the seventh month ... you shall observe the festival of Adonai [to last] seven days: a complete rest on the first day, and a complete rest on the eighth day. On the first day you shall take the product of *hadar* trees, branches of palm trees, boughs of leafy trees, and willows of the brook, and you shall rejoice before Adonai your God seven days. ... You shall live in booths seven days; all Israelites shall live in booths, in order that future generations may know that I made the Israelite people live in booths when I brought them out of the land of Egypt, I Adonai your God. So Moses declared to the Israelites the set times of Adonai.

The law states that the booths should remind us of our wilderness wanderings. Yet we know that the Israelites in the wilderness used tents. Booths were lean-tos of wood and tree branches. They were set up by farmers in the Holy Land at harvest time so the farmers could sleep close to the crops to get the harvest in quickly before the rains came to destroy it. By the time of the P-teller's calendar, of course, most folk knew much more about booths than they did about tents. It made sense to them that the Israelites in the wilderness would do what they did: set up booths.

In this addition to the laws of Sukkot we also find the first mention of the four species that we wave on Sukkot. We do not know what a *hadar* tree was, but the fruit we use for it is the *etrog*, "citron", a bitter kind of lemon. For "leafy trees" we use the myrtle. And we join a branch of myrtle to one of willow and one of palm to make what we call the *lulav*.

The P-teller's calendar adds many details to the mentions of the various holidays in Exodus (see *Mishpatim*), es-

To Consider

The laws of Sukkot mention an eighth day, a second day of rest. This is called *Shemini Atzeret*, "the eighth *atzeret*." Nachmanides thought the word *atzeret* meant "binding"—this last holiday was given to bind all holidays together. The Rabbis in the Midrash thought *atzeret* meant "holding back." They told this story: A king gave a grand seven-day banquet for his children. When it was over, the king said, "I love you so much, it is hard to let you leave. Hold back another day and rest with me." So God says to us: "It's *Shemini Atzeret*. 'Hold back' another day and rest with Me."

Quote to Remember

וַיְדַבֵּר מֹשֶׁה אֶת־מֹעֲדֵי יְהֹוָה
אֶל־בְּנֵי יִשְׂרָאֵל׃

So Moses declared to the Israelites the set times of Adonai.

pecially details about the festival sacrifices to be brought to Adonai. Today the Jewish calendar contains many other holidays, some ancient and some modern. As we check the portion of *Emor* back into the library of the Torah, we should remember that growing and changing is a sure sign that our Jewish religion is very much alive.

Haftarah: Ezekiel 44:15-31

The Rabbis connect the priestly duties in the Torah portion to the prophet's description of the priesthood in a new Temple. Ezekiel predicted this new Temple would be built when the people returned from Babylonia to the Promised Land.

Only the priests of the family of Zadok will remain priests in the new Temple, since they remained loyal to Adonai even when the people went astray (see *Emor* and *Pinchas*).

Ezekiel describes the clothing that the priests will wear when they serve the Temple, saying that they must not wear this clothing outside the Temple. They cannot shave their heads or drink wine before serving Adonai.

> They are to teach My people the difference between the holy and the common, and inform them how to tell the clean from the unclean. When there are disputes, they are to be judges, following My laws of justice.

Their privilege of serving Adonai is all they need. Adonai says, "I am their inheritance" and "I am their property." They will receive their food from whatever is offered to Adonai. They will have no share of the land.

> The priests shall get the best of the first fruits of all kinds, and every offering of every kind you offer. Also, you shall give the priest the first loaf of whatever you bake. [For this,] a blessing will rest on your home.

What Ezekiel teaches here is very much what the Torah teaches. The prophet seems to be looking back to look forward.

A Perfect World

A Sabbath of the Land

The Book of Exodus stated: "Six years you shall sow your land ... but in the seventh year you shall let it rest …. Let the needy among your people eat of it…." This command to give the land one year of rest every seven years was later named *Shemitah*, meaning "untended" or "fallow". According to the law of Shemitah, farmers would not plant or sow, and whatever grew wild on the land in the seventh year would be left for the poor to gather.

The P-tellers of Leviticus revisited this law. This is how the portion begins:

> On Mount Sinai, Adonai spoke to Moses: Speak to the Israelites and say to them: When you enter the land…, Six years you may sow your field…. But in the seventh year the land shall have a Sabbath of complete rest, a Sabbath of Adonai: you shall not sow your field or prune your vineyard. … But you may eat whatever the land will produce during its Sabbath….

In Israel today, when people are chatting and someone says something totally unconnected with the conversation, the other may reply with the popular question: "What has that Shemitah got to do with Mount Sinai?" This is a Jewish way of saying "What has *this* got to do with *that*?" But it also points to a mystery in this portion. Why do the P-tellers suddenly remind us that Moses is on Mount Sinai, then tell us about the law of Shemitah? We can answer that question—but only by looking closely at what else is in this parashah called *Bihar*, "On Mount [Sinai]".

Yoveil—The Jubilee Year

> You shall count off seven weeks of years—seven times seven years… a total of forty-nine years.

Quote to Remember

וּקְרָאתֶם דְּרוֹר בָּאָרֶץ לְכָל־יֹשְׁבֶיהָ…

You shall proclaim release [liberty] throughout the land for all its inhabitants.

Above: Illustration of the "Liberty Bell", from a pamphlet issued for the Columbian Exposition of 1893 (the bell itself is in Philadelphia). The crack appeared the first time the bell was hung and tested in 1753, but the bell rang until 1846, when the crack grew too large for any further use. The bell was ordered for the fiftieth celebration of Pennsylvania's charter, a good reason for quoting from the Torah's portion on the fiftieth year.

To Consider

We know that *shemitah* means "untended" or "fallow". But we do not know what the word *yoveil* means. Some archaeologists and historians believe that it is the horn (*yaval*) of the wild ram, which was supposed to be blown on Yom Kippur to announce the beginning of the year of Yoveil. If so, then the word is another way of saying shofar. But it was translated into Greek as *jubilee*, a word that meant "celebrate". That is why we call the Yoveil year the year of "Jubilee".

Then you shall sound the horn loudly; in the seventh month, on the tenth day of the month—the Day of Atonement—you shall have the horn sounded throughout your land and you shall [celebrate] the fiftieth year. You shall proclaim release [liberty] throughout the land for all its inhabitants. It shall be a jubilee for you: each of you shall return to his holding; each of you shall return to his family. That fiftieth year shall be a jubilee for you; you shall not sow, neither shall you reap....

The P-tellers add a new twist to Shemitah. Every seven years farmers stop working their fields for a year. And every seven times seven years, in the Yoveil or Jubilee Year, farmers stop working the land for an extra year. Would farmers really let the land grow wild two years in a row? Even going one year without working the land could cause grief. When seed is not sown and weeds are not cleared for a whole year, very little grows wild. If the land is not tended for two years, practically nothing would grow in the second year.

In a time when grain was the most important food, wouldn't the people starve in the second year? In fact, we have records showing that even one year without sowing could be too much. The first-century historian Josephus records three times when Shemitah years caused such great famine among the Israelites that many starved to death. Was this what the P-tellers had in mind when they put the law of Shemitah in Adonai's commands to Moses at Sinai?

And did they really mean that every forty-nine years the Israelites should put themselves in even greater jeopardy by not working the land for two years? It seems strange. How could Israelites be expected to mark a jubilee (a great celebration) if they were starving to death?

But there is still more to this strange concept of Yoveil.

Return to Your Land

The law of Yoveil says: "In this year of jubilee each of you shall return to [your family] holding." The idea is that Israelites cannot sell what belongs to Adonai, and the whole land of Israel belongs to Adonai! According to the Torah, when the Israelites conquered the land each tribe was given a part of the Holy Land, and each family was given a piece of land on which to live. But the land did not belong to the family or to the tribe. It was holy land, land owned by God. At the end of every forty–nine years, in the year of Yoveil, all sales of the land were canceled, and every family returned to the land it had originally been given.

Adonai's Promise

In return for the Israelites' keeping the Yoveil year, the P-tellers say Adonai promises that the land will provide more than enough food.

> And should you ask, "What are we to eat the seventh year, if we may neither sow nor gather in our crops?" I [Adonai] will [bring] My blessing for you in the sixth year, so that it shall yield a crop sufficient for three years. When you sow in the eighth year, you will still be eating old grain of that crop; you will be eating the old until the ninth year, until its crops come in. But the land must not be sold permanently, for the land is Mine; you are but strangers resident with Me.

In other words, the P-tellers promise that Adonai will deliver a miracle every forty-nine years! What is the miracle? Adonai will make so much grain grow wild that everyone will be free to celebrate and no one will starve either during the year of Shemitah or the year of Yoveil. In fact, there will be more grain than usual! So much grain that Israelites will still be eating it even two years after the Yoveil year! It sounds too good to be true. And since we know that some sabbatical or Shemitah years did cause starving among the people, it would have to be a miracle to be true at all!

Special Laws for the City Dwellers

Since the P-tellers lived in a time when cities had grown large and many people no longer were farmers, they had to consider how their laws would work for city folk. City folk owned houses in town and worked in trades like bricklaying and sandal-making, butchering and tailoring. Most had never worked on farms. What would happen to them in the

Being Fair in Land Sales

In most years Israelites could buy or sell land. But they had to be careful not to cheat one another. If it was the forty-seventh year, for example, the price could only be set for three years, since in the fiftieth year, the Jubilee year, the person who bought it would have to give it back. In other words, people were not really "selling" the land, only selling a number of harvests. To this law the P-teller adds, "Do not wrong one another, but fear your God; for I Adonai am your God." In other words, "Do not pretend to sell the land (or charge much money for the land) when you know that the land is about to return to you anyway. Behave like God and be fair to one another."

year of Yoveil? If they bought or sold a house, would it return to them in the Jubilee year? The P-tellers said that some towns were "cities" and others were "villages". A true city was one with a wall around it. If you lived in a walled city and you sold a house in it, you could buy the house back during the first year after you sold it. If you did not buy it back, then it was lost to you forever.

But if you lived in a village—a city without walls—any house you sold had to be returned to you in the year of Yoveil. Houses in villages were just like farms. They were protected for your family forever. And of course the houses in the cities of the Levites—the priests who had no land at all—always returned to the Levite families in the Yoveil year.

Special Laws for Slaves

Foreign Slaves

Israelite slaves had to be released in the Yoveil year, but if a slave was not an Israelite, then the Yoveil year did not affect him or her. A non-Israelite slave was treated like property. He or she belonged to an owner and could even be passed down from one owner to another, from one generation to the next. Slavery was common everywhere in the ancient world, and the laws in the Bible make it clear that it was common in Israel, too.

Even in the days of the P-tellers some people grew rich while others became poor. If an Israelite became so poor that he or she was forced into slavery, the P-tellers say, the Israelite should be treated not like a slave, but like a worker. Rich Israelites should not take advantage of poor ones. Israelite slaves should be treated kindly. In the Yoveil year the Israelite slave and his or her family had to be released. The slave and the slave's family would then be free to return to their family home, which Adonai had set aside for them.

> For they are My servants, whom I freed from the
> land of Egypt; they may not give themselves over
> into slavery.

If an Israelite became the slave of a non-Israelite, the law allowed the Israelite's family to redeem him or her at any time. Even if the slave was not redeemed beforehand, the Israelite slave and his or her family had to be set free in the year of Yoveil. In truth, the portion says, all Israelites are slaves, servants of Adonai:

> They are My servants, whom I freed from the land
> of Egypt, I Adonai your God. You shall not make
> idols, or set up carved images or pillars, or place
> figured stones in your land to worship upon, for I
> Adonai am your God. You shall keep My Sabbaths
> and venerate My sanctuary, Mine, Adonai's.

A Perfect World

This sounds all well and good. The basic idea is that every Israelite has a place in Adonai's land. No one can take this place away forever. The land belongs to Adonai and not to the people. It cannot be bought or sold by human beings. At the end of every forty-nine years people would return to the home they had when Adonai first gave them the land. No one who was rich could keep any extra land they bought with their wealth. No one who was poor could be kept from the land Adonai gave them. No Israelite who became a slave could stay a slave. Every jubilee year things returned to the way Adonai organized them. That is the idea of Yoveil attached to the idea of Shemitah.

The idea of Shemitah—a seven-year period—seems to be borrowed from other nations. We have an ancient text from the city of Ugar that tells of a ceremony for celebrating the end of a seven-year cycle. We remember (from the stories of Joseph) the seven-year cycles in ancient Egypt. And we know that Shemitah was observed in the days of the Second Temple.

One thing, however, is certain. There is no trace of the Yoveil year ever being observed! But wait! If there never was a Yoveil year, why are we given all the laws of Yoveil? The answer may be even stranger than the question!

The P-teller and the Greeks

By the time of the P-tellers, the world of the Greeks was well known to the Israelites. And one popular subject for the Greeks was how to create a perfect world. Plato wrote about an imaginary perfect world early in the fourth century B.C.E. in a book called *The Republic*. And he was following the path of other Greeks who had imagined perfect worlds before his time.

So the P-tellers imagined how Adonai's perfect world should look, and they placed their perfect world in the Torah (even as Plato placed his perfect world in *The Republic*). The P-tellers were picturing the way the world *should* be and not the way it *was*. The laws of Yoveil and the laws of Shemitah came together to shape a world where Adonai could prom-

Shemitah in Early Israel

There are a few times when the Bible seems to be speaking of Shemitah during the early days of Israel, the days of the kings and of the First Temple. But we have no way of being sure that Shemitah was ever really observed in those days or of *how* it was observed. Most scholars agree that it was only observed in the days of the Second Temple. We know that the Israelites—those who returned to the Holy Land to build the Second Temple—promised to keep the laws of Shemitah. And the three times that the historian Josephus mentions that great famines were caused by the Shemitah all come from the time of the Second Temple.

To Consider

How did the P-tellers first learn the stories of the Greeks? You may remember hearing about Alexander the Great, who "conquered the world." Among the lands that Alexander conquered was the land of Israel. The Greeks ruled the Holy Land from the fourth century B.C.E. until the time of the Maccabees. Alexander's conquest quickened a slow process. The ideas of Plato and other early Greeks had already reached the Israelites by land and sea just as Israelite ideas had reached the ancient Greeks.

ise the best of everything. Poor Israelites would not remain poor forever, Israelite slaves would not remain slaves forever, no house would ever be sold without the chance of buying it back, and no year would ever come when the land would not give enough grain for everyone. The P-tellers placed their plan for this imaginary perfect Israel in the words of Adonai given to Moses at the mountain called Sinai. That's what Shemitah has to do with Mount Sinai!

Of course, keeping the laws of Shemitah was difficult enough, sometimes even dangerous. But keeping the laws of Yoveil was impossible, and everyone knew it. Later the Rabbis of the Talmud set aside the laws of Yoveil entirely. But it seems that Yoveil, the Jubilee, never happened anyway. It was only an Israelite dream told in the way the Greeks had told about perfect worlds even before the P-tellers imagined the celebration of Yoveil.

Haftarah: Jeremiah 32:6-27

Bihar tells how land returns to its original owner in the Jubilee year. Even sold land can be redeemed. Jeremiah tells about how a parcel of land is redeemed by its rightful family and compares this to the whole nation of Israelites. Even if they are sold into slavery and exile, they are always the property of Adonai, and Adonai can redeem them.

A cousin came to Jeremiah and offered to sell him land that belonged to his family. Jeremiah had foretold that Jerusalem would fall to the Babylonians who now surrounded it. The king put him in prison as a traitor, but he was allowed visitors like his cousin and his scribe/secretary Baruch. It was an act of faith for Jeremiah to buy this land, knowing that the kingdom would fall. Buying it showed the people that Adonai would not desert them.

Jeremiah had the deeds drawn up by Baruch and sealed in a clay jar "so that they will last a long time." (Remember that many of the Dead Sea Scrolls were saved in just this way.)

> For Adonai *Tzeva'ot*, the God of Israel says: Houses, fields, and vineyards shall again be bought in this land.

Jeremiah then offered a prayer to Adonai, ending with the fact that the Chaldeans (Babylonians) had already come to capture the city. "What You announced has come to pass, and now You look at it." In the face of this, Jeremiah says, You [Adonai] told me to buy land though the city is about to fall!

> Then the word of Adonai came to Jeremiah, saying, "I am Adonai, the God of all flesh. Is anything too difficult for Me?"

Terms of the Covenant

Meet Ploni and Almoni

To describe a conversation between two imaginary people, we can assign them common names like Smith and Jones. We say "Smith" said so-and-so, and "Jones" answered thus-and-such. When the Talmud discusses any two imaginary people it calls them "Ploni" and "Almoni".

A covenant is an agreement between people. If you make an agreement, it is obvious that it needs several parts. First comes what is being agreed. For example, let's say that Ploni and Almoni each own a field. Between their fields there is a small stream—just enough water for both fields. If Ploni were to dig a large trench from the stream to his field, Ploni would have more water, and Almoni would not have enough. Likewise, Almoni could dig a large trench, and Ploni's crops would have too little water. So Ploni and Almoni meet and draw up a covenant saying neither of us will dig a trench to take water away from the other. It's a good agreement for both of them.

But Ploni has more workers than Almoni. He sends his workers to the stream with buckets, and they pass the buckets back and forth, drawing water constantly day after day. The little stream can barely flow fast enough to keep the buckets full. Almoni complains. "We had a covenant, and you are breaking it." Ploni says, "Our covenant spoke only about digging a trench. We made no agreement about taking water by buckets." Almoni says, "Our covenant had a reason. It was to keep both of us from using too much water—and you are using too much water."

So they add a second part to their covenant: the reason. Now it is clear why Ploni can not use his many workers to take water from Almoni. The covenant is not just about trenches, but about being fair. But what will happen if one of them breaks the covenant? What if Ploni sends his workers out each night to dig a trench for water and then covers the trench over at daybreak so that it seems it was never there?

A Simple Agreement

Even simple agreements need at least four parts. (1) You have to agree on what is being agreed. (2) You have to agree on the reason for making the agreement. (3) You have to agree on the punishment for not keeping the agreement. And (4) you have to agree on your goal: what you are gaining by keeping the agreement.

A Kingship Covenant

Archaeologists have found copies of many covenants like the one in this portion. Usually one partner was a powerful king. The weaker partner of the agreement might be the ruler or king of a city or a region. Good examples come from the kingdom of the Hittites, a powerful people that ruled much of what is today Turkey. They usually begin, "Thus says [Ploni], king of the Hittites ..." Then Ploni tells the weaker ruler [Almoni] what must be done and why. And Ploni states what punishments will come to pass if Almoni fails to follow Ploni's laws and what blessings will come to Almoni if he obeys. The archaeologists call this a "kingship covenant". God's covenant with Israel in this portion sounds very much like an ancient kingship covenant.

Below: If treaties failed, Hittite soldiers like those from a wall carving in Anatolia would step in to punish the offender.

If Ploni is caught, there should be a punishment—otherwise the covenant is useless. So Ploni and Almoni agree that if one of them breaks the agreement, he will have to pay the other one half of his profit for that season. This is another part of a covenant: the punishment.

Last, there is the blessing: what they each gain by keeping the covenant. Ploni and Almoni agree that by keeping the little stream flowing they will have peace between them and enough water for both of their fields to flourish. This will make them both happy.

A Covenant with Adonai

This portion, *Bichukotai,* "In My Laws", sets out the covenant between Adonai and the Israelites. What is the agreement? What is the reason for the agreement? What happens if the people follow the agreement? What happens if the people break the agreement?

Of course, this covenant is a little different from the simple one between Ploni and Almoni. In their agreement they were equal. In the covenant between Adonai and the Israelites all the requirements and all the punishments are for Israel, because Adonai is much more powerful than Israel. Adonai says,

> If you follow My laws, and faithfully observe My
> commandments, I will grant you rains in their
> season, so that the earth shall yield its produce
> and the trees of the field their fruit. ... You shall
> eat your fill of bread and dwell safely in your land.
> I will grant peace in the land....

Adonai promises that vicious beasts will not attack and the Israelites will always win battles against their enemies. "Five of you," Adonai says, will be more powerful than "a hundred, and a hundred of you shall give chase to ten thousand; your enemies shall fall before you by the sword." Adonai promises that the Israelites will multiply in numbers and the covenant will remain unchanged. Adonai will even dwell among the people.

Then Adonai states the "why" of the covenant—the reason that the Israelites should obey:

I will be your God, and you shall be My people. I Adonai am your God who brought you out from the Egyptians' land to be their slaves no more....

Punishments

>>But if you ... break My covenant, I will do this to you: I will cause misery for you—illness and fever ... and ... your enemies shall eat [your crops]. ... Your foes shall rule over you. You shall flee even when no one is chasing you.

Adonai tells the people that the punishment for not obeying will be seven times worse than the blessing. Rains will not fall, wild beasts will attack, the earth will be hard as metal, roads will be deserted and empty. If the people still refuse to obey, then Adonai will make the punishment even seven times harsher. Adonai will send a powerful nation to attack and defeat the Israelites. Adonai will send disease, and there will be no food. The list of punishments goes on. Adonai will refuse the sacrifices of the Israelites. Adonai will "scatter the Israelites among the nations." The land will be empty, and its cities will fall into ruins.

Looking Back

In the Torah, this portion comes while the people are at Sinai, looking forward to the time when they will be in the Promised Land. Adonai tells the people to obey the commandments in order to gain blessings. And Adonai warns the people against breaking the commandments by stating what will happen to them.

This may be the way it was, but Bible scholars notice that the punishments seem to be historical, too. The punishments seem to look back at what already happened to understand why it happened. If the P-teller (the priest who put this part of the Torah together) is among the people around the time the Second Temple was destroyed, then the punishments ring true. For they tell the story of what really happened when the Assyrians destroyed the kingdoms of Israel (in 722 B.C.E.) and Judah (in 586 B.C.E.) and exiled the Israelites to Babylon.

Laws of Leviticus

The covenant is made up of commandments. The Rabbis of the Talmud spoke of the 613 commandments (*mitzvot*) contained in the Torah. Are there really 613? You could peek ahead at portion *Ki Teitzei* to find the answer. But basically a rabbi named Simlai said there were 248 positive commands—matching "the parts of [our] body"—and 365 negative commands—matching the "sun's days [the year]". This was his way of reminding us to use every part of our bodies and every day of the year to do God's mitzvot. If you really wanted to count the commandments one by one, the Book of Leviticus would be a good place to start. The laws are given in neat lists. And almost everyone agrees that there are 247 commands here—nearly half of the 613 mitzvot.

The P-teller's Idea

The idea of the P-teller is simple and powerful. If the Israelites had obeyed their covenant with Adonai, no nation would ever have been strong enough to defeat or destroy them. It is only because the Israelites broke their agreement that Adonai punished them.

In the face of the Assyrian attack on the kingdom of Israel, some Israelites moved south to Judah; others were carried off in slavery to Babylon, with still others fleeing to the four corners of the ancient world. The ten tribes of the north were "lost" forever. The P-teller is saying that this was not the work of the Assyrians alone. This was the punishment that Adonai brought because the people disobeyed the covenant. Adonai had promised to "scatter the Israelites among the nations," and that is what Adonai did.

Moreover, the P-teller is saying, the southern kingdom of Judah still did not obey Adonai's commands, so the Babylonians were sent by Adonai to destroy the kingdom of Judah. Again the people were scattered—some being carried off to Babylonia, some fleeing to Egypt and other places, and some few remaining to starve and struggle in a land of disease and ruins. It seemed all was lost. But this was not the work of the Babylonians, the P-teller says; this was the punishment for not obeying Adonai's commands.

There is more to the story. The people of Israel did not disappear. The land of Israel was not forgotten.

The Return

The P-teller may have been looking back at what happened, but looking forward, too. Just like the time when the people stood at Sinai, Jews in Babylon were now hoping to return to the Promised Land.

In the covenant in *Bichukotai*, Adonai tells the people that while you "are in the land of your enemies" the land will rest. (Bible scholars believe that "the land of your enemies" probably means Babylon.) The Israelites will remain frightened there—even the sound of a "driven leaf", a leaf being blown by the wind, will terrify them. (Bible scholars believe that the frightening place also refers to Babylon.) Many Israelites will be lost among the enemy (just as, the scholars say, many Israelites became so much like the Babylonians that they had no wish to return to the Holy Land). But some will survive (meaning the ones who still hoped to return). They will be sad for what the Israelites had done in not keeping Adonai's commands. They will pray for forgiveness. Then, says Adonai,

I will remember My covenant with Jacob … My covenant with Isaac, and also My covenant with Abraham; and I will remember the land. … Even then, when they are in the land of their enemies, I will … destroy [the Israelites], canceling My covenant with them: for I Adonai am their God. For their sake, I will remember the covenant with the ancients, whom I freed from the land of Egypt in the sight of the nations to be their God: I, Adonai. These are the laws, rules, and instructions that Adonai set forth through Moses on Mount Sinai, between [God] and the Israelite people.

Even as this P-teller looks back at what happened to the Israelites, the Babylonians have already been defeated by the Persians. This P-teller knows that the Persians permitted the Jews to return to their Holy Land and that a few were brave enough to actually return. In other words, this P-teller knows that the covenant did not end. It was not "canceled" or set aside by Adonai. The people sent to Babylon were punished; they repented; and now they have a chance to build a new kingdom in the Promised Land.

So the Israelites in Babylon are very much at the same point as the people who stood at Sinai. The only difference is that this P-teller knew what had already happened. That is why Bible scholars think that this part of the portion—the blessings and curses of the covenant—was placed here, at the end of the book of Leviticus, the book of priestly teachings. For the priests—either those at Sinai or those in Babylonia—this was a time of looking back and a time of looking forward.

The Last Laws of Leviticus

The last code of laws in this portion, the last laws in Leviticus, explain how sacrifices were turned into the money needed to operate and maintain the Temple and its priests. Some offerings were given as animals, and the Book of Leviticus explained how these animals were sacrificed. Some offerings were given as grain, and the Book of Leviticus explained how the grain was offered. But there were other offerings that could not be given directly.

Quote to Remember

וְזָכַרְתִּי אֶת־בְּרִיתִי יַעֲקוֹב...

I will remember My covenant with Jacob…

The First Book

Leviticus is the third book in the Torah, but already in ancient times it was the first book that Jewish children were given to study. In the Midrash Rabbi Assi taught: "Why do young children begin with [Leviticus] the Law of the Priests, and not with Genesis?—Surely it is because young children are pure, and the sacrifices are pure; so let the pure come and engage in the study of the pure." This may have been one good reason, but scholars believe that there was another. The priests were the first teachers in the schools of the Israelites, and so they began with what was most important to them, the book that held the codes of law of the priests themselves.

To Consider

It sounds a bit strange when the priests talk about "vowing" a person, a place, or a thing to Adonai, but we make "pledges to Adonai" even now. Synagogues and Jewish institutions could not be supported if we did not make contributions to them. The idea that every Jew should give a "fair share" to help support Jewish causes goes all the way back to our Torah.

The Sanctuary Weight

Houses could be "vowed" or pledged to Adonai, people could be pledged, unclean animals (that could not be sacrificed on the altar) could be pledged, and land could be pledged. In each case a certain amount of shekels were brought to the Temple. These laws could only come from a time long after Mount Sinai, since they speak of "the sanctuary weight", a measure first used in Temple times. The portion even tells us the rule of measure when it says "All assessments shall be by the sanctuary weight, the shekel being twenty *gerahs*."

For example, if Ploni decided to give his house to Adonai, the priests would "assess" it (they would state what Ploni's house was worth). Ploni could now make a contribution to the Temple by "buying back" his house "from Adonai". He would give the amount that the priests stated and add one-fifth to it. In this way Ploni could "donate" his house, but the actual donation was in silver shekels.

People could pledge anything of value to Adonai. Whatever was pledged was paid in shekels. If a male between the ages of twenty and sixty was pledged, then the amount to be given to Adonai was "fifty shekels of silver by the sanctuary weight". For a female of the same age the amount was thirty shekels. A male from five to twenty years old was worth twenty shekels, and a female worth ten shekels. From one month to five years a male child was worth five shekels, and a female child was worth three shekels. But if a person was poor and wanted to pledge a male or female to Adonai, the priests would charge an amount based on what that person could afford.

Some things cannot be pledged to Adonai because they already belong to Adonai. The firstborn of an animal already belongs to Adonai. Anything already pledged to Adonai by one person cannot be pledged again by another. One-tenth of all crops—grain or fruit, herd or flock—already belongs to Adonai; it cannot be pledged a second time. But it can be "bought back from Adonai" by paying the value in shekels and adding one-fifth.

Completing the Book

Leviticus ends with the simple statement "These are the commandments that Adonai gave Moses for the Israelite people on Mount Sinai." As we have seen, Leviticus is not so simple after all. Almost all the laws in it come from priests or speak to priests. Looking at the book, you can see that the P-teller was not one priest, but many priests (many P-tellers) who collected these sets of laws at different times and places. Some groups of laws are probably hundreds of years older than others. In the end, though, someone (we called this person the "puzzle-solver") put it all together in one book.

You have now studied the whole Book of Leviticus (*Vayikra,* in Hebrew). Each time we complete studying a book of the Torah we speak aloud the words *Hazak! Hazak! V'Nithazek!* "Be strong! Be strong! And may you be strengthened!" So we say, "Congratulations on finishing a book of the Torah. Prepare yourself! You will need your strength! For the study of Torah never ends!" Go ahead, say the words aloud with strength: *Hazak! Hazak! V'Nithazek!*

חֲזַק חֲזַק וְנִתְחַזֵּק!

To Consider

From Exodus 40:17 and Numbers 1:1 we know that the Israelites spent one month at Mount Sinai. Leviticus ends by saying that its laws were given "on Mount Sinai". Were all the laws in Leviticus given in one month? Bible scholars believe the laws were collected over hundreds of years. Then why should Leviticus state that they were given at Sinai? The idea is what is important, and the idea of Leviticus is that these laws are part of one holy covenant.

Haftarah: Jeremiah 16:19-17:14

The Rabbis connect blessing and curse to the choices made by the people. So does Jeremiah in this haftarah. There are eight sets of sayings here.

Verse 16:19 predicts that all peoples will one day worship Adonai.

Verses 16:20-21 ask "How can human beings make gods?" Adonai will prove that idolatry is wrong. The nations will know that "I am called Adonai."

Verses 17:1-4 predict that Adonai will punish the kingdom of Judah.

> I will make you serve your enemies in a land you do not know, for you have kindled the flame of my wrath, to burn a long while, says Adonai.

Verses 17:5-7 compare those who are to be cursed against those who will be blessed.

Blessed be those who trust in Adonai, who call Adonai their trusted one.

Verses 17:9-10 say that the human heart is deceitful, but Adonai searches the heart and knows the truth.

Verse 17:11 is difficult to translate but seems to mean that unlawful riches eventually lead to poverty (or maybe early death).

Verses 17:12-13 say that God is our "holy Shrine, our Hope", and those who turn away from God are turning from the "Fountain of Living Waters".

Verse 17:14 is Jeremiah's prayer, which has become part of our synagogue service.

> Heal me, Adonai, and I shall be healed. Save me, and I shall be saved; for You are my blessing.

במדבר
Bemidbar
Numbers 1:1-4:20

In the Wilderness

Megillah

In ancient libraries each book was a separate scroll. In Hebrew, a long scroll—especially one that tells a single story (like the story of Esther)—was called a *megillah* (Hebrew for "scroll"). Before the first century C.E. important or long scrolls were also attached to a handle (a rod or roller) of wood to make it easier to roll and store the scroll after reading it. We know such scrolls were attached to wooden handles because of a mistake made by the Jews of Alexandria, Egypt. Not recognizing the meaning of the Hebrew word *megillah*, they translated it into Greek as "handle".

Below: An illustrated copy of the *Megillah* or Scroll of Esther (from the eighteenth century), now preserved in the Library of Congress. Note the plain handle (*left*) for rolling the scroll.

The Torah of Moses

In Babylonia, in talmudic times (before the year 600 C.E.), the books of the Torah were stitched together into one long scroll. The Torah scroll was then so heavy that it required more than one wood roller. The scribes attached each end of the long scroll to its own rod. In the Talmud each rod is called an *amud*, a "pillar". Later, because they were made of wood, and because the Torah was often called "a tree of life", the rollers were given a new name—each was called an *eitz chayim*, "a tree of life".

But the Torah did not begin as one scroll. Originally each book was a separate scroll. To make things even more confusing, any one scroll or even a part of one scroll could be called a *torah*, since the word *torah* just means "a teaching".

Even now some Jews believe that God spoke the whole Torah—all five books—and Moses wrote down the whole Torah—all five books—while Moses was on Mount Sinai. But the Torah itself says that Moses carried down only two tablets of stone on which the laws of the covenant were written.

There is another reason for thinking that the Torah of Moses was originally much smaller than it is today. The Book of Joshua tells how after the death of Moses Joshua built an altar and offered sacrifices at Mount Ebal.

> And there, on the stones, he carved a copy of the Torah that Moses had written for the Israelites. All Israel—stranger and citizen alike ... stood on either side of the Ark of Adonai's Covenant. ...
> Then, [Joshua] read all the words of the Torah, the blessing and the curse, just as they are written in the Book of the Torah. There was not a word of all that Moses commanded that Joshua failed to read in the presence of all the Israelites, including the women and children and the strangers who were with them. [JOSHUA 8:32-35]

Whatever "Torah of Moses" Joshua carved on the stones was short enough to be read to the people as they stood together on the mountain.

Growing the Torah—the J-Tellers

Bible scholars today think that what we now call the Torah was collected to make a history that would unite the people. If so, the Torah might have grown in a fairly simple way.

Once upon a time the land belonged to the Canaanites, the Philistines, and other nations. King Saul united the Israelites; King David conquered the land; and David's son King Solomon built the Temple. Before these kings the Israelites had been separate tribes—not one nation. So imagine that King Jehoshaphat (871-848 B.C.E.—the fourth ruler of the Kingdom of Judah) told his priests, "Collect everything that tells how we became a mighty nation. Write it all down in a scroll." The priests then decided what ideas and stories were important enough to include in their "history".

Scholars believe that the first such "history of Israel" may have been a collection of laws and stories made by a group of priests we now call the J-tellers (remember: the "Y" in *YHVH* comes into English as a "J", just as *Yehudah* becomes Judah and *Yerushalayim* becomes Jerusalem). Of course, the J-tellers believed that the "true" kingdom of Israelites was the Kingdom of Judah, the southern kingdom, the one now ruled by a king of the House of David. Even though old stories claimed that Reuven was the firstborn son of Jacob, in their stories the J-tellers made Judah the most important of the twelve brothers. So, when you think of the J-tellers, though they were probably priests, you can think of them as priests loyal to Judah.

Growing the Torah—the E-Tellers

At the same time, there was another group of Israelites—the ten tribes who had broken away from Solomon's empire to found the northern Kingdom of Israel. This kingdom came to a sudden end in 722 B.C.E. when it was conquered by the Assyrians. Most of its people—the important folk, especially those who lived in the cities—were carried off to Assyria. The

What United the Israelites

Stories and laws gave the Israelites a unified history even before there was a Torah. At the top of the list was the belief in *YHVH* [Adonai], the One God of Israel. The stories told of ancestors and the covenants or agreements they made with *YHVH*. There was a memory of Sinai, where all Israelites were united in a covenant with *YHVH*. The land of Israel also united them, and so did their centers of worship in places like Shiloh, Dan, and Jerusalem.

One People, Different Memories

The laws and stories collected in the north were much like those of the south (after all, the twelve tribes of Israel were once one people, though they had divided into two kingdoms). But there were differences, too. For example, the northern priests thought that God met Moses on a mountain called Horeb, not Sinai. In their stories God often spoke through angels or in dreams. Joshua was an important hero to the northern priests, perhaps because Joshua was from the tribe of Ephraim, the territory at the center of the northern kingdom. The graves of Rachel, Joseph, and Joshua were important to them because they were also in the hills of Ephraim. The E-tellers were probably Levite priests, but you can also think of them as loyal to Ephraim.

ten tribes were "lost". But many villagers and small farmers were not carried off by the Assyrians. At least one temple, the one at Beth El, continued to operate. And some scholars believe that after the disaster of 722 a few northern priests began collecting the laws and stories of the northern Israelites so that they would not be lost along with the tribes and the kingdom.

The northern priests called God either *El* or *Elohim* in any story that happened before Moses arrived at the burning bush. But *Elohim* told Moses a secret four-letter name, *YHVH* [Adonai], at the bush, so after that event the northern priests included this name, sometimes joining it to *Elohim* to show that the two were really the same God. We call these priests the E-tellers, the ones who most often used *Elohim* as God's name.

Growing the Torah—the JE Combination

After the disaster of 722 many northerners fled to the south, and perhaps the E-tellers came with them. Now the only nation of Israelites was the Kingdom of Judah. The king—it may have been Hezekiah (728-699 B.C.E.)—saw that there were two sets of tales of how Israel came to be. He, or one of the kings who followed him, may have called the J-tellers and the E-tellers together, saying, "We are one people now; we should have one history." So the priests worked to join their stories into one collection. This created what some Bible scholars call the "JE" document. Other scholars think that there never was an official E-tellers' document, so that we should speak only of a "J" and not a "JE". But most scholars agree that northern stories were combined with southern stories at some time, so it is useful to think of a "JE" document.

Growing the Torah—the P-Tellers

Meanwhile, the priests of the Temple in Jerusalem had also been collecting the codes of laws and rituals they used for the worship of God. Some codes came from the north and some from the south. Some were ancient even by the time of the first Temple in Jerusalem. Some were more recent.

These became the heart of the scrolls written by the P-tellers—we call them "P-tellers" because they cared most about how priests should behave.

In ancient times the priests also served as the official scribes and record-keepers of the kingdom. They kept lists of who belonged to what tribe, family trees, who made donations, how much was given, and so on. These lists were later used by the P-tellers to help organize the growing Torah. That is why much of the Torah, including this portion at the beginning of the Book of Numbers, reads like the work of accountants.

The work of the priests was suddenly interrupted when the Babylonians conquered Judah and destroyed the Temple (around 586 B.C.E.). The most important Israelites of Judah—including the priests—were rounded up and carried off to Babylonia. The Israelites became known by a new name in Babylonia. Since they came from Judah, they were called Judeans (still later the Greeks called the "Judeans" by the name "Jews").

Only one generation passed before Babylonia was conquered by the Persians. The Persians did not believe in moving conquered peoples to foreign lands. So in 538 B.C.E. Cyrus the Great, King of Persia, decreed that the Judeans could return to their land and rebuild their temple. Around that time, too, the Persian kings were gathering a great library. In it they kept scrolls about all the nations they had conquered. The scrolls told how each nation began and gave the exact laws of each nation. Many scholars think that at this time the P-tellers became more than priests. In order to create one book about the Israelites for the library of Persia, the P-tellers became "puzzle-solvers". They gathered all the scrolls and created a Torah of four books: Genesis, Exodus, Leviticus, and Numbers. It is possible that Ezra the Scribe carried a copy of this book to Jerusalem and read it to the people, calling it "the Torah of Moses".

The Growing of the Torah

This is generally how Bible scholars think the laws and stories were collected to become a single Torah. Later we will meet the author of the fifth book of the Torah, Deuteron-

To Discuss

In the United States today there is a feeling that we are all connected in some way to England. We know this is not true. Most people in the United States either were born here or came from countries other than England. Yet the United States began as thirteen English colonies. The feeling that all of us owe something special to England is similar to the feeling that the twelve tribes of Israel had for Jacob and Moses. The Israelites' idea that they were all part of one covenant is similar to the American idea that we all owe allegiance to one Constitution.

How Many Israelites?

Bemidbar says that there were 603,550 Israelite males above the age of twenty. Historians tell us that if this were true, there would have been more than two million Israelites, more Israelites wandering for forty years than the estimated population of Israelites at the time of King David. With no farms in the wilderness to feed them and hardly any water, the number does not seem to make sense. But we have to remember that as tellers of later ages spoke of the great generations of the past, they often exaggerated the numbers and thus exaggerated the miracles. Surely only Adonai could provide enough food and water for such a mass of people in the wilderness. Their survival had to be a miracle. And after all, that is the point.

omy, and we will see why this scroll was added to make the "*Five* Books of Moses."

So the answer to "When was the Torah written?" is "Many times." The answer to "Where was the Torah written?" is "Many places." But when it comes to "Why was the Torah written?" the answer seems never to have changed. The Torah was always meant to be a book that told us who we are, where we came from, how our covenant with God came about, and how we should behave as "a nation of priests and a holy people". All the sources—the J-tellers, the E-tellers, and the P-tellers—agreed on this: There is only One God, and the Israelites are set apart from other nations by their special covenant with Adonai.

The Book of the Wilderness

Bemidbar means "in the wilderness" or "in the desert". It is the name of this portion and also the Hebrew name of the fourth book of the Torah. It is called *Numbers* in English because it begins with the counting or numbering of the people.

> On the first day of the second month, in the second year following the Exodus from Egypt, Adonai spoke to Moses in the wilderness of Sinai, in the Tent of Meeting, saying: Take a census of the whole Israelite community by clans. … You and Aaron shall record them … from the age of twenty years up, all those in Israel who are able to bear arms.

What follows is a list of the tribes and the head of each tribe. The tribes are Reuben, Judah, Issachar, Zebulun, Ephraim, Manasseh, Benjamin, Dan, Asher, Gad, and Naphtali. And of course Levi, with Moses as its head. The heads of the tribes were called "chieftains" or "elders".

Moses, Aaron, and the chieftains made lists of men from each tribe who were fit to become warriors. The lists are long—they sound like official government records. They end with:

> All the Israelites, aged twenty years and over, enrolled by family clans, all those in Israel able to

bear arms ... came to 603,550. The Levites, however, were not recorded among them ... for Adonai said to Moses, Do not [take warriors from] the tribe of Levi or [count] them with the Israelites. You shall put the Levites in charge of the Mishkan [Tabernacle] ... They shall carry the Mishkan ... and tend it; and they shall camp around the Mishkan. ... any outsider who [comes too near] shall be put to death. ... the Levites shall stand guard around the Mishkan of the Covenant.

The Lists and the Rule

Adonai commanded Moses and Aaron to give each tribe a place to set up its flag and place its camp. Another list repeats the same numbers as before, again totaling the Israelites ready to be warriors as 603,550. Each tribe now had its own campsite around the Tent of Meeting, and each tribe knew where to march when the Israelites were on the move. So *Bemidbar* includes two lists that are almost the same in every way. Why should there be two lists instead of one? The answer may come in another question: Why does one list speak about the Mishkan of the Covenant and the other speak about the Tent of Meeting?

This helps us learn a rule about the way the Torah was put together. The rule was: *The Torah should grow, never shrink.* We have met this rule many times before. When two or more stories (or two or more lists) were both well known, the Torah either arranges them side by side or combines them into one story (or list). Probably, then, there were two lists—the "Mishkan list" and the "Tent of Meeting list"—and both are given in this parashah.

The Levites

For a second time Adonai instructs Moses to put the Levites in charge of guarding the Mishkan, but this time the command includes guarding the Tent of Meeting. Aaron and his sons Eleazar and Ithamar are now the high priests. The Levites are their servants, doing the work of setting up the Mishkan when the Israelites stop and packing it up and car-

To Discuss

The Torah recalls the Levites as one clan—all descended from one family, the family of Levi. But it is hard to say exactly who the Levites were and where they came from. Some Bible scholars think that the Levites were the only group of Israelites who had ever been enslaved in Egypt, and the only group of Israelites who had ever stood at Mount Sinai. These scholars believe that the Levites may have taught the worship of Adonai and the idea of covenant to the Israelites. We know that the Levites helped bring King David to power and served him as priests. There is even a story in the Book of Judges about ordinary Levites being ordained as *kohanim*, high priests, in local shrines. Wherever the Levite priests came from, in time their families were dedicated to serving the priests of the Temple. From that time on only one Levite family—that of Aaron and his sons—served as *kohanim*.

Quote to Remember

וַאֲנִי הִנֵּה לָקַחְתִּי אֶת־הַלְוִיִּם
מִתּוֹךְ בְּנֵי יִשְׂרָאֵל ....

*As for Me, behold, I take the Levites
from among the Israelites....*

Redeeming the Firstborn

The point of redeeming the first-born was to keep the memory of the Exodus fresh in every Israelite home. Many Jews still "redeem" their firstborn son on the thirty-first day after the child's birth in a ceremony called *pidyon haben*, "redeeming the son". The parents give the child to a *kohen*, then exchange the equivalent of five shekels to "buy back" or "redeem" the child. In many places five silver dollars are used, but in Israel the national bank mints special coins for this purpose like the one *below* struck in 1977.

rying it when it is time for the Israelites to travel. And the Levites are special in another way, too—they belong to Adonai.

Adonai spoke to Moses, saying: As for Me, behold, I take the Levites from among the Israelites in place of all the first-born ... among the Israelites: the Levites shall be Mine. For every first-born is Mine: When I smote every first-born in the land of Egypt, I consecrated every first-born in Israel, man and beast, to Myself, to be Mine, Adonai's.

So Moses was told to record the names of the Levites, clan by clan, family by family. And he does this, telling how many Levites there were in each family, and placing each family in charge of some part of the Mishkan. One family was in charge of all the curtains and the hangings, another was in charge of the boards and fittings, and so on.

Those who would camp in front of the Mishkan, in front—before the Tent of Meeting, on the east — were Moses and Aaron and his sons ... and any outsider who came too near was to be put to death. All the Levites who were recorded ... all the males from the age of one month up, came to 22,000.

Adonai claimed all the firstborn of the Israelites in return for sparing the firstborn of the Israelites when the angel of death took the lives of the firstborn Egyptians. So Moses counted all the children in the camp. This number came to 22,273. Adonai took the Levites in place of the firstborn of all Israel, but there were only 22,000 Levites. So Adonai commanded that each of the 273 additional firstborn be redeemed (bought back) at "five shekels per head". This money, 1365 shekels, was given to Aaron and his sons to be used for the worship of Adonai.

Most Holy Things

Some things in the Tabernacle were called "most holy"—the Ark of the Covenant (containing the tablets of Sinai), the Menorah and its lamps and oil vessels, the gold altar, the copper altar, and the tools used in sacrifice Only the High Priests could touch these things. A special family of Levites, the Kohathites, were given the task of carrying them. The High Priests themselves would make the most holy things ready for travel, covering them with skins and putting them on poles. Only then, when they could not be touched even by accident, would the Kohathites lift these things to carry them. The most holy things were thought to be very dangerous even to the Levites. So Adonai told Moses and Aaron:

> Do this ... so that the [Kohathite clans] may live and not die when they approach the most sacred objects... [Do not] let [the Kohathites] go inside and witness the dismantling of the sanctuary, lest they die.

Haftarah: Hosea 2:1-22

The Torah portion tells of Israel's numbers in the wilderness, and the haftarah begins with a promise that the people will grow great in number. God told the prophet Hosea to marry Gomer, a prostitute. They had children, but their marriage seemed doomed from the start. Gomer was unfaithful, and the prophet compared her unfaithfulness to the idolatry of the Israelites. Hosea predicts that Adonai will be like a forgiving husband, taking Israel back if she (Israel) will only give up her faithless ways.

If they turn away from idolatry and return, God promises that "the number of Israelites will be like the sands of the sea, beyond measure or count." Hosea uses names to make his points. The sinful people were called "You are not My people"; when they repent they will be called "the Children of the Living God."

Hosea now speaks of Israel as a prostitute, her people born in shame as she turned toward other gods who promised gifts of wool and linen, oil and drink. God will keep her penned in, unable to find new lovers, until she understands that "I [Adonai] gave her the grain, wine, and oil" to use as offerings to other gods. Now Adonai will take back these gifts. "I will destroy her vines and fig-trees." Adonai will punish Israel.

Afterward, Adonai will take her to the wilderness and "speak to her heart."

> On that day ... I will betroth you to Me forever; I will betroth you to Me in righteousness and in justice, in steadfast love and compassion. I will betroth you to Me in faithfulness, and you shall know Adonai.

Mishkan and Tent

Raise Up Your Head

When the Torah says *naso et rosh*, "raise up the head," this means "count" or "take a census." A student of the Baal Shem Tov, Menahem Nahum of Chernobyl (1730-1787), commented that since when we are counted our heads are "lifted up," Jews should always "hold their heads high in pride" as we remember our ancestors at Sinai.

When We Are Counted

Naso is the longest portion in the Torah. It begins as Adonai commands Moses to "take a census" of the Gershonites and Merarites, two families of the Levite tribe. *Naso* in Hebrew actually means "raise up". *Naso et rosh* means "raise up the head" or "take a census".

Most of the last portion (*Bemidbar*) was also about the census. Another census was reported in Exodus. In the Midrash the Rabbis compare God to a ruler who owned many beautiful jewels. To enjoy the jewels the ruler took them out now and again, looked at them one by one, and counted them lovingly. So God did with the Israelites.

Bible scholars note that the census in Numbers is repeated twice, each time arriving at a total of 603,550. In the first count the Torah refers to the Mishkan as the center of the camp. In the second count it speaks of the Tent of Meeting. So it is time to answer the question: Are the Tent of Meeting and the Mishkan the same, or are they different?

The Mishkan and the Tent

In some places the Torah states that the Tent of Meeting is inside the Israelite camp. If so, then the Tent could be another name for the Mishkan (the Tabernacle). But, in other places the Torah states that the Tent of Meeting was outside the camp. If so, then the Tent cannot be the Mishkan.

Many scholars think the Tent of Meeting was just a simple tent. They claim that the gold, silver, and copper, the heavy hangings and veils, and the other precious items of the Mishkan were more than the Israelites, wandering in the wilderness, could find or afford. Perhaps, they say, the Mishkan was a grandiose legend based on the Temple in Jerusalem.

Other scholars believe that there were two different versions of the years of wandering. The northern tribes told of a

Mishkan, a Tabernacle structure that housed the Ark of the Covenant. The southern tribes told of a Tent of Meeting.

To unite the northern and southern tribes King David brought the Ark of the Covenant to Jerusalem and covered it with a tent, thereby joining the two versions of the story. David's son, Solomon, placed the Ark and its tent in the Holy of Holies in the Temple. By the time the Torah was completed, all the memories were combined—the Tent, the Ark, and the Temple were all included. The Torah never gives a clear answer. It just tells us that the Tent of Meeting, the Ark, and the Mishkan were all holy to the Israelites.

In *Naso*, as the census ends, each clan of Levites knows what it must do to serve the priests and what it will carry when the Israelites march forward.

Purity

The camp of the Israelites is now arranged in areas of holiness. The holiest part is the Mishkan in the center. Around the Mishkan, the Levites, who belong to Adonai, serve as guards to keep common Israelites from touching the most holy things. And around the Levites the Israelites, Adonai's holy people, are camped by families and tribes. Everything about the Israelite camp is holy. And to remain holy, things must remain pure.

The Mishkan has to remain pure, the priests and the Levites have to remain pure, and the Israelites have to remain pure. Why? Because, as the Torah explains, Adonai is dwelling in the center of the camp.

If an Israelite becomes impure—by a disease; by any unusual bleeding, pus, or fluid release; by contact with a corpse; or by hurting others—that Israelite must be sent outside the camp. It is dangerous to have an impure person in the camp because it was thought that others became impure by touching someone who was impure. If people in the camp become impure, then the camp becomes impure, and Adonai might be forced to leave.

The laws in *Naso* are about keeping the camp pure—not just pure in body, but also pure in spirit.

Adonai spoke to Moses, saying: Tell the Israelites:
When a man or woman commits any wrong to-

To Consider
The ancient Israelites thought about holiness (purity) and impurity much the way we think about electricity. A little touch of holiness might make you a little more holy. Touching priests or the Mishkan could be more dangerous. Actually coming into the Mishkan or coming too close to the "most holy things" was extremely dangerous—for ordinary Israelites or for careless priests it meant certain death. It was the same for impure things. You became impure by touching a thing or person that was impure. To become pure again meant bathing and cleaning yourself and waiting until evening. Holiness and impurity were like electricity; they were forces of nature.

Ordeals

Ordeals are an ancient answer to a sticky problem. How can we know what a person does in secret? If there is no witness, how can we tell if a person is guilty of a crime? The ordeal declares that there is always one witness, even when no one seems to be present, and that witness is God. Through the ordeal God is "called" to the witness stand to declare a person guilty or not guilty.

ward another person, thus breaking faith with Adonai … the person shall confess the wrong that was done [and] repay the full amount, adding one-fifth to it … to the one who was wronged. If [the one who was wronged] has no relative to repay, the payment shall go to Adonai for the priest—in addition to the ram of repentance. Likewise, any gift of the sacred donations that Israelites offer shall be the priest's. Each priest shall keep his sacred donations: each priest shall keep what is given to him.

The Ordeal

Naso is also concerned about the purity of marriage. The family is the primary building block of Israelite society. Like the covenant with Adonai, the covenant between wife and husband is sacred and must not be broken. If it is broken, it brings impurity to the camp. If a husband suspects—for good reason or even out of jealousy—that his wife has broken their marriage vows, he may bring his wife to the priest along with a grain offering. The priest tests the wife to see if she was unfaithful. A ritual test like this is an "ordeal".

The ordeal in *Naso* is called *sotah*, "gone astray". It is meant to test whether a wife has gone "off target" with a man who is not her husband.

> The priest shall bring [the wife] forward and have her stand before Adonai. The priest shall take sacred water in a clay vessel and [put in it] some of the dirt from the floor of the Tabernacle …. [Then] the priest shall bare the woman's head and place upon her hands the grain offering of remembrance …. In the priest's hands shall be the water of bitterness that brings on the spell.

The priest tells the wife that if she has gone astray, Adonai will curse her and make her impure among the Israelites. Adonai will cause her "thigh to sag" and her "belly to swell." To this the wife must answer, "Amen, amen!" The priest writes the curses on a piece of parchment and rubs the writing off into the "water of bitterness". The priest takes a little of the grain and burns it on the altar (this sacrifice "calls" Adonai to the ritual). Last, the priest makes the wife drink the water. According to the Torah, if she has been unfaithful to her husband—if her belly swells—she is punished. She is called a curse to her people and she will go childless the rest of her life. But if her belly does not swell, then she is pure and goes away unharmed.

> This is the ritual in cases of jealousy, when a wife goes astray while married to her husband … or when a fit of jealousy comes over a man…. The man shall be clear of guilt; but that woman shall suffer for her guilt.

Of Men and Women

From our point of view, the ordeal of sotah seems entirely unfair. It is not used if a husband or wife is known to be unfaithful—that would be adultery. Adultery is included in the Ten Commandments, and it is automatically punished by Adonai. Sotah is used only if a husband is jealous or suspects that his wife has been unfaithful. There is no ordeal for a husband if a wife is jealous or if she suspects that her husband has gone astray. To our minds, this is not a fair ritual.

The ordeal of sotah comes from early in Israelite history. It is unlikely that the water, the dirt, and the curses rubbed off the parchment could cause a woman any great pain. Of course, if a wife was guilty, the ordeal might cause her to confess her guilt. But the ordeal really was more a way of setting the husband's mind at ease. This helped keep peace in the family and in the camp of the Israelites. The Rabbis tell us that the ordeal was no longer used in the days of the Second Temple, for the simple reason that people no longer believed it worked. Like any "spell" of any magician, it only "works" so long as we believe it works.

It is good to know that the Rabbis also struggled in their time to bring women closer to equality, even in a society that still depended on men to be ready to serve in times of war and where women were still basically concerned with matters of the home and bringing up children.

It is also probable that sotah was not originally an Israelite ritual. "Spells" like this—especially rituals that force Adonai to do something—usually did not find their way into

Who Is Most Important?

As human beings first formed communities they usually found that they needed warriors to protect them or to conquer territories. Men were thought to be more important than women because they were the warriors. Women were still important—to protect the young and sometimes even to fight beside their men when battles went badly. But it was the men who ruled in warrior tribes. Later on, when communities settled down and fighting was no longer the primary measure of worth, women gained in equality. In fact, in a few societies where women were the warriors or served equally in wartime, women were considered more important or entirely equal to men.

Famous Nazirites

The Torah speaks of Nazirites only in *Naso*. But we know from other books of the Bible and from later history that Nazirites were common in Israel. People usually vowed to become Nazirites for a limited amount of time, but a pregnant woman might vow her child-to-be as a Nazirite for a lifetime. Among the famous lifetime Nazirites were Samson and Samuel. Queen Helena of Adiabene, who converted to Judaism in the first century C.E., observed her Nazirite vows for many years. And, according to Christian tradition, Jesus was also a Nazirite.

Below: A carved sarcophagus like the one from the tomb of Queen Helena, who was buried in Jerusalem. In a time of great famine she and her sons, the kings of Adiabene, sent food and money to aid the starving people of Judah. One son, Monobazus, was criticized for this by his own people, but he answered them: "My fathers stored up great treasures here on earth, but I am storing up great treasures in heaven."

the Torah. But the purity of the family was so important, and jealousy was such a quick destroyer of the community, that the Israelites adopted this ordeal and made it their own. They needed something like it—a simple and quick way to remove jealousy. All in all, we can say that sotah was not aimed against women—most people probably knew that it was a harmless test. Instead, it was aimed at keeping peace and purity in the Israelite camp.

The Nazirite

In the Book of Exodus (19:6) Adonai called the Israelites "a kingdom of priests and a holy nation". Every Israelite was special, but there were times when some Israelites felt especially grateful to Adonai or wanted to gain greater favor with Adonai. This was also a matter of purity. Getting "closer" to Adonai meant becoming more like priests—those who could serve in the Mishkan—so becoming purer also meant behaving more like priests. A person who pledged to get closer to Adonai was called a *Nazir* or Nazirite, one who is "set apart" or "dedicated".

A Nazirite man or woman vowed not to drink wine or liquor—not even to eat grapes. No razor could touch a Nazirite's hair; it had to grow long and go untrimmed. (This separated the Nazirites from the priests, who let their hair grow long, but trimmed it regularly.) And a Nazirite vowed not to come near the dead—even if a parent or a sibling died.

> This is the ritual for the Nazirite: On the day that his [or her] time as Nazirite is completed, he [or she, along with many offerings] shall be brought to the entrance of the Tent of Meeting…. The priest shall present [the offerings] before Adonai …. The Nazirite shall then shave his [or her] consecrated hair at the entrance of the Tent of Meeting, and put the locks … on the fire…. After that the Nazirite may drink wine.

The laws of the Nazirites come at the end of the laws of purity. So we learn that purity is the responsibility of every Israelite, from the simplest husband and wife to the person who makes a special vow to be "set apart" for Adonai. Purity is absolutely necessary to make the Israelite camp a place fit for Adonai to dwell among the people.

The Priestly Blessing

Adonai spoke to Moses: Speak to Aaron and his sons: Thus shall you bless the people of Israel. Say to them:

Adonai bless you and protect you!
Adonai deal kindly and graciously with you!
Adonai bring favor on you and grant you peace!

Thus they shall place My name upon the people of Israel, and I will bless them.

The three-part Priestly Blessing is among our most ancient prayers. The Torah teaches: It is commanded by Adonai, pronounced by the priests, and carried out by Adonai. It joins Adonai's name to the Israelite people.

The Spanish commentator Bachya ben Asher (died 1340) counted the Hebrew words in each of the three lines of the Priestly Blessing. He said the three words in the first line remind us of "the foundation for blessings", the patriarchs Abraham, Isaac, and Jacob. The second line contains five words, reminding us of the Torah. The third line contains seven words, reminding us of the seven heavens.

Even though no one knows if there are seven heavens, and it is possible that the Torah was not always five books, and we consider the matriarchs—Sarah, Rebecca, Leah, and Rachel—as being equal "foundations" with the patriarchs, still Bachya's point can help us think of ourselves as blessed while the Priestly Blessing is spoken. We can imagine the first line as the blessing of our history, the second as the blessing of our heritage, and the third as the blessing of our covenant that joins us with heaven.

Offerings for the Sanctuary

On the day that Moses finished setting up the Mishkan ... the chieftains of Israel ... brought their offering before Adonai: six ox-carts [for carrying the Mishkan in its travels] and twelve oxen, an

Quote to Remember

יְבָרֶכְךָ יְהוָֹה וְיִשְׁמְרֶךָ:
יָאֵר יְהוָֹה פָּנָיו אֵלֶיךָ
וִיחֻנֶּךָּ:
יִשָּׂא יְהוָֹה פָּנָיו אֵלֶיךָ
וְיָשֵׂם לְךָ שָׁלוֹם:

Adonai bless you and protect you!
Adonai deal kindly and graciously with you!
Adonai bring favor on you and grant you peace!

The Three Parts

The modern Bible commentator Nechama Leibowitz (1905-1997) said that the first part, "bless you and protect you," speaks of everyday things. The second, "deal kindly and graciously with you," speaks of our hearts and our spirits. The third, "bring favor on you and grant you peace," brings together the world of things and the world of spirit.

To Consider

In the Second Temple priests chanted or spoke the Priestly Blessing every day. For generations, especially in Europe, the Priestly Blessing was spoken only on holy days. Those who thought they belonged to priestly families stood on the platform, covered themselves with their prayer shawls (to concentrate on what they were doing), raised their arms to shoulder height, spread out their fingers to create the letter *shin* with each hand, and chanted the blessing. In Sephardic synagogues the next line ("Thus they shall place My name upon the people of Israel, and I will bless them") is added. In modern Reform and Conservative synagogues the Priestly Blessing is no longer reserved for priests—rabbis often include it as part of important ceremonies or at the end of a worship service. Christian ministers use the Priestly Blessing in much the same way. Although we still call it the Priestly Blessing, we no longer save it for the whole congregation. Fathers and mothers may use it to bless their children at the Sabbath dinner, a rabbi may use it during a Bar or Bat Mitzvah, and rabbis also use it when they ordain new rabbis.

ox-cart for every two chieftains and an ox for each one.

Afterward the chieftains brought their offerings. Each chieftain brought a silver bowl weighing 130 shekels; a silver basin weighing seventy shekels (filled with a meal offering of fine flour and oil); a gold ladle of ten shekels (filled with incense); a bull, a ram, a lamb (for burnt offerings), a goat (for a sin offering), and two oxen, five rams, five billy-goats, and five yearling lambs (as offerings of well-being). The first chieftain brought his gifts on the first day of the dedication. The parade of gifts lasted for twelve days. Every chieftain brought exactly the same gifts.

Nevertheless, each day, each chieftain, and each gift is recorded and listed separately. Modern Bible scholars think this list was the work of an ancient accountant, a priestly scribe whose job it was to record everything exactly and in precise words. Whether the gifts were actually given in the wilderness for the Mishkan or at some other time, the list was included in *Naso* to show how wonderful a ceremony would be held to dedicate a new building to Adonai. Commentators say that even though the gifts were all the same, the long list proves that each chieftain and each tribe wanted to give these gifts freely, from the heart.

The Voice, the Tent, and the Mishkan

> When Moses went into the Tent of Meeting to speak with [Adonai], he would hear the Voice addressing him from above the cover that was on top of the Ark of the Covenant between the two cherubim [sphinxes]; thus [Adonai] spoke to him.

So the portion ends where we began, with confusion about the Mishkan and the Tent of Meeting and how each was used. In Exodus 33 (*Ki Tisah*) we heard how Moses pitched the Tent of Meeting "at some distance from the camp".

> Whoever sought Adonai would go to the Tent of Meeting outside the camp. Whenever Moses went out to the Tent, all the people would rise and … gaze after Moses until he entered the Tent. And when Moses entered the Tent, the pillar of cloud

would descend and stand at the entrance, while [Adonai] spoke with Moses. … Adonai would speak to Moses face to face, as one person speaks to another. And [Moses] would then return to the camp; but his apprentice, Joshua son of Nun, a youth, would not stir out of the Tent.

But in Exodus 40 (*Pikudei*) it is said that the Tent covered the Mishkan, and the cloud kept Moses out.

When Moses finished the work, the cloud covered the Tent of Meeting, and the Presence of Adonai filled the Mishkan. Moses could not enter the Tent of Meeting, because the cloud had settled upon it and the Presence of Adonai filled the Mishkan.

As *Naso* ends it seems that Moses would enter the Tent whenever he wished to speak with Adonai. He would hear Adonai's "Voice" from above the Ark (which we know is in the Mishkan), and "thus [Adonai] spoke to him." Clearly, many different stories were woven together in the Torah, but out of them came one people.

God's Throne

Once the Mishkan was dedicated, the Ark of the Covenant became a sort of throne for Adonai. The Torah says that it was in the Tent of Meeting, so that when Moses went inside "to speak with" Adonai, he heard "the Voice" coming from above, from between the two sphinxes on top of the Ark.

Haftarah: Judges 13:2-25

The Rabbis chose a haftarah about Samson, a life-long Nazirite, to connect with the laws of the Nazirites given in *Naso*. Some of the Judges were prophets; some were military leaders; some judged the people; and some, like Samson, were legendary heroes. In the days of the Judges the Israelites had many enemies, but the fiercest was the Philistines, who were Sea People settled along the coast (see *B'Shalach*). Samson worked all his feats against the Philistines.

Like many great heroes, Samson had his birth announced in a special way. His mother was visited by an angel who told her not to drink wine or beer, nor eat unclean food, for the son she would bear would be dedicated to God as a Nazirite for his whole life. When the angel left, Manoah prayed that the angel return to him and his wife to teach them how to bring up the child. The angel re-

turned and spoke with them. Manoah offered the angel a meal, but the angel could not eat human food and asked that Manoah sacrifice to Adonai.

Manoah asked the angel his name, but the angel said it was impossible to repeat. So Manoah sacrificed a young goat to Adonai, and the angel went up in the flame! Then Manoah was afraid. "We shall surely die," he cried, "because we have seen a divine being!"

But his wife said, If we had been meant to die, Adonai would not have taken our sacrifice and would not have shown us all this and would not have sent us this message.

The woman gave birth to a child she called Samson. The boy grew up with the blessing of Adonai. And Adonai's spirit first inspired him in the land of Dan….

Trumpets and Complaints

To Consider

The Midrash says Moses could not understand Adonai's "pattern" for the Menorah, even when Adonai brought fire to draw a picture in the air. So Adonai said, "Get the artist Bezalel and give him the instructions." When Bezalel finished, Moses was amazed! The Menorah was exactly like the fire picture he had seen. Moses told Bezalel, "I heard the words and saw the pattern, but I could not follow the pattern. But you heard only the words, and made the Menorah exactly like the pattern." So it is with true artists, the Midrash says. Just as the name *Bezalel* means "in the shadow of God", true artists are creators, even as God is the true Creator.

Semichah

When the chieftains "place" or "lay" their hands on the Levites, the Torah uses the word *samchu*, from which we get *semichah*, the name for "ordination". Placing hands on the head or shoulders "ordains" a new rabbi or cantor. After *semichah* a rabbi or cantor is like a Levite, set apart for service to Adonai.

Raising Up: Lamps and Levites

The Israelites are at Sinai. They are making ready and dedicating the Mishkan, the Tabernacle that holds the Ark of the Covenant. The portion is called by its first important word, *Beha'alotcha*, "when you raise up".

> Adonai spoke to Moses, saying: Speak to Aaron and say to him, "When you raise up the lamps [to place them on the Menorah], let the seven lamps give light at the front of the Menorah." … Now [the Menorah] was hammered work of gold [in the] pattern Adonai had shown Moses, so the Menorah was made.

After the lamps are raised up to the Menorah, Adonai says, the Levites must be "raised up" to Adonai. Make them ready to serve Aaron and his sons: Clean them from head to toe. Bring them before the Tent of Meeting. Have the chieftains "lay their hands upon the Levites." And let Aaron declare that the Levites are Israel's "raised" offering to Adonai.

> So you shall set the Levites apart … and the Levites shall be Mine. … [For] I have taken them for Myself in place of all the first born … of the Israelites because every first-born among the Israelites, man as well as beast, is Mine; I consecrated them to Myself at the time that I struck down every first-born in the land of Egypt.

Several times the Torah states that the firstborn son of every Israelite *belongs* to Adonai since Adonai struck down every firstborn son in Egypt. Human life is precious to Adonai, so this was a terrible sacrifice. To make up for it, Adonai claimed the lives of every firstborn of the Israelites, those who were saved. In theory, every firstborn Israelite son should serve Adonai in the sanctuary. Instead, the firstborn are "redeemed"—exchanged for something of equal value—the Levites. Seeing the Levites serving the priests would constantly remind the people of the great sacrifice Adonai made to redeem Israel from Egypt.

Adonai completes "the rule of the Levites" for Moses: They shall work in the Tent of Meeting from age twenty-five to fifty. Then they shall retire. Retired Levites can still help by standing guard over the Tent along with the younger Levites, but they shall do no more work in the Mishkan.

Passover and a Second Passover

>Adonai spoke to Moses in the Sinai wilderness, on the first new moon of the second year after the Exodus from Egypt, saying: Let the Israelite people offer the Passover sacrifice at its set time: you shall offer it on the fourteenth day of this month, at twilight, at its set time; you shall offer it in accordance with all its rules and rites.

While the Torah here commands the Israelites to offer the Passover sacrifice one year after the first Passover (the night they were freed from Egypt), it says nothing about the seven-day holiday of Matzot that we today call Passover. In early Israel, these were two separate holidays (se *Emor*). The seven days of eating matzah could be celebrated by anyone, at home or while traveling. But, as the law states, the Passover sacrifice could only be brought to the Mishkan on a set date.

This commandment is misplaced. The Passover sacrifice should have come a month *before* the dedication of the Mishkan. No one knows why the command was misplaced. But the command led to an interesting incident:

>There were some people who were unclean [because they had touched] a corpse. [They] could not offer the Passover sacrifice on [the exact] day. [They asked Moses and Aaron,] "Why must we be forbidden from presenting Adonai's offering at its set time with the rest of the Israelites?" Moses said to them, "Stand by, and let me hear what instructions Adonai gives about you."

Adonai spoke to Moses, saying: Anyone who is unclean or impure or on a long journey at the set time for Passover

No Before and No After

In the third century C.E. the Rabbis noticed that the command to observe Passover was out of place. They explained with a teaching of the Babylonian sage Rav, who said, "In the Torah there is no before and no after." This became a general rule. Simply put, the Torah is not a history book. It does not always set earlier events before later ones. Instead, the Torah should be studied for what it teaches—what we are, why we were created, how we should behave, and how we should live. Historians might choose to arrange things in order, but the Rabbis said it was more important to know that if we turn the Torah and turn it again, everything we need is in it.

An Amendment

The law allowing a Passover sacrifice to be delayed by a month is a kind of amendment to the law of Passover. Laws often require changes for special cases, and we often keep the original law and just add to it. The priests felt free to add amendments into the story of the people at Sinai, making the amendments part of the laws given to Moses. This was done so often that the story of the Israelites at Sinai as we have it in the Torah takes up most of the Book of Exodus, all of Leviticus, and the first large section of Numbers.

can delay the Passover sacrifice by one month. But only for those reasons. If any other person refuses to offer the Passover sacrifice, Adonai will punish that person severely.

Adonai adds that even a stranger living among the Israelites can offer a Passover sacrifice, but it must be according to the same laws all Israelites follow. "There shall be one law for you, whether stranger or citizen of the country."

One Law for You

The statement of "one law for you, whether stranger or citizen" became a general rule, since the word *ger* or "stranger" can also mean "newcomer". Even now many non-Jews choose to live within the Jewish community. Some follow Jewish laws, and some never do. Some convert to Judaism, and some never do. It makes no difference. Our law is for us and for them. This is hospitality. Rabbi Nathan said that Abraham's tent had four entrances, one on every side, so that Abraham could welcome strangers coming from every direction. And he said we should be like Abraham, welcoming every stranger, treating them as we treat our own family—or even better. There should be "one law". What is good for us is what we should want for them, too.

Of course, the idea that this law is for you, "whether stranger or citizen of the country", must come from a time when the Israelites were "citizens" in their own "country".

The Mysterious Cloud

> On the day that the Mishkan was set up, the cloud covered the Mishkan, the Tent of the Covenant; and in the evening it rested over the Mishkan, looking like fire until morning. It was always so: the cloud covered it, appearing as fire by night. Whenever the cloud lifted ... the Israelites would set out [and] where the cloud settled, the Israelites would make camp.

The Torah pictures the cloud over the Mishkan as a sign that Adonai was present. Some modern scholars explain the cloud in another way. By day the smoke from the sacrifices and the burning of incense in the Mishkan would become a cloud that made it difficult for the Israelites to see the Mishkan. At night the smoke from the oil lamps on the Menorah made it seem that the cloud had turned to fire. When it was time to pack up and travel, the priests were among the first to know. They would take down the Mishkan and stop the sacrifices and the burning, and the cloud would "lift" or disappear. Only when they settled in a new place did the cloud "settle" again above the Mishkan. So the people knew that when the cloud "lifted" it was a sign that they were about to travel from one place to another.

Other scholars think that the idea of the cloud by day and the fire by night comes from a later time, when smoke pots were kept burning at the base of the two huge pillars of Solomon's Temple. The smoke pots formed a cloud by day and a cloud of fire by night. The tellers of the different parts of the Torah may have imagined that similar pillars of cloud and fire appeared to the Israelites in the wilderness.

However we explain the cloud and the fire, the Torah wants us to know that the Israelites were being guided by Adonai, commanded to move when Adonai was ready for them to move, and commanded to settle when Adonai wanted them to settle. Adonai was in charge, and Adonai dwelled among the people in the Israelite camp.

Silver Trumpets

Adonai spoke to Moses, saying: Have two silver trumpets made; make them of hammered work. They shall serve you to summon the community and to set the [tribes] in motion. When both are blown in long blasts, the whole community shall assemble before you at the entrance of the Tent of Meeting; and if only one is blown, the chieftains … shall assemble before you. But when you sound short blasts, the [tribes] encamped on the east shall move forward; and when you sound short blasts a second time, those encamped on the south shall move forward.

The modern Bible commentator W. Gunther Plaut says that the trumpets added sound to the vision of the clouds. We can't always trust what we see—even the magic that Mo-

To Consider

The words used for the different blasts of the silver trumpets—*tekiah* for the long blast and *teruah* for the short blasts—are words we still use today when we sound the ram's horn (*shofar*) in the synagogue. We do not know exactly what these words mean or what the original signals sounded like. We do, however, have pictures of ancient trumpets on the Arch of Titus in Rome (built around 81 C.E.) and on the coins of Bar Kochba (between 132 and 135 C.E.). They were long—three or four feet in length—and straight, with ends that flared open like the end of a modern trumpet (see *page 232*).

Quote to Remember

קוּמָה יְהוָה וְיָפֻצוּ אֹיְבֶךָ
וְיָנֻסוּ מְשַׂנְאֶיךָ מִפָּנֶיךָ׃

Advance, O Adonai! May Your enemies be scattered. And may Your foes flee before You!

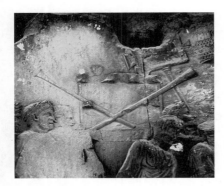

Above: The two silver trumpets of the Second Temple shown being carried by victorious Roman soldiers. Along with the Menorah, the trumpets were taken to Rome after the Romans destroyed the Second Temple. This famous carved relief appears on the Arch of Titus, erected to celebrate the victory over Judea.

ses performed could be performed by other magicians. But the words of Moses were unique, and no one else could ever quite say things in the same way. We need to both see and hear, but hearing is more important. As Plaut says, "The cloud is gone; the sound of the *shofar* remains."

So Adonai called for the priests to sound the trumpets when it was time for the people to assemble, when it was time for them to move, in times of war, on joyous occasions, and on the days of the new moon. The trumpets "shall be a reminder of you before your God: I, Adonai, am your God."

Leaving Sinai

In the second year, on the twentieth day of the second month, the cloud lifted from the Mishkan of the Covenant and the Israelites set out on their journeys ... They marched ... three days. The Ark of the Covenant ... traveled in front of them.... When the Ark was set to move, Moses would say: "Advance, O Adonai! May Your enemies be scattered. And may Your foes flee before You!" And when it halted, [Moses] would say: "Return, O Adonai, You who are Israel's myriads of thousands!"

Before leaving Sinai, Moses asked his Midianite father-in-law to join the Israelites, saying, "Come with us and we will be generous with you; for Adonai has promised to be generous to Israel." But his father-in-law refused, saying, "[I] will return to my native land." In Exodus Moses' father-in-law was named Jethro, but here he is called both Hobab and Reuel. The Midrash said that Jethro actually had seven names! Modern scholars think that there were probably many stories about the Midianites and the Israelites, with the name of the Midianite prophet, priest, and king who became Moses' father-in-law changing from story to story.

Complaining

The people took to complaining bitterly.... Adonai heard and grew angry: a fire of Adonai broke out against them, ravaging the outskirts of the camp.

The people cried out to Moses. Moses prayed to Adonai, and the fire died down. ... Then the Israelites wept and said, "If only we had meat to eat! We remember the fish that we used to eat free in Egypt, the cucumbers, the melons, the leeks, the onions, and the garlic. Now ... there is nothing at all—nothing but this manna to look forward to!"

Even Moses complained. He asked Adonai, Why have you burdened me with these people? Where will I find meat for them? I would rather die than suffer from all their whining. Adonai told Moses to gather seventy leaders at the Tent of Meeting. Adonai would remove some of Moses' spirit and give it to them so that Moses would not have to bear all the burden alone. As for the people, Adonai said to tell them, "Adonai will give you meat and you shall eat. You shall eat ... for a whole month, until [meat] comes out of your nostrils and you hate it."

But Moses argued: "The people with me number six hundred thousand men; yet You say, 'I will give them enough meat to eat for a whole month.' Could enough flocks and herds be slaughtered to satisfy them? Or could all the fish of the sea be gathered for them to satisfy them?" And Adonai answered Moses, "Is there a limit to Adonai's power? You shall soon see whether what I have said happens to you or not!"

So Moses chose seventy leaders and called them to stand around the Tent of Meeting. Adonai came down in a cloud and spoke to Moses, removing part of Moses' spirit and putting it on the leaders. "And when the spirit rested on them, they spoke in ecstasy—but only that one time."

New Prophets

It was different for Eldad and Medad, two of the seventy leaders who had stayed in the camp. The spirit rested on them, too, so that they spoke in ecstasy—but in the camp. A young man ran to tell Moses, "Eldad and Medad are acting like prophets in the camp!" Joshua said to Moses, "Stop them!" But Moses said, "Are you worried for me, [because

Why Did Moses Doubt?

When Moses complained that the people were a great burden, Adonai helped by saying that this burden could be shared with other leaders. Adonai then said that the people would get the meat they wanted—so much meat that they would hate it. Then, even after all the miracles Adonai had done and Moses had seen, Moses doubted Adonai. One lesson Torah teaches is that it is easy for us to forget how God helped us in the past, especially when we want something new or need something else.

A Cushite Woman

A Cushite woman might be from Ethiopia or Sudan—in other words, an African. But commentators like Ibn Ezra think that Miriam and Aaron are actually complaining about Moses' Midianite wife, Zipporah. If so, the word "Cushite" is used to show how foreign Zipporah seemed to the Israelites—she was as much a stranger as an African would be.

you think they are taking my place as Adonai's prophet]? If only *all* Adonai's people were prophets!" Then Moses and the other sixty-eight leaders returned to the Israelite camp. Adonai sent the meat and punished those Israelites who had started all the complaining:

> A wind from Adonai came up, swept quail from the sea and scattered them over the camp …. The people set to gathering quail all that day and night and all the next day …. The meat was still between their teeth, nor yet chewed, when Adonai's anger blazed forth … and Adonai struck the people with a very severe plague. That place was named *Kibroth-hattaavah* ["the graves of craving"] because the people who had the craving were buried there. Then the [Israelites] set out … for Hazeroth.

Jealousy Punished

At Hazeroth, two stories are combined into one. In the first Miriam and Aaron complain that Moses married "a Cushite woman", a non-Israelite. The second story is about jealousy. Miriam and Aaron ask, "Has Adonai spoken only through Moses? Has [Adonai] not spoken through us as well?" Adonai heard them. The text says, "Now Moses was very humble, more so than any person on earth." So it was Adonai who called Moses, Miriam, and Aaron to the Tent of Meeting, where Adonai said to Miriam and Aaron:

> "Hear My words: When a prophet of Adonai arises among you, I make Myself known to [the prophet] in a vision, I speak with [the prophet] in a dream. Not so with My servant Moses…. With him I speak mouth to mouth, plainly and not in riddles, and he beholds the likeness of Adonai. How then did you not shrink from speaking against My servant Moses!" Still angry at them, Adonai departed.

Suddenly, snowy scales appeared on Miriam's skin. Aaron was afraid. He pleaded with Moses, saying, Forgive us for being so foolish. Help her, so that her flesh will not be eaten away! And Moses pleaded with Adonai, saying, "O

God, pray heal her!" But Adonai said, Send her out of the camp for seven days as her punishment.

> So Miriam was shut out of camp seven days; and the people did not march on until Miriam returned to the camp. After that the people set out from Hazeroth and encamped in the wilderness of Paran.

The way this story is told, Moses pays no attention when Miriam and Aaron complain about his marriage or even when they are jealous of his place with Adonai. That is why the Torah notes, "Moses was a very humble man." But Adonai is offended by Aaron and Miriam's jealousy. So Adonai explains how Moses is special. Other prophets are inspired in visions or dreams sent by Adonai, but Moses receives Adonai's words "plainly and not in riddles". Adonai speaks with Moses "mouth to mouth".

Mouth to Mouth

Ibn Ezra explains that "mouth to mouth" means "directly". But other commentators think Ibn Ezra is wrong. The Torah does not say "mouth to ear", meaning that Moses heard Adonai's words. It does not say "mouth to soul", meaning that Moses felt what Adonai spoke. It says "mouth to mouth", meaning that what Adonai said is what Moses said, so what Moses said is what Adonai said. In other words, other people might dream, feel, or hear the words of Adonai, but only the words of Moses could be trusted completely.

Haftarah: Zechariah 2:14-4:7

It is the Menorah that connects the haftarah with the Torah portion. Zechariah lived while the people were building the Second Temple. But the work was going slowly, as other matters became pressing. The prophet urged the people to hurry and complete the Temple.

Adonai promises at the beginning of the haftarah to come and dwell in the midst of the people. God will rule over Judah and choose Jerusalem again.

In a vision Zechariah sees the High Priest Joshua in filthy clothing standing in the heavenly court. As he watches, an angel brings new clothing to Joshua and tells Joshua to be faithful to Adonai. Then the High Priest will "govern My House and have charge of My courts" and be as close to God as the angels. If Joshua does well, Adonai promises to bring forth another servant, "the Shoot" or "Seedling". This must be the new king (or messiah) from the line of King David who will rule over Judah. On that day everyone will invite each other to sit under vines and fig trees.

Zechariah is shown another vision—of a Menorah with a bowl on top that feeds seven bowls, each with a pipe for the lamps. On either side is an olive tree (giving oil to the Menorah). Zechariah said, "What are these?" The angel explained, This is Adonai's word to Zerubabel (governor of Judah):

> Not by might, not by power, but by My spirit, says Adonai *Tzeva'ot*.

The vision ends by saying that the great mountain (on which the Temple will stand) will be leveled like a plain. The topmost stone (the Temple) will at last be seen, and the people will all cry out in joy.

Scouts

Scouts or Spies?

Throughout history most armies have sent spies ahead of them. But the people Moses sent were not normal spies; they were chieftains of the tribes. Chieftains are not trained for secret work, nor would Moses send chieftains into danger. The assignment was just to study the land and its people and to report on life in Canaan. The chieftains went out as normal travelers. They were more like scouts than spies.

The Mission

In the Midrash Rabbi Joshua compares the Israelites to the son of a king. The king looked far and wide and found a wife for his son. The girl was wise and beautiful. She came from a rich and noble family. The king told the prince, "I found you a fine wife." But the prince did not trust his father. He said, "Let me go and see her!"

This greatly annoyed the king. The king said to himself: "What shall I do? If I say, 'I will not show her to you,' he will think: 'She is awful; that is why he does not want to show her.'" At last the king said to the prince, "Go and see her, then you will know I have not lied to you! But because you had no faith in me, you shall never have her for your wife! Instead, I will give her to your son!"

Rabbi Joshua explained: The Holy One assured Israel, "The land is good," but they had no faith, and said, "Let us first send scouts to see the land." Said the Holy One, the Blessed, "If I do not allow them to send scouts, they will say: 'God does not show it to us because it is not good.' Better to let them scout the land. But, since they would not take My word, not one of them will enter the land. Instead, I shall give it to their children." As you read about the scouts, keep Rabbi Joshua's story in mind:

> Adonai spoke to Moses, saying, "Send for yourself men to scout the land of Canaan, which I am giving to the Israelite people. Send one from each tribe, each one a chieftain." So Moses, at Adonai's command, sent [scouts] from the wilderness....

The name of the parashah is Adonai's command, *Shelach-lecha,* "send for yourself." As Rabbi Joshua said, Adonai knew the land of Canaan was perfect. But the Israelites still did not trust Adonai completely. They needed to see for themselves. So Adonai commands, "Send *for yourself,*" meaning "for your own sake".

The Scout Story of JE

JE, the combined work of the E-teller and the J-teller, included a story about the scouts sent by Moses. The hero was Caleb. According to JE, a few scouts traveled into the southern part of Canaan, as far as Hebron. They cut a cluster of grapes—it was so heavy, the story says, that it had to be carried on poles on the shoulders of two scouts. When the scouts returned they reported that Canaan was "a land flowing with milk and honey." But they also reported that the people of Canaan were giants, living in cities too strong to be conquered by little Israel. The scouts said:

> We saw the Nephilim ["those who fell"] there—the Anakites are among the Nephilim—and we looked like grasshoppers to ourselves, and so we must have looked to them.

Caleb disagreed with the other scouts. None of this is true, he said. Have no fear of the land, Caleb told the Israelites, "For we shall surely overcome it." But the Israelites paid no attention to Caleb. They wanted to return to Egypt. Adonai was angered and threatened to kill every Israelite and make a new nation out of Moses.

Moses begged Adonai to forgive the Israelites. Adonai said,

> "I pardon, as you have asked. Nevertheless, … none of those who have seen My Presence and the signs that I have performed in Egypt and in the wilderness—and who have tested Me these many times and have disobeyed Me—shall see the land that I promised to their ancestors …. But My servant Caleb, because he was filled with a different spirit and remained loyal to Me—him will I bring into the land….

According to the JE story, the Israelites were suddenly sorry for being afraid. To prove to Adonai that they were ready to conquer Canaan, they decided to attack the Canaanites and the Amalekites.

> Early next morning they set out toward the crest of the hill country…. [But Moses said,] "This will not succeed [and] you will fall by the sword…." Yet

Nephilim and Anakites

The Nephilim were a legendary people mentioned in Genesis 6:4, where it says they were heavenly beings who suddenly "appeared on the earth." The word *nephilim* means "fallen ones", but the Greek Jews of Alexandria translated it as "giants". Anakites were legendary giants. Joshua later conquered them, leaving only a few survivors. It was said that Goliath, the famous giant slain by David, was an Anakite.

The Faith to Overcome

Rabbi Max Nussbaum (1908-1974) once taught that Caleb's words can help us in positive ways in moments when we feel weak, doubt our strength, question our talents, and suspect our courage. In other words, when we think of ourselves as grasshoppers, we should repeat Caleb's words, *Ki yachol nuchal lah*, "For we shall surely overcome it." If we can only learn to have faith in the strength that God gave us, as Caleb did, then "we shall surely overcome" our problems.

To Consider

In the Torah, changing a person's name always marks a turning point. Think of when *Abram* ["he loved the father"] became *Abraham* ["father of many"], *Sarai* [perhaps from the word for "blinking"] became *Sarah* ["princess"], and *Jacob* ["heel-grabber"] became *Israel* ["the one who wrestles with God"]. So, too, when Moses changed Hosea's name to Joshua. The name *Hosea* [הושע] can be translated as "deliverance". To turn it into Joshua [יהושע] a single *yod* is added. But this change brings the *yod* and the *hey* together. Joshua means "YH [Adonai] is deliverance". Joshua's name marks something new. From this point on many important names in the Bible will include the *YH* that stands for "Adonai". For instance, think of names of prophets like *Elijah* ["My God is Adonai"], *Jeremiah* ["Adonai will raise up"], and *Isaiah* ["Adonai's deliverance"].

they marched defiantly toward the crest of the hill country, though neither Adonai's Ark of the Covenant nor Moses stirred from the camp. And the Amalekites and Canaanites ... came down to [defeat] them at Hormah ["the place of destruction"].

That was the way the JE source remembered the story of the scouts.

The Scout Story Told by P

The P-teller tells a different story, beginning with a list of the chieftains sent out by Moses. (The list is one way we recognize this as a P-teller story.) There are two heroes. One is Caleb; the other is Hosea son of Nun—but the P-teller adds, "Moses changed the name of Hosea son of Nun to Joshua."

According to the P story, the twelve scouts examine *all* of Canaan from the south to the hills of Lebanon. After forty days they return to the Israelite camp at "Kadesh, in the wilderness". They report, "The country we traveled and scouted is one that devours its settlers."

The whole community broke into loud cries. The people wept that night. [Everyone] cried out against Moses and Aaron. "If only we had died in the land of Egypt," the whole community shouted, "or if only we might die in this wilderness! ..." Then Moses and Aaron fell on their faces....

But Joshua and Caleb disagreed with the other scouts, saying, "The land that we traveled and scouted is an exceedingly good land."

If Adonai is pleased with us, Adonai will bring us into that land, a land that flows with milk and honey, and give it to us; only you must not rebel against Adonai. So, have no fear of the people of the country, for they are our prey: their protection has departed from them, but Adonai is with us.

The Israelites refused to listen to Joshua and Caleb. They even threatened their leaders with death by stoning. Suddenly, though, "the Presence of Adonai appeared in the Tent of Meeting to all the Israelites." Adonai spoke to Moses and Aaron. "How much longer shall that wicked community keep muttering against Me? [Tell the Israelites:] 'In this very wilderness shall your carcasses drop. [Not one] of you shall enter the land … save Caleb son of Jephunneh and Joshua son of Nun.'" A very angry Adonai judged the Israelites:

> Your children … shall know the land you have rejected. … You shall bear your punishment for forty years, equaling the number of days—forty days— that you scouted the land: a year for each day." … As for those whom Moses sent to scout the land, those who came back and caused the whole community to mutter against [Adonai], those … died of plague, by the will of Adonai. Of those who had gone to scout the land, only Joshua son of Nun and Caleb son of Jephunneh survived.

The Two as One

There are big differences between the two stories. In the JE story the scouts are gone only a short time and go only a short distance into Canaan. In the P story the scouts are gone forty days and travel through Canaan from south to north and back again. The JE story includes a battle that went badly for the Israelites. There is no battle in the P story. Caleb is the only hero in the JE story, but Joshua is also a hero in the P story. In the JE story Adonai speaks through Moses; in the P story the Presence of Adonai appears at the Tent of Meeting in front of all the Israelites. The P story lists the names of the scouts, and the JE story does not even say how many scouts were sent out.

Other details are almost the same. Both stories call Canaan a "land of milk and honey". (Modern scholars think this refers to a time when the hills of Judea were still forests. Thousands of wild goats—valued for their milk—roamed the hills; and date palms—valued for their honey—were plentiful.) In both stories Moses pleas for Adonai to forgive the Israelites. But in the JE story Adonai threatens to destroy them and start over with Moses, just as Adonai once started over with Noah. And in the JE story, when Moses pleads with Adonai he sounds very much like Abraham pleading for the righteous of Sodom.

Why Caleb?

In Numbers we are told that Caleb was actually a Kenezzite, not an Israelite. The Book of Joshua says that Caleb claimed the land that he scouted for his people, the Kenezzites. Bible scholar Baruch Halpern recalls a tradition that David later married a Kenezzite princess, giving David the right to claim Kenezzite lands. So David would have wanted to celebrate the story of how Caleb "earned" this territory by his loyalty to Adonai. Since the J-teller probably collected stories for the kings of the line of David, he had good reason to remember Caleb. The E-teller also had a good reason. The Caleb story showed the importance of the Ark when the Israelites went to war. The Ark was in the sanctuary at Shiloh before David took it to Jerusalem. And Bible scholars think that the E-teller stories may have been collected by the priests of Shiloh before the fall of the northern kingdom. The JE story of Caleb, then, joined a J story of the southern priests with an E story of the northern priests.

To Consider

Should a person be put to death for breaking the Sabbath? Usually, if a crime is serious, the punishment is severe; but if a crime is minor, the punishment is minor. Yet even the Rabbis thought that putting a man to death for gathering wood on Shabbat was too severe. In the commentary called *Sifrei* they claimed that this was a case that could only happen once! They said it came about this way: The very first Sabbath was observed by every Israelite. If the people could keep just one more Sabbath with devotion to Adonai, then perhaps Shabbat would become a way of life forever. But on the very second Sabbath this Israelite broke the law, destroying the dream that the people would always be devoted to Adonai. That is why he was punished by death. It was because he "killed" the dream.

Both stories end the same way: Adonai decrees that those who came out of Egypt will die in the wilderness. Only their sons and daughters will live to enter Canaan. In the P-story the forty years of wandering are connected to the forty days that the scouts traveled, and the scouts are punished sooner—they die of a plague soon after their return.

Both scout stories contain wonderful word-pictures. On the positive side, the land of Israel will always be called "a land flowing with milk and honey". On the negative, it is also known as a land that "devours its settlers"—a hard place to live. The image of a cluster of grapes so heavy that it had to be carried by two men is well known today as the emblem of the Ministry of Tourism of the modern State of Israel.

The Torah, as we have it now, turns these stories of the scouts into a single story. For this reason we have the riches of both. It is easy to see what we might have lost if we had only one of these stories. That is why it is best to think of the Torah as a kind of library, not just as five "books".

A Cluster of Laws

Shelach-Lecha ends with a cluster of laws. One speaks of the *challah* offering—setting aside "the first yield of your baking" for Adonai. Another repeats the law for strangers: "You and the stranger shall be alike before Adonai—the same ritual and the same rule shall be for you and the newcomer who lives with you." Some of these laws contradict laws in Leviticus—they probably came from a different time and place—and this may be why they were placed here. Suddenly, in the midst of the laws, is a court case:

> Once, when the Israelites were in the wilderness, they came upon a man gathering wood on Shabbat. [They] brought him before Moses, Aaron, and the whole community. He was placed in custody, for [no one knew what should be his punishment]. Then Adonai said to Moses, "The man shall be put to death: the whole community shall pelt him with stones outside the camp." So the whole community took him outside the camp and stoned him to death—as Adonai had commanded Moses.

Of course, breaking Adonai's law of Shabbat was a serious issue. But up to this time it was not known how people should be punished for this. Would Adonai punish them? Should the Israelites punish them? So Moses had the Israelites guard the guilty man while he asked for Adonai's decision. Adonai's judgment was extreme: Put the man to death.

It is a strange decision. Was the story meant to terrify us into keeping the Sabbath? Did the man deserve death just for gathering wood? Modern scholars believe that we have only part of the story here. Something is lost; something is missing. It is a mystery that we will probably never solve. And even though the judgment came directly from Adonai, no punishment like this was ever again inflicted on an Israelite for breaking the law of Shabbat.

Tzitzit

Today we think of the last law in *Shelach-Lecha* as the most important. Adonai told Moses:

> Speak to the Israelites and instruct them to make for themselves fringes (*tzitzit*) on the corners of their garments throughout the ages; let them attach a cord of blue to the fringe at each corner. That shall be your fringe; look at it and recall all the commands of Adonai and observe them, so that you do not follow your heart and eyes to do evil. Thus you shall be reminded to observe all My commands and to be holy to your God. I Adonai am your God, who brought you out of Egypt to be your God: I, Adonai your God.

Rashi says that this law is here because the scouts had followed their hearts and eyes to do evil. From now on Israelites would be reminded to do good by seeing the fringes on their garments.

Nowadays some Jews wear tzitzit all the time, but most Jews wear fringes only on a tallit. The blue thread, part of the fringe in ancient times, is no longer used. The costly blue dye was made from the shells of a particular sea mollusk. But that mollusk became rare, almost extinct, and the special dye became too expensive for common folk, so the custom arose of making the tzitzit only of white cord.

Two Symbols

Above: The scouts carrying a gigantic cluster of grapes has become a symbol for tourism for the modern State of Israel. *Below:* The flag of the State of Israel, designed by Theodor Herzl, the father of modern Zionism, is based on the tradition of making the tallit white with blue stripes.

Later the idea of blue and white as a holy combination gave rise to making the tallit white with blue stripes. In turn this led to blue and white being considered "Jewish colors". It also led to the colors and stripes on the flag of the modern State of Israel, which reminds us of a tallit

Archaeologists notice fringes in paintings of the costumes of many ancient peoples. Fringes were often worn by royal or wealthy folk. But the Torah connects the fringes to "all the commands" of Adonai. In the traditional prayer book this law became part of the *Shema* prayer. When it is recited, worshipers gather the tzitzit in their hand and gaze at them.

Haftarah: Joshua 2:1-24

It is spying that ties the haftarah to the Torah portion. Just as Moses sent scouts to explore the Promised Land, Joshua sent spies to discover the weaknesses of the city of Jericho. Moses' scouts went openly, as travelers. But Joshua sent his two spies "secretly".

When they came to Jericho they stayed at the house of a prostitute named Rahab. But the king of Jericho heard that they were there. He sent word to Rahab, saying, "Bring them out!" She hid the spies and answered, "The men came to me, but I did not know where they were from." They left before the city gates closed, she said. If you hurry, you might catch them.

As the king's men searched, Rahab spoke with the spies.

> I know that Adonai has given you this land. Fear of you has fallen on us …. Swear by

Adonai that you will treat my family as well as I have treated you and give me a sign I can trust…. Save us from death!

Rahab's house was on the wall, so she let the men outside the city on a rope from her window. The spies told her, This will be the sign: When we come to conquer Jericho, tie a red cord at that window and gather your family in the house. As soon as they left she tied the cord of red to the window. The spies hid in the hills three days until it was safe to return to Joshua.

They told Joshua all that had happened and said to him:

> Adonai has put the whole country in our hands; all the people there are scared to death of us.

Rebellions

A Nervous People

Korach (spelled "Korah" in English) is both the name of the parashah and the name of a Levite priest who rebelled against Moses. According to the Book of Exodus, Korah was a close cousin of Moses and Aaron, the son of their uncle Izhar. When we hear Korah's name we automatically think of a traitor—just as we do when someone mentions Benedict Arnold, the traitor who betrayed George Washington. In *Pirke Avot* (5:17) the Rabbis of the Mishnah wrote,

> What is [an example of] a disagreement made for the sake of Heaven? Such was the disagreement between Hillel and Shammai. And what is [an example of] a disagreement not made for the sake of Heaven? Such was the disagreement of Korah and all his company.

The Rabbis mean that some disagreements are good and some are evil. Washington led the thirteen colonies in a rebellion against King George of England. We think of seeking liberty as good, as being "for the sake of Heaven". But the Rabbis say that when "Korah and all his company" rebelled in the wilderness, they had no good cause. Their rebellion was "not made for the sake of Heaven."

Just as we often seek someone to blame when we have made mistakes, the Israelites looked for someone to blame for their mistakes. And who better to blame than Aaron and Moses? So the portion begins with Korah's complaint:

> Now Korah, son of Izhar [a Levite] ... betook himself, along with Dathan and Abiram ... and On son of Peleth ... to rise up against Moses, together with two hundred and fifty Israelites, chieftains of the community, chosen in the assembly, well-known men. They combined against Moses and Aaron and said to them, "You have gone too far! For all the community are holy, all of them, and

Ripe for Rebellion

The Spanish commentator Nachmanides writes that the Israelites were ripe for a rebellion. They were stirred up by many unfortunate events. When they complained to Moses at Taberah (in portion *Be-ha'alotcha*) a fire broke out against them. When they complained that they craved meat at Kibroth-Hattaavah (in *Be-ha'alotcha*) those who complained died suddenly of a plague. And in the last portion, *Shelach-lecha*, when the Israelites believed the majority of the scouts and were afraid to go forward, Adonai punished the whole community. Even those who tried to go forward on their own were met with death.

On and His Wife

Once upon a time there may have been a third rebellion story featuring On son of Peleth, but his name appears just this once and never again in the whole Bible. The rabbis noticed this and tried to explain why On's name appears at all. In a midrash they said this was to remind us of On's wife, who asked him, "What difference will it make if Korah wins? We will just have to serve Korah then, the same way we serve Moses and Aaron now." In this way, the rabbis say, she exposed the truth behind Korah's rebellion.

Adonai is in their midst. Why then do you raise yourselves above Adonai's congregation?"

Many Rebellions Woven Together

Korah and two hundred and fifty others are complaining. Why mention Dathan, Abiram and On son of Peleth? You can probably guess the answer. As with the scouts story, the rebellion in this portion is actually made up of two (or more) stories of rebellion against Moses and Aaron. One is about Korah and two hundred and fifty chieftains. Another is about a rebellion led by Dathan and Abiram.

The story of Dathan and Abiram probably comes from the JE source. It recalls a rebellion against Moses. And it ends when an earthquake swallows up the rebels.

The story of Korah's rebellion against Aaron is probably the work of P. Korah claims that since Sinai, all Israelites are holy. Why should only Aaron and his sons be High Priests? Moses defends Aaron by setting up a test to prove that Adonai chose Aaron as High Priest. P tells this story to show that Aaron and his sons were the "true" High Priests.

The events are confusing in the Torah—there seem to be pieces missing—and the two stories do not seem to fit together. At times Korah seems to be rebelling against Moses instead of Aaron. To study the stories we have to take them apart, always remembering that in the end they are recorded as one story. The simpler of the two stories is about Dathan and Abiram, and we will begin there.

Dathan and Abiram

Dathan and Abiram [of the tribe of Reuben] … rose up against Moses. … Moses sent for Dathan and Abiram … but they said, "We will not come! Is it not enough that you brought us from a land flowing with milk and honey to have us die in the wilderness? Would you also rule over us? … Will you gouge out our eyes [as if we were slaves who revolted]? We will not come!" Moses was very angry and he said to Adonai, "Pay no heed to their offering. I have not … wronged any one of them."

When Moses sent for Dathan and Abiram they refused to come. That was bad, but worse, they doubted Adonai. They called Egypt a "land flowing with milk and honey". They asked Moses, "Will you gouge out our eyes?" meaning "Do you expect us to act like people who cannot see for themselves, like sheep who do whatever you say?" Moses was angry. He said to Adonai, "Pay no heed to their offering." This may be a clue to why Moses sent for Dathan and Abiram in the first place. He may have heard that they were sacrificing to Adonai in the camp of Reuben. This was forbidden—sacrifices were only to be made at the Mishkan. Moses must also have heard that they accused him of doing wrong, so he added, "I have not wronged any one of them."

> Then Moses rose and—with the elders of Israel following him—went to Dathan and Abiram. ... [They] stood at the entrance of their tents, with their [families]. And Moses said, "By this you shall know that it was Adonai who sent me to do all these things; that they are not [plans of my making]: if [Dathan and Abiram] die like all humans die ... it was not Adonai who sent me. But if Adonai brings about something unheard-of, so that the ground opens its mouth and swallows them up with all that belongs to them, and they go down alive into Sheol, you shall know that these men have angered Adonai."

When Dathan and Abiram refuse to come to him, Moses and the elders go to them. Dathan and Abiram stand outside their tents, waiting to see what Moses will do. Moses tells the elders that Adonai will do something extraordinary ("unheard-of") to these people. Instead of dying a normal death, they will be swallowed up alive by the earth.

> Scarcely had [Moses] finished speaking all these words when the ground under [Dathan and Abiram] burst wide, and the earth opened its mouth and swallowed them up with their families. ... They ... went down alive into Sheol. Then the earth closed over them and they vanished.... All Israel standing nearby fled at their shrieking, for they said, "The earth might [also] swallow us!"

To Consider

Dathan and Abiram "went down alive into Sheol." The Israelites did not believe in heaven or hell. Throughout the biblical period it was thought that when a person died he or she went below the earth to a pit called Sheol. Nothing happened in Sheol. It was a place of complete rest. In the Book of Samuel one story tells how a witch brought Samuel's ghost up from Sheol to answer a question for King Saul. The ghost asks Saul, "Why do you disturb me?" Then Saul asks his question and gets his answer. This tells us much of what the Israelites believed happens to us after we die. It may even be based on a kind of pun. The king's name was Saul, which can be translated as "[the one who] asks". And the word Sheol comes from the same Hebrew root and may mean "[the place of] questioning". In a way, then, when the Israelites said that we all go to Sheol when we die, they were saying that what happens to us is a great big question. Even today, if you think of a heaven and a hell, what happens to us after we die is still a great big question.

To Consider

Why are so many stories in the Torah made of more than one story? One reason, pointed out by modern Bible scholar Cyrus Gordon (1909-2001), was that ancient Israelites did not use the kind of logic that we use today. We think things are best explained by going from point to point, from one event to another, in a straight line. Ancient Israelites thought things were best explained by comparing them side by side with other things like them. For the ancient Israelites, then, the best way to think about the rebellions was as two events in one model. To us it looks as though they were confused. To them, our way of thinking might seem equally confusing.

Moses Fell on His Face

When Moses "falls on his face" it seems like Moses does not know what to do. But what exactly does the Torah mean when it says he "fell on his face"? One commentator says it was to pray to Adonai. Modern scholars suggest that "falling on his face" may be an ancient way of saying Moses "called Adonai to come and give him advice."

The elders see Dathan and Abiram, their houses, and their families swallowed up in an earthquake. In an instant they are gone, as if they never were. Thus ends the rebellion of Dathan and Abiram.

Korah and His Rebellion

We can also read the story of Korah by choosing only the bits of the portion that tell about his rebellion.

> Now Korah … betook himself … together with two hundred and fifty Israelites, chieftains of the community, chosen in the assembly, well-known men. They combined against Moses and Aaron and said to them, "You have gone too far! For all the community are holy, all of them, and Adonai is in their midst. Why then do you raise yourselves above Adonai's congregation?"

> When Moses heard this, he fell on his face. Then he spoke to Korah and all his company, saying, "Come morning, Adonai will make known who belongs to [Adonai] and who is holy … [Adonai] will show favor to the one [Adonai] has chosen. Do this: You, Korah and all your band, take fire pans, and tomorrow put fire in them and lay incense on them before Adonai. Then the man whom Adonai chooses, he shall be the holy one. You have gone too far, sons of Levi!"

Korah and his company complain to Moses and Aaron, "You have gone too far! … Why do you raise yourselves above Adonai's congregation?" After Moses "falls on his face" he seems to know what to do. He throws Korah's words back at him, saying, "You have gone too far, sons of Levi!" Then he sets up a test.

To understand the test we need information about fire pans, incense, and the priests. The incense altar did not have fire on it all the time, but incense must be lit in order to burn. Fiery coals were used to light it. These coals and the incense were carried to the altar on fire pans that looked like small shovels. Offering incense was a holy task assigned by Adonai to Aaron and his sons. And even they had to be very careful. If all was not done correctly, the penalty might be instant death.

Korah claimed that any Levite—even any Israelite—should be equal to Aaron. So Moses put him to the test. If so, Moses said, bring your fire pans and let Adonai decide.

Moses continued speaking to Korah, "Hear me, sons of Levi. Is it not enough for you that the God of Israel has set you [Levites] apart from the community of Israel [to serve the Mishkan]? … Do you seek the priesthood too? Truly, it is against Adonai that you and all your company have banded together. For what [has] Aaron [done to you] that you should complain about him?"

Moses said to Korah, "Tomorrow, you and all your band appear before Adonai…. Each of you take his fire pan and lay incense on it, and each of you bring his fire pan before Adonai, two hundred and fifty fire pans…." Each of them took his fire pan, put fire in it, laid incense on it, and took his place at the entrance of the Tent of Meeting, as did Moses and Aaron. Korah gathered the whole company against them at the entrance of the Tent of Meeting.

Then the Presence of Adonai appeared to the whole congregation. Adonai spoke to Moses and Aaron, saying, "Stand back from this congregation that I may destroy them in an instant!" But [Moses and Aaron] fell on their faces and said, "O God, Source of the breath of all flesh! When one person sins, will You be furious with the whole congregation?"

Adonai answered Moses, saying, "Speak to the community and say: Get away from the Mishkan of Korah…." [Moses] spoke to the community, saying, "Move away from the tents of these wicked men and touch nothing that belongs to them, lest you be destroyed for all their sins." Then [the people] backed away from the Mishkan of Korah… and [from] all Korah's people and all their possessions. And a fire went out from Adonai and con-

Quote to Remember

וַיֵּרָא כְּבוֹד־יְהֹוָה אֶל־כָּל־הָעֵדָה:

Then the Presence of Adonai appeared to the whole congregation.

The Presence of Adonai

When the teacher calls attendance you may answer, "I am present," meaning "I am here." But what does it mean when the Torah says that "the Presence of Adonai" appeared or the people saw "Adonai's Presence"? (The Hebrew, *k'vod-YHVH*, is sometimes translated as "the Glory of Adonai." *K'vod* by itself means "honor" or "respect".) The Rabbis thought that "the Presence" or "the Glory" was the cloud that covered the Mishkan when Adonai was there. So, too, at times we think we are alone, and yet we feel that something or someone might be present with us. Perhaps the Torah means this kind of "presence", too. The people suddenly felt that Adonai was present—the kind of feeling you might have when the Holy Ark is opened in the synagogue, when you are called to read Torah, or perhaps even when you are being bawled out by a parent or a teacher.

Offering Incense

Before the Mishkan was built Levites burned incense offerings anywhere they pleased. In *Acharei Mot*, however, Adonai commanded that this be done only by Aaron and his sons and only in the Mishkan. Korah and other Levites could no longer offer the incense sacrifice; nor could any Israelite, even a chieftain. The story makes this perfectly clear: Adonai chose only Aaron and his sons to be the High Priests, the kohanim.

sumed the two hundred and fifty people offering the incense.

The fire pan test was over. Korah and all two hundred and fifty rebels were dead. Adonai commanded Moses to gather up their fire pans—"for they have become sacred" since they were used to offer incense to Adonai. Now the copper fire pans should be hammered to make a covering for the altar. There they would serve as a warning to all Israelites. So Eleazar, Aaron's son, hammered the fire pans to plate the altar. And the P-teller repeats the warning:

It was a reminder to the Israelites, that no outsider—one not of Aaron's family—should presume to offer incense before Adonai and suffer the fate of Korah and his band.

More Rebellion

But the P story is not quite over. The next day the Israelites complained against Moses and Aaron again, saying, "You two have brought death upon Adonai's people!"

Again Adonai tells Moses and Aaron, "Get away from this community that I may destroy them in an instant." But Moses and Aaron "fell on their faces." When they rose, Moses told Aaron: Take a fire pan, take fire from the altar, and burn incense on it as an offering to atone for the people. "For Adonai's fury has gone forth: the plague has begun!"

Aaron took it, as Moses commanded, and ran to the midst of the congregation…. [Aaron] put on the incense and offered atonement for the people; he stood between the dead and the living until the plague stopped spreading. Those who died in the plague came to 14,700—aside from those who died on account of Korach. When the plague stopped spreading, Aaron returned to Moses at the entrance of the Tent of Meeting.

One more time the P story shows that the incense offerings made by Aaron (and his sons) are the only ones Adonai will accept. Only Aaron the High Priest could stop the plague from spreading.

One More P-Teller Story

The P-teller has now proved two things: Only Aaron and his sons can be kohanim (High Priests). And only Aaron and his sons can offer incense sacrifices to atone for sin. But there is more. The chieftains of the tribes may think that they can still perform other offerings of the High Priest. The P-teller has another story to prove that this is forbidden.

Adonai instructs Moses to get a staff from each of the twelve chieftains, including Aaron. Each staff should have the chieftain's name carved on it, including the staff of Aaron. Adonai tells Moses to put the twelve staffs in the Tent of Meeting, in front of the Ark of the Covenant.

> The chieftains gave him a staff for each chieftain of an ancestral house, twelve staffs in all; among these staffs was that of Aaron. Moses put the staffs in the Tent of the Covenant before Adonai. The next day Moses entered the Tent of the Covenant. Behold! The staff of Aaron … had brought forth sprouts, blossomed, and produced almonds. Moses then brought all the staffs [to the chieftains]; each identified and recovered his staff. Adonai said to Moses, "Put Aaron's staff back before the [Ark], to be kept as a lesson to rebels, so that their mutterings against Me may cease, lest they die." This Moses did; just as Adonai had commanded him, so he did.

Again the people were afraid. They cried out to Moses, "We are lost, all of us lost!" The P-teller does not even tell us why they are afraid. It is simple to understand. After each event they were punished and lives were lost. But not this time. This test was just to teach a lesson: No one but Aaron and his sons can be the true priests (kohanim) of Israel.

Instructions to Aaron

The parashah of *Korah* concludes with instructions to Aaron and his family. This time Adonai speaks directly to Aaron. Moses is not addressed here, since he is just a Levite, a servant of the High Priests.

The Quiet Revolution

The P stories in this portion appear to recall a time when other Levite families served as priests in the Temple, even as High Priests (kohanim). But the stories give a clear message: If it was once so, it is not true anymore. Now all High Priests must be from the family of Aaron. The modern historian Ellis Rivkin (1918-) explains this as the "Aaronide Revolution", a quiet revolution that changed the priesthood of Israel forever, turning one priestly family into "higher priests" or kohanim, and leaving all other priestly families as servants or Levites. We can still find traces of this revolution in our ancient writings, but only if we look very closely at the P source.

Below: Fire pan (incense shovel) discovered at Ein Gedi. Pans like these were used by Canaanites, Israelites, and Romans alike to offer incense as sacrifices. Hot coals were shoveled out of a fire, and incense was spread on top to burn.

A Covenant of Salt

Throughout history salt was used in almost everything that was eaten. Salt helped preserve foods. Ancient people spoke of sharing a meal as "taking salt together". Often the Bible speaks of an agreement made through eating together as a "covenant of salt". There is more about this in portion *Vayikra*.

Adonai said to Aaron: You and your sons and [your family] alone shall bear any guilt connected with your priesthood. You shall also [be aided by] your relatives the tribe of Levi…. They shall [serve] you and the Tent … but they must not touch the holy tools or the altar, lest both they and you die. [Also,] any outsider who comes too close shall be put to death.

This special covenant between Adonai and Aaron may be part of the "quiet revolution" that placed the kohanim above the Levites (see above). Here P, the priestly teller, spells out the terms of the agreement: Offerings and sacred donations made by the Israelites to Adonai are assigned to Aaron and his sons. The best of everything that is brought to Adonai—the best of the new oil, the wine, the grain, and the meat—will be the food of the kohanim and their families. "All the sacred gifts that the Israelites set aside for Adonai" belong to Aaron, to his sons, and to his daughters as their "portion for all time". Adonai says, "It shall be an everlasting covenant of salt before Adonai for you and for your offspring as well."

In return, Adonai will give no land to Aaron and the kohanim. Nor will their servants, the Levites, have any land. The kohanim and the Levites will take a tithe from the rest of the tribes, a tenth of everything. But the Levites will also give a tithe—a tenth of all they take—as a gift to Adonai. And that gift will likewise be assigned to the kohanim.

Up to now we have spoken of the P-teller as the record-keeper—the one who kept lists and recorded all the codes of laws—and as the one who recorded all things that were of special interest to priests. But in this portion we can see that the P-teller was not just keeping lists or solving puzzles. The P-teller was also confirming a revolution within the priesthood. Once the Levites served local shrines and altars throughout the land of Israel. But under Solomon the Temple became the only shrine and the only altar for all Israel; and one family—the kohanim, the family that claimed to be descended from Aaron and his sons—became the High Priests for all Israel. The P source explained how the Israelites came to have three "levels" or "divisions" of holiness:

kohanim, Levites, and Israelites. But it is more like a revolution than a simple explanation.

As for the portion of *Korah,* it is filled with miracles: an earthquake that swallows just the right people, the Presence of Adonai appearing to the whole community, a flame that consumes only Korah and his company, a plague that can be stopped only by Aaron and his incense offering, and a staff that blossoms and bears almonds overnight. We think of Korah as the leader of a Levite rebellion, but now you know there was something more happening in this portion; the events were recorded to justify a revolutionary change in the Israelite priesthood.

Haftarah: I Samuel 11:14-12:22

The Rabbis use the question of leadership to connect the rebellion of Korah and the people's demand that Samuel should give them a king. Up to Samuel's time Adonai ruled the Israelites through Judges and Prophets. But the people wanted a king, and Samuel finally gave in to them. "From now on the king will be your leader."

Samuel demands that the Israelites recognize that he never wronged them. They answer, "Witness!" ("It is so!") Samuel repeats for them the wonders that Adonai did for them. Every time the people forgot Adonai, they were given into the hands of their enemies. Then they would ask for help, and each time Adonai sent them good leaders so they could live in safety.

But when the Israelites saw King Nachash of the Ammonites marching against them, they cried out to Samuel, "We must have a king to rule us." Samuel says, This is the king that Adonai has given you. If you obey Adonai, you and your king will be protected. But if you rebel against Adonai, then neither you nor your king will be safe.

You have done wrong to ask for a king, Samuel said, and Adonai will show you by bringing thunder and rain today, in the dry season. So Samuel called to Adonai, who sent thunder and rain that very day, "and the people were in awe of Adonai, and of Samuel." Samuel said, "Do not be afraid:"

Do not turn to emptiness that cannot help or save you.... Adonai will never give you up, for the sake of Adonai's mighty Name, for Adonai has determined to make you God's own people.

Miriam and Aaron Die

The Red Heifer

Chukkat ("law of" or "ritual of") begins with instructions for a ritual. Adonai tells Moses and Aaron what must be done when someone becomes unclean by touching or coming too close to a corpse, a human bone, or a grave. This happened often in ancient Israel. Since family and friends cared for the dying and the dead, most Israelites at one time or another had to touch, move, or bury a corpse. Yet they believed that contact with death made them unclean. So they turned to their priests to make them clean again. Adonai commands the ritual of the red heifer for this purpose.

A heifer is a young cow, one that has never given birth. Adonai instructs the Israelites to bring "a red heifer without blemish" to Eleazar the priest. The red heifer must be sacrificed outside the camp, with Eleazar watching. Eleazar must then dip his finger in the cow's blood and sprinkle the blood seven times in the direction of the Tent of Meeting. The dead heifer must be burned—adding cedar wood, hyssop, and "crimson stuff" (probably red yarn) to the fire. Eleazar and the person who helped him must then wash their clothes, bathe their bodies, and return to the camp. Because they were near the red heifer, they were unclean until evening.

Someone else had to gather the ashes of the heifer and put them in a clean place outside the camp. By touching the ashes this person also became unclean until evening. To finish the preparations, the ashes of the heifer had to be mixed with fresh water. This mixture of water and ashes was called the "water of purification".

Adonai commands: "This shall be a permanent law for the Israelites and for the strangers who reside among you. Anyone who touches the corpse of any human being shall be unclean for seven days. ..." The "water of purification" must be sprinkled on the unclean person on the third day and on the seventh day. Even the person who does the sprinkling becomes unclean until evening and has to bathe.

They Hated Death

The Christian scholar Herbert Danby (1889-1953) was famous for translating the Mishnah from Aramaic into English. Once he was asked, "What was the biggest difference between the beliefs of ancient Egyptians and those of ancient Israelites?" He replied, "The Egyptians treasured most what happens after death; the Israelites loved this life. They hated death and everything about it." In parashah *Chukkat* ("law" or "ritual") we can see for ourselves the wisdom of Danby's words.

Why did touching the ashes or coming near the red heifer make a person unclean, while sprinkling the ashes on an unclean person would make that person clean? Why was this sacrifice done outside the camp and not on the altar in the Mishkan? Why does the priest sprinkle blood seven times toward the Tent of Meeting? Why should this sacrifice be a heifer, not a bull? Why is the color red important—the red skin of the cow, the blood, and the red yarn? These are just a few of the questions that puzzled scholars and commentators through the ages.

Solving the Puzzle

Modern Bible scholars can help here. Thanks to their work, we now know that in Mesopotamia, long before the time of Moses, magician-priests used this kind of ritual. The Israelite priests "adopted" these rituals, changing them slightly—taking out some of the "magic"—making the rituals more "Israelite".

The sacrifice was done "outside the camp", away from the Mishkan, with a cow and not a bull—all of which shows that it was not a normal Israelite sacrifice. The red things— the cow's skin, the cedar wood, the blood, and the red yarn—all stood for blood. Blood was the stuff of life—losing it was bad, and being touched with blood that had been dedicated to God was good (good blood was used to ordain priests in *Titzaveh*). The cedar wood and hyssop gave off a pleasing odor when they were burned, like the incense used in the Mishkan.

By the time of the Talmud, though, the Rabbis had little faith in rituals based on magic. They thought it was proper for us to ask for God's help, but whether we are helped or not is up to God. Magic has a different objective. Magic tries to force God (or demons or spirits) to do what people want. Look at the red heifer as magic, the way the Rabbis did.

The ritual of the red heifer forces God to make a person clean. The priest who sprinkles the blood seven times toward the Tent of Meeting is performing magic. The priest who sprinkles the "water of purification" on an unclean person on the third and seventh day is performing magic. There is no prayer needed, because if the priest's magic is

Similar Rituals

We have met this kind of "magic" ritual before. In portion *Ki Tisah* (Exodus 32) Moses "took the [golden bull-calf] they had made and burned it; he ground it to powder and sprinkled it on the water and so made the Israelites drink it." In portion *Naso* (Numbers 5) the dust of the Mishkan floor was mixed with water to make the "test" called sotah, to see if a wife was unfaithful to her husband. In portion *Metzora* (Leviticus 14) the priest is told to use a mixture of blood, cedar wood, hyssop, and red yarn to cure skin diseases and the same kind of mixture to make a moldy house ritually clean. All of these were difficult for the Rabbis and also for later commentators to explain.

The Sabbath of the Cow

The laws explaining the ritual of the red heifer are read in most synagogues on a Sabbath before Passover, in addition to the usual Torah portion. This connects the idea of making people "clean" with making ourselves and our houses clean for the Passover festival. The day is given a special name, *Shabbat Parah*, "the Sabbath of the Cow".

performed correctly, God is forced to make the person clean. All that the Rabbis could say was that the ritual of the red heifer is a test of our faith. If Adonai told Moses and Aaron to do this, that is what we must do, even if we think it is mumbo-jumbo. So like the priests of old, the Rabbis included the ritual of the red heifer in their law codes.

Thirty-Eight Lost Years

After the ritual of the red heifer is described, the Torah returns to the story of the Israelites' wandering. Everything we heard about the people in the wilderness up to this time—the road to Sinai, the manna, the golden bull-calf, the giving of the tablets of the Law, the scouts, the rebellions—all happened in the first two years after the Israelites left Egypt. The older generation (above the age of twenty) was punished for their lack of faith by not being allowed to enter the land of Canaan (see *Korach*). The Torah says that Aaron died in the fortieth year, and since we read about his death later in this portion, we know that thirty-eight years have passed. The Torah is silent about these thirty-eight years. It seems that the Israelites were settled at a place called Kadesh for all that time. The Torah reports this in two short lines:

> The Israelites all arrived at the wilderness of Zin on the first new moon, and the people stayed at Kadesh. Miriam died and was buried there.

Water from the Rock

After the death of Miriam the Israelites again come to Moses and Aaron to complain. To Moses they say, It would be better for us if we had died with others that Adonai killed, for we are thirsty and our beasts are thirsty. "Why did you make us leave Egypt to bring us to this wretched place, a place with no grain or figs or vines or pomegranates?"

> Moses and Aaron went from the community to the entrance of the Tent of Meeting and fell on their faces. The Presence of Adonai appeared. Adonai spoke to Moses, saying, "You and your brother Aaron take the rod and assemble the community, and before their very eyes order the rock to give

its water ... so the community and their beasts can drink." ...

Moses and Aaron assembled the community before the rock; and [Moses] said, "Listen, you rebels, shall we get water for you out of this rock?" And Moses raised his hand and struck the rock twice with his rod. Out came gushers of water, and the community and their beasts drank.

But Adonai said to Moses and Aaron, "Because you did not trust Me enough to show My holiness to the Israelites, therefore you shall not lead this community into the land that I have given them." Those are the Waters of Meribah—meaning that the Israelites quarreled with Adonai—through which Adonai showed [Adonai's] holiness.

Why did Adonai decree that Moses and Aaron would die in the wilderness? What had they done wrong? Adonai said it was because they "did not trust Me enough to show My holiness to the Israelites." But what does that mean? Rashi explains that Moses was only supposed to speak to the rock, not strike it. But Moses and Aaron were angry with the people, and they struck the rock instead of speaking to it.

Maimonides disagrees with Rashi. He claims that the real sin was not striking the rock, but anger: Moses and Aaron ran out of patience. In Exodus 17 (*B'Shalach*), Moses struck a rock, and water came out for the people. But Moses and Aaron did not speak out angrily then, as they did here when Moses said, "Listen, you rebels...."

In Exodus 17, when Moses struck a rock the first time, the place was named "Massah and Meribah, because there the Israelites quarreled and because they tested Adonai." Here the waters are called "the Waters of Meribah—meaning that the Israelites quarreled with Adonai." Some commentators say that these are one story, not two. But at least one commentator noticed that in Exodus 17, Moses waited until Adonai's Presence was above the rock. This time Moses did not wait. Perhaps this was what angered Adonai most—that when Moses acted, it seemed that Moses and Aaron, not Adonai, produced the miracle. Perhaps that is what Adonai meant by saying, "You did not trust Me enough to show My holiness to the Israelites."

Many Explanations
Many explanations are given for why Moses and Aaron were punished by Adonai at the Waters of Meribah. You can choose any one you like. Each one makes sense. Or better still: If you look closely at the story, you may find a new way to explain what happened. That is one of the miracles of Torah study: Like the water that gushed out when the rock was struck, whenever you strike a verse, new ideas about it rush out in a never-ending stream.

וַיִּרְאוּ כָּל־הָעֵדָה כִּי גָוַע
אַהֲרֹן וַיִּבְכּוּ אֶת־אַהֲרֹן
שְׁלֹשִׁים יוֹם כֹּל בֵּית
יִשְׂרָאֵל:

The whole community knew that Aaron had breathed his last. The entire house of Israel mourned Aaron for thirty days.

To Consider

When Jacob died the Children of Israel mourned for seven days, and the Canaanites said, "This is a most serious mourning." So at the death of a close relative we sit *shivah*—"seven" days of serious mourning. In *Chukkat* the people mourn Aaron's death for thirty days. Later, when Moses dies, the people also mourn him for thirty days. So we observe *sheloshim*, "thirty" days of mourning, by not going to entertainments, not cutting our hair, not wearing new clothing, not marrying, and not attending festive occasions. Both shivah and sheloshim are customs that allow us to properly mourn the death of those we love, even as they set limits on our mourning. Jews show in this way that mourning is important and so is the business of getting on with living our normal lives again.

Modern commentators believe that whatever the sin of Moses and Aaron was, it is missing from the story. They take the last words as proof. The Torah says "the Waters of Meribah ... *through which Adonai showed [Adonai's] holiness.*" Whatever Moses and Aaron actually did to sin against Adonai, the problem was not that Adonai's holiness was not proved. This verse tells us that it *was* proved!

The Death of Aaron

When the Israelites prepared to leave Kadesh, Moses sent messengers to the king of Edom, saying,

> Allow us to cross your country. We will not pass through fields or vineyards, and we will not drink water from wells. We will follow the king's highway, turning off neither to the right nor to the left until we have crossed your territory.

But the king of Edom refused to allow the Israelites to go through his country. If you try, he told Moses, "We will go out against you with the sword." Moses asked a second time, but the Edomites sent out soldiers to bar the way. So, the Torah says, Moses led the people around the country of Edom to Mount Hor.

> At Mount Hor ..., Adonai said to Moses and Aaron, "Let Aaron be gathered to his kin: he is not to enter the land that I have given to the Israelites.... Take Aaron and his son Eleazar ... up on Mount Hor. ... There Aaron shall be gathered unto the dead." Moses did what Adonai commanded. They went up Mount Hor in the sight of the whole community. Moses stripped Aaron of his priestly garments and put them on his son Eleazar, and Aaron died there on top of the mountain. When Moses and Eleazar came down from the mountain [without Aaron], the whole community knew that Aaron had breathed his last. The entire house of Israel mourned Aaron for thirty days.

In his life Aaron was the first to wear the uniform of the High Priest. Now the uniform passes to his son Eleazar, who became the High Priest for the new generation of Israelites who would enter the Promised Land. Aaron silently accepted his death at the place and time that Adonai commanded. One commentary says, "To meet death as Aaron met it, at the end of a good life, is to die on top of the mountain, in sight of the Promised Land."

Meanwhile, the Canaanite king of Arad marched his forces to Mount Hor and attacked the Israelites, taking some of them captive. The Israelites vowed to Adonai, If You let us defeat this people, we will take nothing from them except for the portion that belongs to Adonai. The Torah says, "Adonai heeded Israel's plea and delivered up the Canaanites … they and their cities were destroyed." That place was called Hormah ("destruction").

The Copper Serpent

As the Israelites left Mount Hor they complained to Moses, "Why did you make us leave Egypt to die in the wilderness?" This time Adonai punished them by sending "*seraph* serpents." (The word *seraph* may come from "burning", meaning that the serpents were "fiery" or that their bite caused the Israelites' skin to burn.) Many people were bit by the serpents and died. The rest came to Moses saying, "We sinned by speaking against Adonai and against you. Pray to Adonai to take away these serpents."

> And Moses prayed for the people. Then Adonai said to Moses, "Make an image of a *seraph* and put it on a standard [a pole]. And if anyone who is bitten looks at it, he or she shall recover." Moses made a copper serpent and mounted it on a standard; and anyone bitten by a serpent would look at the copper serpent and recover.

To Consider

Archaeologists have found snakes made of bronze or copper (like the one *below*) in ancient worship sites in Israel. The snake is almost always seen as a symbol of healing. Snakes were scary because they bit and their bite was deadly, but snakes were admired because they could shed their skins and come away in an entirely new body. That is what people want most when they are ill—to shed their illness and come away in a new, healthy body. The Book of Chronicles tells how King Hezekiah (eighth century B.C.E.) removed the copper serpent made by Moses from the Temple and had it destroyed because the Israelites worshiped it like an idol. Either Moses' copper serpent had been used by the Israelites for some four hundred years, or else the story of how and why Moses made the copper serpent was told to explain how the snake was placed in the Temple in the first place!

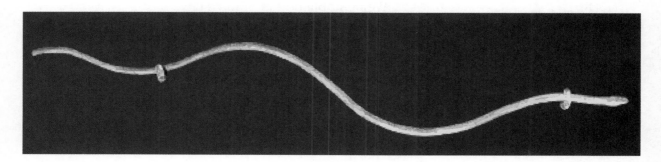

Battles and Popular Songs

King Sihon had his poet-singers write a victory song for him. This is not at all unusual. We remember the "Song at the Sea" from portion *B'Shalach* (Exodus 15), when the Israelites praised God for destroying the Egyptian chariots, singing, "Who is like You, Adonai … / Majestic in holiness / Awesome in splendor, working wonders!" In the same way, "The Star Spangled Banner" was written during the War of 1812 to celebrate the bravery of the Americans. And the popular song that begins "From the halls of Montezuma / To the shores of Tripoli" celebrates many victories of American soldiers and even has a religious name—"The Marines' Hymn".

Israelite Conquests

Now the Israelites moved from camp to camp. (The Torah quotes from a scroll called *The Book of the Wars of Adonai*, telling the exact boundary between the land of Moab and the land of the Amorites.) After a while they arrived at Be'er (the name just means "a well"—perhaps a well-known well). At Be'er Adonai told Moses, "Gather up the people that I may give them water." Then the Israelites sang:

> Spring up, O well—sing to it—
> The well which the chieftains dug,
> Which the nobles of the people started
> With maces, with their own staffs.

This is called "the Song at the Well". Some scholars think it may also be quoted from *The Book of the Wars of Adonai*. Leaving Be'er, the Israelites came near a peak called Pisgah. Here messengers were sent to King Sihon of the Amorites, repeating the message Moses sent to the Edomites.

> Let [Israel] pass through your country. We will not turn off into fields or vineyards, and we will not drink water from wells. We will follow the king's highway until we have crossed your territory.

But King Sihon refused to let them pass. Instead he marched his army out and attacked the Israelites. This time the Israelites fought, defeating King Sihon and capturing the Amorite towns, including Heshbon, their capital.

Heshbon had once belonged to King Ar of Moab. Some time before, King Sihon and his armies had captured it from the Moabites, and the king's poet-singers celebrated his victory with a popular song:

> Come to Heshbon; firmly built
> Well established is Sihon's city.
> For fire came out of Heshbon,
> Flame from Sihon's city,
> Consuming [King] Ar of Moab, …
> His sons are made runaways
> And his daughters are [taken] captive
> By an Amorite king, Sihon.

The Israelites celebrated their victory over Heshbon by adding a new ending to the song: "Yet we [Israel] have utterly thrown [the Amorites] down."

After defeating the Amorites Moses sent spies to the town of Jazer. The Israelites then attacked and conquered Jazer, too. They marched up the road to Bashan, where King Og and his soldiers tried to stop them.

> But Adonai told Moses, "Do not fear him, for I give him and all his people and his land into your hand. You shall do to him as you did to [the Amorites]." [The Israelites] defeated [King Og] and his sons and all his people, until nothing was left to him; and they inherited his country. The Israelites then marched on and made camp in the plains of Moab, across the Jordan [River] from Jericho.

The Victories

Three things stand out in this section about the conquests of the Israelites:

(1) The Torah names a scroll that is not in the Torah and quotes from it. It was called *The Book of the Wars of Adonai*, and no copy of it seems to have survived. All we have are the small parts that are quoted here. It was either a history of conquests or a book of songs praising Adonai in times of war. Bible scholars see this as added proof that the Torah was made up of earlier scrolls that were later combined.

(2) When the Torah speaks of the Israelites conquering lands it often uses the word *yirash*, "inherited". In other words, the lands belonged to them already because of the covenants Adonai made with Abraham, Isaac, and Jacob. It was their inheritance. Clearly war and death were necessary in the conquest. But the outcome depended on Adonai.

(3) In *Chukkat* Moses and the Israelites conquer Hormah. But the Book of Judges (1:17) states that Hormah was conquered much later, after the death of Joshua. Was Hormah conquered twice? In the middle ages Nachmanides believed that Hormah was conquered only once, in the days of the Judges. If so, how could Moses have written about this conquest in the Torah? Abrabanel also thought that Hor-

Conquests and Rights

From the story of King Sihon we can see that war and conquest were common even among the Canaanites. Stronger armies took cities like Heshbon from weaker armies. Sihon and the Amorites captured Heshbon from the Moabites, and the Israelites captured it from the Amorites. But in the eyes of the Torah, no Canaanite nation had any "right" to lands and cities. The Israelites might do the fighting, but it was Adonai who was giving the land to Israel—as an inheritance.

Rabbi Isaac Abrabanel

Isaac Abrabanel (1437-1508) was born in Lisbon, Portugal. He served as treasurer for the royal court of Portugal and later at the court of Queen Isabella of Spain. He attempted to bribe Ferdinand and Isabella to allow the Jews to remain in Spain, but he was among those forced to leave in 1492 following the Edict of Expulsion. He went to Italy, eventually dying in Venice. His commentaries on Torah and Prophets were very modern in spirit. He wrote to help Jews of his time understand how the ancient writings related to the events of their own lives.

mah was conquered only once. He suggested that Moses did not write about Hormah at all—he said that the story was added later. But Nachmanides would not agree with that because he thought that Moses wrote every word in the Torah. So Nachmanides claimed that Moses was able to write about the time when the Israelites conquered Hormah because Moses was a prophet and Adonai showed Moses the future.

For two hundred years archaeologists have searched for the cities mentioned in this portion. Traces of some cities have been found, but either the cities were not occupied in the time of Moses or they show no signs of any warfare around the time of Moses. At present, there is no evidence that the Israelites ever went this way or made any of these conquests. We can believe, like Nachmanides, that Moses saw the future and wrote about it. Or we can agree with Abrabanel that the tales of conquest were added long after the death of Moses. Or we can wait to see if archaeologists ever find evidence to prove these stories of conquest.

Haftarah: Judges 11:1-33

The Rabbis had no trouble connecting this haftarah to *Chukkat*. Both contain tales of the wars of the Israelites under Moses.

Jepthah's mother was a concubine, not a wife, and he fled from home when he was threatened by his brothers. He became a raider leading a small band of outlaws. When Gilead was attacked by Ammonites the elders asked Jepthah to lead them in battle. Jepthah demanded the command of all the troops of Gilead if Adonai gave him victory. Their agreement was repeated before Adonai and the people at Mizpah (see *Bichukotai*).

Jepthah sent messengers to the king of the Ammonites asking what his quarrel was. The king replied that the Israelites took his land when they came up out of Egypt. Jepthah sent more messengers to say that Israel took no land from Moab or Ammon. The Israelites had turned to go around these territories when their kings refused to let them pass through in peace. True, when King Sihon brought the Amorite armies out to fight, Moses and the Israelites fought, and Adonai gave them the lands of the Amorites. True, this land once belonged to you, but you have enough land now. Do not be like Balak, who tried to defeat Israel. Be satisfied with your lot.

But the king of Ammon would not listen, and Jepthah was seized by "the spirit of Adonai". Jepthah vowed to Adonai, "If You hand the Ammonites to me, I vow to sacrifice to Adonai whatever comes out of my house to meet me when I come home safe" (see *Mattot*).

Jepthah then led Israel in battle against the Ammonites, and "Adonai put them in his hand."

Balaam the Prophet

Balak and Balaam

The first word and the name of this parashah is *Balak*, the name of the king of Moab. When Balak saw how Israel defeated the Amorites, he asked his neighbors, the Midianites, to fight with him. "This horde [of Israelites]," he said, "will now lick clean everything around us the way an ox licks up grass." Balak sent messengers to Balaam, saying:

> Behold! A people came out of Egypt and [now they are] settled next to me. Come, put a curse upon this people for me … perhaps I can thus defeat them and drive them out…. For I know that whomever you bless is indeed blessed, and whomever you curse is cursed.

Balaam said to the messengers, "Spend the night here, and I shall answer you as Adonai may instruct me." That night Adonai came to Balaam and told him, "Do not go with them. Do not curse [Israel], for they are blessed." Balaam arose the next morning and sent the messengers away.

Then Balak sent high officials as messengers to plead with Balaam. "Please do not refuse to come. I will reward you richly." At once Balaam answered: Nothing Balak promises is enough, if Adonai my God does not want me to go. But again Balaam asked the messengers to stay overnight. That night God told Balaam, "Go with them. But do what I command you to do."

The Donkey and Balaam

The following morning Balaam arose, saddled his donkey, and went with the officials. The Torah says God was very angry and sent an angel to stop Balaam. When Balaam's donkey saw the angel of Adonai it left the road and went into the fields. Balaam beat the donkey to force her to return to the road.

Dreams and Prophets

Balak sent two sets of messengers to Balaam. Both times Balaam asked them to wait overnight for their answer. Both times Adonai came to Balaam to give him an answer. In *Beha'alotcha* Adonai told Miriam and Aaron, "I speak with [a prophet] in a dream." The Torah doesn't call Balaam a prophet at the start, but every Israelite hearing this story would know that when Balaam hears Adonai answer in the night, this means that Balaam is a prophet.

Confusion?

Is it confusing that the story says God gave permission for Balaam to go with the officials and then says God was "very angry" when Balaam went? By now you probably know the reason for the confusion. Through the years many people told this famous story—always changing it a bit—adding some things and leaving out others. For example, if you tell the story of Balak and Balaam without the part about the talking donkey, it is a serious story. If you include the angel and the talking donkey, it becomes a comic tale. The rule in making the Torah was "always add and never subtract," so the final story comes from earlier tales that did not always agree.

Now the angel of Adonai blocked the path between the vineyards.... The donkey, seeing the angel of Adonai, pressed against the wall, squeezing Balaam's foot. [Balaam] beat her again. Now the angel of Adonai moved forward and stood where it was so narrow that there was no room to turn right or left. When the donkey saw the angel of Adonai again, she lay down under Balaam. Balaam was furious and beat the donkey with his stick.

Adonai opened the donkey's mouth; and the donkey spoke to Balaam. "What have I done to you that you have beaten me three times?" Balaam answered, "You have made a fool of me! If I had a sword, I'd kill you." The donkey said to Balaam, "Look, I am the same donkey you always ride! Do I usually do things like this to you?" [Balaam] answered, "No."

Then Adonai uncovered Balaam's eyes. He saw the angel of Adonai standing in the way, holding a drawn sword. Immediately, [Balaam] bowed low. The angel of Adonai said to him, "Why have you beaten your ass three times? It is I who came out to stop you, for your errand disgusts me. When the donkey saw me, she shied away from me three times. If she had not shied away, I would have spared her and killed you!"

Balaam said to the angel of Adonai, "I was mistaken. I did not know that you were standing in my way. If you still disapprove [of my errand], I will turn back." But the angel of Adonai said to Balaam, "Go with the men. But say nothing except what I tell you to say." So Balaam traveled on with Balak's [officials].

Balak and Balaam

King Balak came out to meet Balaam, asking, "Why didn't you come when I first sent to invite you?" Balaam answered, "I can pronounce only the word that God puts in my mouth."

That night Balak made a feast for Balaam and the next morning he took Balaam to a hill. From there they could see part of the Israelite camp. Going a bit farther, Balaam said to Balak, "Build me seven altars." Then Balak and Balaam offered up a bull and a ram on each altar.

> Balaam said to Balak, "Stay here beside your offerings while I am gone. Perhaps Adonai will grant me a sign, and whatever [Adonai] reveals to me I will tell you." And [Balaam] went off alone.

Adonai gave Balaam the words to speak. So Balaam returned to where Balak and the Moabites were standing beside the altars. Balaam "took up his theme," saying:

> How can I curse whom God has not cursed,
> How [can I] doom when Adonai has not doomed?
> As I see [the Israelites] from the mountain tops,
> Gaze on them from the heights,
> [They are] a people that dwells apart,
> Not counted among the nations
> But who can count the dust of Jacob,
> Or number the dust-cloud of Israel?
> May I die the death of the upright,
> May my fate be like theirs!

Hearing this, Balak said to Balaam, "What have you done to me? Here I brought you to curse my enemies, and instead you blessed them!" Balaam said, "I can only repeat faithfully what Adonai puts in my mouth." Then Balak said, "Come with me to another place … and curse them for me from there." So Balak took Balaam higher, to the very top of Pisgah. Again he built seven altars and offered a bull and a ram on each one. Again Balaam went off alone to seek the word of Adonai.

This time Adonai came to Balaam, saying, "Return to Balak and speak thus." Balaam found everyone waiting beside the altars. Balak asked, "What did Adonai say?" And Balaam "took up his theme," saying:

> No harm is in sight for Jacob,
> No woe in view for Israel.
> Adonai their God is with them,
> … God who freed them from Egypt …
> Lo, there is no omen in Jacob,

To Consider

As the story tells, Balak keeps taking Balaam to higher and higher places. Each time they can see more and more of the Israelite camp. And each time they build seven altars and offer a bull and a ram on each altar. So the drama of the story builds higher and higher. What the Torah really seems to be saying is that there is nothing anyone—even Balaam—can do to change the judgment of Adonai.

Quote to Remember

מַה־טֹּבוּ אֹהָלֶיךָ יַעֲקֹב
מִשְׁכְּנֹתֶיךָ יִשְׂרָאֵל:

*How goodly are your tents, O Jacob,
Your dwellings, O Israel!*

No magic in Israel:
Jacob is told at once,
Israel [knows] what God has planned.

Now Balak said to Balaam, "Don't curse them and don't bless them!" But Balaam said to Balak, "It is as I told you: Whatever Adonai says, that I must do."

This time Balak took Balaam to the peak of Peor, built seven altars, and sacrificed bulls and rams again. This time, though, Balaam did not go off to seek Adonai's words. This time Balaam knew that Adonai wanted to bless Israel. This time Balaam looked out on the whole camp of Israel, and God's spirit seized him. He "took up his theme" and spoke:

Word of Balaam son of Beor,
Word of the man whose eye is true…:
How goodly are your tents, O Jacob,
Your dwellings, O Israel!
Like palm-groves that stretch out,
Like gardens beside a river….
Their kingdom shall be exalted. …
They shall devour enemy nations….
They crouch, they lie down like a lion,
Like the king of beasts; who dare rouse them?
Blessed are they who bless you, [O Israel,]
Accursed are they who curse you!

Balak was enraged at Balaam. "I called you to curse my enemies, and you have blessed them instead," he said. "Go home at once! I was going to reward you richly, but Adonai has kept you from receiving any reward."

But Balaam answered Balak, saying, Even if you gave me your whole house full of silver and gold, I could only speak what Adonai commanded me to speak. I will go home, but first I will tell you what Israel will do to you and your people. Then Balaam "took up his theme" and spoke:

Word of Balaam son of Beor,
Word of the man whose eye is true,
Word of him who hears God's speech,
Who obtains knowledge from the Most High…:
What I see for them is not yet,
What I behold will not be soon:
A star rises from Jacob,

A scepter comes forth from Israel;
It smashes the brow of Moab....
Israel is triumphant.

In a vision Balaam saw the people of Amalek and "took up his theme" again, saying, "[Amalek's] fate is to perish forever." He saw the Kenites and "took up his theme" again, saying, Even though you Kenites live among the cliffs, you shall be conquered by Assyria. And Balaam "took up his theme" again, saying, "Alas, who can survive except God has willed it!" In time, he said, ships will come and conquer Assyria and Eber, too. Even these mighty nations will disappear forever.

Then Balaam and Balak parted company. So ends the tale of how Balaam was hired to curse the Israelites, but instead he blessed them with the words of Adonai.

The Prophet Balaam

The tale of Balaam is a story about a prophet of Adonai. Yet the part about the angel and the talking donkey reads like comedy, pokes fun at Balaam, and claims that Adonai was angry, even though only one verse before Adonai instructed Balaam to go. How could a great prophet not see an angel of Adonai if even a donkey could? Stories like this, featuring talking animals, have been known in fairy tales and folklore forever. This tale, like the one about the talking serpent in the garden of Eden (see *Bereishit*), was probably told by the J-teller.

Yet if we remove the tale of the angel and the talking donkey, we are left with a more serious story. King Balak of Moab and the Midianite leaders tried to pay Balaam to curse Israel, but Balaam could only bless Israel and curse the people who hired him. We may be surprised that a person who could hear Adonai would take money to pronounce blessings and curses. We may be surprised by a non-Israelite who seems to be a prophet of God. We may be surprised how much Balaam sounds like Israelite prophets who also speak in "themes" (or "proverbs") and in poetry. We may even be surprised that *Mah Tovu* ("How goodly"), the blessing given by Balaam, is recited by Jews in prayer services today.

To Consider

When Balaam says, "A star rises from Jacob," some Bible scholars think he is speaking of astrology, predicting the future by "reading" the planets and stars. Even today most people know their "sign"—one of twelve, from Aries (the Ram) to Pisces (the Fish), called the Zodiac. Astrology began before history, but the Zodiac dates back to about 2,600 years ago, when Mesopotamian priests divided the sky into twelve parts and found a "sign" in each part. They divided the sky scientifically, calculating where Earth's equator was and where it would be in the sky above them. Charting the equator, they placed the first sign (Aries) in the spring. Most astrologers use this same chart today, predicting your day or your life based on your sign. But we know now that the earth actually wobbles through space, so while the line the ancient priests drew and the chart they made was accurate in their day, today it should begin close to Aquarius (the Water Carrier). In fact, because of the movement of the earth, the line will pass through every sign of the Zodiac in the course of 25,700 years.

The Balaam Stele

At Deir Alla archaeologists were digging beneath walls toppled by an earthquake. What they found was a large room with benches. In it were 119 shattered bits of plaster covered with black and red letters in old Canaanite Hebrew. The plaster bits once formed a *stele* (a rectangular tablet with a curved top, like many others we know from ancient times). The stele had once hung on a wall in this room. Much of the writing was missing or broken (see *above* for how the archaeologists pieced it together), but the few lines that could be read were amazing.

Even more astonishing is an inscription discovered by archaeologists in 1967. It begins:

> Scroll of [Ba]laam [son of Beo]r, the man seeing the gods; behold, the gods came to him at night … and they said to [Balaa]m son of Beor thus: "The last flame has appeared; a fire for judgment has appeared." And Balaam arose in the morning, … and cou[ld not eat], and he kept weeping. And his people came up to him and they [said] to Balaam son of Beor: "Why are you fasting and why are you weeping?" And he said to them: "Sit! … come, consider the doings of the gods. The gods have gathered together … and they have said … 'Sew up, close the sky with your cloud! [Let] darkness be there, and not brightness….'"

With this discovery we learned that Balaam was well known, even famous, in the days of early Israel. He may have lived in the time of Moses or at any time before the year 760 B.C.E. That's when (archaeologists say) an earthquake collapsed the walls, breaking the inscription into bits.

Was Balaam a Sorcerer?

In the Bible the word for "prophet" is *navi*, which probably means "one who is called [to speak God's words]". Moses is called a navi in the Book of Deuteronomy. Other words for "prophet" in Hebrew include *ish Elohim* ("God's person"), *roeh* ("seer"), and *hozeh* (also "seer"). In the stele rom Deir Alla, Balaam is called a hozeh. In all these ways a prophet is one who is "called" to "see the truth" and "speak" the words of God. As Balaam tells Balak, "I can pronounce only the word that God puts in my mouth."

Balaam not only listens to God, he also searches for signs or omens. This is the work of "diviners", people who look for meaning in the stars, by staring into oil on water in a cup (as Joseph was said to do), by casting lots, or by sacrificing animals to "read" signs on livers and other organs. The Torah includes many times when divining is done by Israelites. This is not exactly "magic", since any signs or omens would have to be "from" God, and the "diviner" only tries to understand them.

Sorcery is the black magic that Balak wants. He hopes that Balaam will pronounce a curse on the Israelites to weaken them so they can be defeated. As Balak has his messengers say to Balaam, "For I know that whomever you bless is indeed blessed, and whomever you curse is cursed." But Balaam refuses to be a sorcerer. In short, the Torah pictures Balaam as a seer, a prophet, and a diviner, but not a sorcerer. That is why some of the Rabbis claimed that Balaam was a great prophet.

The Moabite Women

At the end of this portion the Moabite women tempt the Israelite men. Those who are tempted worship a Moabite god named Baal-peor. Adonai punishes them with death and sends a plague on the Israelites. "Those who died of the plague," the Torah says, "numbered twenty-four thousand."

To Consider

Many of the Rabbis thought that Balaam was a prophet of Adonai. They said he was one of the prophets sent by God to teach truth to the non-Israelite nations. But others among the Rabbis said that even though Balaam did not curse Israel directly, he later betrayed God by giving Balak and the Midianites a plan to weaken Israel. He told them to introduce the Moabite women to the Israelite men so that Israel would learn to worship idols. Afterward God removed the gift of prophecy from other nations of the world—all because of what Balaam had done.

Haftarah: Micah 5:6-6:8

The prophet Micah mentions Balaam and Balak in this haftarah. Micah lived after the northern kingdom had been destroyed and only Judah remained. Like Amos, he thought that Adonai would punish the evils being done in Judah and Jerusalem with destruction of the nation and the Holy City.

Judah will soon be few in number, like drops of dew, like a lost lion cub. The prophet says, You may think your hand is mighty enough to save you, but "on that day" Adonai will destroy your chariots and war horses, your cities and fortresses, your idols and pillars. Any nation (including Judah) that did not obey Adonai will be punished.

Micah uses the language of a lawsuit in which Adonai is accusing Israel of breaking the covenant. "Hear the case of Adonai, you mountains; give ear, you earthly lands." Adonai asks, "What wrong have I done you?" Do you not remember how I brought you up from Egypt, how I saved you from Balak, and how Balaam was forced to answer?

Micah asks, What would be the right way to honor Adonai? "Should I come and bow down?" "Should I bring burnt-offerings of yearling calves?" "Would Adonai be pleased with thousands of rams, ten thousands of rivers of oil?" "Should I offer my first-born child for my sin?" And Micah answers:

> It has been told you, O mortal, what is good—what Adonai requires of you—only this: to do justly, to love mercy, and to walk humbly with your God.

Dividing the Land

Zadok, the High Priest appointed by Solomon, was of the family of Pinchas. Commentators like Abraham Ibn Ezra said that this proves that God keeps a covenant faithfully. Generations later God still honored the "covenant of peace" made with Pinchas. Modern Bible scholars like William W. Hallo think it is more likely that after Zadok became High Priest the P-tellers turned to the past. They found or crafted the story of Pinchas and the "covenant of peace" to show why Zadok deserved to be High Priest. Who came first: Pinchas or Zadok? We may never know.

The Covenant of Peace

At the end of the last parashah Aaron's grandson Pinchas grabbed a spear and killed Zimri, an Israelite man, and Cozbi, a Midianite woman. Zimri's father was a chieftain in the tribe of Simeon. Cozbi's father was a chieftain of the Midianties. As a couple, their influence (and their worship of the Midianite god Baal-peor) caused many Israelites to follow their lead. To punish Israel, Adonai sent a plague that killed thousands, but the plague ended suddenly when Pinchas killed the couple.

This parashah begins with Adonai telling Moses that Pinchas did a good thing. If Pinchas had not killed Zimri and Cozbi, the plague might have wiped out all the Israelites. Adonai rewards Pinchas with a special "covenant of peace", promising that Pinchas and his family after him will always be priests in Israel.

The story of Pinchas teaches us two things: (1) Being a priest (especially a High Priest) usually depended on being born to the right parents. In fact, almost all jobs passed from parent to child in ancient Israel. Children hardly ever wondered about what they would be when they grew up.

And (2) killing for Adonai was rewarded by Adonai. We may no longer agree, of course. We may think that because Pinchas murdered two people, he should have been punished. But remember: Moses was chosen by Adonai even though he had murdered an Egyptian taskmaster. In fact, after making the "covenant of peace", Adonai commands, "Attack the Midianites and defeat them." For the ancient Israelites, war and killing were part of everyday life.

The Census after the Plague

When the plague ended, Adonai commanded Moses and Eleazar the High Priest to take a new census. Adonai tells Moses that the purpose of the census is to count how many

Israelites can be ready to go to war (the war against Midian). The tribe of Levi is counted separately (as it was in the last census; see *Naso*). Including Levi, thirteen tribes are listed in the census. But the tribes of Ephraim and Manasseh are counted as one, since both were children of Joseph. In the last census the total came to 603,550; this time the total of Israelites is 601,730. In the last census the tribe of Levi totaled 22,000; this time there are 23,000 Levites. In the last census each individual was counted. This time the census counts clans ("family-houses") in the tribes. The name of each tribe is given, then its clans are named, then the total is presented. The list looks like this:

> Reuben, Israel's firstborn. Descendants of Reuben: [of] Enoch, the clan of the Enochites; of Pallu, the clan of the Palluites; of Hezron, the clan of the Hezronites; of Carmi, the clan of the Carmites. Those are the clans of the tribe of Reuben. The persons counted came to 43,730.

In the tribe of Manasseh, when it comes to the clan of Zelophehad, the list changes. The Torah says:

> Now Zelophehad son of Hepher had no sons, only daughters. The names of Zelophehad's daughters were Mahlah, Noah, Hoglah, Milcah, and Tirzah.

The count ended, and Adonai gave Moses another reason for the census. Even though the Israelites had not yet conquered Canaan, they were to divide the land according to their clans. Adonai commanded: "Make the share larger for larger groups, make it smaller for smaller groups." And Adonai added, "The land … is to be assigned by lot … whether for larger or smaller groups."

Who Will Divide the Land?

Dividing Canaan would not be an easy task. If larger shares had to go to larger clans, the Israelites could work that out. But if the land had to be divided by casting lots, then God had to do the work (since God controls the outcome when lots are cast). How could it be both ways?

The Bible commentators of the Middle Ages debated this. Rashi said that only lots were used, and God made the

Serah

In the official census records the daughters of Zelophehad were named because Zelophehad had no sons. Another woman was singled out by name in the count of the tribe of Asher. She was Serah, daughter of Asher, head of a clan. She is mentioned two other times in the Bible, whenever the four sons of Asher are named. This is unusual, since most daughters are never mentioned at all. The Bible tells nothing more than Serah's name. We are left to wonder: Why was she so important, so honored? She is a true mystery woman.

Quote to Remember

לָמָּה יִגָּרַע שֵׁם־אָבִינוּ מִתּוֹךְ מִשְׁפַּחְתּוֹ כִּי אֵין לוֹ בֵּן תְּנָה־לָּנוּ אֲחֻזָּה בְּתוֹךְ אֲחֵי אָבִינוּ:

Let not our father's name be lost to his clan just because he had no son! Give us property among our father's kinsmen!

Below: Mesopotamian female worship statue (2600-2500 B.C.E.). Women had models of themselves made to place in household shrines so the statues could pray constantly while the women performed their daily chores. Meanwhile, women's rights in the ancient world varied greatly from place to place.

shares fair for every clan. Nachmanides said that the land was divided more than once. The Israelites first divided it into twelve equal portions; then they threw lots to assign a portion to each tribe. Afterward each tribe assigned right-sized portions of land to the clans.

Abrabanel said that Rashi was wrong, since Adonai tells the Israelites to divide the land fairly. Abrabanel said that Nachmanides was also wrong, since Adonai clearly commanded that lots should be cast, not just for the tribes, but "clan by clan".

Abrabanel proposed an elegant solution: Lots were first thrown to see which tribe received which part of Canaan. Then the Israelites gave more *usable* land to the larger tribes and less to the smaller tribes. Afterward lots were thrown to divide the tribal lands by clan, and it was up to each tribe to be sure to give more *usable* land to larger and less to smaller clans. In other words, the Israelites made sure that the *size* of the portions was fair, but the lots decided the actual *place* of each tribe and clan. That way the work of dividing was shared by God and the Israelites.

Before the land could be divided, the daughters of Zelophehad came forward.

The Daughters of Zelophehad

The names of the daughters [of Zelophehad] were Mahlah, Noah, Hoglah, Milcah, and Tirzah. They stood before Moses, Eleazar the priest, the chieftains, and the whole congregation, at the entrance of the Tent of Meeting, and they said, "Our father died in the wilderness. He was not [with] Korah's company, which banded together against Adonai. [He] died for his own sin, leaving no sons. Let not our father's name be lost to his clan just because he had no son! Give us property among our father's kinsmen!"

The five daughters bring a court case, a legal question. The daughters demand that they be given land like every other clan, even though there is no man in the family. None of them is married. We know this because if any one were married, her share would be with her husband's clan. We also know that their father is dead. Either he died in the Korah rebellion (though he was not a leader in that revolt) or for some other sin ("his own"). Last, the daughters point out, if they do not receive any land, then the clan of Zelophehad ("our father's name") will disappear. If they have land, then when they marry, their husbands can leave their clans and come to the land of Zelophehad, and any children they have will continue the "name" of Zelophehad.

Archaeologists tell us that in other nations—in Mesopotamia to the north and Egypt to the south—women had the right to own and inherit land from their fathers and husbands for more than a thousand years before Moses. But Adonai had given no command to Moses about women and land. Since God would play a part in dividing the land (by the lots), Moses "brought their case before Adonai."

> Adonai answered Moses, "The plea of Zelophehad's daughters is just: you should give them a hereditary portion among their father's kinsmen; transfer their father's share to them."

The Torah concludes by saying, "This shall be the rule of law for the Israelites, in accordance with Adonai's command to Moses." Zelophehad's daughters won their case, but it was a double-edged sword. The Rabbis of the Talmud knew that the law was not quite fair to women, since it only applied if a father died with no sons. But what if there were sons and also an unmarried daughter? Shouldn't she be allowed some of her father's property? In other nations women had such rights. But the law in Israel had been settled by Adonai through Moses, so the Rabbis did not feel free to change it. It would take many generations before women were treated as equals. Even now Jewish women struggle for many rights under Jewish law. But wherever they fight for equality they recall the daughters of Zelophehad, who bravely stepped forward to demand their fair share.

The Next Leader of Israel

Rashi imagines that when Moses saw that land would be passed from father to child, it made Moses think that perhaps his own sons might take his place as the next leaders of the Israelites. But Adonai had a different plan.

To Consider

In the ancient cities of Nuzi and Ugarit we found documents stating that a father's property could be divided among his male and female children after his death. In ancient Elam women had equal rights with men. In Egypt, in the New Kingdom (near the time of Moses), when a man died his property was split, with shares going to his wife and his sons. In all times in Egypt women (wives or daughters) could inherit property and land if it was given to them in a will. The case of Zelophehad's five daughters helped the cause of women's rights by making it clear that Israelite daughters could inherit family land, but only if they would then pass the same land to the next generation in the name of their father—through their sons. Other kingdoms were willing to think of women as very nearly equal, while the Israelites still thought of women as equal only when they could help a clan to survive.

To Consider

Most Bible scholars and most commentators think of the Urim as lots of some kind. As we read in the portion called *Titzaveh*, the Urim usually answered questions with a "yes" or "no" answer (and sometimes with no decision at all). But a few Bible commentators suggested that the Urim (usually called Urim and Tummim) might have been some kind of device for astrology—to allow the High Priest to read the stars and find answers in the sky. In any case, whatever answer the Urim gave, it was always recorded as an answer direct from Adonai.

Adonai said to Moses, "Ascend these heights … and view the land that I have given to the Israelites. After you have seen it, you too shall be gathered to your kin, just as your brother Aaron was…." Moses spoke to Adonai, saying, "Let Adonai, Source of the breath of all flesh, appoint someone over the community who shall go out before them and come in before them, and who shall take them out and bring them in, so that Adonai's community may not be like sheep that have no shepherd." Adonai answered Moses, "Single out Joshua son of Nun, an inspired man, and lay your hand upon him. Have him stand before Eleazar the priest and before the whole community, and appoint him in their sight. Grant him some of your authority, so that all the Israelites may obey him. But he shall present himself to Eleazar the priest, who shall seek for him the decision of the Urim before Adonai. By such instruction they shall go out and by such instruction they shall come in, he and all the Israelites, the whole community."

If Moses was disappointed for his sons, he said nothing. He did exactly what Adonai told him to do. He appointed Joshua as the next leader of the Israelites.

But why does Moses ask for a leader "to take them out and bring them in"? Sforno tells us that it means "to lead them in battle" and "to be in charge of the whole nation." But Rashi notes that even this does not give Joshua the right to declare war. If he wishes to go to war, he must come to the High Priest, who will consult the Urim (see *Titzaveh*) to ask if Adonai commands the Israelites to go to war. (Moses did not need the Urim, since he spoke with Adonai directly.)

The Yearly Calendar

Pinchas ends with a review of the yearly calendar. Bible commentators and modern students of Bible agree that this review is placed here to complete God's instructions for entering the land of Canaan. Adonai spoke to Moses, saying, "Be very careful to present the sacrifices to Me … at the correct times...." The calendar is like the one in Leviticus (see *Emor*). It is based on moon months. It includes the number and kind of animals to be sacrificed on every occasion: normal days, Shabbat, each New Moon (*Rosh Chodesh*), each day of Pesach, Shavuot (the Feast of Weeks), the "day when the horn is sounded" (Rosh Hashanah), the day of "self-denial" (Yom Kippur), each day of "a festival of Adonai" (Sukkot), and the eighth-day "gathering" (Atzeret).

Pinchas

From "a covenant of peace" that calls for war, to a census of soldiers that calls for dividing the land, to a court case on women's rights, to choosing the next leader of the Israelites, to a calendar that calls for festivals and sacrifices—this portion, *Pinchas*, seems to be getting ready for the end of the wandering. Adonai is seen drawing all the strings together to make a single knot; the Israelites who were a ragtag group when they left Egypt will enter Canaan as one people.

Sevens

The number seven appears many times in the calendar at the end of *Pinchas*. There are seven festivals, seven-day festivals of *Pesach* and *Sukkot*, seven festival days when no work is allowed, the large numbers of festivals in the seventh month, and so on. Of course, the number seven is important throughout the Bible, but it seems to be built into this calendar in a special way.

Haftarah: I Kings 18:46-19:21

Oddly enough, it was the people and not the Rabbis who made the connection between the Torah and the haftarah portions here. By the time of the Rabbis, Jewish legend said that the prophet Elijah was really the same person as Pinchas—even though Elijah lived nearly 400 years later. Both were famous for being zealous in their defense of Adonai.

After Elijah killed the prophets of Baal, Queen Jezebel vowed to have him killed the very next day. Elijah fled south to Beersheba in the kingdom of Judah. Alone he went into the wilderness and sat beneath a small tree. He prayed for death, then went to sleep. Twice he was awakened and fed by an angel of Adonai.

He walked forty days and nights to Horeb (Sinai), the mountain of God. The word of Adonai came, asking, "Why are you here, Elijah?" He answered, I have always been faithful to You, but the people have broken their covenant. Now they are trying to kill me. Adonai said, "Go out, stand on the mountaintop...."

Adonai passed by. A furious wind split mountains and shattered rocks ... but Adonai was not in the wind. After the wind, an earthquake, but Adonai was not in the earthquake. After the earthquake, fire, but Adonai was not in the fire. After the fire, a still, small voice.

Adonai commanded Elijah to go back and work with Hazael of Aram, Jehu of Israel, and the prophet Elisha. Adonai would destroy all who had worshiped Baal in Israel. In the last verses Elijah causes Elisha to follow him as his student, later to take over his mantle of leadership, as Adonai commanded.

As Good as Your Word

וַיְדַבֵּר מֹשֶׁה אֶל־רָאשֵׁי הַמַּטּוֹת לִבְנֵי יִשְׂרָאֵל לֵאמֹר זֶה הַדָּבָר אֲשֶׁר צִוָּה יְהוָֹה:

Moses spoke to the chieftains of the Israelite tribes, saying: This is what Adonai commanded.

Tribes

The name of this portion, *Mattot*, means "Tribes". This word for "tribe", *matah*, is a close relative of the Hebrew word *mateh* ("rod" or "staff"). Etymologists—scholars who study the origins of words—tell us that rods were often used as a symbol of leadership. Every Israelite chieftain had a special rod; we learned this from the story of how Aaron's rod blossomed overnight (see *Bemidbar*). So a *matah* or "tribe" could be defined as a "group of families that followed one rod." (For more about rods, see *Va'eirah* and *Bo*.)

If a Person Vows...

Moses spoke to the chieftains of the Israelite tribes [*mattot*], saying: This is what Adonai commanded: If a man makes a vow to Adonai ..., he shall not break his pledge; he must carry out all that has crossed his lips. If a woman makes a vow to Adonai ... while she is young and still in her father's household, and her father learns of her vow ... and does not object, all her vows shall stand.... But if her father [cancels it] on the day he finds out, none of her vows ... shall stand; and Adonai will forgive her, since her father [canceled it].

Should a husband or father be allowed to cancel a woman's vow? There is actually a very good reason: While a young woman still lived at home, her father was responsible for her. If she failed to keep her vow, her father was punished. When a woman married, her husband became responsible. He was punished if she failed to keep her vow. For that reason, a husband or father had the right to cancel a woman's vow as soon as he heard it. On the other hand, if he heard the vow and did not cancel it, the vow stood and had to be kept by the woman. If she failed, it was her husband or father who was punished—he had his chance to prevent this. In the case of a woman who was divorced or lost her husband, any vow she made, she had to keep. She was responsible for herself.

There is something odd in the first verse of *Mattot*. Laws were usually given to the priests or to the Israelites, but the laws of vowing were given to "the chieftains". The Rabbis of the Talmud looked at these laws—all of them about making vows and most of them about what happens when a woman makes a vow—and said that they were given to the chieftains to prevent people from making vows carelessly. For example, if a woman thought that making a vow was a minor thing, or that she might vow and never have to keep her vow (since her father or husband could cancel it), she might be tempted to vow more often. But vowing was so much a part of living together and trusting one another that the laws of vows had to be fiercely enforced. Adonai put the chieftains in charge of enforcing vows.

The Danger of Vows

The Book of Judges tells of a war between the Israelites and the Ammonites. An Israelite leader named Jepthah wanted to defeat the Ammonites. He vowed to Adonai, "If You deliver me victory over the Ammonites, then whatever comes out of the door of my house to meet me on my safe return from the Ammonites shall be Adonai's and shall be offered by me as a burnt offering." He and his army defeated the Ammonites. But when Jepthah returned home, his daughter came out of his door to greet him. Suddenly he regretted his vow. She was his only child, and he had promised to sacrifice her. When she heard of his vow, she agreed to be sacrificed. Afterwards, it is said, the young women of Israel spent four days each year mourning Jepthah's daughter.

The Bible may tell us this sad legend to remind us how carefully we must think before we make a vow. What we say is binding. If we make a promise—especially a vow to God—that promise must be kept. Every vow to Adonai is a covenant. If we give our word, we are bound to keep it.

War against the Midianites

Adonai told Moses that his last task was to lead the Israelites against the Midianites. Each tribe picked an *elef* of men to be the warriors of Israel. The word *elef* usually means "1,000", but many Bible scholars believe that when it comes to armies, it has the meaning of a "unit". Moses sent out twelve units (or 12,000 warriors) led by Pinchas, the army's priest. Pinchas brought trumpets and other things from the Mishkan. (So we learn that this was a holy war, one commanded by Adonai—and the Israelites expected Adonai to fight on their side.) In the end it was a great victory.

The warriors killed all the Midianite men, even the five kings of Midian. They also killed the prophet Balaam, be-

To Consider
Everyone is shocked by the sacrifice of Jepthah's daughter. Didn't Jepthah know the story of Isaac? The Rabbis are especially angry at Jepthah. If he had studied Torah, they said, he would have known the law: The High Priest could set his vow aside because Adonai forbids human sacrifice, or he could have paid the value of his daughter to the Temple instead of sacrificing her. It was ignorance that cost his daughter her life, not the vow that Jepthah made.

Women and Commandments

In shaping Jewish law, the Rabbis divided the commandments into three groups. The first two groups were positive commands. Some positive commands (like going to synagogue to hear the shofar on Rosh Hashanah) had to be done at a fixed time. Since work in the home continued from dawn to dusk, women could not be expected to do these. Other positive commands (like returning a found object to its rightful owner) could be done at any time. Women were required to keep these commands. Men were required to keep all positive commandments. The third group, however, were negative commandments (things you must *not* do)—like not murdering, not working on Shabbat, not stealing, and so on. Men and women were both required to keep all the negative commandments.

cause Balaam had helped the Midianites. They took the Midianites' cattle and riches but destroyed the towns and cities. They took the Midianite women and children as captives. All the booty and captives were brought to Moses, Eleazar the High Priest, and the whole community camped near Jericho.

> Now Moses was angry with ... the army.... Moses said to them, "You have spared every female! Yet they are the very ones Balaam [sent] to cause the Israelites to [worship other gods], so that Adonai's community was struck by the plague. Now, therefore, slay every male among the children, and slay also every woman ..., except for those [pure] women [below the age of marriage].

After the soldiers finished their awful job, they divided the cattle and the riches according to the "law that Adonai commanded Moses." A part of everything went to Adonai, to be given to the priests. Another part belonged to the warriors who had done the fighting. The rest was divided among the community. The commanders of the army, very grateful because not a single warrior of Israel had been killed in the battle, gave additional gifts from their own shares of gold to Adonai.

The Request of Reuben and Gad

After the war with Midian the leaders of the tribes of Reuben and Gad stepped forward to speak with Moses, Eleazar, and the chieftains of the other tribes. "The land that Adonai has conquered for the community of Israel," they said, "is [good] cattle country." The tribes of Reuben and Gad wanted to take the land that had belonged to Midian as their share even though it was not part of Canaan itself. "It would be a favor to us," they said, "if this land were given to [our tribes]; do not move us across the Jordan."

Moses was upset. He recalled when he had sent twelve scouts into the Promised Land and ten of them caused the people to lose heart, so that the Israelites had to wait forty years before crossing the Jordan. Back then only two of the scouts had spoken up for Adonai. Ten of the tribes were now ready to cross the Jordan and conquer the Promised Land, but two tribes did not want to go. If ten scouts had caused the people to suffer before, imagine how terrible the suffering would be if two whole tribes were too cowardly to cross the Jordan. Moses said, "If you turn away from [Adonai] and [Adonai] abandons [the Israelites] once more in the wilderness, you will bring calamity upon all this people."

Making a Bargain

The leaders of Reuben and Gad came closer to Moses. They had a plan.

> We will [quickly] build corrals for our sheep and [walled] towns for our children. Then, we will [hurry to come and] fight at the very front of the army of the Israelites until we have settled them in their home … We will not return to our homes until every one of the Israelites owns a portion [of the Promised Land]. But we will take no share [in the Promised Land], for we have received our share on the east side of the Jordan.

The plan pleased Moses, so he turned it into a bargain:

> If you do this, if you go to battle at the very front of the army, whenever Adonai commands, and every warrior among you crosses the Jordan, as Adonai commands [until the war of Adonai is complete] and the land has been conquered … and then you return [home]—you shall be clear before Adonai and before Israel; and this land shall be your property under Adonai. But if you do not do so, you will have sinned against Adonai; and surely your sin will overtake you. Build towns for your children and corrals for your flocks, but do what you have promised.

Moses then explained the bargain to Eleazar, to Joshua, and to the chieftains. If the tribes of Reuben and Gad kept their end of the bargain, he said, they would receive the land they wanted. If not, they would get a share in the Promised Land, across the Jordan, along with all the other tribes. And the tribes of Reuben and Gad had to repeat their vow in front of all the leaders of the Israelites.

Cattle

The Torah speaks of "cattle". When we think of "cattle" we imagine bulls and cows. Actually, the "cattle" mentioned in this portion was mainly sheep and goats, and probably also donkeys, of which the Israelites had many. Reuben and Gad were tribes known for keeping large herds— they were shepherds. The Bible commentator Isaac Abrabanel thought that it was the addition of more cattle—the cattle taken in the war against Midian—that caused the two tribes to want to settle right there. This, he concludes, was always God's plan.

Below: Map of the land east of the Jordan River that the tribes of Gad and Reuben described as "[good] cattle country".

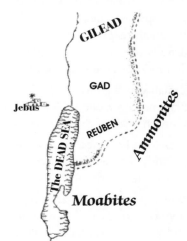

To Consider

Rabbi Meir stated: "Every bargain that is not like the bargain [made with] Gad and Reuben is not a valid bargain." Based on the story of Gad and Reuben, (1) a bargain has to be repeated twice, once in a positive way and once in a negative way; (2) the positive way must be stated first; (3) the bargain must be stated before the punishment for breaking it; and (4) it must be clear to all that the bargain is one that can be kept. This is a good example of how the Rabbis used the Torah's stories as a basis for Jewish law.

The bargain had to be repeated so all understood. This is what Moses meant in saying "you shall be clear before Adonai and before Israel." When we strike bargains, words must be chosen carefully. Every vow, every oath, every promise, every bargain—all must be "clear before Adonai and before Israel."

Haftarah: Jeremiah 1:1-2:3

There is no connection between the Torah portion and the haftarah. This is one of three readings that come just before *Tisha B'Av*, the day on which the Temple was destroyed. It begins with the call of Jeremiah to prophecy, tells the awful message that he is to deliver, and ends with three verses added by the Rabbis to soften the terrible message.

Jeremiah was a priest in the lands of the tribe of Benjamin. The word of Adonai came to him in the thirteenth year of the King Josiah (see *VaYeilech*).

> Before I formed you in the womb, I knew you [and] set you apart. I have appointed you a prophet to the nations.

Jeremiah protested, "I am only a teenager; I do not know how to speak." But Adonai said, "Wherever I send you, you must go. Whatever I command

you, you must speak." And Adonai reached out and touched Jeremiah's mouth and said, "Behold, I put My words in your mouth!"

Adonai gave Jeremiah a vision of an almond tree and a boiling pot ready to pour out on the south. Just as Adonai created the almonds, so now Adonai will turn the kings of the north against Judah. Jeremiah must not be afraid, for Adonai will protect him, but he must speak to the people of Jerusalem and warn them.

But rest assured that in the end, after Judah is punished, those who punished her will fall.

> [For] Israel is holy to Adonai, it is the first fruit of [Adonai's] harvest. Those who eat it [destroy it] shall bear their guilt—evil shall befall them, thus says Adonai.

Marches and Boundaries

מסעי
Masei
Numbers 33:1-36:13

The Way to the Promised Land

The Hebrew word *masei* means "marches" (or "stations on a path"). The portion begins:

> These were the marches of the Israelites who started out from the land of Egypt, troop by troop, led by Moses and Aaron. Moses set down the starting points ... as directed by Adonai, ... as follows:

Egypt to the Sinai Wilderness

The morning after the Pesach sacrifice the Israelites left the city of Raamses, even while the Egyptians were still burying their firstborn sons. "Thus Adonai executed judgment on [Egypt's] gods." The Israelites camped at Sukkot, then at Etham. They turned around to camp at Migdol. Then they "passed through the sea into the wilderness of Etham." They camped at Marah, then at Elim. "There were twelve springs in Elim and seventy palm trees." From Elim they camped at the Sea of Reeds. Leaving the Sea of Reeds, they camped at the wilderness of Sin, at Dophkah, at Alush, and at Rephidim. "It was there that the people had no water to drink." Next they camped in the wilderness of Sinai. This part of the march took one year.

The Sinai Wilderness and the Wilderness of Zin

The Israelites camped at Kibroth-hattaavah, at Hazeroth, Rithmah, Rimmon-perez, Libnah, Rissah, Kehelath, Mount Shepher, Haradah, Makheloth, Tahath, Terah, Mithkah, Hashmonah, Moseroth, Bene-jaakan, Hor-haggidgad, Jotbath, Abronah, Ezion-geber, and Kadesh. This part of the march took thirty-eight years.

From Kadesh (in Zin) to the Plains of Moab

Leaving Kadesh, the Israelites marched to Mount Hor and camped there. Aaron climbed Mount Hor and died. "Aaron was a hundred and twenty-three years old when he died." Then, the Torah says, "In Canaan, the ... king of Arad, living

The Great Journey

The Jewish educator Nachama Skolnik Moskowitz (1953-) says that too often we think of the Israelites *wandering* in the desert. This list shows the forty years as a *journey*—with stops along the way from Egypt to the Promised Land. In truth, the Israelites spent most of their forty years settled in one place or another. They were never lost. Moses was always there to teach them. God was always there to guide them.

The Camps along the Way

The list at the beginning of *Masei* includes forty-two camps. We know where some of these places are; others are unknown. We know generally where the Israelites wandered, but we cannot make an exact map since we do not know where Mount Sinai is located.

in the Negev, learned that the Israelites were coming near." Leaving Mount Hor, the Israelites camped at Zalmonah, Punon, Oboth, Iyim, Dibon-gad, Almon-diblathaim, before (Mount) Nebo, and in Moab near Jericho. This part of the march took place in the fortieth year.

> … At the Jordan [River] near Jericho, Adonai spoke to Moses, saying: Speak to the Israelite people and say to them: When you cross the Jordan into Canaan, you shall unseat all who live in the land; you shall destroy all their [idols]; you shall destroy all their … images; and you shall demolish all their places of worship. You shall take the land and settle in it, for I have assigned the land to you…. But if you do not remove the inhabitants of the land, those you allow to remain shall be stings in your eyes and thorns in your sides, and they shall trouble you in your land … so that I will do to you what I planned to do to them.

The Marches

The word *masei* ("marches") sounds like an army word and the first verse of this parashah says "troop by troop"—not "tribe by tribe" or "clan by clan". At the start, the list tells of the victory of Adonai over the gods of Egypt. The list also tells where water and palm trees were found; and where the people found no water. It speaks of the death of Aaron, but adds that the king of Arad (in the Negev desert) heard that the Israelites were coming. How would the person making the list know that? Even more mysterious is what is missing from the list. The Midrash imagines:

> The Holy One, the Blessed, told Moses: "Write down the stages by which Israel journeyed in the wilderness, in order that they shall know what miracles I did for them."

Maimonides thought that the marching path was given so that people could never claim that the Israelites wandered close by farms (to give them food) or close to wells and springs (for water). In this way all would agree that the Israelites survived only through God's miracles. Both the

Midrash and Maimonides have good ideas, but God's miracles are hardly mentioned in the list. Where are the miracles of the water that came from the rock, the gift of manna and doves, the giving of the covenant at Sinai, and so on?

Bible scholar Graham I. Davies of Cambridge University noticed that this list is like many lists of army movements found in ancient Assyria. It may not be telling us what happened in the forty years of wandering. It may be giving leaders army intelligence—places where supplies were good, places where no supplies were found, and so on. One clue is in the note about the king of Arad hearing of the Israelite approach. Israelite spies may have reported this. The job of spies is to discover what the enemy knows and when.

There is more proof: The list ends with Adonai's instructions to drive out or "unseat" the Canaanites, destroy their idols, and demolish their places of worship. Do it carefully; make sure to drive them all out; otherwise they will continue to attack and "trouble" you—and you will end up being driven out by them! There is no talk of holiness in this list, or of sacrifices, or of kindness to neighbors. Adonai's instructions at the end of this list are the kind given to an army.

Boundaries of the Promised Land

Following the list of "marches" Adonai gave Moses the boundaries of the Promised Land.

> [In the south,] from the wilderness of Zin alongside Edom [starting] from the tip of the Dead Sea … south of Kadesh-barnea … toward the Wadi of Egypt and [ending] at the [Mediterranean] Sea.

> … The coast of the Great [Mediterranean] Sea … shall serve as your western boundary.

> [In the north,] draw a line from the Great Sea to Mount Hor … [ending] at Hazar-enan. That shall be your northern boundary.

> [In the east,] draw a line from Hazar-enan to Shepham [to] Riblah … downward [along] the eastern slopes of the Sea of Kinneret [then] along the Jordan [River, ending] at the Dead Sea.

To Consider

Surely the giving of the covenant at Mount Sinai should be the most important thing to report about the marches of the Israelites. Why is it missing from the list? One modern rabbi suggests that the covenant was given for all time and for all places. So it is not mentioned because this list speaks only of a few times and places. Of course, if the list is a military one, then Mount Sinai may not be mentioned because nothing that happened there was important to the military. It was our spirit that was changed at Sinai, and that is very different from our supplies, our armies, and our wars.

Forty-eight Cities

Later traditions (in the Book of Joshua and in the Book of Chronicles) said that every Levitical city, not just the six cities of refuge (see map *below*), were safe places for those who had spilled blood by accident. The difference was that if a person reached one of the six cities, he or she was automatically granted safety. But if the accidental murderer arrived at one of the other forty-two cities, he or she had to make a formal request for safety. Maimonides said that safety was never quite "automatic". As soon as a city of refuge was reached, the person seeking safety was brought to court for a trial. If he or she was found guilty of murder, the death sentence was carried out at once. But if the court ruled that the murder was an accident, then safety was guaranteed.

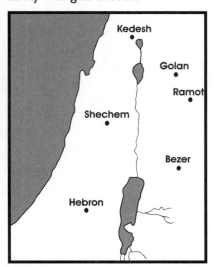

That shall be your land as defined by its boundaries on all sides.

About 1270 B.C.E. Rameses the Great signed a treaty with the king of Hattu (the mighty Hittite kingdom) in the north. The treaty gave boundaries for the land that lay between Egypt and Hattu. This is the land of Canaan. The boundaries in that treaty are almost exactly the same as those recorded here!

Of course, the boundaries of Canaan were well known. Why repeat them? As the Book of Numbers draws to an end, the Israelites have become an army. And an army needs to know its military objective. This boundary list tells the army exactly what territory must be conquered.

The Six Cities

Moses now reminds the Israelites that the land will be divided by lots. He names those who will be in charge of this. All the names are new except for Joshua and Caleb. So we find that the old generation had truly died out, leaving only the two scouts who spoke well of Canaan and were rewarded by being allowed to enter the Promised Land.

What follows, though, is a surprise. Many times we were told that the Levites would own no land. But now Adonai tells Moses that the Levites will be given forty-eight towns scattered around the land of Israel, along with the fields and pastures nearby these towns. Six of these towns will be "cities of refuge", places where a person who killed someone by accident could be safe. Three cities of refuge will be east of the Jordan River, and three will be in Canaan.

Adonai explains this plan to Moses: These six cities will give safety to any Israelites (or strangers among them) who accidentally killed someone. In those days, if a person killed another, even by accident, the relatives of the dead person were required to avenge the killing by killing the killer. Adonai explains that anyone who kills a person on purpose ("with an iron object", "with a stone tool", or with "a wooden tool") is a murderer. Anyone who killed out of hate, on purpose (by striking, pushing, or hurling something), is a murderer. The cities of refuge are not for murderers. Murderers must be put to death. It is the duty of "the blood-avenger", a close relative of the dead person, to kill the murderer. But the six cities of refuge would put an end to revenge in the case of an accidental killing.

If there is any doubt—Was the killing accidental or done on purpose?—the local community must decide. It is up to each local community to protect the innocent and allow the guilty to be punished.

Manslaughter, Murder, and Revenge

Anyone who flees to a city of refuge must stay there at least until the death of a High Priest (this seems to mean that all accidental deaths were forgiven when a new High Priest was appointed). If a "manslayer" (one who kills accidentally) leaves the city of refuge and is killed by a "blood-avenger", the "blood-avenger" is innocent.

> If one person kills another, the manslayer may be executed only on the evidence of witnesses; the testimony of a single witness against a person shall not be enough for a sentence of death. You may not accept a [money] ransom for the life of a murderer who is guilty of a capital crime; he must be put to death. Nor may you accept ransom instead of flight to a city of refuge.... You shall not pollute the land in which you live; for blood pollutes the land. Nothing can redeem the land for blood spilled on it except the blood of the one who spilled it. You shall not corrupt the land in which you live, in which I Myself live, for I Adonai live among the Israelite people.

Throughout the Torah blood is the sign of life and the special gift of God. In the story of Cain and Abel it is Abel's blood that cries out from the ground for revenge. In the sacrifice of animals, blood must be dashed against the altar or covered up by the ground. Because it is the stuff of life, blood separates men from women—women produce it; men may touch it only when absolutely necessary. And anyone who comes in contact with blood—man or woman, priest or soldier—becomes impure and must bathe and wait to become pure again. Murder is the worst of all crimes—it is called "shedding blood"—and it causes the land to be pol-

To Discuss

The word "blood-avenger" is not quite right. The Hebrew is go'el, which really means "the one who redeems." When someone was killed—accidentally or on purpose—that person's blood was lost to the family. The job of the go'el was to balance the scales, to even things out, to restore equality. Blood lost to one family had to be repaid by blood lost to another family. The go'el had to spill the blood of the person who spilled blood. We see this idea of revenge continuing in our own time, especially in movies and on television. But the Torah tried to put an end to this savage tradition. The cities of refuge were set aside so that anyone who spilled blood accidentally could be protected. This did not entirely stop revenge, but it helped by (1) allowing time to pass and anger to cool, (2) punishing the killer by putting him or her into exile for a time, and (3) protecting the community from the accidental "wars" that often flared up when families and clans tried to avenge themselves on one another.

Capital Punishment

Blood must be given for blood taken, according to this parashah. The Israelites had no police force, no sheriffs and no deputies. Close relatives were in charge of putting murderers to death. This was in keeping with the law called the *lex talionis*: "Life for life, eye for eye, tooth for tooth." By the time of the Rabbis, though, the Israelites were opposed to capital punishment in almost all cases (see *Mishpatim*).

luted and corrupted. This is especially terrible in the case of the Holy Land, because not only do the Israelite people live in it, but also God, the Holy One of Israel, lives in it. As Adonai says, "For I Adonai live among the Israelite people."

The Daughters of Zelophehad Again

Now the heads of a clan in the tribe of Manasseh came to Moses and the elders of Israel. They said, All land will be divided by lots, and the daughters of Zelophehad will also be given land. But if they marry men from outside the tribe of Manasseh, the tribe will lose part of its land. Yet Adonai promised that the tribe's land would belong to the tribe forever. Moses told the Israelites:

> The plea of [Manasseh] is just. This is what Adonai has commanded concerning the daughters of Zelophehad: They may marry anyone they wish, provided they marry into a clan of their father's tribe [Manasseh]. No inheritance of the Israelites may pass over from one tribe to another, but the Israelites must remain bound each to the inherited portion of his tribe. Every daughter among the Israelite tribes who inherits a share must marry someone from a clan of her father's tribe, in order that every Israelite may keep his inherited share. Thus no inheritance shall pass over from one tribe to another, but the Israelite tribes shall remain bound each to its portion.

Completing the Book

The Book of Numbers ends by telling how the case of the daughters of Zelophehad was finally settled. The portion records that all five daughters proved righteous. They all married sons of their uncles so that their shares of the land remained within the tribe of Manasseh. There can be no doubt: This report could only be given a long time after the death of Moses. How else could the Torah know what happened to the daughters' lands when the tribe of Manasseh was settled and the daughters were married? The Book of Numbers concludes with:

These are the commandments and regulations that Adonai commanded the Israelites, through Moses, in the plain of Moab, at the Jordan near Jericho.

Finishing

You have now studied the Book of Numbers. As we complete study of a book of the Torah we recite the words *Hazak! Hazak! V'Nithazek!* "Be strong! Be strong! And may you be strengthened!" It is our way of saying, "You have been strong enough to come this far. Continue being strong, for the study of Torah never ends!" So congratulate yourself by speaking the words out loud, with strength: *Hazak! Hazak! V'Nithazek!*

חֲזַק חֲזַק וְנִתְחַזֵּק!

Haftarah: Jeremiah 2:4-28; 3:4

There is no connection between the Torah portion and the haftarah. This is one of three readings that come just before Tisha B'Av, the day on which the Temple was destroyed. This section of Jeremiah speaks of the idolatry of the Israelites and how events will prove that the warnings of Jeremiah are correct.

Adonai asks, What wrong did the Israelites find in Adonai who did wondrous things for them? Yet the priests and the people rebelled against Adonai, chased after prophets who spoke for Baal, and worshiped things that were useless. Look at the other nations: "Has a nation ever exchanged its gods, even if they were unreal gods?" Yet Israel knows the true God and behaves like a "slave" following human masters after false gods—a "double wrong". Now other nations will destroy you.

Did you not bring this on yourselves by turning away from Adonai your God, even while God was leading you on your way?

Do not trust Egypt to save you—"What good will it do … to drink the waters of the Nile?" Don't trust Assyria to help you—"What good will it do … to drink the waters of the Euphrates?" The fault lies with you. Long ago, when Adonai saved you from bondage, you promised, "I will not sin," yet "now on every high place, under every leafy tree", you worship idols, calling wood "My Father" and saying to stone, "You gave birth to me." Let those gods "rise up and save you."

The Rabbis added a verse of comfort to this message, recalling that not long ago the people turned to Adonai, saying, "My Parent, Friend of my youth!"

The Words

"These Are the Words..."

The fifth book of the Torah is *Deuteronomy*, meaning "second law". The name comes from the first Greek translation of the Bible, the *Septuagint*. The first two words in Hebrew are *eilu devarim*, "these are the words...." So in Hebrew the book and this parashah are called *Devarim*, "words".

> These are the words that Moses addressed to all Israel on the other side of the Jordan. … It was in the fortieth year, on the first day of the eleventh month, that Moses addressed the Israelites according to the instructions that Adonai had given him for them.

The first verse says the "words" were spoken "on the other side of the Jordan", so Moses and the Israelites were still outside the land of Canaan. Saying "other side" tells us that whoever wrote these words probably lived on "this side"—*in* the land of Canaan. Since Moses never crossed the Jordan River and never entered the Promised Land, why would he say he was "on the *other* side"? Many traditional commentators say that Moses could write these words, since Moses was a prophet and God spoke to Moses face to face. Modern Bible scholars think that it is highly unlikely that these words were either written or spoken by Moses.

This is not to say that the traditional commentators were wrong and modern scholars are right. The two groups just look at the Torah in different ways and for different reasons. Traditional commentators were concerned with how God wants us to behave and what God wants us to believe. They cared very little about history. For them, all truth was given by God. So for them it was enough to say that God "gave the Torah through the hand of Moses."

Modern Bible scholars are also interested in what the Torah tells us about belief and about living our lives—they not only study the Torah, but also the words of the traditional commentators. In modern times, however, new information about the Torah has come to light. Bible scholars now have ways of discovering what the words of the Torah meant to the people of the Torah. They study archaeology, they compare the Torah with other ancient writings, and they compare Israelite history to the history of other ancient peoples. These new approaches actually open our eyes to more messages and more ideas.

The Book of Deuteronomy

In many ways, Deuteronomy is "the Moses book". According to the book, Moses knew he was about to die. He knew that the Israelites were about to enter the Promised Land. He wanted to finish his work, so he put his teachings into three sermons, each a little different. First he reminded the Israelites of what happened to them—the special way Adonai treated them. Second, he repeated the laws Adonai gave to the Israelites. And third, he blessed the people. At the end of the book Moses climbs Mount Nebo, looks out on the Promised Land, dies, and is buried by God.

The other books of the Torah—Genesis, Exodus, Leviticus, and Numbers—are "told". The Torah does the speaking. But in most of Deuteronomy, Moses does the speaking, using the word "I". Writings of this kind were common in ancient times. Egyptians often carved personal histories on their tombs. In Sumeria, Mesopotamia, and Assyria lawgivers often spoke using the word "I". In Canaan and among the Israelites it was popular to write books that put words in the mouths of long-dead people. For example, the Book of Enoch claims to be the teachings of Noah's grandfather.

The authors—it is likely there are more than one—of the Book of Enoch are unknown to us. They thought people would pay more attention if their words came from the famous Enoch. In the same way, whoever wrote Deuteronomy wanted the words to come from Moses. It is even possible that some of the words *did* come from Moses. Modern scholars think that one part of Deuteronomy may be among the oldest pieces of writing in the whole Torah. But most of Deuteronomy was surely written after the Israelites had settled in Canaan, in the days of the Judges and the Kings.

Two Kinds of Learning

The work of the Rabbis and traditional commentators has been going on for more than 2,000 years. The work of modern Bible scholars began some 300 years ago. But both kinds of Bible study have much to teach us. Today we can learn not only what the Rabbis and commentators tell us about the teachings of Deuteronomy, but also how Deuteronomy came to be and why it became part of the Torah.

Canaanites

Who were the Canaanites who lived in and around the Promised Land? Never a single nation, they were tribal groups ruled by chieftains and small city-states ruled by kings. They worshiped many gods, but especially Baal and his consort, Astarte (carved in relief, *above*). They were not a primitive people, even if they followed primitive religious beliefs. Their pottery was especially creative, and sometimes the potters even showed a sense of humor in their work, as in the pot-bellied figure in the jar *below*.

Knowing this does not make Deuteronomy, or the words of Moses in it, any less important. As we study Deuteronomy we will see how this remarkable book changed the Torah forever.

Horeb/Sinai

Moses begins his first sermon by speaking of the mountain where Adonai made a covenant with Israel.

> Adonai our God spoke to us at Horeb, saying: You have stayed long enough at this mountain. Start out and make your way to the hill country of the Amorites….

Other books of Torah call the mountain Sinai. In Deuteronomy the mountain is called Horeb. Many commentators thought that Horeb was just another name for Sinai. Others said that Horeb was the name of the whole mountain and Sinai was the name for the mountain's peak.

Modern scholars hold a different opinion. Elsewhere in the Torah the name Horeb is used only by the E-tellers who came from the northern tribes of Israel. Tellers from the southern tribes, from Judah, always called the mountain Sinai. It seems there were two memories of where the covenant was given. This section of Deuteronomy, then, was probably a tradition of the northern tribes. You will see a little later in this parashah why modern scholars think this important. In the meanwhile, let's see what else is in Moses' first sermon.

Reminders

Moses reminds the people of the boundaries of "the land that Adonai swore to your fathers—Abraham, Isaac, and Jacob—to assign to them and to their children after them." The boundaries given here are not the same as those given in Numbers (see *Masei*). This time Moses places the northern boundary at "the Great River, the river Euphrates", very far north of the border stated in the last portion.

Moses says that the people were a great "burden" on him, since Adonai multiplied them so that they became "as numerous as the stars in the sky."(Moses adds a little blessing here, saying, "May Adonai … increase your numbers a thousand times more….") Moses claims that he told the people to pick leaders so that he could make them heads of the tribes. (In Exodus it was Jethro who suggested this to Moses, but there is no Jethro in Deuteronomy.)

Moses says that the people soon arrived near the Promised Land. It was then that they said to him, "Let us send people ahead to scout the land for us." (But the Book of Numbers says that God *commanded* Moses to send the scouts.) Moses tells the Israelites,

> I approved of the plan, and so I selected twelve of your men, one from each tribe. They made for the hill country … and scouted it out. They took some of the fruit of the land with them and brought it down to us. And they gave us this report: "It is a good land that Adonai our God is giving to us." Yet you [Israelites] refused to go up [into the Promised Land], and disobeyed the command of Adonai your God. You sulked in your tents and said, "It is because Adonai hates us that [Adonai] brought us out of the land of Egypt, to hand us over to [our enemies] to wipe us out. What kind of place are we going to? Our kinsmen took the heart out of us, saying, 'We saw there a people stronger and taller than we, large cities with walls sky-high, and even Anakites [giants].'"

Moses says, "I told you: Do not fear or worry about [the Canaanites]." You saw, with your own eyes how Adonai fought for you in Egypt, now Adonai will fight for you in Canaan. Even so, the Israelites refused to trust Adonai.

> When Adonai heard your loud complaint, [Adonai] vowed: Not one of … this evil generation shall see the good land that I swore to give to your fathers—none except Caleb … because he remained loyal to Adonai.

In the Book of Numbers, two scouts—Caleb *and Joshua*—bring good reports about the Promised Land. But here Moses only mentions Caleb. Another difference between the two books follows immediately: In Numbers we were told that the reason Moses could not enter the Promised Land

Visit the Bed

The scouts said that there were many giants in Canaan. In this parashah Moses tells the Israelites: "Only King Og of Bashan was left of the remaining Rephaim [a tribe of giants]. His iron bedstead is now in [the city of] Rabbah of the Ammonites; it is nine cubits long and four cubits wide by the standard cubit!" Let's do the math. A standard cubit is about the length of a grown man's forearm (between 14 and 18 inches). If we use 16 inches as our rule, then, King Og's bed would be nine cubits (144 inches) or twelve feet long and four cubits (64 inches) or a little over five feet wide. So Moses is saying, If you do not believe there were giants, you should go to Rabbah and take a look at that bed! Once you see it, you will believe in giants, too!

Spoiled Children

Other books of the Torah also show how the Israelites behaved like spoiled children. They were constantly complaining. When they saw miracles they trusted and praised God. Then they turned around and did foolish things like building the golden calf or chasing after the Midianite women to worship the Midianite god. As soon as the people were punished, they felt guilty again. They would remember God and fear God's anger. This same idea runs through the whole Bible. God remembers good things forever; people are quick to forget.

was that he struck a rock instead of just speaking to it. Here Moses explains:

> Because of you [Israelites] Adonai was angry with me, too, and [Adonai] said: You shall not enter [Canaan] either. Your servant, Joshua son of Nun, shall enter it. … Moreover …, [the] children who do not yet know right from wrong, they shall enter it; to them will I give it and they shall possess it. As for you [Israelites], turn about and march into the wilderness by the way of the Sea of Reeds.

Yet Moses says the Israelites refused to turn back. Because they felt guilty, they decided to show God how brave they were. They went to war against the Amorites. Moses tried to stop the Israelites, saying that Adonai would not be with them in their war, but the people were like spoiled children. They went to war and they were defeated. Then they wept, but Adonai paid no attention to their suffering, because they had ignored the warning and disobeyed.

Afterward the Israelites returned to the oasis at Kadesh and settled there.

After Kadesh

Thirty-eight years later, Moses says, the Israelites set out from Kadesh. They bought food and water from the "children of Esau, who live in Seir." But they made no war against these folk, because the children of Esau were cousins. And they made no war against the Moabites, because Adonai had not promised them the land of Moab. And they made no war against the Ammonites because the Ammonites were "children of Lot" (Abraham's nephew), also distant relatives of the Israelites.

Still, there were other folk to defeat on the "other side of the Jordan". Adonai told the Israelites,

> See, I give Sihon the Amorite, king of Heshbon, and his land into your power. … Do battle against him. This day I begin to put the dread and fear of you [Israelites] upon peoples everywhere under heaven, so that they shall tremble and quake … whenever they hear you mentioned.

Moses tells how Adonai helped the Israelite warriors defeat the stronger armies of King Sihon and King Og. Moses says, "I assigned [the lands of these two kings] to ... Manasseh ... and to the tribes of Reuben and Gad ..." (In Numbers the tribes of Reuben and Gad ask for these lands, but here Moses makes it sound like this was his idea.) He reminds these tribes that in return they agreed to fight in the front of Israel's warriors as the people conquer Canaan. After the conquest they would be free to return home to their families on the other side of the Jordan.

The portion ends as Moses says:

I also instructed Joshua at that time, saying, "You have seen with your own eyes all that Adonai your God has done to these two kings; so shall Adonai do to all the kingdoms [in Canaan]. Do not fear them, for Adonai your God will battle for you."

All the Differences

Devarim often "recalls" things in ways that differ from other books of the Torah. Some differences (like leaving Joshua out of the scout story) are minor; some (like the northern border of Canaan) are major. Early commentators explained these changes away. For example, they said that "the Great River, the Euphrates" actually was the northern border in the days of King Solomon, so God must have promised it to the Israelites. Also, since everyone knew the story of the scouts, Moses took it for granted that everyone knew Joshua was a scout. Besides, Joshua's name is mentioned a little later, so Moses felt no need to repeat it.

Modern Bible scholars, though, suspect that all these changes—large and small—add up to a special set of memories. There was one more main group of Torah "tellers"— the "D" tellers. Up to this point we have found three groups or "schools" of tellers who gave us laws and stories: (1) The J-tellers, who always spoke of Adonai (*YHVH*) and who recalled the memories of the southern tribes; (2) The E-tellers—who spoke of God (*Elohim*) before Adonai's name was given at the burning bush and spoke of Adonai (*YHVH*) afterward—who recalled memories of the northern tribes (some scholars think that the works of these two tellers were later

To Consider

Most Bible scholars believe that the D-tellers—or their followers—gave us even more than the Book of Deuteronomy. They see the marks of the D-tellers in the Books of Joshua, Judges, Samuel, and Kings—and even in the work of some prophets like Hosea and Jeremiah. At one time these books may have formed a single great "history of the Israelites". Back then the Torah may have contained either three books (Exodus, Leviticus, and Numbers) or four books (Genesis, Exodus, Leviticus, and Numbers). Later the Book of Deuteronomy (claiming to be the words of Moses) was split off from the "history" and added to the Torah, making "the Five Books of Moses". The rest of the "history" was placed in the section of the Bible called "Prophets".

To Consider

Modern Bible scholars often speak of "JEPD"—the four tellers of Torah. We should remember two things: (1) Good scholars keep an open mind. Stories that were once thought to be from E-tellers are later said to be from P- tellers, and so on. This does not change the big idea. The Torah is not a single book, or even five books, but actually a library of memories from all the tribes of Israel. And (2) knowing the "tellers" sometimes helps us understand the Torah better, but it does not change the Torah. Through all the ages the most important thing has always been what the Torah means *to us*.

combined to make a "JE" source); and (3) the P-tellers, who present the laws, lists, and stories of the priests and often step in to help solve puzzles by blending or combining stories and laws from other tellers.

To these three groups—"J", "E", and "P"—modern Bible scholars add "D", the Deuteronomist group, the "school" that gave us the Book of Deuteronomy. Some think that the D-tellers worked about the same time as the P-tellers. Some say their work was later and was based on the first four books of the Torah. Some say that their work was earlier, before the time of the P-tellers.

All of these ideas may be correct—the making of Deuteronomy may have come before, during, and after the collecting of the other books of Torah. We are just at the beginning of *Devarim*, but before we are done you will see how the history of this book is a fabulous story of its own—a story chock full of kings and priests and prophets.

Haftarah: Isaiah 1:1-27

There is no connection between the Torah portion and the haftarah. This is the last of three readings before Tisha B'Av, the day on which the Temple was destroyed. The first word of the haftarah is *chazon*, "vision", and the Sabbath on which it is read is known as *Shabbat Chazon*.

These words of Isaiah seem to have been spoken when the northern kingdom was already destroyed and Judah was being attacked along its northern border. The first verse mentions kings up to the time of Hezekiah (see *VaYeilech*).

"The ox knows its owner and the ass knows its master's stall, but Israel" is like a child that does not know its parent. Why do you bring misery on yourselves, destruction like that of Sodom? "Only fair Zion [meaning Jerusalem] is left," but it, too, is already like a "city under siege".

What are your many sacrifices to Me? says Adonai. ... I take no delight in the blood of bulls or lambs or goats. ... I hate your new moons, your festival days....

Adonai says, "Clean yourselves."

Cease to do evil; learn to do good. Seek justice; help the oppressed. Uphold the rights of orphans and the cause of widows. Come now, says Adonai, let us reason together. Though your sins be scarlet, they can become white as snow.

If you return, Adonai says, I will rid Myself of enemy nations. "I will restore your judges as in the beginning. ... Zion shall be redeemed by justice; those who repent will be saved by righteousness."

Hear, O Israel!

Moses Begs for Moses

In Deuteronomy Moses is preaching to Israelites who were never slaves in Egypt. The slave generation had died out—all except Caleb, Joshua, and Moses. Each time that generation had sinned against Adonai, Moses had begged for them to be forgiven.

Moses tells the new generation that he even begged for himself. This portion begins with Moses saying: "And I pleaded [*va-etchanan*] with Adonai at that time...." He was begging to be allowed to cross into the Promised Land.

> Adonai said to me, "Enough! Never speak to Me of this matter again! Go up to the top of [Mount] Pisgah and gaze about—west, north, south, and east. Look well, for you shall not go cross yonder Jordan [River]."

Bible scholars think the first sermon may have ended here, with the next part added later. Even the Rabbis noticed that after this, Moses' mood changed. Nachmanides explained that Moses now turned to the new generation in a new way. He gave them advice as a parent would. He reminded them to be faithful to God and to the Torah after they enter Canaan. As Deuteronomy has it now, the sermon continues with Moses preaching:

> And now, O Israel, listen to the laws and rules that I am instructing you, to do them .... You shall not add anything to what I command you or take anything away from it, but keep the commandments of Adonai your God.... Other peoples ... hearing these laws will say, "Surely, that great nation is a wise and understanding people." For what [other] nation ... has a god so close at hand as is Adonai our God...? What [other] nation has laws and rules as perfect as all this Teaching that I set before you this day?

Never Add or Subtract

When Moses teaches "You shall not add anything to what I command you or take anything away from it," does he mean that no new laws may be added? It seems strange, since we know that new laws are always needed to keep pace with changing times. Scholars think these words are meant for the scribes who will copy the scroll. They must be careful not to change the words—not to add or subtract. In an Akkadian poem (from long before the time of Moses) we find a line praising the poet because "he left nothing out, nor did he add a single line." This is probably what Deuteronomy is saying in these words of Moses.

Sun, Moon, and Stars

Moses cautioned the Israelites not to worship the sun, moon, or stars, since God gave these to other nations to worship. Egyptians worshiped Re, the sun god. Mesopotamians worshiped the moon. And we are constantly reminded that the Greeks and Romans worshiped the planets, since we still call them after gods like Venus, Saturn, Mars, and so on. The first-century historian Josephus said that Moses was pointing out that even though these heavenly bodies were not God, they were God's creations. When other nations worshiped them, they were really worshiping God, even if they did not realize it.

Cities of Refuge

In all there were six "cities of refuge" where a person who accidentally killed someone could find safety (see *Masei*).

Because the new generation were children when Adonai gave the covenant at Horeb (Sinai), Moses reminded them of what they saw and what they heard there. Remember, Moses said, so that you can tell the story "to your children and to your children's children."

> You … stood at the foot of the mountain. The mountain was ablaze with flames to the very skies, dark with thickest clouds. Adonai spoke to you out of the fire; you heard the sound of words but saw no shape—nothing but a voice. [Adonai] declared to you the covenant … the Ten Words; and [Adonai] carved them on two tablets of stone.

Just as there was no shape or form when Adonai spoke from the fire, so the Israelites must never shape an idol—no image of a man or woman, a beast or bird, a fish or insect. They must not worship the sun, moon, and stars—those things were given by Adonai to other peoples to worship, but not to the Israelites. The Israelites belong to Adonai—it was Adonai who brought them out of Egypt. Beware, Moses said, "Adonai your God is a consuming fire, a jealous God."

If the people do forget Adonai and make idols, Adonai promises to destroy them, all but a few. The few will be scattered among other nations. It will be their punishment to be forced to serve "gods of wood and stone, that cannot see or hear or eat or smell." Yet even in foreign lands, if the Israelites seek Adonai with all their heart and soul, they will find that God is full of mercy. Adonai will not forget Adonai's covenant with Abraham, Isaac, and Jacob.

> Know therefore this day and keep in mind that Adonai alone is God in heaven above and on earth below; there is no other. Observe [Adonai's] laws and commandments, which I place on you this day, that it may go well with you and your children after you, and that you may long remain in the land that Adonai your God is assigning to you for all time.

The first sermon ends with Moses telling how he set aside three cities of refuge on the "other side" of Jordan.

The Covenant: The Ten Words

As the second sermon begins the parashah says, "This is the Torah that Moses set before the Israelites..." Moses calls all the people, saying, "Hear, O Israel, the laws and rules that I proclaim to you this day." He reminds the people that Adonai made a covenant with them at Horeb (Sinai). "It was not with our fathers that Adonai made this covenant, but with us, the living, every one of us who is here today." On that day, Moses said, Adonai spoke on the mountain out of the fire. "I stood between Adonai and you at that time to give Adonai's words to you, for you were afraid of the fire and did not go up the mountain."

Moses repeats the "Ten Words" (or, as we call them, the "Ten Commandments") that are also in the Book of Exodus (see *Yitro*). This time some commandments are different. Most of the differences are very small, but the command about Shabbat has many changes. Below are the main parts of the Ten Commandments, as given in this portion:

(1) I Adonai am your God ... You shall have no other gods beside Me.
(2) You shall not make for yourself a sculptured image ....
(3) You shall not swear falsely by the name of Adonai your God....
(4) Observe the Sabbath day and keep it holy....
(5) Honor your father and your mother....
(6) You shall not murder.
(7) You shall not commit adultery.
(8) You shall not steal.
(9) You shall not bear false witness against your neighbor.
(10) You shall not set your heart on ... anything that belongs to your neighbor.

In Exodus the fourth command begins "*Remember* the Sabbath day..." and here it begins "*Observe* the Sabbath day...." The Rabbis of the Talmud said that what was written in Exodus and what was written in Deuteronomy was the result of a miracle: "[Adonai] spoke '*Remember*' and '*Observe*' as a single word—something the [human] mouth cannot speak and the [human] ear cannot hear."

The Differences

The Ten Commandments are presented twice—here and in *Yitro*. They are not exactly the same in both places. The Rabbis and later commentators claimed that Adonai made no mistake. To truly understand the Ten Commandments, they said, we must study the differences and learn both sets of the commandments. Modern Bible scholars, of course, think that the differences are there because the P-teller set down the commandments in Exodus, while the D-teller set down those in Deuteronomy. In the same way, and for the same reason, in Exodus the mountain of God is called Sinai and in Deuteronomy it is called Horeb.

Exploring

Do a little Shabbat exploring in the prayerbook. Look at the *Kiddush*, the blessing we recite over wine on Shabbat, to see if you can find both reasons for keeping Shabbat in it. Next turn to the Sabbath poem *Lecha Dodi*. See if you can find the saying of the Rabbis of the Talmud in one of its lines. While you have the prayerbook in your hands, see if you can find other verses from this parashah. "Know therefore this day" is found in the *Aleinu* prayer. And the *Shema* and *Ve'ahavta* are repeated in almost every service.

The big change, though, comes in the *reason* for this command. In Exodus Shabbat is said to remind us of Creation: "In six days Adonai made heaven and earth … and rested on the seventh day…." In Deuteronomy Shabbat is observed to

Remember that you were a slave in the land of Egypt and Adonai your God freed you from there with a mighty hand and an outstretched arm….

Because the two memories of the Ten Commandments are so much alike, we know that from ancient times the tribes of Israel agreed that these were the basic laws of the covenant. The reason for Shabbat may have been remembered differently by one tribe or another, but everyone knew the command to observe and remember Shabbat.

Moses preached:

Adonai spoke those words—those and no more— to your whole congregation at the mountain, with a mighty voice out of the fire and the thick clouds. [Adonai] inscribed them on two tablets of stone, which [Adonai] gave to me.

Moses says that the people heard Adonai's voice from the fire and felt Adonai's *Kavod* [Presence]. They were afraid that the fire might destroy them and listening to God's voice might kill them. They asked Moses to listen to Adonai and tell them what Adonai wanted them to do—whatever it was, they would surely do it. Adonai said that the people "did well to speak thus." They should return to their tents, but Moses would stay with Adonai to hear all the laws, the rules, and the judgments to be followed in Canaan. Moses would then teach these to the Israelites. So Moses preaches:

Be careful to do as Adonai your God has commanded you. Do not turn aside to the right or to the left: follow only the path [of] Adonai your God….

The *Shema* Prayer

Moses now teaches the Israelites what Adonai taught him, the words of the *Shema*. In time these words would become the single most important statement of Jewish belief. Here the words explain the meaning of the first commandment, "You shall have no other gods before Me."

Hear, O Israel! Adonai is our God, Adonai alone.

You shall love [*ve'ahavta*] Adonai your God with all your heart and with all your soul and with all your might. Take to heart these instructions with which I charge you this day. Repeat them to your children. Recite them at home and when you are on your way, when you lie down and when you rise up. Bind them like a sign on your hand and let them be like a symbol on your forehead; inscribe them on the doorposts of your house and on your gates.

When the *Shema* was written in the Torah scroll, the letter *dalet* at the end of the word *Echad* was always written larger than the other letters. Some sages explained that this was to keep the *dalet* from being confused with a *resh*. It would be terrible to read *acheir* instead of *echad* because *acheir* means "other" or "different". "Other" is no way to think of Adonai. But another custom arose of writing the last letter [*ayin*] of the first word, *Shema*, as a larger letter, too. The Rabbis said that together these two letters, *ayin* and *dalet*, spell the word *eid*, "witness". Thus, whenever we say the *Shema* we are witnesses, as if we ourselves were standing at the mountain when the words were first spoken.

The *Ve'ahavta* paragraph has become almost as important as the *Shema* itself. It calls us to put God's teaching as "a sign on your hand" and "a symbol on your forehead". Many commentators think these words are reminders that we should use our hands (in the things we do) and our heads (in the things we think) in holy ways. But the words come right before the command to put a sign "on the doorposts of your house and on your gates"—which we follow by placing a *mezuzah* on our doors—so the Rabbis thought that the signs for our forehead and hand should also be something real. They called for Israelites to wear *tefillin*—two small leather boxes containing the verses of the *Shema*. Among the Dead Sea Scrolls (dating from 120 B.C.E. to 70 C.E.) we discovered several sets of tefillin, proving that they were worn by Israelites at least as early as the time of the Rabbis. But the debate over whether the *Ve'-*

Quote to Remember

שְׁמַע יִשְׂרָאֵל יְהֹוָה אֱלֹהֵינוּ יְהֹוָה אֶחָד:

Hear, O Israel! Adonai is our God, Adonai alone.

To Discuss

There are many ways to translate the six words *Shema Yisrael Adonai Elohaynu Adonai Echad*. One way (used in this chapter) is "Hear, O Israel! Adonai is our God, Adonai alone." Translated this way, the words explain the commandment "You shall have no other gods...." Another translation is "Hear, O Israel! Adonai our God, Adonai is One." This way the words remind us that Adonai is unique and alone—there is only one God in the universe. Another translation is "Hear, O Israel! Adonai our God is One Adonai." This way the words tell us that Adonai is not made up of "parts" (for example, Christians generally think of God as having three parts), and Adonai cannot be "combined" with other gods (for example, by thinking that any other god is "the same as" Adonai).

To Consider

If the *Shema* is a prayer, it is a strange one. Normally a prayer is spoken to God. But this prayer is not for God to hear. It begins *Shema Yisrael*, "Listen, People of Israel!" It is a prayer we recite to ourselves; it calls on us to hear its words. Because it is not a normal prayer, we sometimes call it a "motto" (a saying we all agree on) or "the watchword of our faith". When guards are posted each night to "watch" over us, we usually set a special password. If someone comes too close, the guard asks, "What is the password?" If the unknown person can repeat the password, it means that he or she is "one of us". This is the meaning of a "watchword". If you repeat the *Shema* every day, it means you are "one of us".

Below: The text inside the *mezuzah* is handwritten on parchment by a scribe. It contains the *Shema* and the two paragraphs after it in the daily service. The reverse side may contain magical texts thought to be protective.

ahavta prayer actually calls us to wear *tefillin* continues. The best we can say is that being a good Jew will always mean using your head and your hand in the service of Adonai.

When it comes to "doorposts" and "gates", archaeologists tell us that it was common all around the Mediterranean for ancient peoples to inscribe verses on them. Since the beginning of our people a *mezuzah*—a case holding verses from Deuteronomy—has marked a home or city as Israelite. The *mezuzah* reminds us of Adonai when we go out and when we come in. Of course, we know that the Torah attached the custom of putting a *mezuzah* on the doorpost to Passover, when the Israelites marked their doorposts with the blood of the *Pesach* sacrifice so that the angel of death would pass over their homes.

Passover

The next section of Moses' second sermon has become part of the *Haggadah* used at the Passover seder.

When, in time to come, your children ask you, "What mean the decrees, laws, and rules that Adonai our God has commanded you?" you shall say to your children, "We were slaves to Pharaoh in Egypt and Adonai freed us from Egypt with a mighty hand."

Moses takes it for granted in the first and second sermons that parents should teach their children. The Rabbis noted that when anyone teaches a child, he or she becomes another parent. So the command to "honor your father and your mother" also means "honor your teachers" as you honor your parents.

People sometimes confuse the meaning of the command to honor parents. Since love between human beings cannot be commanded, Adonai does not command you to "love your father and your mother." There are times when you may hate or dislike a parent or teacher, but you should continue to honor them even though you feel no love for them. If you obey Adonai's command and continue to honor those who try to help you, you will often find that your love for them returns.

A Warning

Again Moses warns the new generation against worshiping the gods and idols of the people they will conquer.

> For you are a people holy to Adonai your God: of all the peoples on earth Adonai your God chose you to be [Adonai's] treasured people. It is not because you are the most numerous of peoples that Adonai ... chose you—indeed, you are the smallest of peoples; but it was because Adonai loved you and kept the oath made to [Abraham, Isaac, and Jacob].

What does it mean to be Adonai's "treasured people"? The modern Jewish thinker Martin Buber (1878-1965) explained that a treasured thing is something set aside—even in a family, it belongs to only one person—so that person has a special feeling for it and a special claim on it. In the same way, Moses said, "Adonai loved you [Israelites]." This love gives Adonai a special feeling and a special claim on Israel. In return, Israel was told just how to love Adonai: "with all your heart and with all your soul and with all your might."

The Chosen People

Why did God "choose" the Israelites? We were never the "most numerous", and we were always the most difficult—stubborn, willful, and disobedient. Why should we be God's "treasured people"? That is a mystery that only God could answer. But it surely shows that understanding what God thinks and how God acts is beyond human reason. In matters of God's choices, all we have is our faith.

Haftarah: Isaiah 40:1-26

This haftarah is the first of seven special selections that preach comforting messages. It is read on the Sabbath after Tisha B'Av, the day of the Temple's destruction. The day is named for the first word, *Shabbat Nachamu*, "The Sabbath of Comforting". The prophet is often called "Second Isaiah". He lived in the sixth century B.C.E. with the Israelites who were exiled to Babylonia, but his work was later attached to the scroll of Isaiah who lived more than a hundred years earlier.

> Comfort, O comfort My people, says your God. Speak caring [words to] Jerusalem. ... For she has received more than enough punishment for her sins at the hands of Adonai.

God is planning a new Exodus, this time for the Israelites in Babylonia, so "prepare a highway." Soon Adonai's Presence will be revealed, and that which Adonai destroyed like faded flowers or withered grass will disappear, while "God's promise holds true forever." Jerusalem will hear "good tidings", and Adonai will come "bringing reward." For God is "like a shepherd ... gathering the lambs."

It is Adonai alone who controls all. "Who can judge the mind of Adonai?" The nations are "a drop in the bucket". Idols cannot compare with God, for God created the world.

> It is God who spreads the heavens out like a curtain, and stretches them like a tent to live in. ... To whom, then, will you compare Me? Who is My equal? says the Holy One.

God created all, and God can restore the Israelites to Jerusalem, for God "knows them each by name." "Not one is missing!"

עקב
Eikev
Deuteronomy 7:12-11:25

All Depends on You

The Second Sermon

In *Eikev* Moses continues preaching his second sermon. The Book of Deuteronomy is made up mainly of three sermons that review the teachings of Moses (see *Devarim*).

It All Depends

The Baal Shem Tov (1698-1760) explained that the word *Eikev* could mean "the end of it". You should always treat any commandment you do as the most important one. After all, any commandment could be "the end of it"—that is, the last commandment you will ever do. And that is the way you should always act: As if everything depends on you.

If You Obey

Eikev means "heel". The word reminds us of Jacob in Genesis (see *Toldot*), when Rebecca gave birth to twins. Esau was born first, but his twin brother was born still holding tight to Esau's heel. For that reason he was named *Ya'akov* (Jacob), from the word *eikev*, "heel".

We still say "on the heels of" to mean something that "follows closely" or "depends on" another thing. This is what *eikev* means in the first verse of this portion. One translation might be: "If you obey these rules and observe them carefully, *then it follows closely that* Adonai your God will faithfully keep the covenant…" Another translation: "Adonai your God will faithfully keep the covenant … *but that depends on* if you obey these rules and observe them carefully." As Bible scholar Jeffrey H. Tigay explains, by rescuing the Israelites from Egypt God kept the oath made to Abraham, Isaac, and Jacob. If the new generation obeys God, then God will keep the oath for them as well. *Eikev*—"*if* you do obey"—means that *everything depends on what you do.*

"And if you do obey," Moses told the Israelites, Adonai will grant you many blessings. You will grow in numbers. Your fields will prosper—you will have "new grain and wine and oil". Your flocks will grow. "You shall be blessed above all other peoples." None of the terrible diseases of Egypt will strike you; they will strike only your enemies. Your people will be healthy, and everyone will be able to have children.

If you obey, Moses continued, you will conquer all the peoples of Canaan. Do not worry that there are many of them, for you saw what Adonai your God "did to Pharaoh and all the Egyptians." Now Adonai will do the same to the peoples of Canaan. Do not be afraid of them, "for Adonai your God is in your midst, a great and awesome God." You will defeat the Canaanites "little by little" until they are "wiped out." You must destroy their idols in fire—not even saving the gold and silver that covers the [wooden] idols. Then you will not be tempted to make new idols with the gold and silver. Above all, never bring an idol into your own house or you will become unholy, for the idol is unholy.

The Blessings of Canaan

Moses preached: In the wilderness Adonai tested you "to learn what was in your hearts: whether or not you would keep [the] commandments." Adonai sent hunger as a test and gave you manna to eat—to show you that people do not "live on bread alone, but may live on anything that Adonai decrees." So, too, your clothing did not wear out and your feet did not swell in all those forty years. After those years of testing, many blessings will be found in Canaan.

> For Adonai your God is bringing you into a good land, a land with streams and springs and fountains coming from plain and hill; a land of wheat and barley, of vines, figs, and pomegranates, a land of olive trees and honey; a land where you may always find food to eat, where you will lack nothing; a land whose rocks are iron and from whose hills you can mine copper. When you have eaten your fill, give thanks to Adonai your God for the good land which [Adonai] has given you.

Moses preached: Adonai gives you the land and all its many blessings. Only you can spoil this wonderful promise. When your belly is full and you live in nice homes you might forget Adonai and say to yourself, "This wealth came to me from my own power and the might of my own hand." Or you might serve other gods and bow down to them. If you forget Adonai your God, then you shall be destroyed like the Canaanites before you.

Now Moses repeated the word *eikev:* It all depends on you, he said. "[If you forget,] then you will be destroyed—because [*eikev*] you did not listen to Adonai your God."

The Golden Calf and the Ark

Moses preached: "Remember, never forget." From the day you left Egypt, you made Adonai your God angry time and

Manna

Jeffrey H. Tigay says that the word *manna* could be translated into English as "whatch'macallit". When the Israelites first saw it they said, *Mah na?*, "What is it?" Manna was the main food for the Israelites through forty years of wandering. The Torah tells how the Israelites sometimes complained about the manna and longed for "the good old days" in Egypt when they ate cucumbers, melons, onions, and garlic.

To Consider

"When you have eaten your fill, give thanks…." The Rabbis took these words as a command from God to give thanks after every meal. They said that Abraham was the first to do this. And they composed the Grace after Meals, *Birkat HaMazon*, to give thanks for the food eaten, to praise the gift of the Promised Land, to remember the Temple where sacrifices were performed, and to remind us that God provides all food everywhere. After all, "food" is really living things feeding living things. Whenever we eat, something living must be sacrificed; something God brought to life must die so that we may live. Thus all eating requires us to praise and thank God.

Bull Worship

Some northern Canaanites, like those settled at Zer (later called Bethsaida), worshiped a bull god, probably not unlike the golden calf (which was also a young male bull). So the Israelites may have learned bull worship from the Canaanites. Some scholars suggest that the story of the golden calf told in Exodus and retold here may have originated in the northern kingdom of Israel and not at Mount Sinai (see *Ki Tisah*). Archaeologists found the carved image of the bull god *above* in scattered pieces. It was probably broken intentionally by the Assyrians when they conquered Bethsaida.

again in the wilderness. You are "a stiff-necked people". When I went up on the mountain to get "the tablets of stone, the Tablets of the Covenant that Adonai made with you," I was gone forty days and forty nights, eating nothing and drinking nothing. But Adonai told me, "Hurry, go down ... for the people ... have been quick to stray from [My] path; they have made themselves a molten image."

Moses retold the story of the golden calf and how he broke the first stone tablets (for the story and its meaning, see *Ki Tisah*). Moses lamented, "As long as I have known you, you have been disobedient to Adonai." The golden calf was the worst sin. The people were still at the mountain, had just heard Adonai's voice, and could still see Adonai's fire.

Moses preached: I begged for the Israelites to be forgiven. I reasoned with Adonai, saying, If You destroy Your people, Egypt will claim: "It was because Adonai was powerless to bring them into the [promised] land, and because [Adonai] rejected them, that [Adonai] brought them out to die in the wilderness." So Adonai's anger was cooled, and the Israelites were saved.

> Thereupon Adonai said, "Carve out two tablets of stone like the first, and come up to Me on the mountain; and make an ark of wood...." I made an ark ... and carved out two tablets of stone like the first; I took the two tablets with me and went up the mountain. Adonai inscribed on the tablets ... the Ten Words ... and Adonai gave them to me. Then I ... went down from the mountain, and I deposited the tablets in the ark that I had made, and they are still in it....

The memory of when the ark was made is not the same here as it is in the Book of Exodus (see *Terumah*). In this sermon Moses makes the ark first; in Exodus the ark is made after Moses returns from the mountain. Both memories agree that the Ark of the Covenant is holy to the Israelites. In Exodus the ark is a part of Adonai's "throne", with a carved cherub (sphinx) on each side. But Deuteronomy never mentions the sphinxes at all.

On the other hand, Deuteronomy tells us much when it states that the tablets "are still in [the ark]." The Hebrew words speak of something permanent, something that has lasted a long time. These words were almost surely written long after the time of Moses, but when? Were they written when the ark rested in Shiloh in the days of the Judges and the prophet Samuel? Or later? Were they written after King David brought the Ark of the Covenant to Jerusalem around the year 1000 B.C.E.? Or later? Were they written when the Ark found its permanent home in the Holy of Holies in the Temple built by King Solomon? Or later? Were they written after the Ark had been stored in the Holy of Holies for so long that no one but the High Priest had seen the sphinxes for hundreds of years? Could it be that Deuteronomy does not mention the sphinxes of the Ark because its memory, its tradition, has entirely forgotten the sphinxes?

But there may be another explanation. The D-teller's story of the golden calf is also about the northern Kingdom of Israel. The first king of Israel, Jeroboam, ordered that two golden bulls be made as symbols of Adonai (just as the sphinxes were symbols of Adonai in Judah to the south). Jeroboam put one gold bull at each end of his kingdom to show that Adonai was always above the people of Israel. In time the northerners may have forgotten that the gold bulls were only "stands" or "pedestals" for Adonai. They may have worshiped the bulls as idols. Not long after, the Kingdom of Israel fell to Assyria. The "ten tribes" were taken off as slaves, never to return.

The sphinxes in Judah could hardly be worshiped as idols, since they were hidden in the Holy of Holies. So when Deuteronomy speaks of the evils of worshiping images (a main idea throughout the D history), it uses the golden calf story to show how idol worship leads to destruction. But when it speaks of the Ark of the Covenant, it does not mention the sphinxes. Of course, there were other idols in Judah that were equally dangerous, and Deuteronomy speaks of them. All these details are clues to when Deuteronomy was completed. It was probably after the fall of Israel, when the Kingdom of Judah became the only Israelite nation.

What God Wants

Moses preached: After Aaron died, Adonai chose the tribe of Levi to carry the Ark of the Covenant, to perform sacrifices,

To Consider

How could carved or sculpted statues of sphinxes or bulls that stood in a place of worship not be idols? It's a tricky question. Adonai commanded that the Ark of the Covenant be made with two cherubs or sphinxes on its cover. But even without the sphinxes, the Ark itself could become an idol if it were worshiped. The seven-branched Menorah could become an idol if it were worshiped. The bull statues set up by Jeroboam as symbols of Adonai did not start out as idols but later were worshiped by the northern tribes. What turns something into an idol has to do with how we treat that thing, what we think it is. The Rabbis said, "Be careful not to turn Adonai's commandments into idols," meaning *do* the commandments, do not *worship* them.

Quote to Remember

לְיִרְאָה אֶת־יְהוָֹה אֱלֹהֶיךָ
לָלֶכֶת בְּכָל־דְּרָכָיו וּלְאַהֲבָה
אֹתוֹ וְלַעֲבֹד אֶת־יְהוָֹה
אֱלֹהֶיךָ בְּכָל־לְבָבְךָ וּבְכָל־
נַפְשֶׁךָ ....

To respect Adonai your God, to always walk in [Adonai's] paths, to love [Adonai], and to serve Adonai your God with all your heart and soul....

Musar

Adonai taught a *musar* or "lesson". In the late 1800s the Jewish world was shaken by modern ideas of freedom. For ages Jews had been forced to live in ghettos and *shtetls*. Students had spent long days studying in a Talmud academy (*yeshivah*). Freedom gave rise to new kinds of Judaism. Many left their studies to join the Chasidic movement, with its *rebbes* and story-tellers. Others came to science and trade through the *Haskalah* (Enlightenment) movement. To save the *yeshivah* system, *Musar*, another new movement, was born. Its goal was to teach ethics—the practical, everyday use of mitzvot and tradition. The core idea of Musar was that when we do good, we become good models for others to follow.

and to give Adonai's blessing to the Israelites. They have no portion of the land; "Adonai is their portion." The priests serve Adonai, so they receive a part of all offerings and sacrifices made to Adonai as their share.

Moses preached: Adonai then commanded, "Up, march on. Lead the people, that they may go in and possess the land that I swore to their fathers to give them."

And now, O Israel, what does Adonai your God demand of you? Only this: to respect Adonai your God, to always walk in [Adonai's] paths, to love [Adonai], and to serve Adonai your God with all your heart and soul, keeping Adonai's commandments and laws ... for your good.

Moses preached: Your God is "the great, the mighty, and the awesome God, who shows no favor and takes no bribe." Adonai your God cares for the orphan, the widow, and the stranger. "You, too, must befriend the stranger, for you were strangers in the land of Egypt." When your fathers went down to Egypt there were only seventy of them; "now Adonai your God has made you as numerous as the stars of heaven."

The Lesson

Moses preached: This is the lesson (*musar*) that Adonai taught you: Remember Adonai's majesty, mighty hand, and outstretched arm. Remember "the signs and deeds" Adonai performed against Pharaoh and Egypt. Remember the Sea of Reeds and how Adonai drowned the army that chased after you. Remember how Adonai provided for you in the wilderness. Remember how Adonai opened the earth and swallowed those who rebelled. You learned all this "with your own eyes." Therefore, keep all the commands that I command you today. If so, you will enter and conquer the land flowing with milk and honey, and you will live long and prosper in Canaan. In Egypt people toiled to bring water to their fields, but the promised land "soaks up its water from the rains of heaven. It is a land which Adonai your God looks after ... from year's beginning to year's end."

Moses preached: You will be rewarded for keeping Adonai's commands. Adonai "will grant the rain for your land in season, the early rain and the late." You shall gather your crops. Adonai will "provide grass in the fields for your cattle." Thus, "you shall eat your fill." If you serve other gods or bow down to them, Adonai's anger will turn on you, and Adonai will stop the rain, the fields will not produce, and you will soon pass away from this good land.

Moses then repeated the words of the *Ve'ahavta* (see *Va-Etchanan*). And Moses preached: If you are faithful to keep all Adonai's commands, Adonai will remove the nations of Canaan for you. "No person shall stand up to you: Adonai your God will put the dread and the fear of you over the whole land in which you set foot, as [Adonai] promised."

Haftarah: Isaiah 49:14-51:3

This is the second haftarah of seven that preach comforting messages as Rosh HaShanah approaches. The prophet called "Second Isaiah" lived in the sixth century B.C.E. among the Israelites exiled in Babylonia. (His work was later added to the scroll of Isaiah who lived more than a hundred years earlier.) The haftarah is very long, with many messages.

The Israelites in exile say, "Adonai has forsaken me," but God is like a mother. "Can a mother forget her babe?" Soon you will be home. "Your ruins … shall soon be crowded with people."

Then Adonai will punish the enemies of Israel. Kings of other nations will serve the Israelites like slaves, and the treasures taken from Israel will be returned so that "all flesh shall know that I am Adonai, your Savior."

The fault was never Adonai's. Adonai did not divorce Israel or sell Israel into slavery. It was for Israel was punished for her own sins.

The prophet says Look at me. "Adonai opened my ear and I did not rebel, I did not turn away." I knew Adonai would help me, even when my enemies insulted me and spit on me. "With Adonai to help me, who can declare me wrong?" All who stand, like me, with God will "walk in darkness" without fear. Those who rebel "shall lie down in pain." All who seek justice, all who seek Adonai can know comfort.

Look back to Abraham your father and to Sarah who bore you: They were alone when I [Adonai] called them, but I blessed them and made them many. Just so, Adonai will comfort Zion….

One People, One Place

Strangely, the mountains of Gerizim and Ebal are not "near Gilgal" (as Moses says). Gilgal is near Jericho. It is the scene of another famous Bible story. Joshua leads the Israelites across the Jordan River, and the river stands aside, letting the Israelites cross over on dry ground, just as they had at the Sea of Reeds. Joshua commands that twelve stones (one for each tribe) be taken from the middle of the river and placed in a heap at Gilgal as a memorial. *Gilgal* means "turning" or "rolling", and Adonai tells Joshua that the place should be remembered because "Today I have rolled away from you the disgrace of Egypt." Why is it mentioned here as being "near" the oaks of Moreh? That we do not know. But you can read the fascinating story of Gilgal in the Book of Joshua, Chapters 3 and 4.

The Confirmation Ceremony

So far, the second sermon of Moses has reviewed the giving of the covenant and the meaning of the Ten Commandments. In *Eikev* the blessings and curses of the covenant were spelled out, and Moses said that everything depends on what the people will do once they enter the Promised Land. *Re'eih* commands a new ritual, a kind of confirmation ceremony for the Israelites. Moses preached:

> See [*Re'eih*], this day I set before you blessing and curse: Blessing, if you obey ... Adonai your God ... and curse, if you do not obey.... When Adonai your God brings you into the land ... you shall pronounce the blessing at Mount Gerizim and the curse at Mount Ebal—both on the other side of the Jordan ... near Gilgal, by the oaks of Moreh.

This "confirmation" ceremony centers on the list of blessings and curses. Moses explains the ceremony later, in the portion called *Ki Tavo*, and the Book of Joshua states that the Israelites did perform the ceremony in Canaan.

The mystery here is why were the twin hills of Gerizim and Ebal chosen for this ceremony? Neither mountain was mentioned before in the Torah. Why are they suddenly important? A little side trip can explain.

The Deuteronomic History

We studied some of the beginnings of the Book of Deuteronomy in the portion called *Devarim*. But there is more to tell. Modern scholars like Martin Noth, Frank Moore Cross, William G. Dever, and Richard Elliot Friedman believe that the books of Deuteronomy, Joshua, Judges, Samuel, and Kings all belong to what is called the "Deuteronomic" history. This history begins just before the death of Moses, when Moses gives sermons repeating the laws of Adonai (remember, *Deuteronomy* means "second law"—the law repeated for a second time). From there the history tells how Joshua and the Israelites conquered Canaan. It tells of the days of the Judges when "everyone did what [he or she] thought was right." It tells of the days of the kings—Saul, David, and Solomon. And it tells what happened after the Israelites split into two kingdoms—north and south. It ends when the Temple was destroyed and the people of Judah were taken off to Babylon.

All the books in the Deuteronomic history speak in similar words and agree on big ideas, so scholars believe they were written by one "school", the D-tellers. The D-tellers also quoted from a library of books. They even mention the names of some: *Sefer HaYashar* ("The Book of the Righteous"), *The Book of the Acts of Solomon*, *The Chronicles of the Kings of Israel*, and *Chronicles of the Kings of Judah*. These are just names to us now, but the books certainly existed, and archaeologists may yet find copies of them. Of course, some books in this library were older and some more recent, so some parts of the "D-history" (short for "Deuteronomic history") are older and some parts are newer.

Throughout the long D-history the tellers repeat one very big idea: that blessings come from obeying God's laws and curses come from disobeying God's laws. This is not the only idea they repeat—it also leads them to another big idea: the greatest blessing is the gift of the Promised Land, and the greatest curse is the loss of the Promised Land.

In making Gerizim and Ebal the place for the confirmation ceremony in *Re'eih*, the D-tellers chose two hills that had been silent witnesses to blessings and curses throughout the D-history. The hills also give us a clue about the D-tellers themselves. We knew (by their language and their stories) that they were northerners. Now we can also guess that the D-tellers lived and worked in the Israelite worship center at Shechem, right at the base of the twin mountains!

What the Mountains Witnessed

Across the valley from Gerizim and Ebal stood "the oak [tree] of Moreh", the first place Abraham stopped in Canaan (see *Lech-Lecha*). Adonai appeared to Abraham, promising,

How Many D-tellers?

Modern Bible scholars do not always agree about how the Bible came to be the way we have it today. For example, some scholars think that an earlier school of D-tellers wrote Deuteronomy, while a later school of D-tellers wrote the rest of the D-history. But all scholars agree that the D-history tells a single long story, using the same kinds of words and repeating the same big ideas from start to finish.

Famous Trees

A tree that has survived for more than a thousand years, like the mighty terebinth *below*, connects earth and heaven in an almost mystical way. Such trees often become legendary as landmarks, attractions, and sites that inspire vision.

Tear Down Their Altars

According to Deuteronomy, the Israelites are required to destroy idols, altars, and worship places of the Canaanites—but only in the Promised Land. This does not require us to destroy any non-Jewish places of worship. In fact, through most of the history of the Israelites in Canaan, this command was either unknown or not practiced. Like other commands in the D-history, it may be part of a plan that hoped to unify the Israelites in their worship of Adonai.

The Plains of Moreh

"The oak [tree] of Moreh" may have been a terebinth tree like the one shown on page 307 (see *below* for a close-up sketch of the terebinth's leaves, branches, and fruit). But some scholars think that the word *elon*, often translated as "oak" or "terebinth," might actually mean "plain" since the hill called Moreh looks out over Israel's Jezreel Plain.

"I will give this land to your offspring" and Abraham built an altar here. But Moreh (or Mamre, as it is called in Genesis) was already well known. Its name, probably from the same root as *re'eih* ("seeing"), means this oak may have been a place people visited to seek visions. The Canaanites "saw" their gods there; Abraham "saw" Adonai there. Moreh was a "high place", a traditional site used by many nations for prophecy and sacrifice. It was also in the fields of Mamre (Moreh) that Abraham purchased his first land—a field with a cave to serve as a family grave (see *Chayei Sarah*).

Beneath Gerizim and Ebal was the city of Shechem, a center of trade, worship, and sacrifice. When King Solomon died his son Rehoboam came to Shechem to meet with the elders of the ten northern tribes. The elders complained that Solomon had mistreated the northern tribes—taking high taxes and forcing their children to become servants and soldiers. Rehoboam turned a deaf ear. He was now king, he said, and he would be even harsher than Solomon. Those were fighting words. When Rehoboam returned to Jerusalem, the northern tribes chose Jeroboam and crowned him king. So it was at the foot of Gerizim and Ebal that Solomon's empire was split into two kingdoms and Shechem became the first capital of the new Kingdom of Israel.

Division proved a curse for both north and south. Never again were the twelve tribes truly united. At times they even fought wars against each other. Never again could they defend themselves against armies from Egypt or Assyria. After the northern kingdom was destroyed, all that remained were memories of the good old days under David and Solomon (the blessing) and the bitter taste of defeat that began when the northern and southern tribes went their separate ways (the curse).

Gerizim and Ebal had witnessed all this—from Abraham to the fall of the northern kingdom. What better place could there be for a ceremony to remind all of Adonai's blessings and curses? This place had seen it all.

Moses Speaks of Unity

But in *Re'eih* Moses spoke of what should unite the tribes: "the laws and rules that I set before you this day." He commanded the Israelites to destroy all Canaanite places of worship, "whether on lofty mountains and on hills or under any blossoming tree." They must tear down Canaanite altars, cut down their idols, and remove all traces of the names of their gods.

What comes next is a towering surprise: Moses told the people that, while Canaanites sacrificed to their gods in many places, from now on Israelites should sacrifice to Adonai in only one place—a place where Adonai's name would be supreme. Moses commanded that all Israelites bring their sacrifices only to that one place. They would eat the meat of their sacrifices there, feasting "before Adonai your God". "You shall not act at all as we now act [in the wilderness]," Moses urged them, because *now* people do whatever they please—they sacrifice and make feasts to Adonai anywhere. In the Promised Land this will not do. All sacrifices will be offered at "the one place" that Adonai chooses.

> And you shall rejoice before Adonai your God with your sons and daughters and with your male and female slaves, along with the Levite in your settlements, for [the Levite] has no portion of the land among you.

What surprises us is that this is a new commandment; and what surprises us even more is that this commandment makes sacrifice to Adonai impossible for many Israelites. Obviously, not everyone will ever live close enough to bring all their sacrifices to "the one place"—to make a feast or to eat the meat. So Moses had commanded something new: sacrifice without worship and worship without sacrifice. This is another big idea of the D-tellers.

In the first four books of the Torah all eating is holy. Human beings must destroy parts of Adonai's creation in order to eat—meat, grain, wine, and oil all mean killing living things. Since Adonai is present whenever blood is spilled, all eating must be both sacrifice and worship. Killing meat for food was done by a local priest at a nearby altar. The blood was dashed on the side of the altar. A part of whatever was killed was given to Adonai as an offering, and the priest (the Levite—this includes Levites and kohanim) took part of that as payment for his service to Adonai.

To Consider

If you live "too far" from the "one place" that Adonai has chosen, you may eat meat whenever you want, as long as it is slaughtered by Levites in the right way. But how far is "too far"? The Rabbis of ancient Israel said that this meant anywhere outside the Temple court. A person could live in Jerusalem and still eat meat that was not slaughtered at the Temple. But recently we have translated one of the Dead Sea Scrolls that contains a different answer. According to this scroll (called "the Temple scroll"), some Jews believed that the phrase "too far" meant "three days' journey".

Offering Daughters and Sons in Fire

Bible scholars do not know exactly what Canaanites did to
"pass their children through fire."
Some agree with Rashi that the
Canaanites often offered children
as burnt sacrifices. Others think
that children were "passed"
quickly through a flame to "pu-
rify" them (see *Acharei Mot*). Or
perhaps the D-tellers are speaking here of a ritual like that used
by the fire-walkers of India who
call on faith and trust as they
walk across heated coals.

The D-tellers now forbid this old system. Whenever you
feel the urge, Moses preached, "you may eat to your heart's
content in your settlements." In other words, Israelites can
now slaughter meat, eat grain, and drink wine anywhere in
Canaan. The D-tellers call this the "blessing that Adonai
your God has granted you." All is free to be taken the way
wild animals are hunted, the way mushrooms and berries
are picked. (Of course, the blood of meat must be treated as
holy: it must be poured out on the ground like water.)

But from now on, sacrifices to Adonai and gift offerings
to Adonai can only be made in "the one place": "the site that
Adonai will choose." Only there will the blood be poured out
on the altar of Adonai; and only there will the eating be a
feast shared with Adonai. The D-tellers speak of "the one
place" time and again. They are clear: Adonai is One. If the
Israelites unite around one center, one priesthood, and one
place of worship, they will be holy because they will be acting more like God: Adonai is One, and Israel can be one.

Warnings

Beware of traps, Moses told the Israelites. Beware of becoming curious about the gods of the Canaanites. Don't say
to yourself, "How did those nations worship their gods? I,
too, will follow those practices." Their ways are dangerous to
you. They do things which are unholy to Adonai—"they even
pass their sons and daughters through fire to their gods."

Again Moses said, Beware "to observe only that which I
command you: neither add to it nor take away from it." And
beware, too, of false prophets.

> If a prophet or a dream interpreter appears
> among you and gives you a sign … saying, "Let us
> follow and worship another god"—whom you have
> not experienced—even if the sign … comes true,
> do not heed the words of that prophet or that
> dream-diviner. For Adonai your God is testing you
> to see whether you really love Adonai your God
> with all your heart and soul.

False prophets and dream interpreters should be put to
death. "Thus you will sweep out evil from your midst." Moses
preached: Beware even of people you love—brothers, sis-

ters, children, wives, or close friends. If they urge you to worship other gods, you should show them no pity. You should stone them to death for their sin. "Thus all Israel will hear and be afraid, and such evil things will not be done again in your midst." If you hear of a town that is worshiping other gods, you should first "investigate thoroughly" and then, if it is true, "put the people of that town to the sword and put its cattle to the sword." Burn the town and all that is in it and leave it as a ruin, "never to be rebuilt." In this way Adonai will not be angry with you for breaking your oath to worship the One God.

What You Are and What You Eat

Moses preached: Even your own body belongs to Adonai.

> You are children of Adonai your God. You shall not gash yourselves or shave the front of your heads [when you mourn]. For you are a people holy to Adonai your God: Adonai your God chose you from among all other peoples on earth to be [Adonai's] treasured people.

> Likewise, Israelites may not eat forbidden foods. Moses then listed foods that were forbidden and foods that were permitted (see *Shemini*). And Israelites may not eat animals that die without being slaughtered. Such animals may be given to strangers who live with you or sold to foreigners. Moreover, you should act kindly toward your animals: "You shall not boil a kid [a young goat] in its mother's milk." Being cruel to God's creation is forbidden. (This was one of the "ten commands" given in *Ki Tisah*.)

The Rest of the Portion

Moses preached: You must give a tithe—a tenth of everything—to the Levites at "the place [Adonai] will choose to establish [Adonai's] name." Every third year, though, the tithe should be given to "the Levite in your community". This tax of the third year will support the local priests and also "the stranger, the fatherless, and the widow in your settlements". To help the needy you must forgive all debts every seventh year. In between you must open your hand to the

Quote to Remember

בָּנִים אַתֶּם לַיהוָה אֱלֹהֵיכֶם לֹא תִתְגֹּדְדוּ וְלֹא־תָשִׂימוּ קָרְחָה בֵּין עֵינֵיכֶם לָמֵת׃

You are children of Adonai your God. You shall not gash yourselves or shave the front of your heads [when you mourn].

The Poor and the Needy

Raising money for the poor and the needy has been a part of Jewish law from Bible times to the present. As the D-tellers put it, "For there will never cease to be needy ones in your land." We human beings have managed to do many wonderful things—from finding cures for disease to walking on the moon. Yet even now we have not managed to find a way to defeat poverty and hunger. As long as there are "needy ones" in our land, we must see tzedakah, the charity given because it is the right thing to do, as our best hope for them.

needy and lend them what they need, "For there will never cease to be needy ones in your land."

Moses repeated the laws for keeping Hebrew slaves (see *Mishpatim*). Then, still speaking of slavery, Moses repeated the laws for the three pilgrim festivals: Passover, Shavuot, and Sukkot. These laws now include the D-history idea of "the one place". On Passover "You may not slaughter the Pesach sacrifice in any of the settlements ... but only at the place where Adonai your God will choose...." The celebration of the Feast of Weeks (Shavuot) is to be held "at the place where Adonai your God will choose to establish [Adonai's] name." And the Feast of Booths (Sukkot) is also to be held "in the place that Adonai will choose." *Re'eih* ends with:

> Three times a year—on the Feast of Unleavened Bread [Matzot], on the Feast of Weeks, and on the Feast of Booths—all your males shall appear before Adonai your God in the place that [Adonai] will choose. They shall not appear before Adonai empty-handed, but each with his own gift, according to the blessing that Adonai your God has bestowed upon you.

Haftarah: Isaiah 54:11-55:5

This is the third haftarah of seven preaching comforting messages as Rosh HaShanah approaches. The prophet is "Second Isaiah", who lived in the sixth century B.C.E. among the Israelites exiled in Babylonia. (His work was later added to the scroll of Isaiah who lived more than a hundred years earlier.) The haftarah is very short.

Adonai speaks to the exiles, calling them "unhappy, storm-tossed" souls with no one to comfort them, but Adonai will give them precious stones as bricks for rebuilding their homeland.

> All your children shall be taught by Adonai, and great shall be the happiness of your children. You shall be established in righteousness, safe from oppression, and unafraid.

The Rabbis said the word *banim*, "children", could also be read *bonim*, "builders". In every generation, the Rabbis said, our children *are* our builders.

Adonai promises to destroy the enemies of Israel. All that is required is for the Israelites to give up false things and turn to Adonai alone. "Open your ears and come to Me; pay attention and you shall live."

> I will make an everlasting covenant with you, [granting you] the true love that I gave to David.

Even those peoples you do not know, "will come running to you," for Adonai has "given you glory."

Judges, Prophets, Kings

The Marks of Deuteronomy

There are definite ways to tell that Deuteronomy is the work of the D-tellers and not of the other tellers (J, E, and P) who completed the first four books of the Torah. The D-tellers have Moses speak in the first person ("as I commanded," "the laws I taught," and so on), and Moses speaks about himself. The J, E, and P tellers speak *about* Moses and what he did or said. The D-tellers call God by the special name "Adonai your God". Names for God in the rest of Torah are generally "Adonai God", "God", or "Adonai". Also the D-tellers speak of "the one place" that Adonai will choose for the altar and the sacrifices. They forbid the people to sacrifice to Adonai anywhere else. The other books of Torah say that altars and sacrifices to Adonai are permitted anywhere.

Moreover, the D-tellers recite many laws concerning city life. In this parashah there are laws about city officials and kings. Of course, Moses lived long before Israelites settled in cities and long before a king was chosen. *Sifrei Deuteronomy* (a collection of comments by the Rabbis) states that Moses knew about these things in advance, since God explained them and gave laws for them to Moses. Rashi and Maimonides basically agree, but they have trouble explaining why many laws and ideas in Deuteronomy are different from those in the rest of the Torah. Did Moses write Deuteronomy? Did the D-tellers? For now let's just note that this second sermon is too long to ever have been spoken out loud. Surely it was written to be read and studied, just as you are doing now.

Judges and Officials

Shoftim is the first important word in the parashah. It means "judges", especially the judges of a court. As the Israelites settled one town after another in Canaan they built walls and gates for their cities. Some gates had large open

Where We Are

Shoftim continues the second sermon of Moses. At the start of this sermon in *Va-Etchanan*, Moses repeated the Ten Commandments. He told the people they could choose between blessing and curse—blessing if they would obey God's laws and curse if they would not. He continued to repeat laws and ideas, but always adding the new "big ideas" of the D-tellers.

Quote to Remember

צֶדֶק צֶדֶק תִּרְדֹּף לְמַעַן
תִּחְיֶה וְיָרַשְׁתָּ אֶת־הָאָרֶץ
אֲשֶׁר־יְהֹוָה אֱלֹהֶיךָ נֹתֵן
לָךְ:

Justice, justice shall you pursue, that you may thrive and live in the land that Adonai your God is giving you.

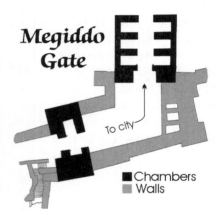

Megiddo Gate

To city

■ Chambers
■ Walls

Above: Diagram of a city gate with inner chambers. People entering Megiddo by foot climbed the staircase (*lower left*), while carts and horses came up the ramp. Everyone first passed the two chambers at the front part of the gate (probably guardhouses). They had to turn left to continue into the city, passing through the second, six-chambered gate. It was in these chambers that town officials may have had offices and judges would sit to hold court. Archaeologists have found examples of six-chambered gates in major cities throughout Israel. All may have been built around the same time.

areas and some had attached rooms. Local courts were often held in these spaces of the city gates. Moses preached about the need for judges and city officials, mentioning the courts held "in the gates of the city". This is one of those "city things" that Moses seemed to know in advance. The portion begins with a memorable statement about treating all people fairly:

> You shall appoint judges and officials for your tribes, in all the settlements that Adonai your God is giving you, and they shall govern the people with due justice. You shall not judge unfairly: you shall show no partiality; you shall not take bribes, for bribes blind the eyes of the wise and upset the plea of the just. Justice, justice shall you pursue, that you may thrive and live in the land that Adonai your God is giving you.

In Hebrew the words "Justice, justice shall you pursue" are *tzedek tzedek tirdof*. In repeating the word *tzedek* Moses is saying "only justice" or "the absolutely fairest, most righteous possible justice". Ibn Ezra, though, commented that the word is repeated for the two ways that justice can be done: "Justice" the first time "if it seems good to you," and "justice" the second time "even if it does not seem good to you." *Tirdof* means "chase after" or "run to find". In other words, you must do everything possible to "catch up with" justice—you should leave no stone unturned as you seek the right decision. It is amazing how much the Hebrew language packs into three little words!

Witnesses and a Supreme Court

Moses stated that any Israelite who worshiped "the sun or the moon or any of the heavenly host, something I [Moses] never commanded" must be stoned to death—but not without a trial. And not without two or more witnesses. No one should ever be "put to death on the testimony of a single witness." If a court case is so difficult that the court cannot decide it, it should be brought "to the place that Adonai your God will have chosen," where the priests will decide the verdict. Once the verdict is decided, you must obey the decision. The priests are like a supreme court; theirs is the highest decision possible.

The King

The next subject is choosing a king to rule Israel. This is logical. Moses has spoken of local government—judges and city officials—and now he speaks about national government. As you read the verses below, listen carefully to the problems that Moses mentioned:

> [If] you decide, "I will set a king over me, as do all the nations around me," you shall be free to set a king over yourself, one chosen by Adonai your God. Be sure to set as king over yourself one of your own people; you must not set a foreigner over you, one who is not [an Israelite]. Moreover, [the king] shall not keep many horses or send people back to Egypt to add to his horses, since Adonai has warned you, "You must not go back that way again." And [the king] shall not have many wives, lest his heart go astray; nor shall he amass silver and gold to excess.

Having a king is always a mixed blessing. A king can unite a country and organize people for large and necessary projects like building towns, walls, and waterworks. But a king can also use power in bad ways: to make the king richer, to force people to do what the king pleases, and so on. Yet when Moses commanded that the king "shall not keep many horses or send people back to Egypt to add to his horses," it seems that Moses was speaking of some special case. What comes immediately to mind when many horses, many wives, and much silver and gold are mentioned is the case of King Solomon. In fact, in the Book of Kings (another book of the D-history) we read how

> Solomon gathered chariots and horses. He had 1,400 chariots and 12,000 horses .... The king [Solomon] made silver as plentiful in Jerusalem as stones.... Solomon's horses were bought from Egypt and [Armenia]. ... King Solomon loved many foreign women ... He had 700 royal wives

To Consider

The D-tellers lived long after Moses, David, and Solomon. By their time there had been judges, city officials, and kings for quite a while. They describe a three-part government. The priests who served Adonai were the highest court of justice. Kings and city officials were the second part of government. And the prophets, who spoke in Adonai's name when they felt commanded to speak, were the third part. In ancient Israel every part of government was expected to follow Adonai's commands, and justice was the work of all three parts.

To Consider

When the D-tellers say a copy of this "Repetition of Torah", the Hebrew words are *Mishneh Torah*. They do not mean a Torah scroll containing five books like the ones in our synagogues. They mean only a copy of the book of Deuteronomy. In Greek the name *Deuteronomy* comes from this Hebrew phrase *Mishneh Torah*, which means a "Repeating" or "Second Telling" of the Law.

and 300 minor wives.... In his old age, his wives turned Solomon's heart toward other gods, so he was not as devoted with all his heart to Adonai his God as his father David had been. [1 KINGS:10:26F.]

Solomon was not the only Israelite king who had too many horses, too much money, and too many wives for his own good, but the D-tellers seem to focus on these things because they "turned Solomon's heart" away from Adonai. In other kingdoms, as Bible scholar Jeffrey H. Tigay explains, people often believed their king was a god or was sent by their god. In ancient Israel God did not make a king over the people; the people decided to have a king.

One more thing sets Israelite kings apart from the kings of other nations. Israelite kings must obey the laws of Deuteronomy. Moses commanded it this way:

> When [the king] is seated on his royal throne, he shall have a copy of this *Mishneh Torah* ["Review of Torah" or "Repetition of Torah"] written for him on a scroll by the Levite priests. Let it remain with him, let him read in it all his life, so that he may learn to respect Adonai his God, to observe faithfully every word of this Torah as well as these laws. Thus [the king] will not lord it over others or change the law to the right or to the left....

Priests and Other Matters

The D-tellers were interested in government, but not so interested in the rules of priesthood. Deuteronomy does not repeat the commands for ordaining priests or for the costumes of the High Priests and other Levites. It often mentions the gifts due to Adonai that are to be paid to the Levites. It states that the Levites live off these sacrifices and offerings. In this sermon it also reminds priests that any Levite can choose at any time to serve at "the place that Adonai has chosen." If they come to this place to serve Adonai, they will receive "equal shares of the dues".

Moses repeated that false prophets and sorcerers are forbidden to the Israelites. To this Moses added, "Adonai your God will raise up for you a prophet from among your own people, like myself; him you shall heed." How will the people be able to tell a true prophet from a false prophet? If what the prophet says comes to pass, then the prophet was sent by Adonai. If not, the prophet is false; the people should pay no attention to him or her.

Moses repeated the command to set aside cities of refuge (see *Masei*). These are for accidental killings only. To this Moses added an example of an accidental killing:

> For instance, a man goes with his neighbor into a grove to cut wood; as his hand swings the ax to cut down a tree, the ax-head flies off the handle and strikes the other so that he dies. That man shall flee to one of these cities and live.

Moses forbade the Israelites to move landmarks "set up by ancestors." Such landmarks were usually piles of stones marking where property lines began and ended.

Moses repeated that false witnesses must be punished. If a person swears that he or she is telling the truth in a court case and it is proved that he or she is lying, "you shall do to that person as he [or she] schemed to do to the other person." Show no pity in punishing the false witness, Moses says; the law is "life for life, eye for eye, tooth for tooth, hand for hand, foot for foot." This law is so old that it is written almost word for word this way in the ancient laws of Hammurabi of Babylon, long before the time of Moses. (For more on this law see *Mishpatim*.)

Making War

Moses now spoke of making war. There were three concerns: (1) how to make the army ready, (2) how to treat the enemy, and (3) how to treat trees.

Making the Army Ready

Moses told the Israelites never to be afraid, even if the enemy has a large army, because "Adonai your God, who brought you from the land of Egypt, is with you." Before a battle a priest will remind the troops that Adonai is with them. Then the commanders will ask four questions:

> "Is there anyone who has built a new house, but has not yet dedicated it...? Is there anyone who has planted a vineyard but never harvested it? Is

Landmarks

When the D-tellers mentioned landmarks "set up by ancestors" they made a slight slip of the lips. How could there be "ancestors" who had set up landmarks if Moses was preaching to the Israelites *before* they entered the land and divided it up among their tribes and families? Even Bible commentators like Ibn Ezra and Nachmanides stated that "set up by ancestors" could only refer to when Joshua divided the land—a time that Moses did not live to see.

Kill All the People?

Why did the D-tellers state that in Canaan, all the people of a captured city must be put to death? Scholars think that when the Israelites were in Babylonia (after 586 B.C.E.) they noticed that the Canaanites had disappeared from the Promised Land. They asked themselves, "How did that happen?" To answer, they wrote the law that Moses spoke in Adonai's name, commanding the Israelites to destroy the Canaanites entirely. The truth was simpler. As the Israelites had used more and more of the Promised Land for their cities, the Canaanites either moved out or blended with the Israelites and other neighboring peoples. They disappeared, but not through out-and-out murder.

there anyone who [is engaged], but not yet married...? ... Is there anyone who is afraid and disheartened?"

Soldiers who answer yes to any of these questions should be sent home. If they are afraid, their fear could make other soldiers afraid, too. If they are too concerned with some major new thing in their lives, they might not be able to give all their attention to the battle.

The Enemy

When the army comes to attack an enemy town there must be an offer of peace. If the town surrenders, then all its people should be made slaves. If the town does not surrender and Adonai gives the Israelites victory, all males must be killed. The women, children, cattle, and everything in the town may be taken as booty—they belong to the Israelites. These are the rules for towns outside the Promised Land.

If a town is conquered inside the Promised Land, then the town and its people and everything in the town must all be destroyed, "as Adonai your God has commanded you." Otherwise the people or the things taken could tempt the Israelites into worshiping foreign gods and doing the awful things that Canaanites do in worship.

The Trees

Moses told the Israelites that a time might come when they would have to lay siege to a city for a long time in order to capture it. If so, the Israelites must not cut down all the trees around the town. Moses asked, "Are trees of the field human that they can flee before you into the besieged city?" When it comes to fruit trees, the Israelites may eat their fruit. When it comes to trees that give no fruit, the Israelites can chop down only enough to make the battering rams and other things they need to conquer the city.

The Unsolved Murder

It may happen, Moses told the Israelites, that a murder victim will be found out in the fields and the crime will go unsolved—the murderer will not be found. In this case a whole town becomes guilty for the murder. But which town? The elders and the city officials must measure the distance from where the victim was found to the towns roundabout to find the nearest town.

The elders of the nearest town must make a special sacrifice to seek forgiveness for the murder. They must take a female cow that has never been worked and bring it to a stream of water that has never stopped flowing. They must break the neck of the cow in the stream. The priests must be present at this ceremony, since Adonai chose them to be God's witness to every case of justice (they are the "supreme court"). With the priests watching, the elders of the town must wash their hands over the dead cow, saying:

> "Our hands did not shed this blood, nor did our
> eyes see it done. Absolve, O Adonai, Your people
> Israel whom You redeemed, and do not let guilt
> for the blood of the innocent remain among Your
> people Israel."

If all this is done, Adonai will forgive the town and remove its guilt, "for you will be doing what is right in the sight of Adonai." And this is where the portion *Shoftim* ends.

That Old Magic

If the special sacrifice of a cow that never worked in a stream that never stopped flowing sounds a little like magic, well, you may be right. As ever, when we find magic rituals they are old practices that were adopted and changed to make them more "Israelite". Like putting new words to an old melody, the meaning changes even if some of the magic rituals remain.

Haftarah: Isaiah 51:12-52:12

This is the fourth haftarah of seven that bring comforting messages as Rosh HaShanah approaches. The prophet is "Second Isaiah", who lived in the sixth century B.C.E. among the Israelites exiled in Babylonia. (His work was later added to the scroll of Isaiah who lived more than a hundred years earlier.)

> I, I am the One who comforts you. What is
> wrong with you, that you are afraid of human
> beings? ... Why do you forget Adonai your
> Maker, who spread out the heavens and established the earth?

It was Adonai who punished the Israelites, who brought them "devastation and destruction", "famine and sword". But it is also Adonai who defends you.

> No more shall you drink from the bowl of My
> wrath. I will put it into the hands of those
> who torment you. ... Awake, awake! Clothe
> yourself in strength, O Zion, dress yourself in
> robes of splendor, O Holy City of Jerusalem!

Adonai will rescue the people as long ago Adonai rescued them from Egypt. "Be sure that My people learn My Name."

> How beautiful on the mountains are the feet
> of the herald who brings good tidings, who
> proclaims peace, the messenger of good tidings who proclaims deliverance—who says to
> Zion: Your God reigns!

Then prepare to leave Babylonia, Adonai says, for "Adonai will [lead] you in front; the God of Israel will be your rear guard."

Laws upon Laws

In Hebrew the 613 commandments are called the *taryag mitzvot*. *Taryag* (תריג) is a Hebrew number. *Tav* [ת] =400; *Resh* [ר]=200; *Yod* [י]=10; and *Gimel* [ג]=3. Many commentators and scholars—including Ibn Ezra, Nachmanides, and Solomon Schechter (1847–1915)—believe that few of the Rabbis actually thought there were 613 mitzvot in the Torah. The number is mentioned only a handful of times in the Talmud. Some scholars say the number was "traditional". Only gradually, in the generations after the Talmud, did the number become accepted as "a fact".

613 Commandments

Maimonides wrote that he found seventy-two commandments in *Ki Teitzei*. So it is fair to ask, How many commandments *did* God give? Except for the "Ten Words" (the "Ten Commandments") named in Exodus, no book of the Torah gives a number. Most Jews today, though, would automatically answer that there are 613 commandments (mitzvot) in the Torah. Maimonides would agree. But how do we know that 613 is the correct answer?

If you try counting one by one, starting with the first mitzvah in Genesis, you soon find that you have either too many mitzvot or too few. Maimonides listed exactly 613, but he often combined two or more mitzvot to make the count come out right. Abrabanel disagreed with the list made by Maimonides; he made his own list. He combined other mitzvot to arrive at exactly 613. Many others also tried counting—so many, in fact, that we have a special name for them, calling them "codifiers", since they tried to make a "code", a list, of the 613 mitzvot in the Torah. This list-making went on for nearly three hundred years. In all that time the codifiers never agreed—every list is different.

But why did the codifiers believe the total had to be 613 mitzvot? One reason was a sermon given by a rabbi in the third century B.C.E. In *Makkot* (23b-24a) the Talmud quotes his whole sermon.

> Rabbi Simlai preached: 613 mitzvot were spoken to Moses, 365 negative commands, matching the sun's days [the year], and 248 positive commands, matching the parts of the human body.

It seems that Rabbi Simlai didn't actually count the commandments. He just took two numbers and added them together: 365 days and 248 parts of the body. He was nearly right about the number of days in the year, but we know he had some bad information about the number of parts in our bodies. Obviously, in his days people *thought* that the body had only 248 parts. Anyway, Rabbi Simlai was preaching a sermon, not stating a fact. He was only pointing out that there are mitzvot to do every day in the year and mitzvot for every part of the body to do.

Other sages used the same number. They never really counted the mitzvot in the Torah. As for Rabbi Simlai, he had not finished his sermon. He went on to say that the 613 mitzvot were later condensed into only eleven mitzvot (by the Book of Psalms), six mitzvot (by Isaiah), three mitzvot (by Micah), two mitzvot (by Habbakuk), and finally only one mitzvah (also by Habbakuk). In other words, the point of Rabbi Simlai's sermon was that all the mitzvot in the Torah could be summed up in a single mitzvah, namely: "The righteous shall live by their faith [in God]."

A Confusion of Laws?

Ki Teitzei means "when you go out", and its first verse reads "When you go out to war against your enemies and Adonai your God delivers them into your power and you take some of them captive...." Looking at it we might think that the D-tellers are still reviewing the laws about war that ended the last portion, *Shoftim*. But that is not what happens in *Ki Teitzei*. The first law given here actually states that an Israelite man can marry a woman taken prisoner in war. Most prisoners become slaves, but a woman married to an Israelite may never be treated as a slave, even if there is later a divorce. The next law, though, is about how property should be divided when a man has more than one wife and loves one wife more than another. It makes no difference which wife he loves best, the law states; his firstborn son must get the birthright, the larger portion of his property.

The next law speaks of what to do with a child who will not obey parents no matter what they do. Parents may bring the child to the elders and declare in public that the child is beyond their control. "Thereupon the men of the town shall stone [the child] to death. Thus you will sweep out evil from your midst: all Israel will hear and be afraid." And the next law tells what to do with the body of a person put to death by the court.

How Many Commandments?

Are there really 613 mitzvot in the Torah? There is no proof. Then why did the codifiers search so hard for exactly 613 mitzvot to list? It was because they trusted the Rabbis of the Talmud. If the number 613 was used by the Rabbis, they thought, it must be a "true" number—their problem was to locate exactly 613 mitzvot in the Torah. We still trust the Talmud today, but not in the simple sense that every word the Rabbis spoke was true; more in the sense that their teachings are wise. The Rabbis were saying that there are many mitzvot in the Torah—and many in this portion called *Ki Teitzei*. Exactly how many is not so important to us.

Stoning a Child to Death

Today we think of the law about stoning a disobedient child to death as very cruel. In ancient nations, though, a father often had the power of life and death over his children—he could kill a child at any moment if the child refused to obey his orders. The Rabbis said this law of the Torah was never used; it was given only to terrify children into obeying their parents. But just in case a parent was tempted to use it, the Rabbis added laws to make it almost impossible for any child to be stoned to death. They said that the law only could be used in the three months after a child turns thirteen, only if the child joined a crowd of "nogoodniks" to taste blood in meat and drink strong liquor when there was no religious feast, only if the child paid for the meat and drink with money stolen from his father, only if both parents are living and not handicapped in any way, and only if both mother and father agreed to take the child to court. Even so, the point of the law stands clear: Obedience to parents is an important step in learning obedience to God.

So the first four laws of *Ki Teitzei* are about (1) marrying captured women, (2) dividing property when there is more than one wife, (3) the disobedient child, and (4) the body of a criminal. It seems like total confusion. The historian Josephus said that Moses gave these laws "scattered", setting them down in whatever order God commanded them. One commentary said that laws may sometimes be beside one another in the Torah, but the things they speak of may be "as far from each other as east from west." Other sages, though, said that the laws were grouped carefully; and we can learn something about each law from the laws before it and after it.

Ki Teitzei is the last group of laws in Deuteronomy, and its laws do not seem to be arranged like a carefully planted garden. Yet in ancient times written scrolls were difficult to make, so few copies of books were made. Laws were often arranged to make them easy to memorize. Sometimes a word in one law matches a word in the next law; sometimes a subject leads to the next subject; sometimes the way a law is written matches the way the next law is written. These were memory cues, and the best students used them to commit whole groups of laws to memory. In fact, in the age of the Rabbis excellent students knew most of the Bible and most of the statements of their teachers by heart. The finest students not only knew the Bible and the teachings of the Rabbis by heart but could discuss them, too.

A List of Laws

Ki Teitzei includes laws about the lifestyle of the Israelites in Canaan. Like most laws in Deuteronomy, these were about everyday things, not so much about sacrifice and the life of priests. Here are some, but not all, of the laws:

Whatever is lost must be returned if you recognize its owner or if someone can prove that he or she owns it. If you see someone on the road who needs help, you must stop to lend a hand. Women should not put on men's clothing, and men should not put on women's clothing.

If you find a bird's nest on the ground and the mother bird is sitting on her eggs, you can take the eggs, but not the mother; "thus you may fare well and have a long life." This seems to be about kindness to animals, like the earlier law, "Do not boil a young goat in the milk of its mother."

When you build a house you must make it safe for people. A flat roof should have a parapet (a railing) so no one will fall off accidentally.

Mixing of "kinds" is not allowed: vineyards should not contain other kinds of crops; oxen and donkeys should not be placed in the same yoke; wool and linen should not be woven into the same garment.

There are laws regarding what to do if a man accuses his wife of being unfaithful (even before the marriage), what to do with people who commit adultery, and what to do when an engaged girl is raped. If a girl who is not engaged is "seized" by a man, then that man must marry her and pay her father fifty silver *shekel*s. Because he caused her pain, he can never divorce her.

There are laws about who shall be part of "the congregation of Adonai". Among those who cannot become Israelites, even when they wish to convert, are the Ammonites and Moabites, "because they did not meet you with food and water on your journey after you left Egypt, and because they hired Balaam … to curse you" (see *Balak*). But Edomites can join the congregation of Adonai even though they were once enemies, for they are the children of Esau, the brother of Jacob, so they are close relatives. And Egyptians can also join—they were enemies, but they also gave the Israelites food and land in a time of famine.

There are laws about how armies should behave. Each warrior should be as pure as possible. Special areas should be set aside outside the camp as latrines or "toilet areas", and each person should have a small shovel to dig a hole and to cover the hole with earth afterward. The reason is simple: When you go out to battle, Adonai goes with you, so the camp should be kept clean and fit for Adonai.

There is a law about runaway slaves:

> You shall not turn over to [his or her] master a slave who seeks refuge with you…. [The slave] shall live with you anyplace [he or she] may choose among your settlements, wherever [he or she] pleases; you must not treat [the runaway slave] badly.

To Consider

One mitzvah in *Ki Teitzei* commands that you always wear tassels ("twists" or "braids") on "the four corners" of your garment. Most garments today do not have four corners, but the robes worn in ancient times did. When we pray we often wear a *tallit*, a prayer "robe" with *tzitzit* or "fringes" at its four corners. (See *Shelach-Lecha* for more on the tallit.) But some orthodox men still observe this mitzvah by always wearing a *tallit katan*, "a little tallit", a small square of cloth with tzitzit at each corner. The tallit katan is sometimes called *arbah kanfot*, "four corners". Because the mitzvah is directed to men and women alike, the Rabbis agreed that women are also permitted (though not required) to wear a tallit or a tallit katan.

Quote to Remember

כִּי תִקְצֹר קְצִירְךָ בְשָׂדֶךָ
וְשָׁכַחְתָּ עֹמֶר בַּשָּׂדֶה לֹא
תָשׁוּב לְקַחְתּוֹ לַגֵּר לַיָּתוֹם
וְלָאַלְמָנָה יִהְיֶה ....

When you reap the harvest of your field and neglect a sheaf, do not return for it; it belongs to the stranger, the orphan, and the widow....

Slavery North and South

Slavery was a hot debate in the United States before the Civil War, and the Torah seemed to be on both sides of the issue. Thomas Jefferson advertised a reward for the return of a runaway slave (*below*), though the Torah commands that runaway slaves be allowed to live wherever they please. Yet the Torah also had laws permitting slavery, providing that slaves were treated fairly and given a day of rest. And it had laws demanding that slaves be set free every fifty years. So pro-slavery folk quoted the Torah as much as anti-slavery folk.

RUN away from the subscriber in *Albemarle*, a Mulatto slave called *Sandy*, about 35 years of age, his stature is rather low, inclining to corpulence, and his complexion light; he is a shoemaker by trade, in which he uses his left hand principally, can do coarse carpenters work, and is something of a horse jockey; he is greatly addicted to drink, and when drunk is insolent and disorderly, in his conversation he swears much, and in his behaviour is artful and knavish. He took with him a white horse, much scarred with traces, of which it is expected he will endeavour to dispose; he also carried his shoemakers tools, and will probably endeavour to get employment that way. Whoever conveys the said slave to me, in *Albemarle*, shall have 40 s. reward, if taken up within the county, 4 l. if elsewhere within the colony, and 10 l. if in any other colony. from
THOMAS JEFFERSON.

Another law forbids Israelites to join Canaanite cults or sell their bodies for pay. Still another forbids Israelites to take back more money than they have lent to one another. (But it is permitted to charge interest on loans to foreigners.) If you make a vow promising something to Adonai, you must keep the vow as soon as possible. "You must fulfill what has crossed your lips," since you "made the promise with your own mouth."

If you go into someone else's vineyard or field, you can eat as much as you like, but you must take nothing out when you leave.

There are laws about divorce, about not taking a man into the army for one year after he marries, and about not taking a person's tools to repay a loan if the person uses those tools to earn a living. Kidnaping is forbidden, and kidnappers must be put to death. You must respect people (and respect their homes) even if they owe you money—you must even return a poor person's coat if he or she needs it as a cover on a cold night. And you must pay wages to the person who needs them "on the same day, before the sun sets" (see *Mishpatim* for more on the coat and wages).

There are laws to protect people: parents, children, widows, strangers, and orphans. Parents should not be put to death for crimes committed by their children or vice versa. "A person shall be put to death only for his [or her] own crime." Equal rights must be shared by all. Whatever falls or is left in the field, the olive groves, and the vineyards during the harvest belongs to "the stranger, the orphan, and the widow". You have to protect the helpless, because "you were a slave in the land of Egypt."

Just a Few More Laws

The list ends with more laws that seem entirely out of place, "scattered" like last-minute details. For example, if the court orders a person to be flogged or beaten a certain number of times, the beating must be done immediately, in the presence of the judge. Up to forty lashes are permitted, but no more. After all, this person is one of you—"a brother", as Deuteronomy puts it.

The next law forbids muzzling an ox while it is "thresh-ing". Oxen were used to break the grain away from the chaff (the stalks and leaves). Naturally they would want to stop and eat some grain from time to time. The law doesn't say so, but it is simple kindness to allow the ox to eat, and it would be cruel not to allow the ox to eat. Isn't the ox due at least a little of the grain that it helps to produce?

The next law states that if a man is married and dies without any son, his brother must marry his wife and bear a son with her. The child will then carry on the name of the one who died. (In Latin, the word *levir* means a "husband's brother". So this is called *levirate* marriage. In Hebrew it is called *yibbum*, from the word for a "husband's brother".) But what happens if a brother does not want to marry the widow? Then the widow has the right to take him "before the elders in the gate" (to the judges) and to pull the sandal off his foot and spit in his face. Afterward, the law says, the brother will be known as "the man without a sandal".

A few final "scattered" laws are about fair weights and measures. People must be honest and fair in buying and selling (see *Kedoshim*).

Amalek

Ki Teitzei ends with Moses preaching a reminder about the nation of Amalek:

> Remember what Amalek did to you on your jour-ney, after you left Egypt—how [they] surprised you on the march, when you were hungry and weary, and cut down all the stragglers in your rear. Therefore, when Adonai your God grants you safety from all your enemies … in the land that Adonai your God is giving you … you shall blot out the memory of Amalek from under heaven. Do not forget!

We studied Amalek in *B'shalach*, where Adonai told Mo-ses, "Write this in a document … I will utterly blot out the memory of Amalek from under heaven." So the command to destroy the Amalekites comes as no surprise. But why is it added here at the end of laws about everyday life? Is the To-rah saying that killing Amalekites should be on the minds of

To Consider

The levirate law may seem strange to us today, but its pur-pose was practical. The Promised Land was divided by tribe, by clan, and by family. If a family dis-appeared, it lost its land. The eas-iest way for a family to disappear was by not having a son to carry on the family name. Therefore, when a man died without a son, his brother should help by father-ing a son for him. It was a dis-grace for an Israelite family to disappear, so if the brother re-fused for any reason, he should be disgraced, too. By the time of the Judges, levirate marriage had a new twist—*any* near relative could take the place of the dead brother. This is exactly what hap-pens in the Book of Ruth, when the right to marry Ruth is passed on by a sandal to Boaz. You can read about it in Chapter 4 of Ruth.

the Israelites every day of their lives? Nachmanides think so, saying, "The story of Amalek must be passed on from one generation to the next." And Rashi says, "Everything that would remind us of Amalek must be destroyed."

In everyday life we tend to forget that we have enemies who would like to destroy us. We think about being tired or hungry, earning a living, playing games, getting married and having children, going shopping or doing business—we have a thousand things to occupy us. We forget about enemies entirely. Yet that is exactly when enemies choose to strike from behind. Enemies like that—terrorists and traitors—do not make peace treaties we can trust. These are the enemies that the Torah calls "Amalek"—those who attack without warning, those who attack without wanting peace.

Haftarah: Isaiah 54:1-10

This is the fifth haftarah of seven that bring comforting messages as Rosh HaShanah approaches. The prophet is "Second Isaiah", who lived in the sixth century B.C.E. among the Israelites exiled in Babylonia. (His work was later added to the scroll of Isaiah who lived more than a hundred years earlier.)

The prophet speaks of Israel as a woman who was divorced, yet her husband [Adonai] takes her back. The haftarah begins "Sing, O barren woman who has never given birth." In Babylonia Israel is a nation unable to live in its own land—so it is like a woman who cannot have children. It wants what it cannot have. But now Adonai will change all that.

Israel should make its tent (its home) larger—much larger:

> For you shall spread out to the right and the left: your children shall drive out other na-

tions. … No more will you remember your disgrace…. For [Adonai] your husband … Adonai calls you "wife" again.

Adonai says, I rejected you "a brief moment", but I take you back "with everlasting love". In an angry moment "I hid My face from you," but now "I take you in unending love."

This is like the days of the covenant with Noah, when Adonai promised never again to cover the earth with waters.

> Now I promise never again to be angry with you or rebuke you—though the mountains may depart and the hills be removed: My love shall never depart from you, My covenant of peace shall not be removed.

Covenants and Curses

The Parts of *Ki Tavo*

As *Ki Tavo* begins, Moses is still preaching his long second sermon to the Israelites. Deuteronomy has thirty-four chapters, and the second sermon stretches over more than twenty-three chapters. There are eleven weekly portions in Deuteronomy, and the second sermon takes up almost six.

Ki Tavo ("when you enter") is the last parashah of the second sermon. The portion divides neatly into three parts: (1) the thanksgiving ritual for bringing harvest offerings to Adonai's "one place"; (2) the covenant ritual to be performed as soon as the Israelites enter the Promised Land; and (3) a catalogue of blessings and curses. Parts two and three do not seem to belong to the sermon. But they are a kind of appendix or addition to it, as we shall see.

All Israelites must give a tithe—a tenth of everything grown or born—to Adonai each and every year. The D-tellers had a three-year formula for the tithe: For two years thanksgiving offerings are brought to the priests at "the one place". In the third year the offerings are brought to a local priest. After that the three-year cycle begins again. In part one of *Ki Tavo* Moses explains the ritual of the two years and the ritual of the third year.

Thanksgiving

Moses preached: Put the tithe of the harvest into a basket and bring it to the special place that "Adonai your God will choose." Hand it to the priest in charge, saying, "In the presence of Adonai … I accept that I have come into the land that Adonai swore to our fathers [Abraham, Isaac, and Jacob] to give to us." The priest will put the basket down in front of the altar. Then you recite the thanksgiving oath:

> My father was a wandering Aramean. Few in numbers, he went down to Egypt [only to become] a great, mighty, and populous nation. The Egyp-

The Meaning of the Tithe

The modern Mishnah scholar Jacob Neusner (1932-) explains that the Rabbis thought about the tithe in two ways. In one way the tithe is "a fair share." All the blessings of the Promised Land come from Adonai. Whatever we harvest, whatever we receive comes because Adonai gives rain and dew at the right seasons. We show gratitude by giving back a tithe as Adonai's "share" of the blessing. Also, in another way the tithe is "rent." The Promised Land belongs to Adonai and the Israelites can stay only so long as they are good tenants. Being good tenants means behaving according to Adonai's commands and paying the yearly "rent."

Quote to Remember

אֲרַמִּי אֹבֵד אָבִי וַיֵּרֶד
מִצְרַיְמָה וַיָּגָר שָׁם בִּמְתֵי
מְעָט וַיְהִי־שָׁם לְגוֹי גָּדוֹל
עָצוּם וָרָב:

My father was a wandering Aramean. Few in numbers, he went down to Egypt, settled there, and became a great, mighty, and populous nation.

Words of Thanks

The opening of the farmer's declaration, "My father was a wandering Aramean," has become part of the *Haggadah*. If the ceremony sounds like a modern Thanksgiving day—with a family feast and words of gratitude to God—it is no wonder. It seems that the Pilgrims based their first Thanksgiving on this passage from Deuteronomy. At the same time, thanksgiving is also older than history. *Below*: A Sumerian king brings a basket of offerings to his god, from a plaque carved around 2450 B.C.E.

tians … oppressed us; they forced heavy labor on us. We cried to Adonai [and] Adonai heard our plea and saw … our oppression. Adonai freed us from Egypt with a mighty hand, an outstretched arm and awesome power, and by signs and wonders. [Adonai] brought us to this place and gave us this land, a land flowing with milk and honey. So I now bring the first fruits of the soil which You, O Adonai, have given me.

You then bow low to Adonai, leaving the basket. Staying nearby, you use part of your offering to make a feast for your family, inviting Levites and even strangers to join you. In this way you and your family and friends feast at "the one place" with Adonai present, at Adonai's "table", the altar.

Moses preached: In the third year, give the tithe close to your home, sharing it with local priests and all who need it. Speaking out loud, you declare to Adonai:

I have removed the [tithe] from the house; given it to the Levite, the stranger, the orphan, and the widow, just as You commanded; I have not broken or neglected any of Your commandments…. Look down from Your holy dwelling, from heaven, and bless Your people Israel and the soil You have given us, a land flowing with milk and honey, as You swore to our fathers.

By observing these thanksgiving rituals, the Israelites renewed the covenant with Adonai year by year (giving Adonai a "share" and paying the "rent").

Moses preached: You pledge to walk in Adonai's ways and observe Adonai's laws "with all your heart and soul". In return Adonai pledges that (1) you are Adonai's treasured people, (2) you will be recognized as "high above all [other] nations", and (3) you will be "a holy people to Adonai your God". (Modern scholars believe that these rituals come from an early age when most Israelites were farmers.)

Renewing the Covenant

Suddenly Moses is no longer preaching. Suddenly Deuteronomy tells us that "Moses *and the elders of Israel* commanded the people, saying...." Many scholars think that the second part of *Ki Tavo* is an appendix to the sermon, attached here because it tells about another ritual. It gives instructions for the ceremony of the blessings and curses—the covenant ceremony—that Moses commanded in *Re'eih*.

For this ceremony the Israelites are commanded to set up large stones and coat them with plaster. On the stones they must inscribe all the words of "this Torah". Next the Israelites must build an altar of uncut stones—"do not strike [the stones] with an iron tool." The Israelites must offer sacrifices on the altar and then share a feast, "rejoicing before Adonai your God." After this is done, the ritual of the blessings and curses begins because "Today you have become the people of Adonai your God."

Six tribes—Simeon, Levi, Judah, Issachar, Joseph, and Benjamin—stand on Mount Gerizim when the blessing is spoken. Six tribes— Reuben, Gad, Asher, Zebulun, Dan, and Naphtali—stand on Mount Ebal for the curse. (Bible scholars agree that this probably means just the elders of each tribe.) The priests proclaim the blessings and curses loudly, so that all the people can hear.

The D-tellers list the twelve curses but not the twelve blessings. Yet they command that the blessings also be spoken. Scholars believe that the blessings were the exact opposite of the curses. The curses all begin "Cursed be the one who...," so the blessings would all begin "Blessed be the one who...." As each blessing and each curse is spoken the people answer "Amen." This was the ceremony of renewing the covenant. It is commanded to be done as soon as the Israelites enter Canaan (see *Re'eih*).

More Blessings and Curses

Part three of *Ki Tavo* is another appendix—a long list of other blessings and curses. There are no instructions given for any ritual or ceremony. The list is attached to conclude the covenant between Adonai and Israel. Ancient treaties and agreements often closed this way, by listing the blessings for keeping the agreement and the curses for breaking it. In fact, many of the curses in this list are also found in a treaty made by King Esarhaddon (680-669 B.C.E.) of Assyria.

Three Covenants

Rabbi Hizkiyah Hizkuni, who wrote his Torah commentary in France in the 1200s, said that there were three covenants made between God and the Israelites. One was made just after the Exodus, another at Sinai, and the third just after the Israelites entered the Promised Land. The third covenant, at Mounts Ebal and Gerizim, was necessary because the people at Sinai (Horeb) had broken the second covenant by worshiping the golden calf.

To Consider

What words were carved on the stones? Moses and the elders said to carve the words of "this Torah". The Rabbis of the Mishnah said that enough stones were used to write all the words of all five books of Moses—the whole Torah. The historian Josephus said that "this Torah" only means "this teaching", and just the blessings and curses were written on the stones. The great scholar Saadia (882–942 C.E.) said that only the most important laws of the Torah were carved on the stones. Another commentator, Abrabanel, noted that while other people make statues to their heroes and carve stones to remember their victories in battle, the Israelites carved a monument to the words of Torah.

To Consider

The Israelites believed in the power of words. A blessing or promise of Adonai would come true, as would a curse. So the superstition arose that this portion of Deuteronomy was dangerous. In many synagogues a volunteer is asked to read the curses. This volunteer's name is not mentioned so that the evils will not be directed at him or her. The volunteer is just called "the one who wishes [to read]." The curses are then read in a low voice, for fear that speaking them out loud might cause them to happen. The rules for reading the curses this way are already in the *Shulchan Aruch* ("The Set Table"), the code of laws written by Rabbi Joseph Caro (1488–1575). They are still followed in Orthodox communities. And many commentators have noted that at one time or another every one of the curses listed in *Ki Tavo* has actually been visited on the Jewish people.

Since the D-tellers probably completed Deuteronomy after 669, they may have copied the Assyrian treaty curses in the same way that they quoted from scrolls in their library (see *Re'eih*). In fact, the custom of placing curses and blessings at the end of covenants goes back at least to the time of Hammurabi (1792-1750 B.C.E.) of Babylon.

The blessings are listed first: If the Israelites obey Adonai, they will be blessed in their cities and in the countryside. Adonai will give them children, and their animals will multiply. Adonai will fight for them against their enemies.

There are only a handful of blessings, but there are heaps upon heaps of curses. Nearly any bad thing that could happen to a person or to a nation is listed. Here are some of the curses:

If the Israelites disobey Adonai, then Adonai will curse them in the cities and in the countryside. There will be heat and drought, blight and mildew. Rain will cease. Crops will fail. There will be calamity, panic, and frustration. There will be madness, blindness, and dismay. Animals will die. Famine will follow. People will die of hunger. Disease will spread among the Israelites and their beasts. Thieves will steal everything. Locusts will eat every blade of grass. Other nations will attack, swooping down like eagles. The Israelites will be conquered and taken off. They will be forced to serve gods of wood and stone. They will be scattered among all the peoples, from one end of earth to the other. And even then the Israelites will find no peace, no place to rest. They will be so poor that they will offer themselves to be sold as slaves, but no one will buy them. The Israelites will become the most inferior of all nations.

When the blessings and the curses are all listed, the second sermon of Moses ends with:

> These are the terms of the covenant which Adonai commanded Moses to conclude with the Israelites in the land of Moab, in addition to the covenant which [Adonai] had made with them at Horeb.

This sermon is sometimes called "The Code of Deuteronomy", since it reviewed the laws and commandments of the covenant. The third sermon will review the history of the Israelites. At the end of the third sermon the blessings and the curses are repeated again.

The Third Sermon of Moses

Ki Tavo contains only the first verses of the third sermon:

> Moses called all Israel to him and said to them: You have seen all that Adonai did before your very eyes in the land of Egypt, to Pharaoh and to all his courtiers and to his whole country: the wondrous feats that you saw with your own eyes, those mighty signs and marvels. Yet to this day Adonai has not given you a mind to understand or eyes to see or ears to hear.

Moses preached: "I led you [Israelites] through the wilderness forty years"—forty years of miracles, forty years in which your clothes and sandals did not wear out, forty years living on manna with no wine or bread. And the whole point of the forty years, Moses said, was so that you might know Adonai your God. "Therefore," Moses said, "be faithful to keep all the terms of this covenant, so that you may succeed in all that you do." With those words *Ki Tavo* ends. The third sermon continues in the next portion, *Nitzavim*.

No Eyes; No Ears

Rabbis, commentators, and Bible scholars all have a little trouble with the statement: "Yet to this day Adonai has not given you a mind to understand or eyes to see or ears to hear." Does it mean that Adonai kept the people from knowing what happened to them, from seeing that Adonai was helping them, from hearing the words that Adonai was trying to teach them? Or is it just an exaggeration?

Haftarah: Isaiah 60:1-22

This is the sixth haftarah of seven that bring comforting messages as Rosh HaShanah approaches. The prophet is "Second Isaiah", who lived in the sixth century B.C.E. among the Israelites exiled in Babylonia. (His work was later added to the scroll of Isaiah who lived more than a hundred years earlier.) The haftarah begins with a verse that was later quoted in the Sabbath hymn, *Lecha Dodi*.

> Arise, shine, for your light has come: the glory of Adonai is shining upon you.

God's light will cause nations to come to you. "Your sons will come from afar; your daughters shall be carried [to you] in safety." When you see this, "your heart will thrill with pride." The best of the animals of all the nations shall be welcome sacrifices on Adonai's altar, adding glory to Adonai's Temple.

The nations that hated you "shall rebuild your walls and their kings shall serve you." Those who refuse will "vanish, their people utterly destroyed." You will become "the joy of all generations ... and you shall know that I, Adonai, am your Savior." Adonai will turn your copper into gold and make Peace your government and Righteousness your ruler.

> Nor more shall the sun be your light by day and the moon glow bright [at night]; but Adonai will be your everlasting light—your God will be your glory .... Your days of mourning shall be ended.

God will make the people righteous to show God's glory, and your nation will grow mighty. "I, Adonai, will hasten it, when the time has come."

נצבים
Nitzavim
Deuteronomy 29:9-30:20

Choose Life

Quote to Remember

אַתֶּם נִצָּבִים הַיּוֹם כֻּלְּכֶם
לִפְנֵי יְהֹוָה אֱלֹהֵיכֶם
רָאשֵׁיכֶם שִׁבְטֵיכֶם זִקְנֵיכֶם
וְשֹׁטְרֵיכֶם כֹּל אִישׁ יִשְׂרָאֵל:

*You stand together this day, all of you,
before Adonai your God—your tribal
chieftains, your elders and your officials,
all the men of Israel.*

Words

We know that the Greek name for this book, *Deuteronomy*, means "Repeated Teaching" or "Second Teaching", and the Hebrew name, *Devarim*, means "Words". Most of *Devarim* is made up of three sermons given by Moses to the Israelites. Each sermon has its own purpose. The first calls on the Israelites to follow Adonai's laws. The second, often called "The Deuteronomic Code", repeats Adonai's commandments, the blessings for obeying, and the curses for not obeying. It requires the Israelites to renew the covenant every year by bringing a tithe of everything to Adonai. And it requires a covenant ceremony—the reciting of the blessings and the curses at Mount Gerizim and Mount Ebal. Moses commands that this ceremony be carried out as soon as the Israelites enter the Promised Land.

The third sermon—almost all of it in this portion, *Nitzavim*—speaks *about* a ceremony and *about* a covenant. Moses (taking Adonai's part) places "this Torah" before the Israelites and commands them to obey it. He tells the Israelites to love Adonai. He reminds them that they have two choices: life and death. Obeying Adonai is choosing life; disobeying Adonai is choosing death. Finally Moses calls on "heaven and earth" to be witnesses as the agreement between Adonai and the Israelites is sealed.

Deuteronomy is the only book that speaks of "this Torah". Yet the Torah we have today, in five books, did not exist in the time of the D-tellers. So when "this Torah" is named, it can only mean the teachings of Deuteronomy—or possibly only the Code given in the second sermon.

The covenant in the third sermon had to be one that was made before the Israelites entered Canaan, while they were still in the land of Moab, at the end of the forty years of wandering. It is not like the covenant made at Sinai (Horeb). There was more action in the Book of Exodus. The *Kavod* ("Presence" or "Glory") of Adonai came down on the mountain. There were earthquakes and fire. Moses went up the mountain to receive the law. A sacrifice was offered, with the blood spattered on the people as the Israelites agreed to accept the covenant. In Deuteronomy the D-tellers replace all that with the power of words. Knowing that the book would be named, as most ancient books were named, by its first important word, they decided to begin their book *Eilu devarim*, "These are the words." And they speak again about "the Word" and its power in *Nitzavim*.

Who Is Making the Covenant

Nitzavim means "standing together" or "assembled". The first few verses of the third sermon are in the previous portion, *Ki Tavo*. In those verses Moses reminded the Israelites that Adonai rescued them from Egypt and gave them victory over their enemies in Moab. This is how most ancient agreements or treaties begin: by giving a brief history. Moses stated the purpose of this assembly:

> You stand together this day, all of you, before Adonai your God—your tribal chieftains, your elders and your officials, all the men of Israel, your children, your wives, even the stranger in your camp, from woodchopper to water drawer—to enter into the covenant of Adonai your God, which Adonai your God is making with you this day....

Sometimes when Torah says that the tribes do something, it means the chieftains or elders of the tribes who represent the tribe. Here the D-tellers make it clear that all the people are assembled. Men, women, and children are here; the leaders are here; the strangers (non-Israelites in the camp) are here; even hired servants like those who chop wood and carry water are here. But there are others, too. As Moses said:

> I make this covenant ... with those who are standing here with us this day before Adonai our God and with those who are not with us here this day.

If everyone is gathered, who are "those who are not with us here"? The Midrash later suggested that at that moment all the souls of Israel—including those not yet born—were

An Extraordinary Discovery

This piece of silver foil was rolled up in an amulet buried with an Israelite girl from the seventh century B.C.E. When it was unrolled and scholars studied the lines, they were amazed to read the oldest quotation from the Torah that we have ever found. The words are the Priestly Blessing (see *Naso*). The family who buried this girl placed the amulet in her grave, trusting that the power of these words would protect her soul forever. And please note: the picture *above* is more than three times larger than the actual piece of foil!

Thinking and Doing

Moses says that someone among the people may already be thinking of doing evil. Just before the witnesses are called, another verse says, "Concealed acts concern Adonai our God; but when it comes to the way people act, it is always up to us and our children to make sure that this Torah is done." Thinking about doing wrong is between you and Adonai (that is, "between you and your conscience"). It is up to all of us to make sure that wrong is not actually done. In the text of the Torah scroll the words "us and our children" have dots over them. Why the dots are there is a mystery. But some scholars noticed that the verse speaks of "us" and not "you" (as in the rest of the sermon). They think this verse may have been inserted to be spoken aloud by the congregation when *Nitzavim* was read in the synagogue.

assembled to accept the covenant. There is truth in this: We are always the products of our parents, and our parents are always the products of their parents. In that sense, you were there, and so were your children who are not yet born.

But if you were not there to agree in person, do you have to accept the covenant? The medieval commentator Abrabanel wrote that this is a question of debt. Those who were there owed Adonai a great debt for rescuing them from Egypt, feeding them in the wilderness, and giving them the Promised Land. When a person who is in debt dies, the next generation has to continue paying until the debt is fully paid. We still owe Adonai for the survival of our people, for our parents and grandparents, for wisdom, and for laws that bring justice and mercy to our world. Since we will always owe this debt, the nation of Israel will continue to survive, and we must continue to repay Adonai. So the D-tellers are correct in every way: All Israelites stood assembled that day—those who were there and those who were not there.

Punishment

Even now, Moses told the Israelites, there may be someone present whose heart is already turning away from Adonai. Someone may be thinking that the curses mean nothing. Someone may be inwardly saying, "I shall be safe, though I follow my own willful heart." Adonai will never forgive such a person, Moses said. Every curse will strike that person, and Adonai promises to blot out that person's name forever.

If many turn away from Adonai, plagues and diseases will strike the land. Visitors from distant places will see how the Promised Land has become like Sodom and Gomorrah, destroyed by Adonai. The nations will all wonder, "Why did Adonai do thus to this land? What was the cause of that awful fury?" And the answer will be "It is because [the Israelites] abandoned the covenant" and "they turned to worship other gods" so that Adonai

> was fiercely angered at that land and brought upon it all the curses recorded in this book. Adonai uprooted [the Israelites] from their soil in anger, fury, and great wrath, and cast them into another land, as is still the case.

God Will Restore You

Moses preached: "When all these things befall you"—when the curses come on you and you are banished to distant lands—it is still not too late to turn your hearts back to Adonai.

> Then Adonai your God will restore your fortunes and take you back in love. [Adonai] will assemble you again…. Even if your outcasts are at the ends of the world, from there Adonai your God will gather you, from there [Adonai] will fetch you [and] bring you to the land … and you shall possess it; and [Adonai] will make you more prosperous and more numerous than your fathers.

Then, Moses said, Adonai will help you by opening your heart and the hearts of your children to love Adonai. With the curses that you suffered, Adonai will curse your enemies. As long as you obey the commands in this Torah, "Adonai will again delight in your well-being … once you return to Adonai your God with all your heart and soul."

Torah Is Not Difficult

Many hearts are moved by the words Moses spoke next. Many of us treasure these words more and more each time we hear them repeated. Moses preached:

> Surely, this commandment which I command you this day is not too mysterious for you, nor is it out of your reach. It is not in the heavens, that you should say, "Who among us can go up to the heavens and get it for us and speak it aloud to us, that we may observe it?" Neither is it beyond the sea, that you should say, "Who among us can go across the sea and get it for us and speak it aloud to us, that we may observe it?" No, the Word is very close to you, in your mouth and in your heart, to observe it.

The Word (meaning, "this Torah") is not a long distance away. It is not above us or out of our reach. We don't need to send messengers for it or ask others to read it aloud for us. It is "very close to you".

To Consider

When other nations see the destruction of the land of Israel, Moses said, they will ask why. They will be told that Adonai punished the people as Sodom and Gomorrah were punished, and that the people were sent out of the land. The D-tellers add to this "as is still the case". When you read that this is "still the case", it is a hint as to when this sentence was written. If the people are "still" out of the land, then the sentence must have been written after the destruction of the Temple, when the Israelites, the people of Judah, were carried off to Babylonia. In those days cities were ravaged and burnt by the Babylonians; hunger and plague were everywhere. So this sentence was written after the year 586 B.C.E., meaning that the Book of Deuteronomy was not fully completed until at least six hundred years after the time of Moses!

Good and Evil

Some say that people who do evil are often rewarded, while people who do good often suffer. Deuteronomy says that doing good always means choosing life, and doing evil always means choosing death. Think about a teeter-totter in a playground. Is it better to be "up"? Or is it better to be "down"? As with a seesaw, when we do evil we may seem to be rewarded for a while, and when we do good we may seem to suffer sometimes. Yet things are not always what they seem. Being on top can sometimes be bad; being on the bottom can sometimes be the best thing. Sometimes it is the way we look at things that makes them seem good or evil.

At times, though, words don't translate an idea properly. For example, the words "in your heart" meant something special in ancient times. The heart was thought to be the place of memory. And the words "in your mouth" meant "by repeating it out loud", since books were scarce and people memorized and repeated them to one another. So the last sentence could be better translated as "The Word is very close to you; you can memorize and teach it so that you will always know what to do."

The Choice

The D-tellers now put a choice before the Israelites. This is not a choice about agreeing to Adonai's commandments. The people have already accepted the covenant. Now it is a personal choice. Every person must choose between being a part of the people or not. And the stakes are very high. A person who chooses to be a part of the community of Israel will surely live. But a person who chooses not to follow the ways of Israel will surely die. In Moses' words:

> See, I set before you this day life and good, death and evil. For I command you this day, to love Adonai your God, to walk in [Adonai's] ways, and to keep [Adonai's] commandments, laws, and rules, so that you may thrive and increase, and so that Adonai your God may bless you in the land you are about to enter and possess. But if your heart turns away and you … are tempted into the worship and service of other gods, I declare to you this day that you shall certainly die; you shall not long endure on the soil that you are crossing the Jordan to enter and possess.

The Witnesses

An official agreement requires witnesses in order that those who agreed cannot later argue, saying, "You really said such-and-such," or "I really meant such-and-so." The witnesses can testify, "This is truly what was said and what was meant." So Moses called two "witnesses" to seal the agreement between Adonai and the Israelites.

I call heaven and earth to witness against you this day: I have put before you life and death, blessing and curse. Choose life—if you and your children would live—by loving Adonai your God, heeding [Adonai's] commands, and holding fast to [Adonai]. For thereby you shall have life and shall long endure upon the soil that Adonai swore to your ancestors, Abraham, Isaac, and Jacob....

The agreement is sealed. The covenant is recorded for all time. If you question what was said, ask the witnesses. Of course, "heaven and earth" here really stands for "all of Creation". The D-tellers mean that everything in the world tells us that Adonai brings blessing—life and good—to those who do what is right and what is just; and everything in the world tells us that Adonai brings curse—death and evil—to those who worship false gods and do harm to others.

To Consider

Deuteronomy is the only book of the Torah that commands the Israelites to "love" Adonai. Other books command "respect for" or "fear of" Adonai. All the same, the "love" that Deuteronomy commands is not the kind of love we think of today. We speak of *love* as "longing for" or "caring deeply about", while the D-tellers mean *love* as "acting as you are commanded to act." Deuteronomy cares less about your inner feelings than about how you behave. The things you do *prove* your love for Adonai.

Haftarah: Isaiah 61:10-63:9

This is the seventh and last haftarah of comforting. It usually falls on the Shabbat just before Rosh HaShanah. The prophet is "Second Isaiah", who lived in the sixth century B.C.E. among the Israelites exiled in Babylonia. (His work was later added to the scroll of Isaiah who lived more than a hundred years earlier.)

The prophet praises Adonai, who is about to "make a glorious victory spring up before all the nations." The nations will see how Adonai delivers Israel from exile and makes her like "a crown of beauty in the hand of Adonai." Before you were called "Forsaken" or "Abandoned"; now you will be "The Holy People", "The Ones Redeemed by God", the "Sought Out", and the "City Not Forsaken".

Adonai says, I am like a wine grower with red clothing from treading grapes all alone. (This is the line recalled in "The Battle Hymn of the Republic", where it says God "is trampling out the vintage where the grapes of wrath are stored.") I expected help, Adonai says, but in the end I alone punished Israel.

God said: They alone are My people, children who will not be false to Me. So God became their Savior.

It is a powerful prophecy, saying that Adonai suffers when Israel suffers, like a parent forced to punish a child. So the prophet speaks of Adonai using the image of a human, a wine grower, coming out of the hills of Edom.

Afflicted in their affliction, the Divine Presence saved them. In love and pity God redeemed them, carried them, and raised them high in all times past.

Josiah and Deuteronomy

Questions

In 721 B.C.E. Assyria came south like a wolf to swallow up the Kingdom of Israel. Cities were taken and burned. Important folk—rulers, officials, judges, priests, and elders—were carried off as slaves. Some people fled, reaching the Kingdom of Judah to the south, but the ten tribes of the north were lost. The prophets had feared this disaster. Hosea and others warned the king not to fight Assyria, but the king refused to listen. Now there was only the Kingdom of Judah—the land of the tribes of Judah and Benjamin.

Some northern priests made it to Jerusalem, carrying precious scrolls and even more precious memories. These were all who were left of the E-tellers. In Jerusalem they met the J-tellers and possibly combined their works into a new JE source. Later the Aaronide priests (the P-tellers) re-worked all the memories, codes, stories, rituals, and laws into three or four scrolls of Moses (see *Bemidbar*).

Some D-tellers may also have fled to the Kingdom of Judah, carrying bits and pieces (or maybe an early telling) of Deuteronomy and the other books of the long history they were completing—the books of Joshua, Judges, Samuel, and Kings. Like everyone else, all the tellers were looking for answers to some big questions: Why had Adonai allowed the Assyrians to defeat the ten tribes? Where was Adonai when cities like Shechem and Samaria fell? Where was Adonai when holy places like Beth El and Dan were demolished? What had gone wrong? Could the remaining Israelites trust Adonai to save them?

Hezekiah, Manasseh, and Amon

King Hezekiah heard some of the answers in the work of the tellers and in the words of prophets. The tellers said that Adonai *brought* the Assyrians to destroy the northern tribes *because* the northern tribes worshiped idols and turned

The Horned Altar

In 1973 archaeologists found proof of Hezekiah's reform in the ruins of ancient Beersheba. They discovered a very large horned altar, but it was found in pieces. The stones of the altar had been taken apart and used in repairing a part of the town wall. The archaeologists put them back together again (*below*) just to see the kind of altar that Hezekiah had destroyed. In this way they learned that Hezekiah had done exactly what Deuteronomy commanded and exactly what the Book of Kings said that he did.

away from Adonai's commandments. Hezekiah also heard the D-tellers teaching about "the one place". Gathering all these thoughts, Hezekiah worked out a plan. He pretended to bow to the Assyrian king. But really he was hurrying to unite the people and to strengthen the Kingdom of Judah.

To unite the people Hezekiah commanded that all sacrifice to Adonai be done in "one place", the Temple in Jerusalem. He cleaned the Temple, removing all the idols that kings before him had placed in it. He even found and destroyed a copper serpent in the Temple—it was said that Adonai told Moses to make it (see *Chukkat*), but now it had to be destroyed, for the people were worshiping it like an idol. Throughout Judah he tore down idols and local altars.

To prepare for war Hezekiah ordered his engineers to dig tunnels, cement huge storage pits for water, rebuild city walls, and erect towers for defense. Their feats of engineering made him famous as king who was a great builder. But he never completed all the work he wanted to do.

In 704 B.C.E. a new king, Sennacharib, took over in Assyria. All around smaller kingdoms tested the power of the new king by rebelling. Against the advice of the prophet Isaiah, Hezekiah joined their rebellion. Later Sennacharib inscribed what happened on a stone monument: In 701 he laid siege to forty-six cities of Judah, crushed and burned the city of Lachish, and made Hezekiah "a prisoner in Jerusalem, his royal city, like a bird in a cage." Jerusalem was only saved by a miracle (see 2 Kings 19:34-35). Isaiah had been right, and Hezekiah had been wrong. The Kingdom of Judah suffered and licked its wounds like an injured lion.

Hezekiah died in 687, and his son Manasseh became king. Manasseh undid all the good that his father had done. He built altars everywhere, bringing Baal worship back to Judah. He "passed his children through fire" as Canaanites did. He murdered innocent people, making Jerusalem "run with blood". Because of Manasseh, the Book of Kings said, Adonai swore to destroy the Kingdom of Judah.

Manasseh died in 642. He would be remembered as the worst king in the whole history of Judah. His son Amon was very much like him—in fact, Amon was so hated in his own time that he was murdered after just two years as king. It was then, in 640 B.C.E., that Amon's eight-year-old son

To Consider

In Hezekiah's time the main sources of Jerusalem's water were outside the walls of the city. The Bible tells how Hezekiah's engineers made a tunnel to bring the water into the city and created "the pool of Siloam" to hold the water. In 1888 an ancient Hebrew inscription was found in a tunnel under Jerusalem. It told how two groups tunneled under the hill—one from the city and the other from outside. "When there were still three cubits to be cut through, there was heard the voice of a man calling to his fellow … and when the tunnel was driven through, the quarrymen split the rock … axe to axe; and the water flowed…" It was a wonderful moment in ancient engineering, the result of careful work. No wonder Hezekiah was known as a great builder. No wonder he had an inscription carved and placed right in that tunnel, where the workmen had met head-on.

To Consider

Archaeologists say that Manasseh actually did much good for the people of Judah, repairing and re-building what was destroyed by the Assyrians. If we had only the words of the D-tellers, we would think that Manasseh was one of the greatest villains of Jewish history. But in other places the Bible has good words about him. The Book of Chronicles tells how Manasseh was once thrown in jail in Babylon. In prison he turned to Adonai, praying for help. When he was released and returned to Jerusalem he was a changed man. He offered sacrifices to Adonai and rebuilt the walls of Jerusalem. You can read the story in 2 Chronicles, Chapter 33.

Josiah became king of Judah. The Book of Kings tells us lit-tle about Josiah's childhood years, but Josiah was destined for greatness.

Josiah's Reform

The year was 622 B.C.E. The place was Jerusalem. King Josiah was twenty-six years old. Like his ancestor Hezekiah, he decided to repair the Temple of Solomon. He sent a scribe, Shaphan, with instructions for Hilkiah the High Priest to begin the repairs.

> Then the High Priest Hilkiah said to the scribe Shaphan, "I have found a scroll of the Torah in the House of Adonai." And Hilkiah gave the scroll to Shaphan, who read it. The scribe Shaphan then went to the king and reported …, "The high priest Hilkiah has given me a scroll"; and Shaphan read it to the king. [2 Kings 22:8ff]

When Josiah heard the words of the scroll of the Torah he was terrified. He tore his clothing the way a mourner would. He told Shaphan, Hilkiah, and other officials to inves-tigate whether this scroll was truly Adonai's teaching. They found the prophetess Huldah in Jerusalem and asked her. She told them that the scroll contained the very words of Adonai. Adonai would surely bring disaster to Judah, but because Josiah's heart was softened when he heard the scroll, the disaster would not come in his time.

Josiah was determined to save his people. He gathered the elders at the Temple. He read the covenant scroll to them—every word. He stood by a pillar and made them vow to be true to the covenant with Adonai: to "follow Adonai and observe [Adonai's] commandments, rules, and laws with all their heart and soul. And all the people entered into the cov-enant."

Josiah ordered that everything used for worshiping Baal, Asherah, and "the worship of heaven" be removed from the Temple and burned. He cleaned the Temple from top to bottom. He destroyed places in Jerusalem where for-eign worship was practiced—including some that were built in the days of Solomon. He destroyed idols and altars throughout the land, even in what was left of the north. Then he commanded the people:

> "Offer the Passover sacrifice to Adonai your God as commanded in this scroll of the covenant." Now the Passover sacrifice had not been offered in that manner in the days of the chieftains who ruled Israel, or in the days of the kings of Israel and the kings of Judah. Only in the eighteenth year of King Josiah was such a Passover sacrifice offered in that manner to Adonai in Jerusalem. ... Thus Josiah brought to pass all that was written in the Torah scroll that the priest Hilkiah had found in the House of Adonai. There was no king like [Josiah] before who returned to Adonai with all his heart, with all his soul and with all his might, for everything in the Torah of Moses; nor did any [king] like him arise after him. [2 KINGS 23:19FF]

The national reform of Josiah was the last glorious moment for the prophets and the priests, for the kings and the people of Judah. A few years later Josiah was killed in battle at the city of Megiddo. The Kingdom of Judah would struggle on for a short time under weak kings until, in 586 B.C.E., it was conquered by Babylonia.

The Found Scroll

You have studied almost all of Deuteronomy. You have heard how, not long before the Temple's destruction, "a scroll of the Torah" was found there. So you can see why modern Bible scholars believe that the scroll found in the Temple was the work of the D-tellers, the Book of Deuteronomy that we have been studying. Here is the evidence:

(1) Only Deuteronomy calls itself "the book of the Torah". (2) It is the only book of the Torah that commands that all sacrifice to Adonai must be done at "the one place". (3) Only Deuteronomy speaks of "the worship of heaven" (which could mean either astrology or the worship of the sun, moon, and stars as gods—both are mentioned). (4) It is the only book of the Torah that commands a Passover sacrifice in Adonai's "one place".

Passover

It may be surprising for us to hear that Passover was not observed with sacrifice and feast for hundreds of years. But we should remember that in those days, the important spring holiday was Matzot, the week of eating unleavened bread. It was only later that the two became one holiday, Passover as we know it today (see *Emor* and *Beha'alotcha*).

And there is more: The story of Josiah, told in the Book of Kings, uses words and phrases taken directly from Deuteronomy, saying things like "with all his heart, with all his soul, and with all his might" and "follow Adonai and observe [Adonai's] commandments, rules, and laws." And it is Deuteronomy and the D-tellers alone who speak of "Adonai your God". And think: What was it that so terrified Josiah when he first heard the scroll? It surely must have been the power of the words—especially the curses.

Who Wrote Deuteronomy?

Was Deuteronomy written for Josiah as a plan for his reform—a kind of constitution for a new Judah? Probably not. Too much in the words of Deuteronomy points to the north, not to Judah. When the D-tellers spoke of "the one place", they probably did not mean the Temple in Jerusalem. They never said where "the one place" was, but the only holy places mentioned in Deuteronomy were all in the north: Gilgal, Shechem, Moreh, Ebal, and Gerizim. They probably meant one of these, most likely Shechem.

Yet when Josiah heard the words "the one place", he thought of the Temple in Jerusalem. Never mind that the other tellers—J, E, and P—only spoke about where Adonai's *Kavod* or "Presence" could be found. Josiah knew that the Temple was named "the House of Adonai". So it is easy to see why he thought that "the one place", "where Adonai's *name*" would be found, was the Holy Temple.

Was Deuteronomy written by northern priests? Not necessarily. Look at the works of the P-tellers. Priests give us lists of names and laws of sacrifice; they explain how priests should behave and what priests should wear; they explain what the altar should look like and how the Mishkan should be built. Priests give details of the rituals and the lives of priests. But Deuteronomy is more interested in the covenant, the blessings and the curses, and how common Israelites should behave in the Promised Land. So the D-tellers were probably not northern priests.

Look back at what Josiah's great-grandfather Hezekiah did. Hezekiah also seemed to be following parts of the D-tellers' plan. Perhaps Deuteronomy was not yet complete in Hezekiah's time. Or perhaps Hezekiah had a copy of it. Either way, Hezekiah ran out of time before he could complete his plan for reform. But Deuteronomy was probably very nearly complete when Hezekiah died. Perhaps the scroll of Deuteronomy was stored in the Temple then and forgotten. The next kings, Manasseh and Amon, had no use for it. They filled the Temple with idols and foreign worship, undoing Hezekiah's work. It was only when Josiah decided to repair and clean the Temple building that the book was discovered by accident.

Who wrote Deuteronomy? Some parts sound as if they were written by prophets, possibly Hosea and others. Some parts sound as if they were written by royal scribes in the north. Whoever wrote it (we call them the D-tellers), they were clever. They had devised a plan to unite the people. They had a belief in the One God that they passed on to us in the *Shema* and the *Ve'ahavta*, in their love of Passover, and in reminding us of our duty to teach our children. They had a belief in the power of words that remains strong in us to this day. They may not have been rulers or elders or priests, but they believed deeply in the covenant with Adonai. They left us their beliefs and their love of God.

VaYeilech

In this portion, *VaYeilech* ("he went"), Moses seems to be taking care of many last-minute details. He announced to the people:

> I am now one hundred and twenty years old, I can no longer be active. Moreover, Adonai has told me, "You shall not go across yonder Jordan." Adonai your God will … cross over before you [to] sweep those nations from your path…. (Joshua is the one who shall cross before you, as Adonai has spoken.) Adonai will [defeat those nations as Adonai] did [defeat] the Amorites….

You can see even in this little bit of *VaYeilech* that more than one teller is at work. Even in these few lines there is some confusion about who will "cross over before" the Israelites. Will it be Adonai or Joshua?

The Five Books of Moses

Was "the scroll of the Torah" found in the Temple in 622 B.C.E. really the Book of Deuteronomy? We can only answer with a strong "Maybe." Will we ever know who the D-tellers were? We can only answer with a strong "Probably not." What we know for certain is that even though some of the mitzvot in Deuteronomy disagree with mitzvot given in the other four books, Deuteronomy was added to them so that today the Torah is only complete if it contains "the *five* books of Moses".

Hazak V'Amatz

The words *Hazak v'amatz* mean "be strong and firm." They are repeated twice in this portion—once by Moses to the people and once by Adonai to Joshua. In the Book of Joshua they are spoken again, by the people to Joshua. Today we hear them spoken whenever Jews wish to urge one another to be brave.

Twice-Told Things

Before this portion, nearly all of Deuteronomy is the work of the D-tellers. (A few verses show that other hands probably touched it here and there.) But this portion, which is only thirty verses long, is a confusion of parts from different tellers. The best way to see this is to look at things that happen twice in *VaYeilech*—but never quite in the same way.

Appointing Joshua

In the sight of all the people Moses appoints Joshua to be the next leader, saying, "Be strong and firm, for it is you who shall go with this people into the land that Adonai swore to their fathers to give them … And Adonai … will be with you; [and] will not fail you or forsake you." This sounds like the D-tellers.

A few verses later Adonai calls Moses and Joshua to the Tent of Meeting and appoints Joshua as Israel's next leader, even though Moses has already appointed him. Adonai tells Joshua, "Be strong and firm: for you shall bring the Israelites into the land that I promised them on oath, and I will be with you." "The Tent of Meeting" is nowhere in the work of the D-tellers, but it is known to the tellers called J and E.

The Scroll of the Torah

Moses completed writing the scroll of the Torah and handed it "to the priests, sons of Levi, who carried the Ark of Adonai's Covenant, and to all the elders of Israel." He commanded them to read it to the Israelites every seven years. But a few verses later "Moses instructed the Levites who carried the Ark of the Covenant of Adonai, saying: Take this book of Torah and place it beside the Ark of the Covenant of Adonai your God, and let it remain there…."

Both of these pieces sound like the D-tellers. But since they disagree on what happened, we think they probably came from two *different* D-tellers.

The Poem

The poem that we will read in the next portion, *Ha'azinu*, is introduced twice in this portion. Once Adonai tells Moses: "Write down this poem and teach it to the people of Israel; put it in their mouths, in order that this poem may be My witness against the people of Israel." This sounds like the JE source, or perhaps the P-tellers.

The second time Moses tells the people, "Gather to me all the elders of your tribes and your officials, that I may speak all these words to them and that I may call heaven and earth to witness against them." The idea of "heaven and earth" as witnesses is a favorite of the D-tellers.

The Witness

Adonai tells Moses that the poem will be a witness against the people of Israel. But Moses tells the people that these words and "heaven and earth" will witness against them. The first does not seem to be from D-tellers, while the second definitely is.

The Coming Sin

Adonai tells Moses that the Israelites are sure to sin. They will

> go astray after the foreign gods … in the land that they are about to enter; they will forsake Me and break My covenant that I made with them. Then My anger will flare up against them, and I will abandon them and hide My face from them.

A few verses later Moses tells the people:

> I know that, when I am dead, you will act wickedly and turn away from the path that I commanded you, and that in time to come misfortune will befall you for having done evil in the sight of Adonai.

But Moses does not say that Adonai told him this. This last sounds like the D-tellers, who have *Moses speak about Adonai* instead of having *Adonai speak through Moses*, as the other tellers normally do.

How Was the Poem Given?

In one place we read "That day, Moses wrote down this poem and taught it to the Israelites." Later we read "Moses recited the words of this poem to the very end, in the hearing of the whole congregation of Israel." Both of these could be memories of the D-tellers, but one speaks of writing and teaching the poem, while the other claims that the poem was given as a sermon.

Keeping It All

As in the rest of the Torah, the rule that was followed in bringing the laws and stories, the memories and traditions together was that of keeping it all. Bits and pieces that disagreed with one another were set side by side or combined to make one new version, but nothing was thrown away. Knowing that helps modern Bible scholars to study the way the Torah was made (see *Balak*.)

Again, we would have to think that these two pieces may come from more than one D-teller.

Mystery

There is no mystery about what happens in *VaYeilech*. Moses gets ready to die. Joshua is appointed (by Moses, by Adonai, or by both) as the next leader of the Israelites. Moses writes out the words of Deuteronomy ("this Torah"). He gives the scroll to the priests to keep beside the Ark. He commands that the words be read every seven years to the people. Moses tells the people that he knows they will fail to keep Adonai's commands. He writes a poem and teaches it, or gets ready to recite it, to the Israelites.

The only mystery is how in this one chapter so many pieces were stitched together like a quilt. In the end it is surely one blanket, but every piece of it has a pattern of its own.

Haftarah: Isaiah 55:6-56:8

In *VaYeilech* Moses tells the people that he knows they will sin when he is gone, but they can always repent, and God will forgive them. This haftarah calls on us to repent—it is only read if *VaYeilech* falls before Rosh Hashanah.

Some scholars think the hopeful words here come from a "Third Isaiah". If not, they belong to the "Second Isaiah" who lived with the exiles in Babylonia in the sixth century B.C.E. Either way, they are joyous.

> Seek Adonai while there is still time. Call out while God is near. Let the wicked forsake their ways; and the sinful, their thoughts. Let them return to Adonai, who will show them mercy; to our God, who is quick to forgive.

Adonai says, "My thoughts are not like yours. My ways are not your ways." God's words are like rain falling earthward. They do what they are sent to do.

> Go out with joy and be led forth in peace. Before you, mountains and hills shall break out in joyful song—the trees of the field shall clap their hands.

Adonai says, "Keep justice and do what is right." The time for being saved is near. The one who keeps the Sabbath is happy; the one who does no wrong is glad. To strangers and those who feel like outcasts, Adonai says, "I will give you an everlasting name that will never be cut off." Even if foreigners keep the Sabbath, Adonai will "bring them to My holy mountain and make them joyful in My house of prayer." This is Adonai's promise: I will bring home more than I have already.

The Song of *Ha'azinu*

Give Ear

Ha'azinu means "give [your] ear" or "listen". It is the first word of a poem presented by Moses. When English speakers hear "give ear", they are often reminded of the speech of Mark Antony in William Shakespeare's play *Julius Caesar*, "Friends, Romans, countrymen, lend me your ears." However, there is a difference. Moses is not calling for the Israelites to listen. As the poem begins he is calling on heaven and earth to hear his words:

> Give ear, O heavens, let me speak;
> Let the earth hear the words I utter!
> May my teaching come down as the rain,
> My speech [be like] the dew....
> For the name of Adonai I proclaim;
> Give glory to our God!
> The Rock!—[Adonai's] deeds are perfect,
> Yea, all [Adonai's] ways are just;
> A faithful God, never false,
> True and upright is [Adonai].

Rashi says that Moses calls on heaven and earth because they are permanent—they will always be there. Elsewhere in Deuteronomy Moses calls heaven and earth as witnesses, but this time, as we were told in the last portion, *VaYeilech*, the poem itself is the witness.

How can a poem be a witness? What is it a witness to? The poem recites the debt that the Israelites owe Adonai for rescue, miracles, and the gift of the land. Adonai is always doing what is just and what is fair. But (in the past and in the future) it is the Israelites who go astray—time after time they turn away from Adonai and worship other gods. The poem says "the Israelites often deserve punishment." This is how a poem can be a witness. At any time this poem can testify "here is why the punishment is sent" and "here is why the Israelites deserve it."

Quote to Remember

הַאֲזִינוּ הַשָּׁמַיִם וַאֲדַבֵּרָה
וְתִשְׁמַע הָאָרֶץ אִמְרֵי־פִי:

Give ear, O heavens, let me speak;
Let the earth hear the words I utter!

The Rock!

God is often called "the Rock". Most scholars think this is a comparison, as when God is called a "shield", meaning that God protects us. In the same way, a rock can provide us protection, and by its nature it is solid and reliable. A few scholars, however, think that this title reminds us that Adonai may have once been thought of as a "mountain god". After all, Moses (and later the Israelites) first "met" Adonai at a mountain.

Dull and Witless

Adonai calls the Israelites "dull" and "witless" people. Why choose these two words? In the Book of Jeremiah Adonai says, "They deserted Me and did not keep My commandments." The Talmud explains: Only a "dull" (stupid) people would be protected and rescued by Adonai and then "desert" Adonai. Only a "witless" (non-thinking) people would receive a gift like the Torah and not learn from it.

To Consider

The word "no" (לא, in Hebrew) is the word "god" (אל) spelled backwards. The poem seems to say that when the Israelites turn away from Adonai and worship "no-gods", they are getting things backwards. Adonai decides to punish them in the same way, by sending an enemy that is "no-folk", that is, a backward enemy who worships false gods. When they turn their "no" to "yes"— when they get it right and turn their "no" around—both the enemy and the Israelites will realize that there is only One God.

Like Children

The poem calls the Israelites "unworthy". They are like children with a good home who do not realize they have a fine parent, Adonai. They are "dull" and "witless". If only they knew how well Adonai had treated them, they would not act in evil ways. But how can they know? The poem answers:

Remember the days of old,
Consider the years of ages past;
Ask your father, he will inform you,
Your elders, they will tell you.

Your elders, your parents, know that Adonai found the Israelites the way you find something in the desert, in the wasteland. Adonai watched over them as an eagle watches over her nestlings. There was no other god at Adonai's side helping to feed and clothe Israel. But the Israelites grew fat and greedy—they forgot who fed and protected them. They angered Adonai with awful behavior. They sacrificed to "demons" and to "no-gods", even to new gods that people dreamed up. All the while they forgot the God who raised them.

Punishment

"Adonai saw and was vexed." Adonai decided, "I will hide My face from them, and see how they fare in the end." Since the Israelites served "no-gods" and wasted themselves, Adonai sent a "no-folk" (an unknown people, "a nation of fools") against them. Adonai would punish them with "misfortunes", "famine", "plague", "fanged beasts", and "venomous creepers". The enemy's "sword shall deal death" even as Adonai's other terrors would be striking every Israelite—"young man and maiden alike", infants and elderly alike.

Adonai was angry enough to destroy the Israelites entirely, except for one thing. Their enemies—people of little wisdom—would crow. They would think, "Our own hand has defeated [Israel]" and "None of this was caused by Adonai!" If they were wise, they would know that no nation could defeat the Israelites unless "their Rock had sold them, Adonai had given them up." The enemies of Israel may celebrate when Adonai punishes Israel, but the wine they drink will be from the grapes of Sodom and Gomorrah. It will be the "venom of asps, the pitiless poison of vipers". If they were smart, they would learn a lesson from Israel's punishment.

One day, Adonai says, the enemies will make some mistake; their foot will falter. Their time for punishment is coming soon enough. Once the Israelites have been punished enough, it will be time for the enemies of Israel to be punished. Adonai will ask them, Where are your gods? "Let them rise up to your help, let them be your shield!" But their gods will not answer. Adonai will say,

See, then, that I, I am the One;
There is no god beside Me.
I deal death and give life;
I wounded and I will heal:
None can save [you] from My hand.

Then Adonai will punish Israel's enemies fiercely, with a "flashing blade". When I judge them, Adonai says, "I will make My arrows drunk with blood, even as My sword devours flesh." Then "the long-haired enemy chiefs" will be the slain and the captive.

The Poem Ends

When the Israelites deserve punishment, Adonai must punish them. To do this, Adonai must turn away. Adonai says, "I will hide My face from them." This is the way Adonai punished the earth in the flood, the way Adonai punished Sodom and Gomorrah. But Adonai refuses to destroy everything; Noah and his family were saved from the flood, and Lot and his family from Sodom and Gomorrah. Just so, most of the Israelites will be destroyed, but some few will survive.

When the punishment is over, Adonai hopes the lesson will be learned—not just by the Israelites but by all nations. The Israelites are the model, and the poem says, "O nations, praise [Adonai's] people!" Let the other nations remember, the poem concludes, that if they take the blood of the Israelites, Adonai will take their blood. Adonai will "cleanse the land" by removing the enemies of the Israelites, and also by removing the Israelites if they are unworthy.

Demons

The word for "demons" is *sheidim*. It is used in *Ha'azinu* and once more in the Bible, in Psalm 106, where it says that children are sacrificed when demons are worshiped. Rabbi Manuel Gold (1933-) points out that demons were not always evil spirits. In the Akkadian language *sheidim* were friendly spirits, protectors of the people. They were minor gods (scholars call them "demigods"). By the time of the Rabbis, though, demons were thought to be evil and dangerous. People even took out "insurance policies" against them by having a local scribe inscribe curses to stop or catch the demons on special bowls. The bowls were buried upside down in a corner of the house. Since all demons were thought to come from beneath the earth, the bowls prevented them from entering the house. It was thought that any demon who stopped to read the message on the bowl would be snared by it.

To Discuss

The first-century historian Josephus reported that copies of *Ha'azinu* were kept in the Temple. Not long ago, archaeologists exploring the caves in which the Dead Sea Scrolls had been discovered found a copy of this poem that had never been attached to any other scroll. This copy may have been used by the priests for their weekly reading of *Ha'azinu*, or it might have been used to help priests memorize the poem. Finding a copy that is on its own sheet of parchment shows how important the poem was.

Below: Some Dead Sea Scrolls were found in pottery jars of a shape otherwise unknown. Some scholars believe that these jars were made especially for hiding the scrolls.

Moses came, together with [Joshua], and recited all the words of this poem in the hearing of the people. [Afterward, Moses] said to them: Take to heart all the words [of this poem]. Repeat them to your children, that they may observe faithfully all the terms of this Torah. For this is not a trifling thing for you: it is your very life....

Ha'azinu

The Talmud tells us that the *Ha'azinu* poem was divided into six parts. One part would be read each Shabbat, while the priests were offering the *musaf* (the "additional" sacrifice of the Sabbath day) until all six parts were read. Then the reading would begin again on the next Sabbath. Nowadays the *Ha'azinu* portion is always read on a Sabbath near or during the High Holy Days. Because it was used in the service of the Temple and because the way it uses words (and some of the words in it) is older than the rest of Deuteronomy, scholars believe that the *Ha'azinu* poem may be an old composition that was later added to Deuteronomy.

Some scholars think that the poem refers to a particular punishment—something that actually happened to the Israelites. But scholars do not agree on what disaster it might be that caused the poem to be written. Some say that the "punishment" in *Ha'azinu* was the fall of the Kingdom of Israel. Others say that the poem is earlier. Possibly the enemy, the "no-folk", were unknown raiders off the desert. Such raids occurred time and again in the days of the Judges. On one thing all the scholars agree: This poem is old, but not as old as the Song at the Sea (see *B'Shalach*).

After the Poem

The P-tellers added a few verses right after the *Ha'azinu* poem.

That very day Adonai spoke to Moses: Climb these heights of Abarim to Mount Nebo ... and view the land of Canaan.... You shall die on the mountain that you are about to climb, and shall be gathered to your kin, as your brother Aaron died on Mount

Hor and was gathered to his kin; for you both broke faith with Me among the Israelite people, at the waters of [Meribah].... You may view the land from a distance, but you shall not enter it—the land that I am giving to the Israelite people.

How do we know that these verses came from the P-tellers? Chiefly because it was the P-tellers who believed that the reason Moses and Aaron could not enter the Promised Land had to do with a sin at Meribah—either Moses striking the rock instead of speaking to it or Moses and Aaron not waiting for Adonai's *Kavod* ("Presence") to appear before acting (see *Chukkat*). It cannot be the D-tellers, since they believed that Moses could not enter the Promised Land because the Israelites listened to the scouts instead of trusting in Adonai (see *Devarim*), and that Aaron was punished because he made the golden calf.

Many modern scholars suggest that this section by the P-tellers used to be part of the ending of the Book of Numbers. Later, when Deuteronomy was added to the Torah, it was moved here, after the *Ha'azinu* poem.

Haftarah: 2 Samuel 22:1-51

The poem by Moses is connected by the Rabbis to a poem from David that is found twice in the Bible—in the Book of Samuel and in the Book of Psalms (18). The first lines say that David wrote this poem/prayer after he was saved from his enemies, especially Saul, who tried to kill him.

David praises Adonai as "my rock", "my fortress", "my shelter", "my shield", and "my deliverer".

> In my torment I call to Adonai ... in Your Temple You heard me. My scream reached Your ears.

God is pictured as a warrior riding down from heaven on a cherub (sphinx), launching arrows to scatter David's enemies. Adonai saw that David was innocent. "Your laws of justice are before me.

I have not turned away." And Adonai was faithful to the faithful.

God gives victory to the righteous. "You make my stride long and my ankles do not waver as I chase down my foes and destroy them."

> They cry for help, but there is none; [my enemies plead] to Adonai, but get no answer.

David has been permitted to destroy his every enemy, and Adonai has helped. David has been preserved "to be a leader of nations." So David thanks Adonai and sings praises to God's name.

> You are a tower of victory to Your king. You show love for your anointed one, for David and his descendants forever.

The Death of Moses

Cyrus the Great

The Persians led by Cyrus the Great (*above*) conquered Babylonia in 538 B.C.E. Shortly thereafter he issued a decree allowing captive peoples to return to their native homes. The decree was recorded on a stone shaped like a cylinder (*below*) that is now in the British Museum. A copy was made to be displayed at the United Nations building in New York City, because this decree was said to be the first statement in history of the rights of nations.

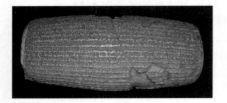

The Five Books of Moses

As part of the synagogue Torah service, Jews recite the words "This is the Torah that Moses placed before the Children of Israel—from the lips of Adonai." From our studies we know that the Torah is not one book, but a library of books. It was collected and expanded in many times and places. Laws, lists, and stories were remembered and recorded by different tellers—sources like J, E, P and D (see *BeMidbar*). This is only natural. Even powerful rivers like the Amazon, the Nile, and the Mississippi have their start in lots of gentle streams that flow downhill to join together.

When did the sources first join together to form the complete and powerful Torah? No one can give the exact date, but a little history can help us guess.

In 622 B.C.E. King Josiah was given the "scroll of the Torah" that was accidentally found in the Temple. We are fairly sure that this scroll was the Book of Deuteronomy, the only book that calls itself "Torah" (see *VaYeilech*). In 586 B.C.E. the Babylonians conquered the Kingdom of Judah and took the captive Judeans north. This began the Babylonian exile. It is likely that the Judeans carried with them all the pieces of what would become the final Torah.

After 538 some Judeans returned from Babylonia to rebuild the Temple. In 458 Ezra left Babylonia to join them in Jerusalem. The Bible tells us that Ezra was a scribe, an expert in "the Torah of Moses", who came to teach "the Torah of Adonai" to the people. Nearly twenty years passed before the people gathered and "asked Ezra the scribe to bring the scroll of the Torah of Moses with which Adonai had charged Israel." For seven days Ezra read the Torah to the people. A few years later the Book of Chronicles was completed. It was the first book of the Bible to know all five books of Moses and to call them "the Torah".

So here is our guess: Before the Judeans went to Babylonia, "the Torah" was only the Book of Deuteronomy.

During the years from 586-538, a final editor (or editors) in Babylonia completed the Torah as we know it today out of all its many sources.

Some scholars think that the final editor was a P-teller. Other scholars call the final editor by a different name, the "R", the "Redactor", a fancy name that means "an editor who puts things in writing" or "an editor who selects things." If Ezra was "an expert" in the Torah of Moses, he must have studied it before leaving Babylonia. Since he read it to the people in Jerusalem, he must have brought a Torah scroll to Jerusalem. From what we know, then, the Torah as we have it today was completed in Babylonia.

The final editor copied the Book of Deuteronomy almost entirely from the work of the D-teller. But at the very end, R (or whoever was the final editor) tacked on a few "last-minute" items. One was the poem *Ha'azinu*, which was once a separate scroll but was thought to be the work of Moses. Another was Moses' last "blessing" to the tribes.

The Blessing

Vezot HaBerachah means "This is the blessing." The portion begins, "This is the blessing with which Moses, servant of God, bade the Israelites farewell before he died." Some scholars think this blessing is a single poem, perhaps the oldest in Deuteronomy. Others say that many short poems were arranged to create for Moses a farewell blessing like the one Jacob gave to his children at the end of Genesis.

Moses says that Adonai came like flashing light out of the wilderness—he names many places, including Sinai, Seir, and Paran—to rule over Israel. Then suddenly the poem is interrupted by a verse that talks *about* Moses, saying: "Moses charged us with the Torah, the inheritance of the congregation of Jacob." The Rabbis loved this verse so much that, along with the *Shema*, they said it should be taught to children from the time they could speak. In the Middle Ages commentators thought the verse was an answer to be given by the people to the start of the poem. Later scholars often agreed, saying that the poem was probably written to be spoken out loud, and this verse was meant to be spoken by the congregation.

Quote to Remember

תּוֹרָה צִוָּה־לָנוּ מֹשֶׁה
מוֹרָשָׁה קְהִלַּת יַעֲקֹב:

Moses charged us with the Torah, the inheritance of the congregation of Jacob.

To Consider

The Torah says, "Moses charged us with the Torah, the inheritance of the congregation of Jacob." Nachmanides noted that it says "the *congregation* of Jacob", not "the children of Jacob". From ancient times, he taught, many people have chosen to join the congregation of Jacob. The inheritance belongs as much to them as to those born as Jews. Our inheritance is the Torah, so people who convert are rewarded by having many more commandments to follow than non-Jews. As a Chasidic rabbi once stated, "It is not the study of Torah that makes us Jews. Being a Jew means living in such a way that we *become* Torah with our lives."

A Kind of Marriage

We read this last portion of the Torah on *Simchat Torah*, "[the holiday of] Celebrating the Torah". In many synagogues the poem is broken up blessing by blessing so that many people can have an *aliyah* (be "called up" to the Torah). In some synagogues the verses are repeated until every adult has had an aliyah, then repeated again when all the children present come up together for one aliyah. Whoever has the honor of reading the last verses of Deuteronomy is called the *hatan Torah*, the "bridegroom of the Torah". After the last verse is read, the first verses of Genesis are read. The person honored with this aliyah is called the *hatan Bereishit*, the "bridegroom of Genesis". The celebration goes on as we march and dance with the scrolls of the Torah as if we were at a great wedding. After all, the covenant between Adonai and the people of Israel is surely a marriage made in heaven.

Next Moses "blesses" each tribe. Some blessings tell us about a tribe, as when the poem says that the tribe of Reuben is "few in numbers". Sometimes a blessing asks Adonai to help a tribe, as when it says, "Listen, O Adonai, to the voice of Judah … help [Judah] against its foes." Sometimes a blessing compares a tribe to an animal, as when it says that the tribe of Gad is "like a lion [ready] to tear off arm and scalp." The largest blessing is reserved for the tribe of Joseph (made up of the two tribes of Joseph's sons, Ephraim and Manasseh). And even though there are twelve tribes blessed, there is no mention at all of the tribe of Simeon.

Much of what is said in the blessings can no longer be explained. The blessings may refer to events or stories that are not in the Bible, or to things we don't know. Of course, archaeologists may one day discover objects and writings that will help explain these mysterious verses. For now, though, two things are very clear: (1) The blessing tells about the tribes *after they were settled* in the Promised Land—it knows where they were settled *in the days of the kings*, Saul, David, and Solomon. (2) The poem generally speaks kindly of the tribes, asking for their blessings *to continue*. These two things tell us that the blessings were written long after the time of Moses.

The blessings end as they began: speaking to all the Israelites and praising Adonai. Moses says: "There is none like God, riding through the heavens to help [the Israelites]." Since Adonai drove their enemies out, "Israel dwells in safety…. In a land of grain and wine, under heavens dripping dew."

> O happy Israel! Who is like you,
> A people saved by Adonai,
> Your protecting Shield, your Sword triumphant!
> Your enemies shall come cringing before you,
> And you shall tread on their backs.

This was surely a popular poem celebrating the protection of God and God's help as a shield and a sword against enemies, while at the same time celebrating the bounty of the land. Nothing makes it sound like "Moses' last words to the Israelites", but it seemed to the final editor that it could be, so the poem was set here, just before the death of Moses.

The Death of Moses

The Book of Deuteronomy, and the whole Torah, ends with the death of Moses. The story is told in just a few sentences.

> Moses went up … to Mount Nebo, to the summit of Pisgah, opposite Jericho, and Adonai showed him the whole land…. Adonai said to him, "This is the land which I swore to Abraham, Isaac, and Jacob, saying, 'I will assign it to your children.' I have let you see it with your own eyes, but you shall not cross there." So Moses the servant of Adonai died there, in the land of Moab, at the command of Adonai. [Adonai] buried him in the valley in the land of Moab…; and no one knows his burial place to this day. Moses was a hundred and twenty years old when he died; his eyes were undimmed and his body still was youthful. And the Israelites bewailed Moses … for thirty days.

The translation says Moses died "at the command of Adonai", but the Hebrew really says "at the mouth of Adonai". This led the Rabbis to speak of God's "kiss of death". We may use this expression to mean a terrible thing that leads to someone's end, but the Rabbis thought of it entirely differently. Nothing could be a finer way to die, they imagined, then to be blessed with a final kiss from God.

The Torah says "no one knows his burial place to this day," which of course means that these words were written after the death of Moses. But the Rabbis and later commentators agreed that the reason Moses' final resting place remained unknown was so that later people would not turn his grave into a place of worship. It says "his body was still youthful," and Ibn Ezra said that the words used here really mean "he had no wrinkles on his body"—even though he was not as strong in his old age as when he was young, his body showed no signs of age. It says, "Moses was a hundred and twenty years old when he died." In Babylonia this was considered a perfect age, because the Babylonians based their arithmetic on the number sixty rather than the number ten, as we do now, and 120 was twice sixty. So the meaning is probably "Moses died at the perfect age"—the exact right moment for a great hero to die.

Who Buried Moses?

The Rabbis of the Talmud asked, "If Moses was alone when he died, who buried him?" Rashi tells us that the Rabbis had two opinions; some said that Moses buried himself, while others said that it was God who buried Moses.

The period of wailing and mourning for Moses came to an end. Now Joshua son of Nun was filled with the spirit of wisdom because Moses had laid his hands upon him; and the Israelites heeded him, doing as Adonai had commanded Moses.

This section is both an ending of the story of Moses and a new beginning for the people of Israel. After the traditional thirty days were over the people were ready to follow Joshua, because he was "filled with the spirit of wisdom" when Moses blessed him. But if we listen closely to the words, we can hear an important comparison between Joshua and Moses. The words tell us that the Israelites did what Joshua asked them to do, but also that Joshua asked them to do what "Adonai had commanded Moses." Moses was the one who gave Adonai's commands to the people. Joshua would lead them according to those commands. Joshua would never be as great as Moses. And that is how the book ends, too:

Never again did there arise in Israel a prophet like Moses—whom Adonai singled out, face to face, for the various signs and wonders that Adonai sent him to display in the land of Egypt, against Pharaoh and all his servants and his whole country, and for all the great might and awesome power that Moses displayed before all Israel.

It says "face to face", but this does not mean that Moses saw the face of God. It only means that Adonai spoke to Moses one on one, the way a friend speaks to another friend. Moses is remembered for being the only prophet who ever spoke to Adonai in this way. Some scholars think that the words are here to show that from this time on, any prophet who claimed to speak "face to face" with Adonai certainly be a false prophet.

Who Wrote the Story?

If Moses never returned from the mountain, who wrote these words about Moses' death to include them in the Torah? Some of the Rabbis said that Adonai told Moses to write these words before he climbed the mountain to die. Others said that the few words about Moses' death and burial were written by Joshua. Ibn Ezra said that the whole story was written by Joshua. In modern times, too, experts disagree. Some say that the whole story was told by the D-tellers. Some say that it was collected from stories known to all the tellers—J, E, P, and D—and composed by the final editor. If so, it is the perfect story to end our study of the Torah—even as it is the perfect story to end the Torah.

The End of Our Study

The Rabbis said that a book was holy if it "makes the hands unclean". They taught a strange law: If you touched a holy book, then your hands could not touch the *terumah* offering—the one raised by hand and waved—without making it unclean. All we need to know is that when the Rabbis spoke of a book that "makes the hands unclean" they meant the book was holy enough to be included in the Bible. In Greek these books were known as the *canon*, the official set of books. When a book was included in the Holy Scriptures (the Bible), it was said to be *canonized*.

The Torah, the Five Books of Moses, was the first canon of the Hebrew Scriptures. Not long after the Torah was canonized, the Deuteronomic history (Joshua, Judges, Samuel and Kings) and the writings of various prophets were added to it. For a while the canon was called "The Law and the Prophets". But other books seemed equally holy—books like the scrolls of Ruth and Esther, Psalms, and Proverbs. The Rabbis discussed which of these scriptures ("writings") also "made the hands unclean" and should be added to the Bible. In the end they closed the canon of the Bible, calling it *Tanach*—a name made from the first letters of *Torah*, *Nevi'im* (Prophets), and *Ketuvim* (Writings). *Tanach* is the complete Hebrew Scriptures, the Bible we know today.

As you complete the study of the Book of Deuteronomy you will want to repeat out loud the words that Jews have spoken through the ages, whenever the reading of a book of Torah is complete: *Hazak! Hazak! V'Nithazek!* "Be strong! Be strong! And may you be strengthened!"

חֲזַק חֲזַק וְנִתְחַזֵּק!

Quoting from Torah

It was not until the sixteenth century that the *Tanach* was divided into chapters and verses. Before then, when a person quoted a verse from the Torah, he or she just mentioned in what *parashah* ("portion") the quote was found. The rest of the books were quoted without any mention of where the quote was found. Unless you knew the entire Bible by heart, it was difficult to find a biblical verse. Of course, before printing became common, learning the entire Bible by heart was just part of a good Jewish education.

Last-Minute Stories

Many scholars believe that the final editor of the Torah, whether it was a P-teller or the R-editor, added a few stories at the last minute. *Ha'azinu* and the blessings found in this portion may have been two of them. More surprising, the last-minute additions may have included the story of how God created the world in seven days (see *Bereishit*) and the tale of the Tower of Babel (see *Noach*).

Miracles

You have studied the whole Torah portion by portion. I hope you have discovered that the Torah is speaking to you about the ways you behave and the things you believe. You should not behave exactly as the people in the Torah did—often their stories are given to help us understand how *not* to behave. And you should not believe all the things they believed—what we believe changes with where and when we live. Even in the time it took to put the Torah together, beliefs kept growing and changing.

Yet the Torah will always set a mark for us, as if it were saying, "This is our God, and this is our covenant. This is where we were, and this is what we learned." Imagine where you were when you began your study of Torah. See where you are now. It was like that for me, too. Years ago I began writing this book, and now, like a little miracle, it is finished. Of course, the Torah shows us that we should be grateful for every miracle, the big and small alike.

Haftarah: Joshua 1:1-18

The Torah portion, ending with the death of Moses, is always read on Simchat Torah, and the haftarah is the very beginning of the next book of the Bible, the Book of Joshua. Deuteronomy and the Book of Joshua may once have been part of a larger work, the D-history (see *Re'eih*).

After Moses died Adonai told Joshua to lead the people across the Jordan River into the Promised Land. "Be strong and have courage," Adonai says "I will be with you as I was with Moses."

> Let the Book of this Torah never depart from your lips. Meditate on it day and night. Take care to carry out all that is written in it. Then shall you be successful in what you do, and then shall you do well.

Then Joshua gave orders to the chieftains of the Israelites, instructing them to get the camp ready to move.

Joshua reminded the tribes who would keep land on the far side of Jordan of their bargain with Moses (see *Mattot*). They promised: "We will do everything you command us and go anywhere you send us."

> We will listen to you, just as we always listened to Moses. Our only prayer is that, just as it was with Moses, may Adonai your God be with you! … Only be strong and have courage!

The slogan "Be strong and have courage!" was often applied to Joshua, and the words occur several times in this haftarah (see *VaYeilech*).

The Torah

Reading the Torah

There are fifty-four portions (*parshiot*) in the Torah. But this was not always true. When and why did the parshiot come to be? The "why" part is easy. The Torah was divided into parshiot to arrange it for reading in the synagogues. The "when" part takes a little explaining.

Bible scholars believe that the custom of reading the Torah aloud in the synagogue probably began some time in the third century B.C.E. How do they know? For one thing, the *Septuagint*, the first Greek translation of the Torah, was completed in the first half of the third century. And we know it was translated to be used in the synagogues in Alexandria, Egypt, where the Jews spoke Greek. Also the philosopher Philo of Alexandria and the historian Josephus Flavius both speak of public Torah readings as an "ancient" practice. And they lived in the first century C.E.

The Torah, though, was not yet divided into portions. It was only divided into scrolls. Since it was written on five scrolls, it was "the Five Books of Moses". The Mishnah tells us that by the end of the second century C.E. the Torah was being read on Mondays, Thursdays, and Shabbat, and there were special readings for festivals and other occasions. But the readings still were not portions.

In one place in the Mishnah Rabbi Meir says that a small amount of text was read on Shabbat morning, the next piece of text on Shabbat afternoon, with more text read on Monday and Thursday. The next Shabbat the readers would start wherever they left off on Thursday. In another place Rabbi Judah says that wherever the reading ended each Shabbat, it began there the next Shabbat.

Dividing the Torah

The Talmud of Babylonia was completed around the year 600 C.E. It tells us that in the Land of Israel the synagogues

The Septuagint

The name *Septuagint* comes from the Latin word *septuaginta*, meaning "seventy". There was a legend that seventy-two elders of Israel, six from each tribe, gathered together in Alexandria, Egypt, to create a translation of the Torah into Greek. According to the legend, the translation was made during the reign of Ptolemy II Philadelphus (285-244 B.C.E.). It is a sweet legend, but a little fanciful. If you think about our history, you know why. Ten of the tribes were lost in 722 B.C.E., almost five hundred years before the "elders" met in Alexandria!

Old Traditions Die Hard

For a while after the Babylonian Talmud was completed, the custom of completing the Torah in three years continued in the Land of Israel. But many Babylonian rabbis came south, and the Land of Israel soon joined the rest of the Jewish world, completing the Torah once each year. But old traditions die hard. Around the year 1170 a famous Jewish traveler, Benjamin of Tudela, visited Cairo. He found two great synagogues there. One used the fifty-four portions of Babylonia, while the other was still reading the Torah "the old way" and completing it only once in three years.

completed reading the Torah once every three years. The Torah was split into parts called "divisions" or *sedarim*. The number of sedarim changed from place to place—some synagogues used 153 sedarim, others used 155 sedarim, and still others used 167 sedarim.

The Talmud also tells us that in Babylon and other communities outside the Holy Land the synagogues completed the reading of the Torah once each year. This must mean that the Five Books of Moses were now divided into the fifty-four portions or parshiot that we use today.

Fifty-Four?

Of course, you know that there is a problem with the number of parshiot. There are only fifty-two weeks in the solar year. But you probably also know that the Jewish calendar as we have it today is a combination of the solar year and the lunar months. Some Jewish years are "leap" years and contain an extra month (*Adar Sheni*, the "Second Adar"). In those years every parashah is read on its own Shabbat. But in normal years some portions are paired and read together on Shabbat in order to complete the reading of the Torah in one year. It gets even more complex when we remember that festivals have their own special readings, and there are some Sabbaths on which we read special portions in addition to the weekly portion.

Haftarah Readings

To each weekly Torah portion a reading called the haftarah is added. The word *haftarah* may mean "a parting [message]". Some commentators thought it was named this because the haftarah was the last thing read in the services of the Second Temple. Not everyone agrees. One commentator says it is called "a parting" because when it begins we leave behind the Torah. The exact haftarah selections were not fixed at first. Different communities had different traditions about what book to read, and the choice may at times have been somewhat random. The history is a bit hazy.

The Talmud mentions the reading of the haftarah but gives no list. The New Testament mentions that a haftarah was read in the synagogues of Israel but does not tell us more than that. It was some time later that the Rabbis began to organize a single list attaching each haftarah to a particular Torah portion. Most of the time they tried to connect haftarah readings to things happening in the Torah—for example, connecting the Song of Deborah to the Song of Moses (*B'shalach*). A third of the time, though, they chose a haftarah based on the time of the year or the approach of a festival. Today the readings are generally the same everywhere (though a few times each year Sephardic Jews read a different haftarah portion from Ashkenazic Jews).

Of course, there are special haftarah readings for every special occasion. This fits with the main purpose the Rabbis had in mind in adding the haftarah reading: They wanted us to know that the words of the prophets were also the words of God—which is why the prophets are part of our Bible.

What the Torah Is

You have met many of the Torah's famous people; many well-known rabbis and sages; and a host of commentators, Bible scholars, archaeologists, Egyptologists, and linguists. All of them have helped us in our study.

When you began you might have thought of the Torah as one long history of our people from the beginning of time to the death of Moses. Now you know better. It is not one long history. It is not history at all.

The Torah is a collection of the stories, wisdom, and laws of the Israelites. It is all cleverly arranged to look like a history, but the reason it came into being was to make one people out of many tribes. Most of the people who first read it were priests. As we have seen, much of it was written by priests and for priests. There is nothing wrong with this picture, since Israelite priests believed that Adonai had given them two missions: to tell the difference between what was clean or holy and what was unclean or un-Godlike; and to teach the people the meaning of the Torah of Moses. In other words, just like the Rabbis would later, the Israelite priests thought of themselves as judges and sages.

As for the Torah, we know a lot about how and when it was put together. But these things are less important than

The Maftir

The person who is the last to be called to read from the Torah is usually the one who reads the haftarah. The name for this reader is the *maftir*, "the parting one". The maftir is often a young person celebrating a Bar or Bat Mitzvah. Often, reading the haftarah is the last big thing they have to do in their ceremony. For them it is a real "parting".

God and Us

The Torah teaches that we are created "in the image of God". It is up to us to behave as if we are created in God's image. As the philosopher Martin Buber once said, "God does not want to be believed in, to be debated and defended by us, but simply to be realized by us." The more we behave in God-like ways, the more God enters our world.

what the Torah tells us about itself and about us. The stories and the codes of law in the Torah come to teach us how we should live our lives and what we should think about ourselves and our world.

Having completed a study of the portions of the Torah, we can be proud of most of what was recorded so many generations ago. The Torah lets us know that we are "a kingdom of priests and a holy people". If we can learn to live up to that ideal, we will not only be people who study Torah, we will be people who live Torah lives.

A Tradition of Ending

In the Middle Ages it was a tradition for Jewish authors to end their books with a short prayer giving thanks to God, the Author of life. So I end with this traditional prayer:

תַּם וְנִשְׁלָם, שֶׁבַח לָאֵל, בּוֹרֵא עוֹלָם:

Done and fulfilled, thanks to God,
Creator of the Universe. *Amen*.